RUSSIAN RESEARCH CENTER STUDIES, 95

Published under the auspices of the Davis Center for Russian and Eurasian Studies, Harvard University

Closer to the Masses

STALINIST CULTURE,
SOCIAL REVOLUTION,
AND SOVIET NEWSPAPERS

MATTHEW LENOE

HARVARD UNIVERSITY PRESS
Cambridge, Massachusetts
London, England 2004

Library of Congress Cataloging-in-Publication Data
Lenoe, Matthew E. (Matthew Edward)
    Closer to the masses : Stalinist culture, social revolution, and Soviet newspapers /
Matthew Lenoe.
       p. cm -- (Russian Research Center studies ; 95)
    Includes bibliographical references and index.
    ISBN 0-674-01319-0 (hardcover : alk. paper)
     1. Press and propaganda--Soviet Union--History. 2. Communism and culture--Soviet
Union--History. 3. Socialist realism--Soviet Union--History. I. Title. II. Series.

PN5277.P7L46 2004
302.23'0947--dc22

                                                                           2004042214

To Mari Tsuchiya Lenoe

Contents

Closer to the Masses

~ Introduction

T HIS BOOK TELLS THE STORY OF the transformation of Soviet newspapers in the time of the New Economic Policy (NEP) and the First Five-Year Plan.[1] It is a story of purges, political intrigues, transformation of language, and social upheaval, but it is above all a story about the origins of Stalinist culture.[2] Between 1925 and 1930, Soviet newspapermen, under pressure from party leaders to mobilize society for the huge task of industrialization, molded a new master narrative for Soviet history and a new Bolshevik identity for millions of novice Communists. They began to present everyday labor as an epic battle to industrialize the USSR, a battle fought against shirkers and saboteurs within and imperialist enemies without. Party members were the vanguard of the socialist forces in this imagined battle, heroic warriors responsible for leading and inspiring the foot soldiers, "the nonparty masses." The images and metaphors created by NEP journalists became the core of Stalinist culture in the mid-1930s and strongly influenced the development of socialist realism, Stalinism's official literary genre.

The story of the transformation of Soviet newspapers begins during the New Economic Policy of 1921–1928 and continues through the "Great Break" of 1928–1932. The NEP was the Bolshevik leadership's effort to revive the economy and reconcile peasants to Soviet rule by legalizing small-scale trade, leasing factories to private entrepreneurs, and replacing forced grain requisitions with a set agricultural tax. Many Communists viewed the NEP as a temporary retreat at best, or a counterrevolutionary concession to the bourgeoisie at worst. In 1928–1929, faced with a decline in sales of grain to the state, the regime opted to force peasants to join state-controlled collective farms and to invest large amounts in the construction of heavy industry. The result was a social, economic, and political revolution—the "Great Break." A sharp increase in levels of state coercion and a crackdown on private "speculation" accompanied this move. During this period Joseph Stalin, already "first among equals" in the Central Committee leadership, crushed "Rightist" opposition to the new program within the party and established a personal dictatorship.

The transformation of Soviet newspapers was an integral part of the Great Break. In fact the party's change of economic course was accompanied by an equally deep shift in priorities not just for the newspapers, but for culture and propaganda as a whole. During the NEP years, newspapers, the education commissariat, artists, psychologists, and others pursued with great seriousness the job of reshaping the language, culture, and thinking processes of "the masses" and turning them into politically conscious citizens of the new socialist state. Those involved in the project often referred to this as "making the New Soviet Man." I designate it the "NEP mass enlightenment project."[3] But with the Great Break the party Central Committee put the creation of the New Soviet Man on hold, insisting instead that all cultural efforts and resources be used to mobilize the population, and especially the party activists, for the immediate job of industrialization. In the Leninist lexicon of agitation and propaganda (agitprop), this was a shift from "enlightenment" to "mobilization."

The shift from enlightenment to mobilization was not one of rhetoric (discourse about the New Soviet Man continued) but one of practice. A number of changes in practices signaled the end of the NEP mass enlightenment project, among them the decline of studies of audience response to the mass press, the abandonment of experimental methods in pedagogy and psychology, and a decline in the regime's monitoring of popular moods.[4] But most important for this book's story, the Central Committee leadership in 1929–1931 retargeted newspapers all over the USSR at rank-and-file party activists, homogenizing the NEP press network, which had previously included newspapers differentiated according to target audience and intended to reach all segments of the Soviet population. The primary task of the newspapers was now to mobilize party cadres for economic tasks.

The CC executive apparatus headed by Stalin played a central role in reshaping Soviet newspapers, but other important agents and forces were involved. The CC leaders acted within complicated social, political, cultural, and economic contexts. Thus this book uses a methodology that emphasizes the context within which human beings create particular cultural objects. Sometimes designated "the production of culture" method, this approach entails studying cultural artifacts in their larger social, economic, and cultural contexts. Sociologist Wendy Griswold has diagrammed the approach as a "cultural diamond" of four points, all connected to one another, representing a cultural object, its creator(s), its audience, and the social world. One of the earliest cultural sociologists, Michael Baxandall, began his study of fifteenth-century Italian painting not with an aesthetic analysis of particular works but with an examination of the instructions issued to the painters by their purchasers. Baxandall sought to explain Italian Renaissance paintings by studying the conditions of their production—the relationship between artist and purchaser, the availability of particular raw materials, the representational conventions of the time, and their connections to religious, theatrical, and other practices.[5] My study too is an attempt to explain cultural artifacts—Soviet newspapers—by examining the conditions of their production. Shortages of newsprint, Leninist theories of propaganda, and the changing economic priorities of the regime all contributed to the transformation of Soviet newspapers. Most important, party recruitment of young men from the lower classes in the 1920s created the new audience that Stalinist leaders strove to reach with their newspapers during the First Five-Year Plan. The transformation of the Soviet press was tightly bound up with the Bolsheviks' own social revolution from above.[6]

The social origins of Stalinism became an important topic in Western scholarship with the publication of major works by Roger Pethybridge, Moshe Lewin, and Sheila Fitzpatrick in the 1970s. Although their arguments were quite distinct, these scholars all proposed that the life experiences or the "traditional" cultural background of lower-class recruits to the party in the 1920s and 1930s strongly influenced Stalinist culture and politics.[7] In this book I take a closer look at the social influence on the development of Stalinist culture. I examine reader response to the newspapers and party officials' attention to that response, and I also examine the social background and life experiences of the young journalists who molded Bolshevik culture. In short, I aim to describe possible mechanisms by which popular thinking interacted with official propaganda to shape Stalinist culture.

I prefer the production of culture approach to currently fashionable postmodern methods, and in particular to Michel Foucault's methods for the study of culture, because practitioners of the former seek to specify *who* develops a particular cultural object, under what constraints, with what purposes in mind, and with what effects. Examining the conditions of production of a cultural artifact enables one to see where that artifact fits into political and social hierarchies, and who uses it for what. But postmodernists in general and Foucault in particular tend not to address these questions. Let us take the example of Foucault's book *Discipline and Punish*, which traces changes in the treatment of criminals from the late seventeenth century to the mid-twentieth. In this work Foucault explores both the methods of punishment (later "treatment" or "rehabilitation") and the theories behind the methods. If his purpose is simply to *describe* the changing geography of punishment, then his work is useful, but hardly revolutionary. But at points in the book Foucault indicates that he is formulating a kind of explanation of change. He does so in terms of the spread throughout the Western world of a new "micro-physics of power" based on myriad small "technologies of power," such as the many standardized movements of eighteenth-century military drill. The causative power seems to lie in the discourse and concrete practices of punishment themselves, which evolve and spread seemingly without human intervention. Individual decisions, political struggles, economic change, and social upheaval all disappear.[8]

Frank B. Farrell, in *Subjectivity, Realism, and Postmodernism: The Recovery of the World,* has composed a critique of postmodern methods that deserves attention from historians. Farrell writes of a notional triangle, with the three linked corners representing the world, the "speaking or acting self," and the cultural practices/discourses "relevant to determining what selves and the world are like." In postmodernism, Farrell argues, "all determinative power flows to the position of cultural practice and interpretation." Culture determines completely who the self is and what the self thinks the world is. The world itself has no effect on the self, and the self cannot escape the cultural categories and schemas that determine an individual's perceptions and actions. In Foucault's works, Farrell writes, "how the world is and what selves are like . . . offer very little constraint on how our discourses . . . articulate the world into proper classifications. . . . Discourse/power configurations . . . seem to create selves and objects out of nothing." Culture alone has the "God-like power" to create the world.[9]

Postmodern claims for the dominance of discourse and micro-practices of power over self and world have contributed to recent arguments that the Soviet Union, Imperial Russia, and the liberal democracies of the "West" share or shared something called "modernity" with many nefarious consequences. Proponents of the "shared modernity" thesis argue that differences between Leninist and liberal democratic regimes in forms of property, levels of coercion, and political organization are less important than they appear. They assert that power in both regime types is constituted by very similar discourses and micro-practices, all coming under the general rubric of "modernity." Among these are the management of space by distant bureaucracies, the regimentation of labor, intelligence reporting on popular mood, and the provision of various welfare benefits to the population. Advocates of the "shared modernity" thesis do not deny that there are differences between Leninist and liberal democratic regimes, but they do downplay them. Thus Kate Brown, in her article "Gridded Lives: Why Kazakhstan and Montana Are Nearly the Same Place," minimizes the difference between free and forced labor, and Yanni Kotsonis in *Russian Modernity* plays down the differences between free elections and more coercive forms of "mass participation in politics."[10]

Advocates of the "shared modernity" thesis also emphasize the common sins of Leninist regimes and liberal democracies, including the exploitation of labor, genocidal attacks on indigenous peoples, and the deployment of "science" to justify racial and ethnic bigotry. The USSR committed gross injustices, they assert, but the liberal "West" committed the same injustices. Peter Holquist summarized such claims nicely in 1997 when he wrote that "insofar as Soviet Russia presents a problem, it is a problem *of the modern project itself*" (italics added).[11]

The call for rigorous comparative studies of the Soviet Union and non-Leninist societies is stimulating and probably the most important development in Soviet studies in many years. The reminder that "bourgeois" democratic states have engaged in many of the same abuses that Leninist states have is well taken. And bringing the many "technologies of power" into history is certainly important. One need not be a Western triumphalist, however, to question the usefulness of the umbrella term "modernity" as an explanatory or descriptive device. With reference to the history of Soviet newspapers and propaganda, at least, it obscures more than it explains.

Soviet agitprop did develop within the broader context of a worldwide revolution in propaganda that one could call "modern." The years from about 1870 to 1945 saw a remarkable coincidence of changes in communications technology with the expansion of universal manhood suffrage (and ultimately universal suffrage, period). The first transatlantic telegraph line connected London and New York in 1869, and in the next few decades imperial states and private companies laid down a global network of telegraph cable. Also in 1869 the so-called Agency Alliance Treaty divided up news coverage of the world between Reuters, a British wire service; Havas of France; and the Bernard Wolff Agency in Berlin. By the 1890s telegraph cables linked Asian, American, European, and African cities in a single network, making possible newspaper coverage of events halfway around the globe on the day after they occurred. The result was an immense compression of the globe in the human imagination—it became possible, indeed routine, for educated newspaper readers to debate and discuss events around the world that were reported to them almost in real time. The advent of practical wireless telegraphy and the spread of telephone lines in the first decade of the twentieth century further shrank the world.[12]

A revolution in the mass distribution of information accompanied the increased speed of news transmission. In 1871 William Bullock created the first commercially viable rotary press, which made it possible for daily papers to reach circulations in the hundreds of thousands (compared with thousands at the turn of the nineteenth century). The growing population of literate city dwellers in North America, Europe, and Japan was the audience for the new high-circulation papers. Economies of scale and greater production efficiency in general made it possible to sell newspapers for pennies an issue, bringing an entirely new class of readers into public life. Beginning in the late 1920s the availability of cheap radio sets in some societies once again revolutionized the mass distribution of information.[13]

Simultaneous with changes in communications technology was a trend toward expansion of the franchise in most European and North American societies, and in a few other places, notably Japan. Moreover, mass political participation took the form not only of voting, but of joining labor unions, striking, demonstrating, participating in city political machines, writing letters to government authorities or to newspapers, and so on. Mass politics, combined with the spread of the idea of popular sovereignty, presented ruling elites with novel problems of controlling the feelings and opinions of their subjects. Whoever wielded, or desired to wield, political and economic power—whether the young samurai who made the Meiji Revolution in Japan, the Tsar and his advisers in Russia, or John D. Rockefeller—had to face these problems.

It is certainly useful to recognize that in the broadest sense elites all over the globe had to deal with the emergence of mass politics. But the solutions arrived at by different elites differed drastically one from another. In the United States and in the Soviet Republic, for example, two completely distinct paradigms emerged for managing mass politics during the 1920s—the "science" of public relations and the Bolshevik system of agitation and propaganda.

As described by the most famous of its founders, Edward Bernays, the science of public relations involved manipulating mass opinion by playing to the deepest desires and unspoken cultural assumptions of the populace. Bernays prescribed a course of study for the would-be PR counsel that involved learning the new "science" of psychology and the preferences and assumptions of different social, occupational, and religious groups. The most effective PR campaigns, he asserted, used people's desires for sex, security, food, and social status to make their point. And they did not directly challenge people's cultural assumptions (for example about proper family structure, the role of government in the economy, or racial hierarchies). Bernays's public relations was ultimately about understanding individual desires through psychology and marketing surveys and then stimulating and using those desires to mold popular opinion.[14]

Soviet agitation and propaganda as it evolved during the 1920s was based on entirely different principles and procedures. Appeals to individual desire for sex, wealth, prestige, or even security were taboo for ideological reasons. And although there was movement toward working with the audience's preexisting cultural assumptions, especially after 1929, Soviet propagandists through Stalin's death did not develop statistically rigorous survey or polling methods. In fact they rarely used statistical data at all. Nor did they develop the finely graded categorizations of the population by hobbies, occupation, religion, and so on advocated by Bernays. They remained content with the coarse system of class distinctions inherited from prerevolutionary Marxist intellectuals, dividing the populace into proletarians, peasants, capitalists, nobles, and the urban petty bourgeoisie.

As this book shows, Soviet journalists and propagandists in the 1920s and early 1930s strove to reach their audiences with rational explanations of party policy, exhortations to heroic sacrifice, and appeals to class resentments. Ultimately they found the last two more effective than the first. By the middle years of the First Five-Year Plan they had focused their efforts on mobilizing party activists with calls for heroic sacrifice and denunciations of internal class enemies. The Soviet press of the early 1930s instilled in party members an identity as warrior heroes battling for socialism, presenting them with images of the coming millennium, and promising them that industrialization would make the Soviet state even more great and powerful than the wealthy capitalist democracies. This could not have been further from Bernays's prescription for appeals to individual desires and cultural orthodoxies. Even though both Soviet agitprop and American PR were in some very large sense responses to common problems of "modernity," they differed in their most basic assumptions.

This book is divided into two parts. Part 1, "Soviet Newspapers in the 1920s," gives an overview of three aspects of Soviet newspaper production that are crucial for understanding Part 2 and the book's overall argument. Chapter 1 looks into the theories of press function that informed Bolshevik journalism and links these theories to changes in the language of Soviet newspapers between 1925 and 1933. Chapter 2 explains how newspapers were financed and distributed in the USSR throughout the 1920s and into the 1930s. Chapter 3 examines reader responses to the newspapers and argues that Soviet journalists and officials paid attention to those responses in the 1920s.

Part 2, "The Creation of Mass Journalism and Socialist Realism," is a narrative of the transformation of Soviet newspapers and the origins of socialist realist literature. Chapter 4, "The Creation of Mass Journalism," shows how newspaper writers in provincial industrial centers created new forms of journalism to mobilize worker activists in 1926–1927. Chapter 5, "Mass Journalists, 'Cultural Revolution,' and the Retargeting of Soviet Newspapers" shows how practitioners of the new "mass journalism," mostly young Communist reporters, took over *Pravda, Izvestiia,* and other major central Soviet newspapers in 1928–1930. This takeover was facilitated by the Central Committee executive apparatus as part of a two-pronged offensive to retarget the press at rank-and-file party members and undermine "Rightist" opponents of Stalin at the central newspapers. Chapter 6, "The Central Committee and Self-Criticism, 1928–1929," tells the story of mass journalists' participation in the self-criticism campaign of 1928–1929, their attacks on provincial party organizations, and the intervention of Stalin and other Central Committee secretaries to halt their "excesses" in September 1929. Chapter 7, titled "Mass Journalism, Soviet Sensations, and Socialist Realism," examines the strong influence of mass journalism on the creation of socialist realism, the official literary genre that became a keystone of high Stalinist culture in the 1930s.

~ I
SOVIET NEWSPAPERS IN THE 1920S

~ 1

Agitation, Propaganda, and the NEP Mass Enlightenment Project

BETWEEN 1925 AND 1933 the layout and tone of the Soviet central press underwent an obvious change. Issues of *Pravda* and *Izvestiia* from the period of the New Economic Policy (1921–1927) contain journalistic genres familiar to today's Western reader: the papers feature wire service reports written in an "objective" style, editorial commentaries, economic analyses, and short satirical pieces about everyday life. The shrill declamation of the same newspapers in the early 1930s, by contrast, seems alien and bizarre. Exclamation points, commands, military metaphors, and congratulations from party leaders to factories for surpassing their production plans dominate. The newspapers alternately castigate readers like angry parents, and exhort them to battle like officers urging their troops forward. Boldface headlines proclaim the triumphs of worker "shock brigades," the "mobilization" of young Communists for construction labor, and other "victories on the labor front."

Changes in layout accompanied changes in prose style. Issues of *Pravda* and *Izvestiia* from the NEP era present headlines in a single typeface, carry few illustrations, and roll continuous columns of small-type print from page top to bottom. Editions of *Pravda* from 1933, on the other hand, resemble high-circulation American newspapers of the time in arrangement of text, headlines, and photographs. Articles are shorter and the typeface of headlines is varied. Photographs, absent in 1925, appear. International news has been displaced from the front page by "all-Union" news from the great construction sites and new factories of the First Five-Year Plan (1928–1932).

Superficial changes in style and layout were connected to deep changes in content and ideology. Between the NEP years and the early 1930s *Pravda* and *Izvestiia* shifted from complex coverage of news and party policy to the presentation of Soviet society as an army at the command of the "generals" in the Politburo. By 1930 both newspapers were organized almost entirely around the fulfillment of tasks set by the party Central Committee (CC). Mostly these involved raising production. Lead editorials explained the task, reports from the factories showed how activists worked to carry it out, and collective letters from the activists themselves pledged to achieve even more in the future. All of these pieces presented production as war—worker activists were "soldiers of socialist construction," construction sites and factory shop floors were "the front." Almost half of all headlines took the form of commands given to the readers ("Complete the Dnepr Dam in One Year!"). The newspapers, and by implication the party leadership, were addressing Soviet subjects as soldiers under orders.

The story of the transformation of the Soviet press in the late 1920s bears on the larger question of continuity and change between NEP Bolshevism and the "high Stalinism" of the 1930s and 1940s. The jarring shift in the language and layout of central Soviet newspapers would seem to fit the dichotomy of "soft" NEP/"hard" Stalinism that dominated Western historiography of the USSR in the 1970s and 1980s. *Pravda* and *Izvestiia* in the NEP years had a relatively moderate tone, often reporting facts and events without providing an explicit evaluation of them. In contrast the tone of both papers in the early thirties was shrill. Writers larded their work with value-laden language, superlatives, and epithets, pounding readers with the "correct" interpretation of the news. Thus, the central newspapers' progression from moderation to shrillness would seem to mirror the regime's development from soft to hard.

This analysis is, however, shallow. An examination of journalistic practice and Bolshevik theories of propaganda reveals important continuities between the NEP and high Stalinist eras. Throughout their history Bolsheviks saw themselves both as tutors of the masses and as their leaders in the war between the classes. The party press, too, could play the role of tutor or commanding officer, depending on the situation. During the Civil War of 1918–1921, naturally, Bolshevik newspapermen strove to mobilize the population for victory, taking on the role of officer. With the war's conclusion, CC agitation-and-propaganda (agitprop) officials ordered much of the press to gear down its militant rhetoric and adjust to the long-term task of tutoring the masses, raising their "cultural level." But throughout the NEP years some so-called mass newspapers, targeted at Communist youth and factory workers, continued to embody the role of military officer, instructing and exhorting their readers to battle with class enemies. Thus, when the exigencies of the party's forced-draft industrialization drive prompted Bolshevik leaders to enlist the *entire* press, including *Pravda* and *Izvestiia*, in the task of rallying society for the First Five-Year Plan, journalists turned to the experience of NEP mass newspapers. The shrill tone of Stalinist newspapers, their presentation of labor as combat, and their martial rhetoric all had precedents in NEP and Civil War journalism. In this respect Stalinism had solid roots in earlier Bolshevik culture.

NEP Newspaper Work

On November 4, 1917, ten days after the Bolsheviks seized power, the Central Executive Committee of the Congress of Soviets authorized the closing down of bourgeois newspapers and seizure of their assets for use by "organs of Soviet Power." By late summer 1918 the Soviet leadership had shut down all non-Bolshevik daily publications and banned advertising. During the years of the Revolution and Civil War hundreds of local party and Soviet institutions published their own news sheets, often of only two to four pages, and distributed them for free. Paper, printing equipment, and trained journalists were all in short supply.[1]

Even at the highest levels Bolshevik journalism during the Civil War was an improvisation. At the central party organ, *Pravda*, Mariia Ilichna Ulianova, Lenin's sister, was de facto head editor of the paper during the Civil War. She was also in charge of all the administrative and secretarial duties of the editorial offices, distributing pencils from her desk and determining employee eligibility for food rations. From the spring of 1918 *Pravda* was housed in the former offices of I. D. Sytin's publication *Russkoe slovo (The Russian Word)*, the highest-circulation newspaper in prerevolutionary Russia. The building was unheated and the newspaper disposed of no automobiles at all. According to the unpublished memoirs of N. M. Rabinovich, who was at the time a courier and researcher for *Pravda*, Ulianova and the other editors were groping for the right tools to transform *Pravda* from an underground oppositional newspaper to the official organ of the Soviet government and Communist Party. They spent much time reading old issues of *The Russian Word* in their search for useable journalistic models.[2]

In the winter of 1921–1922, in the first months of the New Economic Policy, the party's Central Committee made advertising legal again, ordered the closing down of hundreds of the provincial newspapers that had appeared during the Civil War, and terminated the practice of free distribution of the press. But despite the concentration of assets and the opening of new sources of income, Bolshevik newspapers continued to operate in an atmosphere of scarcity and improvisation throughout the 1920s. From 1921 to 1926 the number of typesetting machines and printing presses in operation in the Soviet republics declined as prerevolutionary equipment wore out and few new purchases were made. In fiscal year 1922–1923 production of paper and cardboard was 18.2 percent of 1913 production in the Russian Empire. Soviet production did not reach the 1913 level until 1928–1929. Experienced journalists were in short supply and experienced Communist and socialist journalists in even shorter supply. The founding of the State Institute of Journalism (GIZh) in 1924 barely made a dent in the problem.[3]

Bolshevik journalism relied heavily on equipment, physical plant, and even personnel inherited from the prerevolutionary press through the late 1920s. The central Soviet newspaper distribution agency during the Civil War, Tsentropechat, was the nationalized remainders of publishing entrepreneur A. S. Suvorin's prerevolutionary distribution network. This network passed to other agencies and ended up largely in the hands of the central party organ, *Pravda*, at the end of 1922.[4] In the first days of their rule the Bolsheviks confiscated the printing and editorial facilities of major commercial publications, including the popular Petersburg newspapers *Birzhevye vedemosti (Market Report)* and *Kopeika (Copeck)*, and on October 27, 1917, *Pravda* took over the presses of *Den' (The Day)*, a relatively low-circulation commercial paper in St. Petersburg.[5] After the Soviet government's spring 1918 move to Moscow, *Pravda* and *Izvestiia* shared space in the former headquarters of *The Russian Word*. *Izvestiia* in particular continued to rely on nonparty veterans of *The Russian Word*. Until 1926 the paper's entire Moscow News department was almost entirely staffed by *Russian Word* veterans.[6]

Three interlinked institutions were involved in Soviet newspaper production—the editorial offices *(redaktsiia)*, where the work of writing, copy editing, and laying out each day's edition was done, the print shop *(tipografiia)*, where the edition was typeset and printed, and the publishing house *(izdatelstvo)*, which handled the business side of production such as advertising and distribution, and which usually did planning and production of books, calendars, and other nonserial publications. Major publishing houses, such as *Pravda*'s, published several newspapers and journals and so included several different editorial offices. Before 1925 most Moscow print shops operated under an umbrella printing trust known as Moscow Polygraphic (Mospoligraf). From 1925 onward newspapers began taking over individual print shops. Conflict between the editorial office workers and printers over production deadlines and quality was constant. Once newspapers took direct control over print shops, conflicts also flared about wages, benefits, and working conditions.[7]

Employee numbers seem to have expanded at the newspapers during the 1920s, although there were significant cuts during the 1926–1927 belt-tightening campaign *(rezhim ekonomii)*. At the CC's mass worker paper *The Worker Gazette* on January 1, 1926, there were 171 editorial office employees, 391 blue-collar printers, and 392 employees handling business and accounting work at the publishing house and the print shop, and an additional 131 unclassified employees, for a total of 1,085 employees. The editorial offices themselves were divided into a number of departments, which corresponded to sections of the newspaper. At *Izvestiia* in December 1929, for example, the editorial offices employed 172 persons in eight departments—International News (15 staff members), National News (72), Economic News (7), Soviet Construction and Worker/Peasants' Inspectorate Page (8), Cultural Department and Literature Section (8), Party Department (2), Bureau of Investigation and Legal Consultation (this department handled reader letters denouncing crimes and disorders in the state apparatus—11 persons), and the Secretariat (49), which coordinated the work of the other departments to produce a single edition of the paper. Of these employees about 50 were engaged in clerical work (typists, archivists, couriers). Another 60 or so were consultants and correspondents who worked abroad or in other parts of the Soviet Union. There were, then, somewhere just over 60 persons engaged in actual "literary work" (writing and editing) at the editorial offices.[8]

The head editor of major central newspapers was usually a first- or second-level party leader who lacked the time to do real journalistic work (Nikolai Bukharin at *Pravda* and Ivan Skvortsov-Stepanov at *Izvestiia* were typical). The actual job of running the paper was done by the second-in-command *(sekretar* or *zamestitel zaveduiushchego)*, who worked closely with the heads of the various departments. The department heads, together with the head editor and his deputy, made up the editorial board *(redkollegiia)*. With the exception of the head editor, these were the men and women (a very few women) who really ran the newspaper.

Every newspaper, like every Soviet workplace, had a party organization, and in practice many important decisions about newspaper production were made at the organization's meetings. Party members generally made up somewhere between one-quarter and one-third of editorial office employees at the major central newspapers. In 1926, for example, when *The Worker Gazette* editorial offices employed about 170 persons, there were 56 party members and candidates in the paper's party organization.[9] At *Izvestiia* in December 1929, 46 of 177 editorial staff employees belonged to the party.[10] A relatively high proportion of high-ranking editors and writers were Communists compared to other occupational groups. According to a 1929 survey done by the Section of Press Workers (the journalists' labor union) 97 percent of head editors and 61 percent of department editors were Communists.[11] At *Izvestiia*, meetings of the party organization (or "party cell") in the late 1920s covered many of the same topics and included many of the same active participants as meetings of the editorial board. According to party rules, editors were not supposed to serve on the three-man bureaus that guided party cell work, as this concentration of authority was deemed unhealthy. In practice, however, this rule was sometimes violated (*Izvestiia* editor Ivan Gronskii, for example, was elected to the party cell bureau in March 1930).[12]

During the Russian Revolution and Civil War there was a drastic contraction of the Russian newspaper network because of material shortages and the Bolsheviks' shutting down of all opposition and commercial newspapers. Jeffrey Brooks has demonstrated that the quantity of all print materials available to the general population dropped sharply after the Revolution and did not reach something like prerevolutionary levels until the late 1920s. Soviet historians of the press put the total circulation of daily newspapers in prerevolutionary Russia at 2.7 million to 3.7 million copies. On Press Day (May 5) of 1924, they state, total circulation of Soviet dailies was 2.5 million—circulation still had not reached that of the last prerevolutionary years. The number of dailies published also declined under Soviet Power. In 1914 there were 824 daily newspapers in the Russian Empire; in 1928 there were 201 dailies in the Soviet Union.[13] Nor did the largest Soviet dailies equal the

1917 circulation of the prerevolutionary giant *The Russian Word*, 1,000,000 copies, until early 1930, when *Pravda* reached that number.[14]

NEP "Pluralism" and Central Committee Control of the Press

Western accounts place the development of the Soviet press network in the context of growing party control over Soviet society and Joseph Stalin's rise to power. They tell how circulation rose, paper supplies, printing equipment, and financing improved, and the newspaper network expanded. Simultaneously party control over the press tightened. Growing censorship culminated in Stalin's complete domination of the newspapers. The dissenting or dissonant voices that had occasionally been heard in the press were silenced.[15]

Soviet histories of the press also focused on the expansion of central control, but with an accent on the positive. Through the newspapers, "culture," meaning in the Soviet context everything from brushing your teeth to attending the ballet, spread into the countryside. The party CC defeated the Left Opposition and Right Deviation and ended "factionalism." Like the Western accounts, Soviet histories described increasing circulation, improving typographical equipment, and steadily rising budgets.[16]

The narrative of growing central control seems right, as far as it goes. It accurately describes the relationship between the CC departments responsible for the press and the hundreds of provincial newspapers in the USSR.[17] *Krasnaia pechat (Red Press)*, the Press Department's organ between 1922 and 1928, was filled with guidance on layout, content, writing style, and political line. Denunciations of specific newspapers for journalistic incompetence or political deviation were also common. Constant injunctions against "bureaucratic language," "sensationalism," coverage of trivia, and the airing of the party's dirty linen bespoke the intense desire of CC functionaries to control the press. Through *Red Press* the Press Department pressured provincial papers to fall in line with ongoing propaganda campaigns, to devote more space, for example, to the "industrial crisis," or the alliance of workers and peasants, or the "scissors crisis."[18]

But the story of the party leaders' expanding control over the press does not account for the change in tone of the *central* newspapers between 1925 and 1933, precisely because *Pravda* and *Izvestiia* were already under close CC supervision by the early 1920s. Even a cursory comparison of CC journals with these papers demonstrates that editors were following the party leaders' agenda. On January 22, 1925, for example, *Izvestiia*'s domestic coverage was entirely devoted to the anniversary of Lenin's death. Articles and editorials appeared on "Lenin's Precepts—A Communist Oath," "Lenin and the Komsomol," "Lenin on the Labor Union Movement," "The Party without Lenin," and "A Cadet's Memories of Lenin." The newspaper reported on gatherings at workers' clubs, factories, villages, and soviets to mourn the dead leader. Its coverage closely followed guidelines laid out by the January 7, 1925, edition of *Red Press*, which suggested topics such as "One Year Without Lenin" and "Lenin and the Komsomol."

In 1933, too, *Izvestiia* followed the CC executive apparatus's agenda closely. The January 1933 edition of *Kommunisticheskaia revoliutsiia (Communist Revolution)*, the organ of the CC's Department of Culture and Propaganda, opened with two articles by Stalin. The first, "Results of the First Five-Year Plan," emphasized the rapid growth of industrial production in the USSR compared with that in the bourgeois countries and asserted the need to wipe out the residuum of "hostile classes." "On Work in the Countryside" criticized shortcomings in local party organizations' management of collective farms. Other pieces on the results of the First Five-Year Plan followed, as well as a notice that several Moscow economic enterprises had organized a "socialist competition" to see which could best fulfill the decisions of the January CC Plenum. Like *Communist Revolution*, *Izvestiia*'s January 19, 1933 edition emphasized problems at collective farms, rapid industrial growth, and the persistence of "hostile class elements" in the Soviet countryside. The front page headlines were "Political Departments Must Decisively Improve the Work of Rural Organizations," "Let Us Strengthen Revolutionary Vigilance at Every Post! Smash the Class Enemy!," and "Under the Leadership of the Central Committee—To the Victories of the Second Five-Year Plan." On the front page there also ran greetings from the Moscow and Leningrad party organizations, promising to fulfill the directives of the January CC plenum and improve work in the countryside. On later pages there were more articles covering the high output of specific factories and collective farms.

The CC executive managed the newspapers with the same toolbox from the early NEP years right through Stalin's death in 1953. Top CC officials kept journalists on a tight leash by setting their agenda, cutting funding to newspapers that published unacceptable material, and controlling information flow, editorial appointments, subsidies, and paper supplies. Prepublication censorship, on the other hand, was not important in determining content. Until the end of 1927 *Izvestiia* and all party newspapers were free from prepublication censorship by Glavlit, the Central Directorate of Literature. At other papers a single Glavlit censor was present at press time, and he or she focused almost exclusively on questions of military secrecy. After 1927, when Glavlit representatives were placed at all Soviet newspapers, the editors of major central organs still had the clout to override censors' decisions and publish what they thought appropriate.[19]

Agenda-setting was the most important CC tool for controlling the press during the NEP and after. There were a number of institutional mechanisms for determining the newspapers' agenda, including CC circulars, conferences with newspaper editors, and the publication of instructional journals. *The Worker Gazette* and *Pravda* also had the right to send representatives to Politburo, Orgburo, and Secretariat sessions, where they would learn what themes the leadership considered important. Through all of these channels CC agitprop officials informed newspaper editors about priority propaganda campaigns, proper presentation for different target audiences, and desirable articles. There was also a form of extraordinary agenda-setting, in which the Politburo, the Orgburo, or the Secretariat ordered a central newspaper or newspapers to publish a specific article.[20]

Much agenda-setting within the Soviet press, however, was informal. Senior and deputy editors were usually prominent party officials who were in constant touch with the CC agenda through attendance at high-level party meetings. Nikolai Bukharin, editor-in-chief of *Pravda* until 1929, was a Politburo member. During 1929, a year in which Bukharin, under intense attack for his "Right Deviation," exercised little control over the paper, Leonid Kovalev, head of the Department of Party Life, chief of the newspaper's party organization, and de facto senior editor, attended Orgburo and Secretariat sessions. At *Izvestiia* Ivan Skvortsov-Stepanov (head editor from late 1925 until 1928) was a member of the Central Committee and in the first months of 1928 was attending Politburo sessions regularly. Skvortsov-Stepanov's successor, Ivan Gronskii, reported in his memoirs being in regular touch with Stalin by telephone during the struggle with the Right Deviation in 1928–1929.[21]

Through their control of *Pravda* and *Izvestiia* CC leaders were able to set the agenda for the entire Soviet press. Numerous sources report that even in the early 1920s provincial newspapers followed the lead of the central newspapers, often reprinting their articles verbatim. A combination of party discipline, the shortage of capable writers, and fear of reprimand from above prompted provincial editors to cleave tightly to the central press's line. Agitprop officials even complained at times that the provincial press was following the center's lead *too* slavishly.[22]

Central party institutions also used postpublication sanctions to keep the press in line. Between 1923 and 1928 the CC's Agitprop and Press departments, as well as the higher-level Politburo, Orgburo, and Secretariat, regularly censured central newspapers for all kinds of slips, from publication of pessimistic forecasts of the ruble's exchange rate to premature release of official information. Offending papers were sometimes written up in *Red Press*. The Central Control Commission (CCC), the organ responsible for judging breaches of party discipline, reprimanded editors for publication of "pornography," "sensationalistic" denunciations of party officials, and the like. In some cases the CCC recommended that the CC fire responsible editors.[23]

The CC executive apparatus also strove to centralize information sources. One of the Politburo's goals when it established the central all-Union wire service Telegraph Agency of the Soviet Union (TASS) in July 1924 was "the achievement of the necessary . . . control over and concentration of all information in one general direction."[24] In June 1925 TASS received a monopoly on the distribution of international news within the USSR. In addition the wire service was to disseminate all-Union news and "supervise" the use of international and all-Union news by the republic-level wire services. In January 1928 the Orgburo and Politburo confirmed TASS's monopoly on the production of international news and extended it to the area of domestic Soviet (or "all-Union") news. TASS was supposed to serve as the clearinghouse for all published information above the local level, although in practice the major central newspapers had their own correspondents in the provinces and abroad.[25]

The top CC organs had the authority to hire and fire editors at any newspaper in the USSR, and they had to approve editorial appointments down to the level of provincial papers and sometimes below. Needless to say, this gave them great influence over content. The most obvious example was the packing of the *Pravda* editorial board with Stalin supporters in the summer of 1928, which enabled Stalin to dominate the paper even though its head editor, Bukharin, was his chief political opponent.[26]

Central Committee authority over paper supplies and financing for newspapers was yet another potent instrument of press control. Throughout the history of the Soviet Union, party leaders considered paper a strategic material, best rationed through a centralized distribution system. As a matter of routine the Committee on Press Affairs (Komitet po delam pechati) attached to the Council of People's Commissars (Sovnarkom) managed paper supplies, loans, and subsidies for the press, but the CC executive organs made most important decisions and many not-very-important ones. Central newspapers such as *Pravda* or *Komsomolskaia pravda*, for example, had to apply to the Secretariat to receive extra newsprint to publish supplements for special occasions such as the anniversary of the October Revolution. The CC secretaries could and did cut financing and paper supplies to publications that displeased them.[27]

The formal introduction of *khozraschet* or "financial autonomy" for state-owned enterprises at the beginning of the NEP in late 1921 did not loosen central domination of the press or force newspapers to be more responsive to readers' tastes. In practice party officials applied *khozraschet* only to newspapers they disapproved of or thought they could dispense with. All of the CC newspapers continued to receive subsidies, both direct and indirect, throughout the NEP. A financial umbilical cord linked them to the Central Committee, and party leaders held the scissors that could cut that cord.[28]

The relatively moderate tone taken by the NEP newspapers, then, did not reflect the "pluralism" of NEP society at large, as some scholars have claimed.[29] If "pluralism" means open debate between individuals of differing political convictions, it is not a good word to apply to Soviet society in the 1920s or to the central Soviet press. During the period covered by this paper open polemics between opposing factions within the Communist Party rarely appeared in either *Pravda* or *Izvestiia*. Writers in these newspapers could express opposition to the "general line of the party" only in muted and indirect language. Even when they disagreed among themselves party leaders remained obsessed with maintaining an appearance of unity in the press and public pronouncements. Lying beneath policy debates within the party was a very stable base of common assumptions about the tools and goals of governance, including the necessity of maintaining party unity and suppressing public dissent. This base of common assumptions remained solid throughout both the NEP and Stalinist eras.

The submerging of intra-party conflict grew from the ideological anxieties of the NEP and the strictures against "factionalism" endorsed by the Tenth Party Congress in 1921. Many party members thought that NEP measures to loosen central economic controls might allow a recrudescence of capitalism. Within the party the NEP was thought of as a temporary retreat, a purchase of time to rally a proletariat shattered by the Civil War. Bolshevik leaders, accustomed to thinking about economic and social processes in terms of martial metaphors, concluded that in the NEP, as in any retreat, discipline and unity were necessary to prevent a rout. Resurgent "bourgeois" elements might interpret open dissent within the party as a sign of weakness and expand their activities from the purely economic to the spheres of ideology and politics. A siege mentality took hold among the Bolsheviks. As Stephen Cohen has put it, "the atmosphere of relaxation fostered in the country by NEP triggered an opposite course inside the party."[30]

Prominent Bolshevik journalists reacted to the threat of bourgeois resurgence by reaffirming the party's right to silence opposition, first asserted in November 1917 when the Petrograd Soviet shut down "bourgeois" and "counterrevolutionary publications." In early 1923 the Fourth Conference of the journalists' labor union (*Soiuz rabotnikov pechati* or SRP) passed resolutions denying the right of remaining independent periodicals to criticize the party. Conference delegates condemned the idea of an independent press, affirming that the Soviet state would create its own "truly healthy, truly comradely, truly proletarian criticism."

In pursuit of a "truly proletarian criticism" the Fourth Conference of the SRP endorsed freedom of criticism for the party press and its "worker/peasant correspondents." Worker-peasant correspondents, ordinary working people who wrote to the newspaper with accounts of disorders in their factories and villages, were supposed to serve as a check on corrupt or power-hungry Communists. Sergei Ingulov, SRP secretary and CC Press Subdepartment head, expressed great faith in their ability to "control distortions" in Soviet society and provide a check on the arbitrary power of state and party officials. "Worker correspondents," he opined, "writing the full truth in clear language, do not have to use half-truths or lies."[31]

But the journalists' enthusiasm for "truly proletarian criticism" contradicted party leaders' determination to maintain unity during the NEP retreat. Within a few weeks of the SRP conference the CC Orgburo issued a secret directive asserting that "the editorial staffs of local newspapers . . . are unconditionally subordinate to their (local) party committees." The directive prohibited the publishing of critical material about a party committee without the express permission of the committee itself.[32] The effect of this directive was to set up a hierarchy of criticism—a newspaper could find fault with party organizations lower down the administrative pyramid, but not with those on the same level or higher. Thus, *Pravda* could attack a provincial party committee, but a provincial newspaper could not attack central party organs. This hierarchy was not always observed, but it did provide high-ranking authorities with a powerful tool for silencing criticism "from below." Even within the party, the CC leadership tightly circumscribed freedom of expression.

The change in tone of the central Soviet newspapers, then, cannot be explained by the notion that various "voices," representing different groupings and ideological orientations within the party, were silenced one by one, until only the CC's "general line" remained. The different voices that the reader discerns in an edition of *Izvestiia* from 1925 do not depend on the political orientation of the writers. They are not the voices of Bukharinites, or Stalinists, or Zinovievites, much less Mensheviks or Kadets. Rather, they are the voices of the foreign correspondent writing a wire report, the editor exhorting citizens to buy Industrialization Bonds, the satirist describing his visit to the provincial Executive Committee, or the party leader explicating the meaning of the alliance between workers and peasants. They are voices that differ one from another because they come from different sources—a telegram from the TASS or Russian Telegraph Agency (ROSTA) wire services, a speech by a CC member, a communiqué from a city soviet Press Bureau—and are written for different purposes, with different audiences in mind. Historian Jeffrey Brooks has put it this way: "Even when leaders agreed, the press accommodated many voices and several distinct discourses, each linked with types of authors and targeted audiences."[33]

Defining the Voices of the Soviet Press

Pinning down the components of the increasingly shrill rhetoric of the early thirties is not a question of pluralism, but of the various voices that arose from the interplay of information sources, subject, intended audience, and Bolshevik thinking about agitation and propaganda. Some of these voices were more shrill than others. A TASS telegram from the Far East might read to today's North American reader like "objective" reporting. This is in part because no first person narrator intrudes, in part because concrete events, places, persons, and dates, rather than abstractions, are discussed, in part because of the paucity of value-laden language, and in part because any judgments passed are likely to be qualified with modals of probability such as "possibly," "may," or "might." On the surface, the purpose of the article is to inform the reader of an important event. On the other hand, an editorial titled "All Hail the Builders of the Auto Construction Factory!" will be larded with superlatives *(ogromnii, bystreishii)*, words expressing emotion *(entuziazm, ustoichivost')*, value-laden vocabulary, and exclamation points. The purpose of this sort of editorial was not simply to inform, but to exhort industrial workers to greater efforts and transmit a sense of solidarity in a common struggle.

One of the most characteristic (and shrillest) genres of Stalinist journalism was this type of exhortative article, usually headlined with a direct or indirect command ("Let's Pick Up the Pace of Industrialization!") and narrated in the first person plural. This kind of article was really a directive for party activists. It came with an easy-to-remember slogan attached and was often part of an agitprop campaign running for weeks, even months at a time. Typically such a piece described a party directive to the activists, recounted successes and failures in its implementation, and gave instructions about how to proceed in the future. This genre, very prominent in editions of *Pravda* and *Izvestiia* from the early thirties, also appeared in NEP-era issues, albeit much less frequently. Conversely, "neutral" wire service reports, quite common in 1925, had become rare by 1933. Both types of articles persisted over time, but the amount of space devoted to each changed.

I will identify the voice of a given Soviet journalistic piece by its *source*, its *intended audience*, its *purpose* in the Bolshevik scheme of agitation and propaganda, and certain lexical and grammatical features (imperative verbs, for example). The difficulty with using these kinds of criteria to identify individual voices is that they are merely indicators or tags. When the reader senses that two pieces are written in the same voice, he or she is responding to a complex network of syntactic and semantic cues. These might include sentence structure, transitivity of the verbs (are they verbs of mental process, mental state, physical action, etc.), person of the narration, the presence or absence of modals of probability, opinion, or desirability ("probably," "in my opinion," "unfortunately"), communicative function of the verbs (to command, for example, or to question), the use of nouns referring to abstractions or concrete objects, or the types of agents (institutions, individuals, social classes). All of these play a role in creating the impression of a single, discrete voice. It is possible to describe the complex net of syntactic and semantic attributes that define the voice of a single text, or even to compare the voices of several different texts. It is also possible to show change over time in the work of a single author by analyzing the frequency of certain syntactic/semantic structures, for example verbs of different transitivities. But when looking at the composition of an entire newspaper, the multiplicity of authors, subject matter, targeted audiences, and purposes make such detailed analyses extremely difficult.

The ideas of M. A. K. Halliday, Roger Fowler, and other functional linguists are helpful in linking the two levels of analysis presented above—semantic/syntactic properties and the text's source, intended audience, and purpose. Halliday is interested in elucidating how the situation in which a text is produced, including the social and cultural environment, influences the syntactic and semantic structure of that text. Following Bronislaw Malinowski, Halliday calls the social, cultural, and physical environment in which text is produced the "context of situation." He explains the global relationship between text and context this way: "the context of situation, the context in which the text unfolds, is encapsulated in the text, not in a kind of piecemeal fashion, nor at the other extreme in any mechanical way, but through a systematic relationship between the social environment on the one hand, and the functional organisation of language on the other." There are two interesting consequences of the strong (albeit not complete) determination of text by context. First, context of situation can be inferred from grammatical and lexical features of the text (indeed, if it could not we would not understand written texts at all), and second, people in similar situations will use similar language. A given situation will tend to evoke a specific body of vocabulary, set phrases, intonations, and so on. Halliday dubs this body of lexical, grammatical, and phonological features a "register." He offers the international language of the air, in which pilots use a limited vocabulary to communicate with other aviators and air traffic controllers, as a clear-cut example.[34]

Halliday's work suggests that, in a given historical context, newspaper articles from the same source, with the same intended audience, and for the same purpose will generally contain similar vocabulary and grammatical structures.[35] To use Halliday's terminology, they will be written in the same register. The concept of register justifies the use of attributes such as source, audience, and purpose as a proxy for detailed linguistic analysis in defining voice. It also undergirds my definition of the voice of a newspaper piece by its source, its purpose, its intended audience, and a few discrete grammatical features, such as imperative verbs or narration in the first person plural. Under this definition, a short wire service report aiming to inform relatively well-educated readers about a discrete event would have one voice; a profile of a heroic "shock worker" intended to motivate other factory operatives to work harder would have another.

Because Bolshevik use of the press was highly self-conscious it is not difficult to define the purpose and intended audience of a given article. Soviet newspapermen were aware of the possible uses of different sorts of journalism, such as the leading editorial (*peredovaia*), the theoretical article, the wire service telegram, and the feuilleton, in promoting the party's agenda. They talked about their journalistic practice in terms of Lenin's theory of agitation and propaganda, which recognized various functions of the press—educating readers, motivating them to action with emotional appeals, and organizing them for political action or economic production. These functions were known respectively as "propaganda," "agitation," and "organization." In thinking about their work's effect on readers, Soviet journalists used these categories, and this book will do so also.

I have attempted to elucidate the categories that will be useful in analyzing the change in tone of the central press in the late 1920s, and to dispose of the notion that suppression of political dissent had anything directly to do with that change. The increasing shrillness of Soviet newspapers resulted from a shift in the distribution of different voices in the newspapers, not the shutdown of some putative NEP pluralism. To understand why Bolshevik journalists and press officials chose to turn up the volume on some voices and turn it down on others, we next turn to the theory of agitation and propaganda that informed their decisions.

Agitation, Propaganda, and the Functions of the Press

In his 1985 book, *The Birth of the Propaganda State*, Peter Kenez argues that mass mobilization using agitation and propaganda was integral to the functioning of the young Bolshevik state. While affirming the importance of the Soviet agitprop apparatus itself, Kenez considers that Bolshevik theories of agitation and propaganda had relatively little effect on practice. In particular, he claims that the central distinction between agitation and propaganda made first by Giorgii Plekhanov, one of the socialist thinkers who introduced Marxism to Russia, and elaborated by Lenin is "not useful."[36] However, the fact that Bolsheviks sometimes used the two terms loosely does not mean that the distinction was not made in practice and debates about practice. "Fighting agitation," which appealed to the masses' emotions with a few simple slogans, and "propaganda," which made its points by presenting more complex explanations, represented two poles of the Bolsheviks' relationship with "the people." Theorists and journalists writing in the central agitprop journals *Red Press*, *Zhurnalist* (*Journalist*—formally the organ of the journalists' labor union), and *Communist Revolution* repeatedly articulated this distinction, although they were not always rigorous in applying the word "agitation" to one pole and "propaganda" to the other.

Throughout the 1920s Soviet newspapermen and agitprop officials carried on an active discussion about how to improve the press and use it more effectively to influence the masses. The phrase "closer to the reader" or "closer to the masses" was code for this issue. At stake was not only the question of what effective propaganda might be, but of what role newspapers and other journals were to play in the new socialist society. The background to this discussion was Lenin's categorization of press function, made in his 1901 article "Where to Begin." In later discussions of the function of the press, Soviet journalists and theorists would encapsulate this theory with one quote from the article: "The newspaper is not only a collective propagandist and a collective agitator, it is also a collective organizer."[37]

The concepts of agitation and propaganda represented opposite poles of Bolshevik thinking about selling their policies and worldview to the masses. They had been part of European socialist discourse at least since the 1870s. German social democrat Wilhelm Liebknecht described the functions of the press as "Teach, propagandize, organize," and Russian social democratic pamphleteers were making the agitation/propaganda distinction by the mid–1890s.[38] Lenin himself probably borrowed the two categories from Plekhanov. He elaborated upon the distinction in his 1902 book, *What Is to Be Done?*:

> The propagandist dealing with, say, the question of unemployment, must explain the capitalist nature of the crisis, the causes of its inevitability in modern society, the necessity for the transformation of this society into a socialist society, etc. In a word he must present "many ideas," so many, indeed that they will be understood only by a few. The agitator, however, speaking on the same subject, will take as an illustration a fact that is most glaring and most widely known to his audience, say the death of an

unemployed worker's family from starvation, the growing impov-
erishment, etc., and utilizing this fact, known to all, will direct his
efforts to presenting a single idea to the masses, e.g., the sense-
lessness of the contradiction between the increase of wealth
and the increase of poverty. He will strive to rouse discontent
and indignation among the masses against this crying injustice,
leaving a more complete explanation of this contradiction to the
propagandist.[39]

According to Lenin, propaganda involved extended theoretical explanations of the socioeconomic processes that underlay surface phenomena such as unemployment. By appealing to audience members' reason,
the propagandist aimed to cultivate in them a whole new worldview.
Propaganda was a process of *education* that required a relatively sophisticated, informed audience. Agitation, on the other hand, motivated the
audience to action by appealing to their emotions with short, stark
stories. The agitator did not seek to change his listeners' worldview, but
to mobilize them. Agitation was the tool of choice for unsophisticated,
even ignorant audiences when quick action was required. Definitions
from the first edition of *The Great Soviet Encyclopedia* link propaganda
with education and agitation with organization/mobilization.

Propaganda signified "illumination" *(osveshchenie)* of an issue through
the presentation of information and explanation in an extended format.
Within the concept nestled the idea of teaching, of raising the "cultural
level" of the masses. For the Bolsheviks this meant teaching peasants
and proletarians to read, drawing them into political life, transforming
their worldview, even instructing them in hygiene. Propaganda was
thus linked with the long-term project of educating the downtrodden
Russian masses to be worthy citizens of the socialist utopia that the
Bolsheviks were constructing.

Agitation meant riling up the populace, motivating it to action by
presenting selected facts and simple slogans. Agitation was more superficial than propaganda. Whereas propaganda was suited to the serious,
long-range tasks of "cultural construction," agitation was considered appropriate for wartime or other crisis situations. Agitation was
also closely related to Lenin's third function of the press, "organization." Indeed, the boundaries between the two categories were unclear.
As a tool for exhorting people to action, agitation was an adjunct to
organization.[40]

As originally formulated in "Where to Begin" the organizational function of the press referred to the fact that the task of producing and distributing an illegal newspaper would compel the Social Democrats, then an underground political party, to set up a network of correspondents, agents, and distributors. This network could then be used to carry out other revolutionary tasks. In the prerevolutionary context of a secret, conspiratorial party, the organizational function of the press had quite a different meaning from that which it took on once the Bolsheviks governed Russia. After the Bolsheviks came to power, their propagandists (including Lenin himself) redefined the press's organizational function to mean the mobilization of labor to increase economic productivity. The years of the First Five-Year Plan found newspapermen visiting the shop floor to organize "socialist competitions," "production reviews," and "production meetings," to elicit denunciations of shirkers and incompetents, and to collect workers' ideas for increasing efficiency. All of this activity was supposed to raise productivity and contribute to the growth of Soviet industry. In contemporary commentary these forms of journalism were referred to as "organization" and sometimes "agitation."

The NEP Mass Enlightenment Project

The transition from War Communism to the New Economic Policy was not just a temporary retreat from maximalist, statist economic policies, but also a commitment to the long-term project of creating citizens of the coming Communist utopia through education—what I called in the introduction the NEP mass enlightenment project. This meant "Cultural Construction," instructing the masses in everything from politics to hygiene. It was necessary to drop the strident agitation of the Civil War, which had aimed to mobilize the population around a few slogans, and begin to educate the people. In Bolshevik terminology, the press had to gear down from agitation to propaganda. In 1923 I. Vardin, editor of the CC Agitprop Department journal *Communist Revolution*, described the difference between the Civil War and the early NEP press this way: "Then the paper was an agitation sheet with an 'Official' section (of party and state directives). The Soviet newspaper of our day doesn't have that deadly clichéd quality; it is free of the 'agit-drum,' and full of letters, articles, notes on the life of workers, peasants, Red Army men."[41]

During the early years of the NEP, publicists and party leaders writing in *Red Press* and *Journalist* focused on the educational/ propagandistic function of the press. In the newspapers themselves "Cultural Construction" was a dominant trope. In 1924 *Izvestiia* regularly published a special section under that rubric. Advocates of Cultural Construction argued that to transform the Soviet Union from an agrarian into an industrialized nation, it was necessary to raise the masses' cultural level and prepare them for the complex political and productive tasks they would have to fulfill in a modern society.

As the Civil War wound down in the spring of 1921 the party leadership was already directing the press to move from agitational, emotional appeals to more sophisticated propaganda. A CC circular from April 4, 1921, laid out a program for the local press to adhere to, including headings for various sections of the newspaper ("The Urban Economy," "Popular Education," "Red Army Life"). It also instructed the local committees that "by collecting facts about local construction, summing up and describing experience in local work, the province or county (uezd) paper should inculcate in the masses a can-do feeling, it should offer them practical, business-like aid in overcoming obstacles and achieving positive results in local socialist construction. The agitation of general, abstract judgments should be replaced by an agitation of facts."[42]

In the first years of the NEP the CC Press Department regularly cautioned leading party organs such as *Pravda* to avoid the simplistic agitation of Civil War journalism. In a February 6, 1924 directive the CC ordered that "the leading party newspapers should orient the party members politically, avoiding superficial 'agitationism' or a narrowly institutional approach to questions, giving instead more facts and planned-out, systematic illumination of them."[43]

During this period the CC press journal *Red Press* constantly used the verb *osveshchat'*, "to illuminate," in describing what newspapers did. The press was to "illuminate" the tasks of socialist construction, the importance of the alliance between workers and peasants, the new tax structure. Party propagandists believed that by using the searchlight of Marxist-Leninist theory to burn through the mystifying fog of culture and tradition, they could "illuminate" the world as it truly was, exposing the realities of class conflict and production relations. Once the laboring classes saw the mechanisms of their own exploitation they would naturally come to support the party and Soviet Power. The Soviet press's job was to explain carefully to its readers the old regime's machinery of oppression and the necessity of temporary sacrifices to stabilize Bolshevik rule and build socialism. Coverage of domestic economic issues by *Pravda* and *Izvestiia* in 1924 and 1925 reflected these assumptions. Articles on monetary reform, the alliance between proletariat and peasantry, state wage policy, and like topics cited a complex range of causes for economic difficulties.

Behind the efforts of Soviet journalists to educate and indoctrinate the masses lay a sincere conviction that Soviet Power was a benevolent power, and that the masses would understand this if the press simply "illuminated" the political and economic situation properly. The peasant or "backward" worker was an intelligent human being. He was educable. It was necessary to meet him halfway when explaining government policy, to comprehend his point of view. This conviction was at work in the central press of the early and middle 1920s. *Izvestiia* ran a section devoted to explaining new laws and taxes to its readers. The paper's wire service reports and reportorial material frequently showed the Soviet government taking some action that would benefit the masses—feeding the hungry, rebuilding a washed-out bridge, and so on.[44]

A central part of the mass enlightenment project was the construction of a newspaper network differentiated by target audience. To reach the heterogeneous population of the Soviet Republic, agitprop officials needed to target particular newspapers at particular social groups. The differentiated press network had its origins in a special commission set up by the CC Agitprop Department in December 1921. Headed by Iakov Doletskii, head of the official wire service ROSTA and including Lev Sosnovskii, *Poor Peasant* editor and prominent Civil War journalist, the commission was charged with organizing a streamlined, cost-effective newspaper network under the direction of central party organs. On January 17, 1922, the CC Secretariat approved the commission's proposal for 232 newspapers, exclusive of the labor union, Red Army, and commissariat presses. They were to be divided into "leading" organs for party and Soviet officials, "special peasant newspapers," "mass newspapers" for less educated urban audiences, Komsomol (Communist youth) newspapers for youth, and newspapers for ethnic minority groups (Jews, Poles, Germans, Armenians, Kazakhs, etc.).[45]

By 1924 the press network, particularly in Moscow and Petrograd, was further differentiated, including newspapers tailored to the varying reading abilities, interests, and education levels of a range of social groups. The CC itself published separate newspapers for party activists (*Pravda*), factory workers (*Rabochaia gazeta* or *The Worker Gazette*), and peasants (*Krestianskaia gazeta* or *The Peasant Gazette*). Evening newspapers such as *Vecherniaia Moskva (Evening Moscow)* were for urban office workers and professionals (usually nonparty), youth newspapers such as *Komsomolskaia pravda (Komsomol Truth)* were for Komsomol activists, and so on. According to a February 6, 1924, circular from the CC Press Department, the job of the differentiated press network was to spread knowledge among workers and peasants and "raise their cultural level." Propaganda—explanation, education, enlightenment—was the order of the day. The peasant press was to explain to its audience the party's rural policies, such as the tax in kind. The worker press was to explain to factory operatives party policies in relevant areas such as wages. The "leading press," charged with providing political guidance and explications of central policy for party cadres, was cautioned to avoid "superficial agitation."[46]

A second central part of the NEP mass enlightenment project was the establishment of the so-called "worker-peasant correspondents movement." During the Civil War some Soviet newspapers, including *Pravda*, began actively soliciting letters from working-class and poor rural readers. Mariia Ulianova at *Pravda* encouraged the early development of the movement. By 1923 the CC Agitprop Department was collecting information from newspapers on their correspondents and trying to standardize the methods for working with them.[47] In November 1923 the Agitprop Department in conjunction with *Pravda* ran the First All-Union Conference of Worker Correspondents. Correspondents from all over the Soviet Republic convened in Moscow to hear reports, pass resolutions, and found the movement's official journal, *Raboche-krestianskii korrespondent (Worker-Peasant Correspondent)*.[48] Editors and agitprop officials expected worker-peasant correspondents to perform a variety of functions, among them monitoring local officials, providing intelligence on popular mood, and selling subscriptions to the newspapers. They also expected that by writing to the papers about public affairs and participating in local study circles the correspondents would improve their writing and reasoning abilities and learn how to participate responsibly in government. The workers and peasants, in other words, would master "culture."

Like other aspects of the NEP, the mass enlightenment project in the press was controversial. Given the later transformation of Soviet newspapers under his leadership, it is worth noting that Joseph Stalin, who had by 1922 already attained a powerful position in the CC executive apparatus, was impatient with it. In the spring of 1922 he challenged Old Bolsheviks Konstantin S. Eremeev and Viacheslav Karpinskii's plan for the Central Committee's new mass worker newspaper, *Rabochii* (*Worker*, later renamed *The Worker Gazette*). Influenced by thinkers from the Proletarian Culture movement *(Proletkult)* who advocated the construction of an entirely new proletarian culture to replace the bourgeois culture of the old regime, Eremeev and Karpinskii wanted the new paper to be "a newspaper by the workers, and not a newspaper for the workers." Their orientation was propagandistic. The new paper would consist almost entirely of worker letters and "be a large, serious popular organ of propaganda and agitation, and not an agitational broadsheet of the type of the first years of the proletarian revolution."[49]

Although the Eleventh Party Congress approved Eremeev and Karpinskii's plan for *Worker* on April 1, 1922, Stalin had already secured the Central Committee Orgburo's approval of an alternative project, which ordered the editors to model *Worker* on the "militant" Civil War newspapers *Bednota (Poor Peasant)* and *Gudok (The Siren)*. Eremeev and Karpinskii, who thought that Stalin was forcing *The Worker* into a superficial, agitational mode inappropriate for the long-term project of "enlightening" the workers, offered their resignations in protest. In early May 1922, the Central Committee Secretariat replaced them with a new head editor, N. I. Smirnov. Stalin, through his dominant position in the Central Committee's executive apparatus, thus secured the continuation of the militant, agitational style of Civil War journalism at the Central Committee's own mass worker newspaper.[50]

Stalin reiterated his support for agitational/mobilizational journalism in a vituperative exchange with Sergei Ingulov on the pages of *Pravda* in May 1923. In this debate, Stalin contended that the paramount function of the press in Soviet society was mobilizing the masses around party directives. "The press," he wrote, "is the single tool by which the party daily speaks to the working class." According to Stalin Civil War agitation exemplified what the relationship between the party and the masses ought to be—"tens and hundreds of thousands of workers respond[ing] to the call of the party press." Ingulov took issue with Stalin's narrow understanding of the relationship between the party and the populace, arguing that the party should not just speak *to* the masses; it should be engaged in a conversation with them. Through the worker and peasant correspondents who wrote in to the newspapers the masses could advise and interrogate the party. There should be "a conversation" between rulers and ruled.[51]

Studies of the reader and stylistic reform were a third pillar of the

NEP mass enlightenment project at the newspapers. To communicate their message effectively, party propagandists concluded that they needed more information about the reading habits and comprehension of "the laboring masses." On April 27, 1922, the CC Secretariat recalled Iakov Shafir, a party member and linguist, from assignment in Georgia. In the coming years Shafir would serve as the CC point man on issues of journalistic style and reader response to the press, reviewing children's books for the Agitprop Department, studying reader response to various newspapers, and publishing articles on the reform of writing style.[52]

Professional linguists from outside the CC executive apparatus also contributed to the party's style reform efforts. To cite one important example, members of the Moscow Linguistics Circle, a group of university-affiliated linguists with funding from the Commissariat of Enlightenment, published studies of newspaper language throughout the NEP years. In June 1923 the Circle had on its agenda the study of contemporary newspaper language, of "social dialectology" (the specialized language of various social/occupation groups, from bureaucrats to criminals), and of the transformation in Russian literary language wrought by the Revolution. Circle members who published works on the style of the mass press included formalist critic Viktor Shklovskii, professor of linguistics Dmitrii Ushakov, and Grigorii Vinokur, one of Ushakov's graduate students and later a prominent Stalinist literary critic. Their participation in the CC Agitprop Department's style reform campaign was typical of early Soviet scholars' efforts to merge their own mass enlightenment projects with the party's own.[53]

Between 1924 and 1929 the CC, the Moscow Party Committee, the Commissariat of Enlightenment, the journalists' labor union, the central state publishing house (GIZ), and various newspapers all sponsored studies of reader comprehension and newspaper readership. These studies aimed to discover what newspaper genres readers preferred, which newspapers they read, and what vocabulary and grammar structures were most difficult for them to understand. Ultimately the authors of reader studies hoped to adjust newspaper style and content to the needs and abilities of working-class and peasant readers. Although early Soviet reader studies were methodologically flawed (to name two problems, none selected random samples and few used anonymous questionnaires), they did represent a serious attempt to improve communication with workers and peasants.[54]

Suspicion of popular culture and tastes in general created great tensions within the NEP mass enlightenment project. Educated Russians tended to believe that the masses would *not* select salutary reading material on their own, and Marxist doctrine reinforced their view of common working people as "dark" and "ignorant." To fulfill their social and political functions, then, Soviet newspapers had to be popular but also salutary in content.[55] They had to sell without being sensational—without running the stories about sex, crimes, scandals, and the lives of the rich and famous that were the staple of Western tabloids. For Soviet editors and writers this was a difficult conundrum. Editors and publicists agreed that *Pravda* and *Izvestiia* were unattractive to the mass reader because they were formatted like the serious, "thick" journals of political and literary commentary. The masses were not ready for this. Their levels of culture and political consciousness were too low. Thus, the problem of the mass enlightenment project in the newspapers was to strike the right compromise between changing the presentation of news so as to appeal to the reader, and educating the reader to appreciate intellectually sophisticated commentary on economic, political, and literary life.[56] Soviet debates about reforms in newspaper style, layout, and the worker-peasant correspondents' movement were all permeated by this problem.

Russian Marxists had no doubt that yellow journalism (called by Russian intellectuals "boulevardism" after the cheap, sensational tabloids for sale on Paris boulevards) facilitated the exploitation of the masses under capitalism by distracting their attention from the realities of class struggle and wage slavery. Yet they could not get over the feeling that there was something to be plucked from the experience of the Western popular press apart from the forbidden fruit of "bourgeois sensationalism." Was the secret of the capitalist tabloids, they asked, their variegated and attractive layout, their photographs, or their content? Did they address issues relevant to workers' lives? In a January 1923 issue of *Journalist* there appeared a long article about the English tabloid *The Daily Mail* and its owner Lord Northcliffe. The author concluded that Northcliffe's paper communicated effectively with the masses by explaining the problems of workers' daily existence in terms of bourgeois ideology. *The Daily Mail* attributed individual success or failure in life to the individual's moral qualities (diligence versus laziness, morality versus depravity) rather than to economic relations (the capitalists' exploitation of the working class). Although these explanations were incorrect, they did help the masses make sense of their daily lives. Soviet journalism's job was to help the masses understand their daily lives by providing the *correct* explanations. This statement of the Soviet press's mission as education and enlightenment was in tune with the general atmosphere of early NEP journalism.[57]

One way of attracting "mass readers" was to use more photographs and adapt more varied layouts and typefaces. But many early Bolshevik journalists were suspicious even of these superficial concessions to popular taste, feeling that a "serious political organ" should not have a flashy exterior.[58] Nonetheless, as early as 1923 contributors to *Journalist* argued that the mass newspaper of the future would have to abandon the old "Soviet" layout for a less monotonous system based on the practice of American or Western European newspapers.[59] In 1927 *Journalist* reprinted excerpts from an American journalism text, *Editing the Day's News*, which explained how to lay out "pyramid headlines" (printed one atop another), "streamer headlines" (running the whole length of the page), and "jump headlines" (headings given extra emphasis by the white space around them). The author of *Editing the Day's News*, George Bastian, also described how varied typefaces and photographs could be used to liven up a newspaper. *Journalist* noted that even such staid organs as *Pravda* were beginning to use "American techniques" of layout.[60] By the end of the First Five-Year plan all of the important mass circulation central papers had adopted many features of the "American system," publishing more photographs and varying the typefaces of their headlines. But these changes were quite small compared with the adoption of entirely new and wholly Soviet methods for producing "sensational" news.

End of the Mass Enlightenment Project and the Invention of Mass Journalism

As the NEP era wore on, discussion of the press's role in society shifted back in the direction of agitation and mobilization. Soviet newspapers' retrograde movement from the propaganda/education pole of press function to the agitation/mobilization pole was driven ultimately by Soviet leaders' desire to increase economic productivity and industrialize the USSR. By 1925 party leaders were deeply concerned with the linked problems of low industrial productivity and endemic grain shortages. By raising productivity they hoped to lower the price of manufactured goods, bringing them within the range of peasant budgets. Peasants purchasing industrial products needed cash, so they would be motivated to sell more grain to the state on the open market. In addition to raising the state's stock of grain, higher productivity would mean more profit to invest in further Soviet industrialization. The difficulty was to squeeze more production out of industrial workers without provoking resistance or rebellion. Party leaders' solution was the "belt-tightening" campaign of 1926.

The belt-tightening campaign, or *rezhim ekonomii*, provided the decisive push that propelled the Soviet press toward mass organizational journalism. At the very outset of the campaign, in late February 1926, the chairman of the Supreme Council on the Economy (VSNKh), Feliks Dzerzhinskii, called on newspapermen to facilitate cost-cutting by putting factories "under the microscope," auditing their expenditures and production processes.[61] In response to the party's call, editors at so-called "mass worker" and Komsomol newspapers pioneered new forms of organizing journalism, forms that became the backbone of Soviet press coverage during the First Five-Year Plan. All of these involved direct intervention by newspapermen in the production process. In Tver, a textile center north of Moscow, *Tverskaia pravda* editor Aleksei Ivanovich Kapustin organized a series of audits of local factories, which he dubbed "production reviews" (*proizvodstvennye smotry)*. The Komsomol newspapers *Komsomolskaia pravda* and *Changing of the Guard* (Leningrad) began organizing and publicizing "contests" (*konkursy)* for maximum output between factories and individual workers. Such contests, christened "socialist competitions," became a prominent feature of Soviet news coverage during the First Five-Year Plan and after. Another innovator in organizing journalism was *The Urals Worker,* a mass worker paper published in Sverdlovsk.[62]

The mobilizing journalism of the 1926 belt-tightening campaign was new in that newspapermen actually went in to the factories and helped organize production. Its rhetoric, however, was the agitational rhetoric of the Civil War, full of military metaphors and exhortations to action. By joining new forms of journalism such as the socialist competition with the militant rhetoric of the Civil War, newspapermen aimed not just to organize the shop floor, but to galvanize factory activists by equating industrial production with the epic military struggles of the revolutionary years. This presentation of industrialization as war—indeed, as a kind of ritualistic replay of the Revolution and Civil War—would became the dominant metaphor of the First Five-Year Plan.

The Shock Campaign

The organizers of the new journalism referred to themselves as *massoviki*, or "mass activists," and their work as *massovost*, or "mass work." In the context of newspaper work I will translate these terms as "mass journalists" and "mass journalism." The mass journalists' most important tool was the *udarnaia kampaniia*, or "shock campaign," a militant agitation campaign coordinated around a particular party slogan or task. The term *udarnaia* or "shock" referred to the elite shock troops trained by various powers in World War I. Newspaper shock campaigns were permeated with military metaphors of this sort.

The language of the shock campaign, with its command-form headlines, military metaphors, grandiose superlatives, and vocabulary of urban revolt and class war, was a complex amalgam of elements that had entered the speech and writing of Bolshevik activists over a twenty- to thirty-year period. Even before the turn of the century, Russian revolutionary emigrés in Europe had picked up foreign words related to class struggle, strikes, and revolutions, such as *barrikady* (barricades), *avangard* (the avant garde), *organizovat* (to organize), and *proletariat*. During World War I and the Civil War a whole constellation of military terms, such as *front*, *liniia* (line), and *otriad* (detachment) entered the Bolshevik vocabulary. During the Revolution and Civil War Bolshevik publicists also borrowed some phrases from popular speech, such as the sailors' peremptory command *Daesh'!* (very roughly translatable as "Do it!" or "Give it everything!").[63] The militant and military language of the Civil War Bolshevik press owed a great deal to Red Army chief Leon Trotsky's grandiloquent exhortations to action, issued often from his command train. Trotsky's addresses to common soldiers and activists were full of imperatives ("To the Urals, revolutionary proletarians! To the Urals, conscious peasants! Comrade Communists, forward!") and superlatives ("the most grandiose victories").[64] There was probably also extensive cross-fertilization between the German Spartacist press and the Bolshevik newspapers.[65] All of these elements came together in the Civil War agitation of the Soviet press. The shock campaign's militant language was not invented by mass journalists in the 1920s, or by Stalin and his supporters during the First Five-Year Plan. It had been part of the repertoire of Bolshevik journalism since the Civil War.

The shock campaign was supposed to mobilize the masses, to get them to close ranks around the party and undertake some task, such as raising productivity or paying the agricultural tax. In theory at least it involved every part of the party's agitprop apparatus, and not just the newspapers. Local activists might organize discussion groups and exhibits, collect funds, teach adult education classes, and distribute pamphlets or even "agit-toys," which taught children lessons about class struggle.[66] Because the shock campaign was aimed at readers with little or no education, it required a simple presentation, with easy language and straightforward thematic organization. Contributors to *Communist Revolution* and *Red Press* agreed that the ideal press campaign repeated a single slogan over and over, avoided difficult technical terms, continued for a prolonged period of time, and was maximally militant.[67]

Command-form headlines were a key element of the shock campaign. *Red Press*, the CC Press Department organ, made this explicit in January 1924 when it praised *The Perm Star* for its use of militant "shock language" in a productivity campaign. One of the newspaper's exemplary headlines from the campaign was "Tanner! Before the war you processed an average of 127 skins a day! Now you process only 108. Fifteen percent are missing. Get to work!"[68]

Some journalists in the mid-1920s saw the shock campaign as a way to make the newspaper exciting without stooping to the vulgar sensationalism of the prerevolutionary boulevard press. In 1925, for example, M. Levidov, a regular contributor to *Journalist*, argued that the shock campaign was actually a means of rehabilitating sensationalism in an acceptable form. Levidov thought the fear of "boulevardism" had become an unhealthy obsession. He complained that in the NEP Soviet newspapermen wrote their pieces too cautiously, giving them humdrum titles such as "On the Question of . . ." and "On the Occasion of. . . ." They "guaranteed their work against sensationalism, boulevardism, and coincidentally against [the readers'] interest." "Why this petty bourgeois fear of boulevardism?" Levidov asked, and went on, "Was not our revolution a boulevard revolution?!" He endorsed the work of mass newspapers such as *The Worker Gazette*, *Worker Moscow*, and *Poor Peasant*, recommending that *Pravda* and *Izvestiia* imitate their "militant shock character." His prescription for a lively newspaper was short articles, concentration of material on the front page, and militant agitational rhetoric.[69]

Critics attacked the shock campaign for exactly the same reasons Levidov praised it. They polemicized against its "naked 'meetingism', the striving, not to educate, not to explain, but to strew slogans around, to pound the war drums of agitation." In an article written for the 1929 anniversary of the October Revolution, Sergei Ingulov, just removed from the leadership of the Newspaper Section of the CC Agitprop Department, criticized mass journalists newly ascendant in the central press for immoderate militance, sensationalism, and superficiality. Ingulov put his argument in the context of Soviet press history, placing the origins of the shock campaign in the crude agitation of the Civil War. But wartime agitational journalism was not appropriate for the prolonged tasks of economic reconstruction and cultural enlighten-ment. Calmness and reasoned propaganda were necessary, not the hys-terics, "self-promotion," "pathos," or "meetingism" of the shock campaign. Ingulov's criticisms defined quite clearly the shock campaign and its place in Soviet thinking about agitation and propaganda. They placed the campaign's origins in the Civil War era and pinpointed its "shrillness," militance, and mobilizing purpose.[70]

During the middle years of the NEP the CC mass newspapers *The Peasant Gazette* and *The Worker Gazette* devoted proportionally more space to shock campaigns and used more militant language than either *Pravda* or *Izvestiia* (see Table 3 below). Shock campaigns dominated *The Peasant Gazette* in particular. Targeted at peasants and rural activists, this CC newspaper was full of command-form headlines and simple statements of propaganda schemas. A piece on getting ready for the winter sowing would be labeled *"Gotovsia k sevu i peresevu!"* ("Prepare for the Winter and Spring Sowings!"). Political commentary might be headed "What Is Trotskyism? Trotskyism Is Lack of Faith in the Power of the Revolution." *The Peasant Gazette* presented a limited number of propaganda schemas, most of them explicitly labeled. For example, one preoccupation of the party leadership in 1925 was transforming the concept of the *smychka*, the alliance of peasant and worker that had made the Revolution of 1917, into the concept of trade between the countryside and the city, the exchange of industrial goods for produce and grain. *The Peasant Gazette* presented this straightforwardly as *"Gorod-derevne, "* or "From the City—to the Countryside." *The Peasant Gazette* also frequently ran headlines that imitated informal popular speech, as for example, *"Ekh zhizn' ty nasha kustarnaia!"* ("Oh, Life, You're Our Workshop!") or *"Doloi svistunov!"* ("Stick It to the Pick-pockets!")[71]

In 1925 such language and presentation was considered inappropriate for *Pravda* and *Izvestiia*, which were aimed at supposedly more sophis-ticated party officials and the urban intelligentsia. However, *The Peasant*

Gazette of 1925 foreshadowed 1933 issues of *Pravda* and *Izvestiia*. Rural party and Komsomol activists wrote in to the paper, reporting their activities using military metaphors. Most of these reports followed a three-part formula—successes, failures, and tasks for the future. They had titles such as "We're Succeeding" and "We Must Reform Our Party Cell." The newspaper also included the projections of a "shining future," which would become one of the defining tropes of socialist realism and 1930s Soviet journalism. At the bottom of page three of *The Peasant Gazette*'s January 20, 1925, issue, for instance, there appeared a drawing of a village at night, with lights shining from the windows of the houses, and below this, the caption "Just a few more years and Lenin's lamps will burn in every hut!" *The Peasant Gazette* also featured "ardent greetings" on the occasion of a conference or convention—a phenomenon rare in the *Pravda* or *Izvestiia* of 1925. A comparison of the newspapers' coverage of the All-Union Teachers' Conference held in early 1925 is instructive. The peasant newspaper trumpeted "*The Peasant Gazette* Sends Ardent Greetings to the Conference of Red Teachers!," whereas the leading organs simply headed their coverage "The All-Union Teachers' Conference." In terms of the Bolshevik theory of agitation and propaganda, *The Peasant Gazette* was dominated by agitational journalism and the shock campaign, whereas coverage in 1925 editions of *Pravda* and *Izvestiia* was more propagandistic, educational, and informative in character.[72]

We can use the working definition of voice sketched earlier in this essay to specify the characteristics of the shock campaign. The shock campaign was actually a chorus of several voices, all "singing" the same party slogan. Its *purpose* was to mobilize readers to carry out tasks set by the party. Its intended *audience* was the ordinary party or Komsomol activist—relatively uneducated and "backward." The grammatical and lexical indices of the shock campaign were command- or implied command-form verbs and vocabulary of war and struggle. But the campaign material came from several different sources—the Bolshevik activist or factory worker writing in from the "front," the party leader delivering a triumphant speech to a conference, the correspondent reporting on successes and failures in "battle," and the editor outlining the next "campaign." Different sources thus defined different voices, but the voices were united by a single target audience, a single purpose, a single party slogan or task, and a single vocabulary of war and struggle.

The shock campaign projected an image of the party, and indeed of all of Soviet society, as an army responding to the commands emanating from the "General Staff"—the Central Committee. The peculiar signature of the shock campaign was the use of military metaphors and "fighting" vocabulary. Factory operatives and party activists were "soldiers of socialist construction"; the factories, mineshafts, and collective farms "the front." Orders were couched in command-form headlines. "Loyal soldiers"—worker correspondents, collective farm chairmen, Red Army soldiers—reported in from their posts at the "front," describing successes and setbacks and committing themselves to carrying out the orders of the center no matter what the cost. "Generals"—Stalin, Kirov, Molotov, Ordzhonikidze—visited the "front" to congratulate the "soldiers" and distribute medals. In this drama editors played the role of low-level officers, perhaps platoon or squad leaders, passing along the generals' orders, explaining them, exhorting the soldiers to carry them out effectively.

Between 1925 and 1933 the shock campaign came to dominate domestic coverage in *Pravda* and *Izvestiia* (see Tables 1 and 2). The total space devoted to campaign-related material increased by about 50 percent. At the later date more than two-thirds of the domestic news was part of one campaign or another. Reports "from the front" giving accounts of victories and denunciations of shirkers and traitors took up far more space than in 1925. The central press in 1933 depended more heavily on verbatim transcriptions of party directives and party leaders' speeches. These took up just over 25 percent of domestic coverage as compared with 10 to 20 percent eight years earlier. Not only that, but in 1925 a significant proportion of this kind of party material emanated from local organizations, whereas in 1933 almost all of it came from the CC. In the meantime "Chronicle" material, the short news items about crimes, accidents, and cultural events that had filled the back pages of *Pravda* and *Izvestiia* in 1925, virtually disappeared. In 1925 *Izvestiia*'s coverage of a flood in Leningrad took up half a page. In 1933 such an item would have merited no more than a tiny paragraph on the back page. The percentage of space devoted to other genres, such as economic analysis, popular science, and book reviews, also dropped. The shock campaign "chorus" was drowning out other voices.

The fighting tone of the headlines also increased dramatically during the period under study. In 1925 around 10 percent of domestic headlines and headings in *Pravda* and *Izvestiia* contained shock language (command-form verbs and military language). In 1933 more than

Table 1. Space devoted to ongoing campaigns as a percentage of total domestic coverage—*Izvestiia*

	1925	1933
1. Total page area in sample (in square inches)	16,679	11,279
2. Total page area devoted to domestic coverage	12,492	9,329
3. Editorials, commentary on ongoing campaigns	19.2%	18.0%
4. Directives from party/Soviet institutions, leaders' speeches	19.9%	26.5%
5. Reports on campaigns in progress, successes, setbacks	7.9%	14.8%
6. Reports from "loyal soldiers"	0.0%	5.1%
7. Greetings and congratulations from leaders to "soldiers"	0.4%	3.8%
8. Total percentage of space devoted to ongoing campaigns	47.3%	68.2%

Note: See appendix for information on the compiling of this table.

Table 2. Space devoted to ongoing campaigns as a percentage of total domestic coverage—*Pravda*

	1925	1933
1. Total page area in sample (in square inches)	15,706	10,345
2. Total page area devoted to domestic coverage	12,894	8,407
3. Editorials, commentary on ongoing campaigns	10.5%	13.1%
4. Directives from party/Soviet institutions, leaders' speeches	11.2%	27.7%
5. Reports on campaigns in progress, successes, setbacks	6.5%	20.0%
6. Reports from "loyal soldiers"	0.0%	8.3%
7. Greetings and congratulations from leaders to "soldiers"	0.0%	1.9%
8. Total percentage of space devoted to ongoing campaigns	10.3%	78.8%

Note: See appendix for information on the compiling of this table.

Table 3. Percentage of shock headlines for various newspapers, 1925 and 1933

Newspaper	Shock Headlines (%)	
	1925	1933
Pravda	10.4	48.2
Izvestiia	8.4	42.7
The Peasant Gazette	42.8	—
The Worker Gazette	23.6	—

Note: See appendix for information on the compiling of this table.

40 percent did. As Table 3 demonstrates, both "leading" papers were converging with the CC mass newspapers *Worker Gazette* and *Peasant Gazette*, which were already running many shock headlines in 1925. This was because *Pravda* and *Izvestiia* had been retargeted at a new mass audience—the hundreds of thousands of working-class activists who entered the party in the late 1920s and early 1930s.

There were other changes in the leading papers. Both printed more photographs and illustrations in 1933 than in 1925, and used a larger range of typefaces. Articles, other than transcriptions of party leaders' speeches, were shorter. In essence, the domestic coverage of both central organs became one big campaign pushing breakneck industrialization and collectivization under the overarching slogan of "socialist construction." Daily departments such as "On the Industrial Front" presented the struggle to accomplish these tasks as a war. Not only was more space devoted to official campaigns, but there was also a contraction in focus from a diverse party agenda to an obsession with raising industrial and agricultural production.

Between 1928 and 1930 the shock campaign came to dominate *Pravda, Izvestiia,* and other central newspapers that had previously had a relatively moderate, propagandistic tone (such as *Trud—Labor*—and *Evening Moscow*). These newspapers were remodeled along the lines of NEP mass worker and peasant papers such as the CC's own *Peasant Gazette* and *Worker Gazette*. This did not happen by a process of drift, but under direct CC orders. Under pressure from the party leadership to mobilize activists for the regime's new crash industrialization program, newspapermen resorted to the shock campaign as their favored mode of agitational, organizational journalism. They retargeted their newspapers at a new generation of young lower-class male activists just entering the party, and they abandoned the NEP mass enlightenment project. The increasing shrillness of the Soviet press in the late 1920s thus grew out of the exigencies of forced-draft industrialization and the party's determination to use the newspapers as a mobilizing tool.

But CC decisions did not and could not completely determine the direction that Soviet journalism took during the First Five-Year Plan. Newspapermen and middle-level agitprop officials created the new forms of mobilizing journalism. They did so in the context of existing Bolshevik culture, and they responded to the perceived reading tastes of activist youth. Even the newspapers' tightening focus on their activist audience did not derive solely from CC initiatives—it was accelerated by the Soviet economy of shortage. Political decisions, social change, cultural assumptions, and economic pressures interacted to shape the Soviet press.

~ 2

Newspaper Distribution and the Emergence of Soviet Information Rationing

T HROUGHOUT THE 1920S Soviet propaganda officials struggled to ensure that key newspapers reached their target audiences. Radio was in its infancy, and the telephone and even telegraph networks did not extend beyond larger cities, so newspapers were an essential means of communicating with the populace. Even more important, the press was a vital conduit for Central Committee (CC) orders to party officials and activists in the provinces. Keeping this conduit open was not easy. Previous studies of newspaper distribution during the New Economic Policy (NEP) have outlined the immense material difficulties faced by press officials, including newsprint shortages, lack of funds, and poor transport and communications infrastructure.[1] Building on these studies and on new archival evidence, this chapter argues that the repeated crises of newspaper distribution in the NEP were part of a complex process in which the party's determination to get newspapers to its support base interacted with state subsidization of the mass media to drive press distribution in the direction of a central rationing system. The result by the early 1930s was the rationing of information to privileged strata in an emerging quasi-caste hierarchy. The story of early Soviet newspaper distribution is thus part of the larger story of the emergence of a privileged status group of party officials and activists who served the Soviet state. The case of newspaper distribution shows that the emergence of this status group was overdetermined— conditioned by multiple causes, including Bolshevik leaders' self-identification as an avant-garde party, their decision to industrialize the Soviet Union at a breakneck pace, their use of the press to mobilize a far-flung network of activists and officials, their central control of the economy, and their rejection of market mechanisms for the distribution of goods.

I view the development of early Soviet society as a process of stratification into various status groups (collective farmers, party officials and activists, etc.) and, following Max Weber and Ken Jowitt, I see this process as the routinization of the party's "impersonal charisma." My understanding of the process of routinization is strongly influenced by the work of Janos Kornai, who argues that "the classical system" of state socialism, by which he indicates something like the high Stalinist system, is "coherent." By this Kornai means that various elements of the classical system, such as the Communist Party's monopoly on political power, state ownership of property and the means of production, reliance on bureaucratic as opposed to market coordination of the economy, the economy of shortage, and the official ideology all reinforce one another. This chapter focuses on the mutual reinforcement of Bolshevik avant-gardism and the economy of shortage. Constant shortages (of newsprint and other goods), which had their roots in the state domination of the economy, drove upper-level party officials to institute rationing to ensure that their own bureaucrats and activists had the information and the material goods they required. Shortage thus increased the perquisites of the bureaucracy and accelerated its evolution into a privileged Weberian status group, an evolution already driven by Bolshevik self-identification as an exclusive, avant-garde group with a special claim to political power.[2]

State Subsidy of the Press

In the 1920s and 1930s the Central Committee Orgburo or Secretariat made the most important decisions about press financing and distribution based on advice and information provided by CC agitation-and-propaganda (agitprop) officials. (The Committee on Press Affairs of the Council of People's Commissars administered the details of the business side of press affairs.) Approval by the CC Politburo of Orgburo/Secretariat decisions was routine. As this chapter demonstrates, after 1928 the party CC took over more and more of the decisions related to press financing and distribution. The whole press management apparatus became more centralized. Most important, the distribution departments of individual publishing houses were eventually closed

(1931–1932) and replaced with a single centralized distribution organ, Soiuzpechat. Private distribution agents were also eliminated from the distribution system beginning in 1928.

As part of their crash efforts to propagandize the population during the Civil War the Bolsheviks distributed the newspapers for free through factories, barracks, schools, "reading huts," party organizations, and village soviet offices.[3] With the end of the Civil War, however, party leaders determined to overhaul the financing and distribution of the press to cut costs and ensure direct CC control of the newspapers. Between November 1921 and January 1922 the Council of People's Commissars and the CC Agitprop Department and Orgburo slashed central subsidies to the press, ordered that newspapers be sold rather than handed out gratis, and took over ideological and financial supervision of the provincial newspaper network from the Russian Telegraph Agency (ROSTA). Newspapers were supposedly put on a "self-financing" regime *(khozraschet)*, but the CC also made provisions for continuing press subsidies by local executive committees and the Commissariat of Internal Affairs. The goal of these decrees was to cut the size of the Soviet press network and shift operating costs from the central budget to consumers, enterprises, and local government.[4]

The central decision to shift to paid distribution of the press triggered catastrophic drops in circulation and the closing of many newspapers, in an episode that became known as the Press Crisis.[5] The crisis disrupted the newspaper distribution system, fraying the already weak lines of communication between the CC and provincial party organizations. In the spring of 1922 party officials from Orenburg, Arkhangelsk, Azerbaijan, Ustiug, Semipalatinsk, Irkutsk, Zaporozhe, Simbirsk, and the Chuvash regions all complained to the CC that they were not receiving Moscow newspapers. *Pravda* in particular carried vital information about central policy decisions and the political situation. Failure to deliver it to provincial party committees meant an almost complete breakdown in communications.[6]

The near-collapse of the provincial press network prompted the CC to restore some of the central subsidies to the press, mandate free distribution of newspapers to key institutions, and order Communist party members to subscribe to *Pravda*.[7] As early as February 1922 the CC announced that it would fund two subscriptions to a package of central newspapers for every province party committee and one subscription for every county committee.[8] In late April the CC Secretariat, alarmed by the rapid fall in the circulation of *Poor Peasant*, provided free subscriptions for township *(volost)* executive committees and a number of other rural government offices.[9] In early summer of 1922 the CC Secretariat restored subsidies to the provincial press, earmarking 107,753 gold-backed rubles for local papers.[10] Throughout 1922 and 1923 the CC continued to provide funds for *Poor Peasant* and the new mass worker paper *Worker*.[11]

Even as they declared the press "self-supporting," then, party officials continued direct and indirect subsidies to ensure that subscribers within their power base would receive newspapers. Free distribution was one way of achieving this, as was ordering party members to subscribe. Yet another was bulk distribution of papers to essential institutions at discounted rates. This practice, which had dominated the distribution system during the Civil War, was known as "collective subscription."[12] In 1921–1922 collective subscriptions made up a large proportion of total newspaper circulation. In the third week of January 1922, for example, they accounted for 57 percent of the circulation of the three leading Petrograd newspapers.[13] Collective subscriptions remained important throughout the NEP years. There were many reasons for this, but one was the CC's continued subsidization of such subscriptions. The November 28, 1921, Council of People's Commissars decree transferring the press to paid distribution mandated that newspaper prices be determined by production costs, *except in the case of collective subscriptions.* There it was permissible to sell papers below cost. The party leadership was willing to pay to make sure that their message reached their support base in the barracks, the factories, and the party/ state offices.[14]

In the later NEP years most Soviet newspapers continued to require state subsidies. Of the three major CC newspapers only *Pravda* recorded a profit for the three fiscal years between 1926 and 1928. *The Worker Gazette* reported profits in 1927 and 1928, and *The Peasant Gazette* for 1928 only. And these official figures certainly exaggerate profits. The three major CC newspapers all received extensive hidden subsidies, including tax exemptions, favorable rates for postal and railroad delivery, controlled prices for newsprint, and state loans converted into outright grants. A 1929 Workers' and Peasants' Inspectorate (Soviet acronym RKI) report stated that none of the CC publishing houses kept a complete accounting of expenditures and that *Pravda* had in fact *lost* money in 1928, even while reporting a profit. One version of the RKI's report also noted that *The Peasant Gazette*, nominally in the black, was in fact losing money during the first months of 1929.[15]

The profitability of an NEP newspaper depended heavily upon its target audience. As discussed in Chapter 1, Soviet newspapers during the NEP were differentiated by target audience, with some aimed at urban workers, others peasants, and so on. Papers that sold to white-collar urbanites usually made money, whereas those aimed at peasants, youth, workers, and national minority groups tended to lose money. But party officials were quite willing to subsidize huge losses at peasant, youth, and worker papers in order to "enlighten" these groups. The story of the CC peasant newspaper *Peasant Gazette,* founded in late 1923, exemplifies this.

A high priority for the Press Subdepartment of the CC in the years 1923–1924 was getting the newspapers to rural residents. Newspapers were supposed to be one of the key links in the *smychka,* the alliance of peasantry with proletariat that would build socialism. Unfortunately, information reaching the Press Subdepartment in 1923 demonstrated that not even the so-called peasant press was reaching the "rural fast-nesses." According to the Subdepartment's data the circulation of rural county newspapers was static. And as of November 1, 1923, only 42 county newspapers out of a total of 121 targeted the peasantry. Their circulation totaled a pathetic 19,500 out of a total print run of 188,020 for all county organs.[16] Nor were the province-level newspapers doing much better. According to Agitprop Department data from 1923, there were only 26 provincial peasant newspapers in the entire federa-tion, only 9 of them in European Russia. The total onetime print run of these papers was 85,000, but in reality 90 percent of these issues circulated in the provincial capitals and the bordering counties. Press Subdepartment data indicated that few newspapers made provisions for individual subscriptions, and street prices were prohibitively high, often 15 to 30 rubles an issue.[17]

To solve the problem of getting the party's message to the country-side, CC Agitprop officials decided to publish a new national peasant newspaper, *The Peasant Gazette.* The newspaper's primary task would be to sell the new party policy of alliance between the peasants and the proletariat, whose concrete expression was the establishment of a tax in kind on agricultural produce and the liberalization of trade. From the beginning Agitprop officials understood that the paper would have to be very cheap for individual peasants to buy it. To keep costs down it would come out only once a week (later twice a week), and collec-tive subscriptions by clusters of peasant households would be encour-aged. Even so, the paper would require large subsidies, both direct and indirect.[18]

Expectations proved correct. When the Central Committee began publication of *The Peasant Gazette* in late 1923, subscription grew at a rapid clip, but the paper ran a large deficit. But because of its determination to reach the "wild peasants," the CC was willing to subsidize the paper liberally. During the fiscal year 1923–1924 *The Peasant Gazette* received 23,000 rubles a month in direct subsidies from the People's Commissariat of Finance for a print run of 150,000, and an additional 400 rubles for every 10,000 issues printed above 150,000. From October 1924 monthly funding was set at 25,000 rubles, or 300,000 rubles for the fiscal year 1924–1925. When the People's Commissariat of Finance reduced this to an annual total of 200,000 rubles (or 16,667 rubles per month), *The Peasant Gazette*'s editor and financial manager protested, asserting that at the current circulation of 400,000 the paper lost 39,479 rubles a month.[19]

Like peasant newspapers, the Communist Youth League (Komsomol) papers targeted an impoverished audience, and like the peasant newspapers they were consistent money losers. The central Komsomol paper, *Komsomolskaia pravda*, founded in 1925, lost money throughout the NEP period, as did its sister in Leningrad, *Changing of the Guard*, and most of its provincial cousins.[20] *Komsomolskaia pravda*, which began publication May 1, received 125,000 rubles from the Central Committee in start-up funds and ran a deficit each month through August 1925, when the paper lost 7,450 rubles.[21] It went on losing money through 1928.[22] *Changing of the Guard* too was a sinkhole for subsidies. In February 1926 the publishing house of the newspaper *Leningrad Pravda* complained to the Komsomol Press Department that in the six and a half months since July 16, 1925, when *Leningrad Pravda* took over publication of *Changing of the Guard*, the latter had lost 72,795 rubles. Lowering expenses for the paper was not possible, according to the complaint. The current price of 60 kopecks did not cover costs, but raising the price to the one ruble, 30 kopecks that would cover them would make *Changing of the Guard* too expensive for Komsomol youth.[23]

Party officials often attached unprofitable newspapers aimed at priority audiences to evening urban newspapers, which generally made high profits. The evening paper would serve as a cash cow for the less profitable organ. This was in fact one of the primary functions of urban evening newspapers in the early Soviet press network. The evening papers targeted the urban intelligentsia and white-collar workers, social groups that many inside the party considered "alien," but whose members were more ready and able to buy a newspaper than blue-collar laborers and peasants. To reach this audience, the evening newspapers pushed the boundaries of ideologically acceptable journalism, printing "sensational" accounts of crimes and disasters, sports news, financial information, and the like. Their relatively nonpolitical content and "petty bourgeois" audience made the evening newspapers an object of suspicion within the party. But no one could deny that they made money.

The 1923 debate over publication of a new paper in Moscow, to be called *Evening Moscow*, epitomized the combination of ideological suspicion and financial allure that characterized the party leadership's attitude toward the evening papers. The publishers of *Ekonomicheskaia zhizn (Economic Life)*, a financial newspaper published by the Council on Labor and Defense, seem to have initiated the discussion in the hope that they themselves could publish *Evening Moscow* and cover their large operating losses. According to a report delivered by G. I. Krumin, the editor of *Economic Life*, in July 1923, the main purpose of the new evening paper would be to serve "the development of market trade" under the NEP and rapidly transmit information about prices to the financial public. The paper was to publish state decrees of interest to businessmen and information on postal tariffs, address changes, train schedules, and tram routes. It would carry relatively more local news (court and so on) than other Soviet newspapers. By publishing "healthy sensations, but without stooping to yellow journalism, naturally," *Evening Moscow* ideally would "guarantee a massive in-flow of advertising" and earn a profit.[24]

The Orgburo approved an evening newspaper for Moscow, but with the proviso that it be published by the Moscow province party committee's publishing house, *Rabochaia Moskva (Worker Moscow)*, whose flagship newspaper targeted proletarians.[25] This was a deliberate choice to provide financial support to a mass worker paper aimed at factory party and labor union organizations. For Central Committee officials these had priority over *Economic Life*'s audience, which consisted largely of private businessmen ("NEPmen") and officials in the trade and financial commissariats.

In spite of the nominal transition to "self-financing" most Soviet newspapers continued to receive subsidies in one form or another throughout the period of the NEP. Party leaders provided this money to the press to ensure that newspapers reached audiences with a high political priority, most importantly the collective body of party/state officials and Communist activists designated by the term *obshchestvennost* (sometimes translated as "civil society," but perhaps better rendered in the Soviet context as "official society"). But during the NEP the party did strive to win the support of groups outside the bounds of *obshchestvennost*, such as peasants and nonparty youth. Subsidies for *The Peasant Gazette* and Komsomol newspapers were one expression of this striving. Also, during the NEP, party press officials were willing to countenance market-driven distribution and newspaper content when these helped to finance newspapers with higher-priority audiences, as is demonstrated by their use of urban evening newspapers as cash cows. However, at the end of the NEP, distribution priorities and tolerance for market-driven newspapers narrowed dramatically.

Newspaper Distribution and Collective Subscription

Each type of newspaper had its own methods of collecting subscriptions and delivering the papers, which ran the gamut from almost exclusive reliance on collective subscriptions for the labor union organs to dependence on street sales for the urban evening newspapers. Newspapers aimed at priority audiences, such as Red Army troops and factory operatives, sold for the lowest prices, ran the highest deficits, and made the most use of collective subscriptions. As the party expanded through the NEP years, *Pravda*, the essential newspaper for every Communist, converged with the distribution profile of the mass worker newspapers. *The Peasant Gazette* developed a distribution system that used postmen and the paper's own peasant correspondents who received a commission for selling subscriptions.[26] Using this method the peasant newspaper managed to generate a large number of individual subscriptions by mail This system was unique for the Soviet Union of its time.

By the fall of 1923 the transition to paid distribution had been made successfully, as the proportion of newspaper issues distributed for free dwindled to insignificance. In terms of distribution methods the major Moscow newspapers at this time fell into three groups. *Poor Peasant* and the mass worker newspapers *Worker Gazette* and *Worker Moscow* distributed more than half of their print runs through collective subscriptions (from factories and labor union organizations, for example). At *Pravda* about one-fifth of circulation went to collective subscribers. *Economic Life* and *The Trade and Industrial Gazette* (the organ of the Supreme Council on the Economy) had no collective subscribers to speak of. These were the quintessential "NEP newspapers," selling to businessmen and state enterprise managers who bought them or subscribed on an individual basis. These readers sought financial and trade information.[27]

The Worker Gazette, the CC's mass worker paper, epitomized the distribution methods used by mass papers, including labor union organs. In 1923 the newspaper's distribution department divided the Russian Republic into ten regions and put a "plenipotentiary agent" in charge of recruiting subscriptions and monitoring delivery in each one. The agents worked through party committees, labor union committees, and individual party cells. In addition to lecturing these groups on the "tasks of the press" and collecting subscribers, *The Worker Gazette* representatives recruited worker correspondents who were supposed to write to the newspaper, enlist new subscribers, help with delivery of the paper, and participate in the so-called Friends of the Newspaper clubs, which also functioned as study circles. Apart from the possible satisfaction and prestige gained if their correspondence appeared in the central newspaper, such worker correspondents had a monetary incentive to help *The Worker Gazette*. Friends of the Newspaper clubs received a 5 percent commission on subscriptions they collected.[28]

The Friends circles were in reality adjuncts to the factory labor union committees that negotiated the relationship between party, administration, and workers. *The Worker Gazette*'s distribution department stipulated that they be organized by the factory committees in coordination with local *Worker Gazette* "Bureaus" (i.e., the newspaper's agents). The circles were supposed to set up *"Worker Gazette* corners" in their enterprises, run study circles and sports clubs, organize lectures on new technologies at the labor union clubs, promote "revolutionary weddings," notify the newspaper of their factories' production successes, and so on.[29]

The Peasant Gazette, which was supposed to reach "wild peasants" unconnected to official society, had to use different distribution methods. Although its first subscription campaign relied almost exclusively on official rural institutions, the paper's managers ultimately built a distribution system that reached hundreds of thousands of individual rural residents. The evidence for this is the voluminous archive of reader letters that the newspaper left behind (containing an estimated 800,000 reader letters), surveys of village correspondent social status, and official reports on newspaper distribution, which consistently singled out *The Peasant Gazette*'s methods as unique. Unlike the other central newspapers, which sold through their own local agents, the railway press distribution network, the party, the Komsomol, and the labor union committees, *The Peasant Gazette* used individual correspondents and rural postal carriers to sell subscriptions and deliver the newspaper. According to one 1929 report by the Central Control Commission, the post office distributed 80 percent of *The Peasant Gazette*'s circulation. Village correspondents (about 10,000 were involved in distribution in the late 1920s) handled most of the remainder. One of the main reasons for the peasant newspaper's success was its massive mailing list, "like those of American newspapers," that contained the addresses of post offices, rural mail carriers, cooperative stores, schools, village soviets, ward *(raion)* offices, and state farms. In 1929–1930 there were more than four million addresses on this list. The newspaper's distribution department used the mailing list to reach actual and potential subscribers with advertising materials, including a free *Peasant Gazette* calendar, and a variety of pamphlets and brochures. A second key to success was the newspaper's "instructors," who kept in contact with the village correspondents. Maintaining such a large distribution apparatus was not cheap. Compared with *Pravda* and *The Worker Gazette*, each of which spent about 10 percent of their annual budget on distribution, *The Peasant Gazette* used 20 percent.[30]

In spite of the success of *The Peasant Gazette* and the urban evening newspapers in reaching nonparty members, distribution of the Soviet press continued to be weighted toward *obshchestvennost* throughout the NEP. A high proportion of newspaper subscriptions went directly to party/state institutions such as labor union committees, party cells, army barracks, and rural government offices. Officials continued to provide subsidies to ensure that the newspaper reached these organizations, which constituted the party's base of support. A December 1926 report on newspaper distribution in Moscow to CC secretary Viacheslav Molotov illustrates the point. Even in the Soviet capital, where the proportion of individual subscribers and purchasers of newspapers was probably higher than anywhere else in the Soviet Union, the labor union newspapers *Labor* and *The Siren* continued to deliver more than 90 percent of their circulation through collective subscriptions. Their most important distribution channel was labor union committees. At the other end of the spectrum, even *Izvestiia*, known for catering to white-collar urban residents who subscribed as individuals, distributed just over one-third of its Moscow circulation to collective subscribers. At *Pravda*, *The Worker Gazette*, and *Worker Moscow*, between 42 percent and 45 percent of all Moscow circulation went to collective subscribers. *Pravda* in particular had substantially *increased* its proportion of collective subscriptions between late 1923 and late 1926. Whereas something under 21 percent of *Pravda*'s Moscow subscriptions were collective in November 1923, 42 percent were collective in December 1926. *Pravda*'s distribution profile was converging with those of the mass worker newspapers *The Worker Gazette* and *Worker Moscow*. It is telling that the central party organ's circulation had increased more rapidly than that of either mass worker paper since 1923. The large circulation increase taken together with the rise in the proportion of collective subscriptions suggest that *Pravda*'s distribution department was increasingly targeting factory organizations and lower-level party activists (the *nizovoi aktiv*) as opposed to urban street sales. The paper was shifting its focus from educated urban readers and the party intelligentsia to the mass of party members.[31]

The shift in *Pravda*'s distribution by late 1926 was a precursor of dramatic changes to come in the Soviet press network. In 1928–1930 the CC Department of Agitation and Propaganda, supported by the Stalinist CC leadership and by young Communist journalists, retargeted much of the Soviet periodical press at party activists and officials—in other words, at *obshchestvennost*. Two important forces were driving this shift, which, as seen above, was under way well before 1928. The first was the push to industrialize the Soviet Union that began in 1926. As the industrialization drive accelerated, party leaders began to insist that the press's top priority must be mobilizing *obshchestvennost* to participate. This crowded out other functions that had characterized the Soviet press earlier in the NEP, such as making money and "enlightening" peasants and nonparty youth. The imperative to mobilize officials and shop-floor activists for the industrialization campaign prompted newspaper managers to rely even more heavily on collective subscriptions than before, as the best and cheapest method of ensuring that the papers reached the collective body of *obshchestvennost*.[32]

The second force tending to limit the Soviet press to circulation within the bounds of *obshchestvennost* had nothing to do directly with the conscious decisions of party leaders. It developed in a process unrecognized at the time from the incentives set up by the CC officials' subsidization of the press and their insistence that the newspapers mobilize various groups rather than seek profits. Newspaper editors and business managers strove to maximize circulation to prove to higher officials that they were succeeding in their assigned mobilization tasks. Assured of continued central subsidies, they did so regardless of cost. The result was that newspapers quickly used up available newsprint supplies. Shortages of newsprint ultimately forced the CC leaders to ration the newspapers in high demand, such as *Pravda* and *Izvestiia*, to various priority audiences within *obshchestvennost*. The next section describes this process in more detail.

Newsprint Shortages and the Rationing of Information

During the 1920s the Soviet press went through three cycles of circulation expansion and contraction. In each case newspapers began the expansion by subsidizing subscriptions through direct discounts and the extension of easy credit. Central government grants and loans (often never repaid) made this possible. Eventually, expanding circulation outran the supply of newsprint, and paper shortages ensued. The Central Committee responded with measures to cut print runs, lower production costs, reduce the proportion of discounted subscriptions, and force the newspapers to tighten credit to subscribers. Party leaders intervened in this fashion in early 1922 (the Press Crisis), in 1926, and in 1929–1930. Finally, in 1930–1931 Central Committee officials set up a system of centralized rationing of newspapers to control newsprint supplies and direct information to preferred audiences.

The Press Crisis of 1922 and Central Committee efforts to cut circulations and subsidies were described at the beginning of this chapter. The 1926 belt-tightening campaign in the press was quite similar. It began with a financial scandal at *Izvestiia*, the Soviet Union's number two newspaper after *Pravda*. *Izvestiia* had reported the highest profits of any central Soviet newspaper in 1923 and early 1924, but in 1925 it ran into financial difficulties. For that year the newspaper's expenditures were up about 450,000 rubles or 36 percent over 1924.[33] Officers of the Workers' and Peasants' Inspectorate brought in to investigate discovered that *Izvestiia*'s claims of large profits in 1923–1924 were mostly a conjuring trick. The episode became known in Soviet journalism circles as the *steklovshchina* (Steklov-gate) after the newspaper's former editor.

Under Steklov, it turned out, *Izvestiia* had inflated print runs by sending extra copies above and beyond distribution agents' orders. ROSTA's distribution department, for example, generally ordered 20,000 to 22,000 copies of each issue in the first half of 1925, but *Izvestiia* delivered 24,000 to 26,000 copies.[34] The newspaper accepted an unlimited number of returns from such deliveries.[35] *Izvestiia* also offered subscribers and distribution agents unlimited credit, with no real deadline set for repayment. In late August 1925 *Izvestiia*'s new business manager estimated that distribution agents and *Izvestiia*'s own distribution offices in the provinces owed the newspaper around 800,000 rubles. There was no prospect that this balance would be repaid, but it had nonetheless been entered on the paper's accounts as income.[36]

In response the Inspectorate ordered 15 percent cuts in *Izvestiia's* staff, forbade the inflation of circulation by sending extra copies of the paper to distribution agents, mandated strict limits on the return percentage, and set a forty-day limit on repayment of credits by distribution agents. *Izvestiia* was not to offer credits to agents before they had demonstrated the ability to repay, nor was it to include on its balance sheet "income" owed by subscribers and agents who had failed to repay credits.[37]

Izvestiia's measures to raise circulation were commonplace at Soviet newspapers. The fundamental motivation was to demonstrate to officials at the Committee on Press Affairs and the Central Committee that a given newspaper was fulfilling its party-mandated mission, whether that be mobilizing party members, teaching "wild peasants" modern agricultural techniques, or propagandizing urban youth. High circulations could then justify higher subsidies. At the levels of the CC agitprop apparatus and Orgburo, newspaper editors often lobbied for more subsidies, using high-circulation numbers as an argument.[38]

Because artificial inflation of circulation was so common, the Soviet press ran short on newsprint in the first days of 1926. By February domestic paper factories had a half-year backlog of orders.[39] On January 22, 1926, the Orgburo passed a resolution ordering that newspapers cut paper use, and suggesting ways to do this. The Press Department moved to implement the resolution, merging the two Leningrad evening newspapers, limiting the number of pages for all central newspapers, and cutting the publication of supplements.[40] Cost-cutting at the newspapers also entailed limiting the credits offered to distribution agents and seeking more individual subscriptions.[41] According to Aleksandr Iu. Pismen, head of the *Pravda* distribution department, the central party organ tried to arrange direct delivery of subscriptions to individuals through the post office and apartment building supervisors. Judging by Pismen's comments in two separate reports, however, as of March 1927 delivery of newspapers to individual residences was more of a hope than a reality.[42]

Apart from the attempt to increase individual subscriptions, measures to control newsprint consumption had some temporary success. *Izvestiia's* print run of 588,000 in February 1925 dropped to 457,000 in February 1926 and 409,000 in October. At *Pravda* and *The Worker Gazette* the Central Committee measures stopped the runaway consumption of newsprint, and circulations held steady throughout 1926 (at about 490,000 for *Pravda* and 265,000 for *The Worker Gazette).*[43] Many provincial newspapers lost high proportions of their circulation.[44]

But the 1926 central reform effort ultimately failed to squeeze out of the distribution system discounted collective subscriptions, loose credit policies, or high return rates. Central Committee officials, intent on reaching key supporters with their message, continued to provide subsidies, direct and indirect, to reach preferred target audiences. Circulations began to climb again. As early as April 1928 there were signs of a developing paper shortage. On the 23rd of that month the Orgburo approved the purchase abroad of 11,700 tons of newsprint and 3,500 tons of book paper above planned imports. To conserve existing supplies the Orgburo also began rationing paper to publishers, including the major central newspapers. It cut off paper supplies entirely to some publications considered of secondary importance, such as the antireligious journal *Atheist* and *Fur Industry.* On May 3, 1928, the Politburo approved these measures.[45]

In May 1929 the Central Committee had to take action again, as a Council of People's Commissars report projected a shortfall of 5,800 tons of paper and warned that no funds were available for purchases abroad. On May 11 the Secretariat ordered the Agitprop Department to warn all newspapers that current paper allocations would not be increased. In an effort to control the upward spiral of circulation, the Secretariat barred all periodical publishers from printing promotional supplements such as calendars, forbade them to promote subscriptions with prize lotteries, and called a moratorium on most advertising to sell subscriptions. An early draft of the resolution prepared by Sergei Ingulov, chief of the Agitprop Department's Newspaper Sector, blamed the paper crisis on the rapid increase in periodical circulation. Ingulov accused publishers of exceeding their paper allocations and warned that further violations of consumption norms might lead to the collapse of the entire press network.[46]

In 1930–1931 the Central Committee leaders began setting circulation numbers for central newspapers and major provincial organs to control newsprint consumption. In February 1930, the Secretariat set print runs for *The Peasant Gazette, Poor Peasant, Kustar i artel ("Artisan and Cooperative"),* and a number of journals. The earliest instances of the Secretariat setting print runs for *Izvestiia* and *Pravda* recorded in the central party archive are March 1931 and June 1931 respectively. Previous to this the Central Committee executive apparatus had rationed paper supplies to central newspapers rather than setting print runs, and had done so only at times of severe newsprint shortage.[47]

CC bureaucrats did not set print runs based solely on political considerations or analyses of market demand. Officials in the Culture and Propaganda Department (the successor to the Agitprop Department) were subject to intensive lobbying by commissariats, labor unions, and the newspapers. For example a September 10, 1936, report to the Orgburo by B. M. Tal, director of the Press and Publishing Department (successor to the CC's Agitrop and Kultprop departments) complained of "continuous" petitions on the subject. Although much of this lobbying took place at the Agitprop/Kultprop/Press Department level, from which detailed documentation is not available, some petitions did reach the Orgburo. On February 21, 1931, for instance, the Orgburo raised the circulation of *Labor* in response to a petition; just over two weeks later the Secretariat rejected editor Anastas Mikoian's request to raise the circulation of the central cooperative organ *Snabzhenie, kooperatsiia, i torgovlia (Supply, Cooperatives, and Trade)* by 70,000.[48]

Because of CC responsiveness to such lobbying and because of other considerations, both of ideology and of institutional politics, newspaper allocation did not approximate demand. When a newspaper's print run exceeded demand, the paper became surplus *(nedefitsitnye)*. Distribution agents were loaded down with extra copies that they could not sell. When the central authorities set a newspaper's print run below actual demand, the paper became scarce *(defitsitnye)*, disappearing from kiosks. To ensure that scarce newspapers reached the sectors of the population whose support they counted on, Central Committee officials were forced to ration them. Ultimately, then, the introduction of a centralized rationing system for newspapers was the result of the continuing heavy state subsidies to the press.

The first step toward central rationing of the newspapers was centralized distribution. On August 16, 1930, the Council of People's Commissars issued a decree concentrating responsibility for all newspaper distribution and subscription in the Commissariat of Posts and Telegraphs (the newspaper distribution department in the postal commissariat was named Soiuzpechat in 1932). The new system eliminated the multiple distribution systems run by newspaper publishers during the NEP, and it squeezed private agents out of the subscription recruitment business. From the point of view of party press officials, it got rid of the "parallelism" and "unhealthy competition" that had characterized newspaper distribution during the NEP.[49]

The new distribution system was built around "control numbers." These were the subscription recruitment quotas set for local post offices, party organizations, factories, and other official organizations by contract between newspaper publishers on one hand and the postal commissariat on the other. The system was a pyramidal cascade of control numbers, with the Orgburo or Secretariat at the peak setting print runs for major Soviet newspapers. After the Orgburo set the print run for a newspaper, its publishers negotiated with the postal commissariat distribution quotas for various cities and regions of the USSR. The system of control numbers cascaded right down to individual mail carriers and subscription agents, who had their own subscriber recruitment quotas. In larger cities and towns the CC publishers maintained agents who negotiated control numbers with post offices and monitored their fulfillment. The August 1930 Council of People's Commissar's decree also mandated that the postal commissariat pay fines to newspaper publishers in the event it failed to sell the requisite number of newspapers.[50]

Distribution agents used the system of control numbers to rid themselves of surplus newspapers. Among the latter were such obscure organs as *Moskovskii stroitel (Moscow Construction Worker)*, *Arkhitekturnaia gazeta (Architecture Gazette)*, and *Lesnaia promyshlennost (Timber Industry)*, but also large central papers such as *The Peasant Gazette* (often surplus in the 1930s), *Labor*, and *Za industrializatsiiu (Industrialization)*. Agents set distribution quotas for party committees, factory committees, civic activists, and mail carriers. Often they attached a "subscription package" *(komplekt)* of various surplus newspapers to *Pravda* or *Izvestiia* subscriptions. Enterprises or individuals refusing to buy the subscription package could not receive *Pravda* and *Izvestiia* either. Kiosk salespeople got rid of surplus newspapers in a different way, selling them "in bundles of five or ten issues for use as wrapping paper."[51]

The establishment of a pyramid of control numbers for distribution increased the reliance of some Soviet newspapers on collective subscriptions (this was the simplest way for local postal distribution agents to fill their subscription quotas) and hence accelerated the tendency for them to circulate within the bounds of *obshchestvennost*. It had a drastic effect, for example, on *The Peasant Gazette*'s unique distribution system. The CC's peasant newspaper, which had once targeted the individual peasant and maintained probably the highest proportion of individual subscribers of any mass-circulation central Soviet paper, was now distributed "by a compulsory, forced procedure" to collective farms. Collective farm management would buy a number of subscriptions, docking the farmers' pay without consulting them. According to a 1936 report, the chairman at one collective farm in Moscow had subscribed to 417 rubles' worth of newspapers in the peasants' names, but without their permission. One woman interviewed by investigators complained, "Don't ask me how the collective farm subscribed to two newspapers, *The Peasant Gazette* and the county paper, for me. . . . I can't read. I certainly don't need them." *The Peasant Gazette*, once the regime's most effective channel for reaching "the nonparty masses," had become just another organ for *obshchestvennost*, in this case for collective farm officials.[52]

The most prominent scarce newspapers were *Pravda*, *Izvestiia*, and *Komsomolskaia pravda*. Demand for these organs was inflated not just by their low (subsidized) prices, but also by their function as authoritative sources of political information. All three papers provided essential guidance on central policy and the party's "general line." For party members, subscription to *Pravda* was a necessity. As a result many firms, state institutions, and party organizations paid for subscriptions to *Pravda* and/or *Izvestiia* for their employees, especially at the managerial level. This caused little or no financial pain for institutions that could increase their budgets easily by appealing to the state. For individual households, on the other hand, newspaper subscriptions were a real drain on the budget. The ultimate result was that the state paid for free circulation of its official newspapers to its leading cadres. Institutional and enterprise subscriptions drew off most of the supply of the big central papers, making purchase difficult for those who lacked access to the press through their place of employment, the party, or the Komsomol.

By 1931 ideological and political imperatives motivated Central Committee officials to move beyond setting print runs to adjusting the rationing system directly. Party leaders were often unhappy with the distribution patterns that emerged from the negotiations between publishing houses and postal agents. By late 1931 they were routinely ordering adjustments in the number of newspapers allocated to various institutions or social groups with the aim of ensuring that groups whose support the party most depended on were well supplied with the authoritative central organs *Pravda, Izvestiia,* and *Komsomolskaia pravda.* In rationing the newspapers party officials established what historian Elena A. Osokina has called a "hierarchy of consumption," privileging social groups whose support the party considered essential—first and foremost the circles of *obshchestvennost.*[53] This was a departure from the NEP, when party officials had generally used indirect methods such as discounted subscriptions to channel newspapers toward desired audiences, and when their commitment to reaching subscribers outside official society was much stronger (as witnessed by the example of *The Peasant Gazette*).

To implement rationing of the scarce central newspapers Soiuzpechat developed a system of "subscription coupons" *(talony na podpisku)* in 1932. Only those holding such coupons could subscribe to the scarce central newspapers. Souizpechat allocated the coupons among factories, administrative organs, and other state institutions in accordance with the rationing guidelines set by the Central Committee. It also set up a network of "closed kiosks" to which only privileged people holding "subscription tickets" *(abonementy)* had access.[54] The result was that the authoritative central newspapers simply became unavailable to the general population. According to Central Committee reports from 1933 and 1936 *Pravda, Izvestiia,* and *Komsomolskaia pravda* were unavailable at Moscow and Leningrad kiosks, most of their circulation going by collective subscription to government institutions and economic enterprises.[55]

Central Committee reports on distribution of the newspapers reveal the party leaders' communication priorities in the early to mid-1930s. These were propagandizing the armed forces, mobilizing factory Communists for industrialization, and communicating with the party's outposts in the countryside. Red Army units (especially the political propaganda departments attached to them) and Commisariat of Internal Affairs troop detachments apparently enjoyed the highest priority, followed by party and Komsomol organizations, central government offices, higher educational institutions, and points where newspapers reached a collective audience, such as factory workers' clubs. Somewhat lower on the list were state farms, collective farms, and their attached Machine Tractor Stations. Lower-level government offices and smaller industrial enterprises had an even lower priority.[56] Taken together these priorities outline the sharpening boundaries of a new Stalinist elite.

Shortage, Information Rationing, and the Stratification of Soviet Society

Throughout the 1920s and 1930s Central Committee officials attributed the continuing difficulties in press distribution to industrial backwardness and the inefficiency and laziness of distribution agents. In these accounts Soviet industry was simply unable to satisfy the demands of the newly liberated masses for print materials, and newspaper distribution managers sold their product in bulk to institutions because they were too lazy to recruit individual subscribers.

Yet the crux of the problems exercising party press officials was not inadequate paper production or administrative incompetence, but rather a process identified by Janos Kornai as "the reproduction of shortage." In his *Contradictions and Dilemmas* Kornai shows how the easy availability of subsidies in a state socialist economy leads to a very high demand for factors of production (raw materials, labor, capital), which in turn generates hoarding by enterprises and shortages. Kornai's model of the individual firm's behavior in a socialist economy describes the functioning of Soviet newspaper publishing houses very well.

In Kornai's terminology the ready availability of state subsidies means that the individual enterprise has a "soft budget constraint." If the firm loses money, its managers can expect some form of aid from the state. This may take the form of price controls, tax breaks, state grants, regular subsidies, easy credit, or investment without expectation of return. In short, "the financial situation of the firm does not constrain action." For enterprises operating under "hard budget constraints" (market prices, no tax breaks or subsidies, credit on conservative terms) profitmaking is a survival imperative; for enterprises under the soft budget constraints of a state socialist economy, profit making is largely irrelevant. A different set of imperatives takes hold. Kornai enumerates some of these—"Let it cost what it may." "Once we have a contractor, we shall not stop the investment just because we have no money." "If there is a loss, the state budget will take over."[57]

Kornai's model of the soft budget constraint corresponds closely to the reality of newspaper financing in the USSR. As discussed above, even during the NEP party leaders continued to subsidize Soviet newspapers in spite of their nominal commitment to *khozraschet* or "self-financing." Statements such as "if there is a loss, the state budget will take over" above precisely describe the attitudes of Soviet newspaper editors and business managers during this era and after. To use Kornai's terminology, Soviet newspapers were an almost pure case of soft budget constraints. Because of their proximity to the Central Committee and their high political priority as bearers of the party's messages to the populace, central newspapers had a "softer" budget even than most other Soviet enterprises. Kornai postulates a continuum running from pure hard budget constraints to pure soft budget constraints—Soviet newspapers lay at the end of the "soft" side of this scale. They benefited from all five of the budget-softening conditions listed by Kornai: price setting, a soft tax system, free state grants, soft credit, and investment on soft conditions. Through direct contacts with the highest levels of the party leadership, the big Moscow-based papers were able to influence the price of raw materials and the price of the product (in Kornai's terms, the newspapers could influence "input as well as . . . output prices"). The largest central newspapers, and probably provincial newspapers as well, were tax-exempt. Newspapers received state grants in the form of contributions to the purchase of new printing plants and regular subsidies. Credit was very soft—it was granted without regard to a newspaper's financial prospects. Loans were often forgiven and converted into outright grants. Investment was also soft, as the state frequently put money into publishing operations with little expectation of monetary payback.[58]

In Kornai's model, a typical firm in the socialist economy strives constantly to increase its production in response to "taut central plans" or other signals from the central authorities.[59] In the case of early Soviet newspapers the main drive to increase production came from the center's demands that the press carry out political tasks. Agitprop officials were ready to take a financial loss to get the party's messages to the populace. The readiness of bureaucrats to fund the mass press created an incentive to inflate circulation by lowering prices, offering subscribers unrestricted credit, and dumping newspaper subscriptions on workers through mandatory payroll deductions. Inflated circulation then provided an argument for more subsidies. Inflated circulation also meant high consumption of newsprint, and ultimately, shortages of newsprint.

The firm's "soft budget constraint" in Kornai's model also helps to explain the prevalence of collective, institutional subscriptions. In state socialist economies, Kornai argues, enterprises with their soft budgets have a purchasing advantage over individual households, which are dependent on fixed wages and whose budgets are thus hard. The firm can afford to overspend in the expectation of state aid. The household cannot, for its income is fixed. State enterprises thus tend to suck up consumer goods that otherwise might have been available for purchase by individual households.[60] From the point of view of the newspaper's distribution agents, then, enterprises had more ready supplies of cash and were more likely customers than individuals.

There were further advantages to dealing with firms rather than individuals. In the first place, it was quicker and simpler. In the case of collective subscription by a factory's labor union committee, for example, selling twenty copies of the paper required the consent of only one person, the committee chairman or subscription plenipotentiary, rather than twenty individuals. In the second place, factory directors, foremen, labor union committee secretaries, and other authorities could easily pressure their subordinates to subscribe. For the newspaper distributor, in short, selling subscriptions to enterprises was simpler, surer, and more profitable than selling them to individuals. The advantage of institutional subscribers on the market for print materials reinforced the tendency, already inherent in the party's press distribution priorities, for newspapers to circulate within *obshchestvennost*.

When print runs became so high as to threaten a breakdown in paper supply, central authorities would tighten financial discipline over newspapers and attempt to force them to switch to individual subscriptions. The history of the printing and distribution of Soviet newspapers between 1922 and 1965 is a series of such cycles—inflated print runs, paper shortage, central response. Between 1922 and 1930 Soviet publishing went through three such cycles. Although paper shortages plagued the USSR throughout the 1920s, supplies bottomed out three times, in 1921–1922, 1925–1926, and 1928–1929. Each time the CC agitprop officials responded with an attempt to puncture the inflated print runs of the newspapers. In 1922 they put a stop to free distribution and shut down many provincial newspapers. In 1926 they tried to force newspapers to tighten credit policies toward subscribers and distributors. Finally, between 1928 and 1930 the CC officials capped circulation by taking responsibility themselves for allocating newsprint and setting print runs. The capping of circulation in turn forced central authorities to ration the newspapers, to ensure that they reached priority sectors of the population. The history of early Soviet newspapers is a case study of the process by which the firm's soft budget constraint generates shortages that in turn necessitate central rationing.[61]

During the First Five-Year Plan (1928–1932) the developing economy of shortage became tightly intertwined with the abandonment of the NEP mass enlightenment project, the rise of a new Stalinist elite, and a dramatic transformation of official discourse. As already noted, Bolshevik leaders during the NEP strove to educate the masses, to raise their level of "culture" and "political consciousness." Newspapers such as *The Peasant Gazette* they viewed as teaching tools. But the enlightenment project was a source of tension within the party. The party's need to insulate itself from the "uncultured" and "politically backward" masses, along with the "revolutionary vanguard" self-image promoted by Lenin, undermined the project. Stalin and other leaders believed that limited regime resources needed to be devoted first and foremost to the mobilization of cadres to carry out practical tasks of the moment.[62] The decision for rapid industrialization in 1928 only increased the sense of many Communist officials that they could not afford to devote resources to the long-term project of transforming the population's psyches. In an atmosphere of crisis Bolshevik leaders insisted on using the press to mobilize activists for the do-or-die task. They abandoned for the moment the goal of transforming the psychology of the population at large.

But it was not just ideology, political culture, and the industrialization drive that undermined efforts to include the masses in the Soviet project. The party/state's control of the economy did so as well. As Kornai has shown, state ownership and centralized coordination drive state socialist economies in the direction of shortages and, ultimately, rationing. This alone tends to distance party members, especially state officials, from the nonparty populace, because Communists have priority in rationing (the party leadership needs to secure its support base). Party members, or at least those at higher levels of the party, together with other groups whose services are essential for the regime, such as highly qualified technical specialists, come to form a privileged status group, viewed with envy and resentment by the rest of the population. In the case of newspapers, central ownership and coordination led to the rationing of information and ultimately to the undermining of the mass enlightenment project. Newsprint shortages generated by the press's soft budget constraint forced CC apparatchiks to ration, and when they did so, they gave priority to party members and state officials. This process strengthened the tendency of the major central newspapers to circulate within the bounds of *obshchestvennost*, a tendency that originally derived from the party's insularity and avant-gardism and was reinforced by the industrialization drive. The Central Committee ended up rationing the newspapers, and hence rationing information, to those members of official society higher in the "hierarchy of consumption."

Nothing was left for secondary tasks such as mass enlightenment. In the press the economy of shortage heightened the leaders' sense of operating in an environment of scarcity and drove them toward rationing the newspapers to the indispensable audience—again, the cadres. The party leaders lacked material and human resources for their industrialization drive. In straitened conditions they had to channel available funds, talent, paper supplies, and so on into the primary tasks of maintaining the loyalty and reliability of the activists and of official society as a whole.

The rationing of newspapers persisted at least to the end of the Stalin era. A 1953 description by emigré Arkadii Gaev outlined a distribution system essentially unchanged since the early 1930s (the one element Gaev did not mention was the *talony*—subscription coupons).[63] Rationing of *Pravda* in the early 1950s was still tantamount to rationing information. Although Gaev and others have claimed that the whole Soviet press simply repeated *Pravda*'s content, a reading of newspapers from the early 1950s shows that the Central Committee organ provided unique and important guidance to party cadres.[64]

The rationing of information in general persisted until the collapse of the Soviet system and included more levels than those detailed in this chapter. Alex Inkeles in 1950 and Vladimir Shlapentokh in 1985 both noted the tiered character of Soviet agitprop efforts and information dissemination. Distinct messages were conveyed to "the masses," rank-and-file activists, and the apparatus of full-time party and state officials. The messages were kept distinct through the use of different channels, such as oral agitation meetings, secret limited-circulation information bulletins, and the newspapers.[65]

The mutual reinforcement of the party's avant-gardism, the industrialization drive, and the central control of the economy points toward what Kornai has called "the coherence of the classical system." In *The Socialist System* Kornai argues that various features of the "classical system" (i.e., the Stalinist system) of Marxist-Leninist state socialism, including the party's monopoly of political power, official ideology, state ownership of the economy, shortage, and bureaucratic planning, "develop a coherence." The different elements "exhibit affinity" for one another. Mixed systems, for example those that attempt to combine the party's monopoly on power with market coordination of the economy, are inherently unstable. Kornai writes that the classical system is "a fabric so closely woven that if one strand breaks, it all unravels sooner or later."[66] This chapter has described one example of the coherence of the classical system. Communist avant-gardism, the push to industrialize, and central control of the economy reinforced one another, all three tending to drive the party and the populace apart into separate status groups. The NEP mass enlightenment project, at least as embodied in NEP newspapers, did have its origins in a genuine Bolshevik concern with "raising the cultural level of the masses," but it did not fit with avant-gardism, rapid industrialization, or a state-run economy, which became keystones of the Soviet system. As a result the NEP compromise between the newspapers' functions of mobilizing *obshchestvennost* and mass enlightenment was unstable. When resources were short and tasks urgent, the Central Committee insisted on rationing information to its cadres, at the expense of other social groups.

~ 3

Reader Response and Its Impact on the Press

As PART OF THE NEW ECONOMIC POLICY (NEP) mass enlightenment project Bolshevik leaders and agitation-and-propaganda (agitprop) officials sought feedback on reader response to the official press, aiming to adjust their propaganda to audience preferences. They used a variety of sources, including worker-peasant correspondent letters, reports from grassroots party agitators, and interviews with secret police (OGPU) informers. Party agitprop departments also sponsored numerous studies of newspaper readership and reader preferences during the NEP. Through these channels the assumptions and predilections of ordinary Soviet subjects influenced official culture. The producers of official culture, in turn, aimed to transform the everyday culture of their subjects, so that there was constant mutual influence.

In the 1920s reader letters to the newspapers were a particularly important part of the state's mechanism for gathering intelligence on popular moods and adjusting propaganda to them. They were, in a sense, the Soviet equivalent of opinion polls in late-twentieth-century liberal democracies. Lenin himself had regularly perused reader letters forwarded to him by the *Pravda* editorial board. When officials at the Central Committee (CC) Press Section organized *The Peasant Gazette* in late 1923, they stipulated that the newspaper should use reader letters to gather information on the mood of the peasantry.[1] By 1926 most, if not all, central newspapers put together summary reports *(svodki)* on the reader letters they received and forwarded them to high-level party and state organs, including the Central Committee, the Komsomol CC, the Moscow province party committee, the People's Commissariat of Agriculture, and the Central Committees of labor unions.[2] The highest levels of the party leadership, including Stalin, Viacheslav Molotov, and Lazar Kaganovich, read these *svodki* and the individual reader letters that newspaper editors forwarded to them. They also requested intelligence on specific topics. In late February 1927, for example, Molotov asked *The Peasant Gazette* to provide him with a report on peasant attitudes toward the threat of war.[3]

It was not the reality of reader response to the press, but party officials' *perceptions* of that reality that influenced propaganda production. Thus, although this chapter assumes that reader studies, informer reports, and other sources roughly reflected real reader response, this assumption is not essential to the argument—that the producers of official culture used available response data to mold their production. These producers disposed of much information on reader response and this, combined with the producers' own preconceptions about "the masses," helped to shape official culture.

Sources on reader response revealed four trends of particular importance in motivating the future direction of Soviet propaganda and the development of Stalinist culture. First, party members and aspiring party members read the central press's coverage of politics carefully, using it as a guide to action. This was as the Bolshevik leaders intended. Second, almost no readers, including the young male activists who dominated the party and Komsomol rank-and-file, actually found domestic political stories interesting. Third, what *really* interested the young activists was coverage of wars, military affairs, science, adventure, and technology. Fourth, the denunciation of "class enemies" for sensational crimes went over well with both activists and "the laboring masses."

During the later years of the NEP Soviet journalists, literati, and agitprop officials strove to develop print genres that would *both* convey a political message *and* galvanize young male activists, drawing them into participation in "the work of socialist construction." In doing so they used the perceived preferences of these activists for narratives of heroism, adventure, and military glory. Two results were the development of mass journalism in the newspapers and socialist realism in fiction.

Political Education and Marching Orders: Reading for Activists

For lower-level party activists, officials, and Komsomol members, reading the central newspapers was a prerequisite for knowing which production and propaganda campaigns the Central Committee was emphasizing, what the current "general line" was, which party leaders were in favor or disfavor, what kind of local events to organize, and so on. *Pravda, Izvestiia, Komsomolskaia pravda,* and other major Soviet papers carried political information essential for party members striving to maintain or improve their official positions. They also taught aspiring Communists the key terms and phrases of the new official language.[4] The ordinary Communist or Komsomol member's reading of *Pravda* resembled in some ways the banker or broker's daily perusal of *The Wall Street Journal.* Knowledge of the paper was a "professional" necessity.

A large majority of *Pravda* and *Komsomolskaia pravda* readers were party or Komsomol members throughout the 1920s. Activists responding to reader preference surveys at both papers clearly indicated that they read for vital political information. Respondents to *Pravda*'s 1929 survey of its readership, for example, wanted access to extended political and economic commentary by party leaders. Of all respondents 81 percent wanted to see the full texts of party leaders' speeches in *Pravda,* rather than summaries. The author of a short piece covering the *Pravda* survey for *Gazetnoe khoziaistvo (Newspaper Management)* concluded that readers saw in *Pravda* "a serious aid in learning the most important elements of socialist construction."[5] According to an article published in *Pravda*'s in-house newsletter, *Pravdist,* survey respondents had asked for more coverage of lower-level rural and factory party organizations, and more information on the party's education system.[6] Such requests would typically have come from rank-and-file party activists seeking publicity for their own grassroots work and further political education to promote their career chances in the party/state bureaucracy.

A March 1930 anonymous survey of the reading habits of the *Komsomolskaia pravda* editorial staff sheds more light on party members' approach to the newspapers. Staff members described their newspaper reading as "serious," "a duty," or a "tribute" of time paid as part of their professional and party work. All characterized their fictional reading as "diversion" without serious value, something to unwind with before bed. "I relax with *Don Quixote,*" one said. "First thing in the morning I read the newspaper. My daily tribute payment *(dan)*. And nothing more. I have no time. I come to work at the office early in the morning and stay until ten or eleven at night. In the evening I find something easy, fiction." A second editor described how he relied on the daily newspaper and party theoretical journals for necessary guidance in politics and read classical belles lettres for relaxation. "I entertain myself with the classics," he began. "To find reading time I've got to scrape for every free minute. Apart from editorial staff work, I study at the university. I read in the cafeteria, on the tram. [Reading is] my first duty. I consider the following journals obligatory: *Vestnik komakademii [Communist Academy Bulletin]*, *Pod znamenem marksizma [Under the Banner of Marxism]*, and *Bolshevik*." Like the central party and Komsomol papers, party journals were required "professional" reading for Communists, especially those with full-time jobs in the party/state apparatus.[7]

For aspiring activists as much as for high-ranking party members the Soviet press was an essential source of political guidance. For young villagers, reading *The Peasant Gazette* was a way of expanding one's horizons, acquiring knowledge about the outside world, learning how to behave like an activist, and ultimately perhaps escaping "the rural fastnesses." This was certainly the case for Ivan Sergeevich Eroshchenko, a twenty-two-year-old Ukrainian villager from the Kharkov region, who wrote to *The Peasant Gazette* in 1925 in hopes of visiting the newspaper's Moscow editorial offices. In his letter, Eroshchenko, who wrote in non-native Russian with numerous spelling and grammar errors, credited *The Peasant Gazette* with helping him replace his cloudy "uncomprehending thoughts" with the light of knowledge. "When I began arming myself with *The Peasant Gazette*," he exclaimed, "then from the newspaper's printed page I learned knowledge, and I understood that for our newly unfolding life, knowledge is necessary."[8]

Eroshchenko used *The Peasant Gazette* as a guide to turn himself into an activist. After receiving instructional materials from the paper, he attempted to organize a Friends of the Newspaper Circle in his village. Unfortunately, he reported to the editors, "it is difficult, comrades, to organize an avant-garde of activists from the peasantry because the politically unconscious mass of peasants *(sic)*." When Eroshchenko read from the newspaper to his "circle," those attending remained "in order," but "when it came time for payment of dues for subscription to *The Peasant Gazette*, then they instantly became not understanding and no longer activists *(sic)*." Eroshchenko followed official rhetoric, blaming his failure on "the peasant who is dark, the peasant who is illiterate . . . infected with the prayers of the saints, capitalists, religion."

Eroshchenko was on the way to learning official language, and this was part of his larger project of constructing a career as a Communist activist (and perhaps ultimately official or journalist). He wrote to *The Peasant Gazette*'s editors that he wanted to become a peasant correspondent for the paper and visit its Moscow editorial offices. He requested a map of the capital and a train ticket to Moscow. "I want to achieve great knowledge, for my life, to direct it to serve the great State where the power of peasants and workers [reigns], but in me there is an unsated lack of literacy. but all the same . . . even if just a little, I have a strong pull toward science *(sic)*." Eroshchenko closed with a desperate plea that the editors not ignore his letter. "Dear comrades! Do not leave your friend Eroshchenko out in the sticks! And I want to go visit you in the editorial offices so that you may arm me with knowledge, and send me back to the countryside for the struggle with darkness and primitiveness."[9]

Eroshchenko's move from newspaper reading to civic activism was typical of more energetic, youthful readers. Many Soviet subjects who aspired toward education or an active public life went beyond passive consumption of the newspapers to join reading circles, write for the local press, and solicit subscriptions. Party agitprop officials and activists created numerous outlets for these aspirations. They set up "wall newspapers" (broadsheets, often handwritten) and *mnogotirazhki* (low-circulation workplace newsletters run off on old-style platen presses), organized Reading Circles and Friends of the Newspaper clubs, held public discussions of articles in the central press, and encouraged readers to write to the newspapers. Many young readers with political, educational, or literary aspirations used these channels to become local activists or enter Soviet journalism in the 1920s.

Reading for Diversion: Popular Science, Adventure, and War

Political education was a "duty" for activists, but very few readers actually enjoyed reading about the party's agenda. Many sources indicate that both activists and the "nonparty masses" got more pleasure out of nonpolitical topics such as news of life abroad, local human-interest stories, sex scandals, crimes and disasters, humor, adventure and exploration, and popular science and technology. In *Worker Moscow*'s 1928 readership survey, for instance, 74.5 percent of all respondents requested expansion of the Moscow city news department, and 74.3 percent asked for more international news. The third-most-favored department was science and technology (72.6 percent of respondents). Many fewer readers requested expansion of the departments of party life and labor union affairs. Surveys at *The Worker Gazette* (1925–1926) and *Evening Moscow* (1926) showed similar preferences, with readers favoring above all international news, Moscow city news, and popular science stories.[10]

One of the highest priority audience for the press in the 1920s was young men and boys from "the laboring masses." Bolshevik leaders deliberately strove to fill the rank and file of their party with working-class youth, and most new recruits were male. Recognizing this group as the core of the party-under-construction, agitprop officials monitored their reading preferences closely, seeking the most effective rhetorical strategies to mobilize them. The Komsomol's Agitprop Department in particular focused on this task. Komsomol studies in the mid-to-late 1920s found that young men wanted to read about warfare, adventure, science, and technology more than any other subjects. Editors and even the CC leadership responded to these findings by adjusting the content of the newspapers.

During the year between September 1925 and September 1926, for example, the Kiev Komsomol newspaper *Molodoi Bolshevik (Young Bolshevik)* solicited comments and suggestions about content from its readers. In response to these requests the editors expanded the Popular Science section, running articles on radio, military technology, medicine, agriculture in foreign countries, book printing, and paper making.[11] Comments by young "child correspondents" (mostly teenagers) to the editors of the Young Pioneer paper *Iunyi Leninets (Young Leninist)* in December 1926 show a similar pattern. According to the editors, the child correspondents' favorite department was I Made It Myself. The correspondents wanted to see a number of new departments introduced to the paper, namely Chemistry, Aviation, Film, and Chess and Checkers. They also requested expansion of the department of Science and Technology.[12]

Documents submitted by the Komsomol and the CC Agitprop department in support of a summer 1928 CC Orgburo resolution "Measures for the Improvement of the Youth and Children's Press" show similar reader preferences. The Komsomol's report to the Orgburo on the youth press noted a rapid rise in the circulation of youth periodicals with a focus on science and "adventure stories." The section on books cited unspecified library studies to claim that after adventure fiction by foreign authors such as Jack London, books "of a popular science type" were the most popular among youth. In response to these findings the report called for expansion of press coverage of science and technology in the press and in Komsomol cultural activities.[13]

Library reader studies in the 1920s confirmed the trends reported in surveys of newspaper reading preferences. In the later 1920s the most active readers in Soviet society were teenagers and young adults. Judging from scattered contemporary studies, nearly 60 percent of visitors to Soviet libraries were between the ages of twelve and eighteen.[14] And young men needed to read the regime's texts on politics, society, and history to get ahead. According to a 1926 report by the Komsomol CC Agitprop Department on the reading habits of Soviet youth, most borrowers of books from the social sciences and history departments were young men who aspired to membership in the party or Komsomol. Books from these departments were necessary study aids for the political education circles that prepared aspiring Communists. Authors of the report claimed that the vast majority of requests for "sociopolitical literature" from the social sciences department were young males, many of them Komsomol members, who read these books "for study and practical goals." A librarian at the Perm province central library was quoted as saying, "Literature of a political character does not elicit any particular interest—it is read to the extent that it is necessary for study in political education circles. Great interest is noticeable [only] among youth preparing for entrance into the Komsomol."[15]

In contrast to officially sanctioned texts on politics and society, works that dealt with the technological wonders of modernity were genuinely popular. The 1926 Komsomol Agitprop Department report cited above noted that the highest number of requests for nonfiction books (41.7 percent of all reader requests for nonfiction) went to the department of Applied Sciences. The popularity of Applied Sciences, the report claimed, was caused in part by young males' high demand for books on technology and machines, including works on electricity, radio, the telephone, airplanes, and automobiles. Worker youth in particular were interested in technology and its applications.[16] The interest of young male activists in air travel, radio, automobiles, and other novel technologies helped to motivate the elaboration of technological themes in early socialist realist literature and in journalistic

"Soviet sensations"—the stories of Arctic exploration and aviation adventures that riveted Soviet readers in the 1930s.[17]

The most requested genre in library studies was fiction. Reader tastes in fiction foreshadowed the development of "Soviet sensations," the formulation of socialist realism as an official literary doctrine, and the militarization of newspaper language in the late 1920s. In particular the predilection of young men for war stories and adventure tales strengthened these trends. Komsomol CC Agitprop Department reports frequently remarked upon the phenomenon. The 1926 report stated that young men "showed great interest in literature of a heroic character, in historical novels on the revolutionary movement, on the civil war in general, in adventure literature, and etc." According to a 1926–1927 Kiev library study, Jack London, the American author of tales of adventure and man's struggle with nature, was first among fiction authors requested, and B. Kellerman, the German adventure novelist, was fourth. Novelists who wrote about war were also popular in the Kiev study.[18]

As Komsomol and party agitprop officials sought to develop new styles of fiction and journalism that would both attract readers and mobilize activists, they kept in mind the popularity of war stories and adventure tales. Data on reader response influenced a number of resolutions on the press drafted by the Komsomol and party agitprop departments and ultimately passed by the respective Central Committees. The 1926 Komsomol Agitprop Department report cited above, for example, was filed with a draft resolution on Komsomol literature and seems to have influenced it. The resolution called for more realistic representation of heroes, and for more "intense emotionalism" that would "infect the reader" with enthusiasm and the desire to pursue Komsomol work. It ordered Komsomol writers "to acquaint the novice [activist] with the heroic struggle of the international proletariat, the party, and the Bolshevik underground." The resolution, in short, proposed to use activists' liking for tales of heroism and violent revolutionary struggle to mobilize them.[19] A revised version was ultimately approved by the Komsomol CC Bureau. Similarly, the party CC's summer 1928 resolution "Measures for the Improvement of Youth and Children's Press," which among other things called for the newspaper and book press to undertake "the inculcation into youth of the militant traditions of the Bolshevik Party" and the publication of youth books on technology, was based in part on reader studies and library borrowing data gathered by the Komsomol Agitprop Department.[20]

Based on their reader surveys agitprop officials in the Komsomol and party apparatuses believed that young male activists responded most enthusiastically to coverage of new technologies and to tales of adventure and wartime heroism. These preferences exercised a strong influence on the development of high Stalinist journalism and literature. Soviet newspapermen in the late 1920s strove to appeal to activists' perceived tastes by militarizing their language and presenting labor as proxy combat, a replay of the civil war. They also evolved a genre of "Soviet sensations" that included coverage of technological breakthroughs, intrepid rescues, glorious construction epics, and heroic explorations in Siberia and the Arctic. Soviet novelists developed the themes of labor as heroic combat, and technology as symbol and portent of socialist modernity, integrating them into socialist realist production novels of the 1930s.

Thus, the reading preferences of party activists in the 1920s, or at least those preferences as perceived by agitprop officials and writers, helped to mold the high Stalinist culture of the 1930s. Taking the analysis one step further, it is clear that the party leadership developed high Stalinist culture as a part of the social revolution that they themselves were making. Having chosen to create a "proletarian" party by recruiting hundreds of thousands of young men from the working class, the party leaders strove to mold a culture that would mobilize them for action.

Scapegoating, Show Trials, and Mass Mobilization

The theme of hidden enemies, whether "class enemies" or "enemies of the people," was central to Stalinist culture from the First Five-Year Plan forward. Indeed, the master narrative of industrialization as heroic combat that stood at the center of Stalinist culture required enemies. This theme can be traced back to Marx's theory of history as class warfare, but Soviet journalists and agitprop officials refashioned it during the NEP years for use as a tool of mass mobilization. Specifically, they learned that popular resentment of party privileges and stagnant living standards could be channeled by placing blame on corrupt officials and putative class enemies. They also found that rank-and-file activists, party and Komsomol, responded with enthusiasm to the denunciation of class enemies. Thus, the elaboration of the theme of hidden enemies during the NEP years and after developed from a fundamental tenet of Bolshevik ideology (history as class warfare) but was elaborated in response to the moods and deep cultural assumptions of the populace. The moods and reactions of Communist activists to central propaganda were important in driving this elaboration.

Some party officials, usually those accused by the press of corruption, understood the scapegoating function of trials of corrupt officials and press exposés of class enemies (see the case of Bezdezhskii, described below). Others genuinely believed that class enemies were everywhere and that they were the chief obstacle to the success of the Soviet Union. But even they understood that press campaigns against corruption and class enemies were effective tools for mobilizing activists and redirecting popular anger. Scapegoating, whether conscious or not (i.e., whether the accusers actually thought the accused were guilty or not), had become a key part of the mechanism of the Bolshevik state by the end of the NEP.

The theme of hidden enemies grew out of the watchdog or denunciatory function of the NEP press. During 1922–1923, as Central Committee Press Department officials worked to reshape the newspaper network slung together in ad hoc fashion during the Civil War, they wrote of *razoblachenie* or *izoblichenie*, meaning "exposing" or "unmasking," as one of the important functions of the press. They asserted that Soviet newspapers should monitor the state apparatus and economic enterprises for corruption and inefficiency. Lenin himself articulated this idea vis-a-vis economic enterprises in a September 1918 article, "On the Character of Our Newspapers." In the piece, published in *Pravda*, the Bolshevik leader called for more coverage of work at individual factories. According to Peter Kenez, "he wanted detailed reports of which factories did their work well, of which ones did not, and of how success was achieved; *above all, he wanted to unmask the guilty—those who did not do their work. They were class enemies* (emphasis added)."[21] Throughout the 1920s and 1930s the Soviet press would serve as unmasker of corrupt bureaucrats, enforcer of labor discipline, denouncer of enemies, and monitor of mood in the factories and the fields. In effect official newspapers were supposed to substitute for the market competition and relatively open politics that provided some check on corruption and economic inefficiency in bourgeois societies.

But press exposés of official corruption and incompetence were not just a means of controlling the party/state apparatus—they were also a way to send messages to specific groups or the populace at large. The message might be a warning that certain activities would not be tolerated. The most dramatic form of exposé, and the one that sent the strongest message, was coverage of "show trials" *(pokazatelnye protsessy)*. During the Civil War provincial and local newspapers regularly covered the trials of "speculators," "bandits," thieves, and arsonists in an effort to discourage illegal trade, armed opposition to the Bolsheviks, and ordinary crime.[22] Trials of people accused of economic crimes such as shirking, embezzlement, and administrative malfeasance remained a standard part of the party's agitprop repertoire in the NEP era, their proper use and presentation discussed at the highest levels of the party hierarchy. With the resurgence under the NEP of retail trade and the reappearance of factory managers in suits, show trials became an important way of convincing workers and party cadres that the Bolsheviks still represented the dictatorship of the proletariat. The trials demonstrated that the party remained vigilant and ready to punish those class enemies who took advantage of the new economic conditions.

The systematic coverage of show trials grew out of party leaders' anxiety that workers might perceive the introduction of the NEP, which legalized certain forms of private business and allowed market forces to influence wages and employment, as a betrayal. One important indication of this concern was the Politburo's creation on September 6, 1923, of a commission on "informing the worker masses of the state's economic achievements." The commission was supposed to come up with ways of persuading workers that the temporary sacrifices of the NEP were yielding economic results. The party leaders wanted to ensure regular newspaper coverage of salary increases, factory openings, measures against unemployment, the introduction of health and disability insurance for workers, decreases in the cost of living, and so on. The commission assigned to the task included representatives from a number of the most important central state institutions. These included the Central Control Commission, the Workers' and Peasants' Inspectorate (RKI), the Council on Labor and Defense, the Supreme Council on the Economy, the Central Council of Labor Unions, the Commissariat of Finance, the Commissariat of Transport and Communications, and Gosplan, the central economic planning board.[23]

One of the publicity tools discussed by the committee (known as the Baranskii Commission after its chairman) was the show trial. In a report on press coverage of the RKI, the state watchdog bureau, members of the Inspectorate's own Information and Publishing Department explained how and why they proposed to publicize show trials. According to the report, hyper-optimistic news reports of Soviet economic successes were creating problems: "Totally optimistic information leads to completely unexpected and undesired results, as practice has shown. During the autumn slow-down strikes workers stated directly: 'You praise yourselves constantly, that (*sic*) everything everywhere is going well, so why then don't you raise our wages?'" The report then emphasized that news coverage must include not only positive achievements, but also the reasons for failures:[24]

The Department has begun and will continue a campaign to publicize materials from show trials, undertaken at Central Control Commission instance.

The most important thing which these trials must demonstrate is that there exist flaws (*nedostatki*) within the [Soviet] apparatus itself which everywhere render our responsible managers helpless in the struggle with malfeasance and irresponsibility (*beskhoziaistvennost*).

For this reason it is absolutely natural to connect the unmasking of deficiencies with the positive work of perfecting the apparatus.

And in the agitation campaign the emphasis is being made precisely on this connection.[25]

In short, Soviet administrators needed show trials of corrupt or putatively officials and managers to pinpoint the blame for economic difficulties and explain to workers why their salaries were not going up. The RKI along with its party analogue, the Central Control Commission (CCC), ran the investigations and publicized the trials. Embedded in the procedure itself was the assumption that economic problems were not structural, but had their origin in the corruption and incompetence of individual workers and managers. Newspapermen and CCC/RKI officials sought to direct worker frustration at stagnant living standards against corrupt individuals. Although this may not have been conscious scapegoating, journalists, party leaders, and agitprop officials over the course of the NEP became increasingly aware of the utility of this tactic for mobilizing the "laboring masses" and redirecting popular resentment away from party leaders.

Propaganda and police officials used show trials in the 1920s, as later, mostly to send messages to their audience—they did not discuss the question of the innocence or guilt of the accused in their planning. They generally assumed that the prosecutor or security organs had already determined that the accused were guilty before the case came to trial. In accordance with the trials' central purpose, Komsomol and Party agitprop departments tried to ensure that newspapers' very popular Court Chronicle departments covered only trials "with an instructive, educational function."[26]

Even in January 1924, while the Baranskii Commission was still preparing its report, the central Soviet press was using coverage of trials to send specific messages to the population. Newspapers referred to many of these explicitly as "show trials" (an alternate translation is "instruction trials"). In the month of January alone the Central Council of Labor Unions organ *Labor* covered seven show trials and ran two articles calling for the organization of yet more such spectacles to promote action against specific social and economic disorders. Accounts of the trials generally ran at the bottom of one of the newspaper's back pages (pages four, five, or six), often in a semiregular section headed "From the Courtroom." Although inconspicuously placed, coverage of show trials was routine and telegraphed clear messages about Soviet Power and its enemies.[27]

One message *Labor* strove to convey was that in spite of NEP concessions to private traders Soviet Power was still battling to defend worker rights. A good example of this covered by *Labor* in January 1924 was the trial of the Martyshevskiis, a couple who ran a sweatshop where eight young women worked fifteen to seventeen hours a day making stockings for irregular pay without any health insurance or other benefits. The long hours and the lack of benefits violated Soviet labor law. The reporter also introduced the element of sexual exploitation, noting that the husband, aided by his wife ("the 'madam'") had made "hooliganistic attacks" on his female employees. In a story on a similar case one of *Labor's* Odessa correspondents reported on the trial of the head of a restaurant cooperative at the local food workers' labor union. Like the Martyshevskiis, the chief of the cooperative was accused of working his employees up to sixteen hours a day and failing to provide any form of insurance benefits for them. He had also funneled off 60 percent of the cooperative profits for his own use and failed to provide workers with work clothes.[28]

Although broadly similar in purpose to show trial coverage after 1927, *Labor's* 1924 pieces were completely different in tone. There was no abuse of defendants as "bastards," "scum," "reptiles," "wreckers," or "spies." The worst epithet applied to any of the accused in January 1924 was "madam," to Martyshevskii's wife. Even terms such as "class-hostile elements" did not appear. In short, coverage was propagandistic, attempting to indict the enemies of Soviet Power with narratives of their crimes, delivered in a relatively neutral tone.

Denunciation, Reader Letters, and Popular Anger

During the 1920s effective presentation of show trials depended in part on feedback from reader letters and other intelligence sources. Both the denunciatory and information-gathering functions of the Soviet press depended on a massive inflow of letters to the newspapers. Indeed, Soviet newspapers received a volume of mail probably unprecedented in world history. For the Bolsheviks, these letters were input from below, a manifestation of mass, democratic participation in Soviet Power. In the mid-1920s reader letters to the newspapers helped to catalyze important changes in the presentation of party propaganda, not out of any desire to carry out the popular will but rather because of the felt need for more control over popular moods.

As noted at the beginning of this chapter, Soviet newspapers during the NEP regularly compiled reports on popular mood based on reader letters. Editors forwarded these reports to a variety of instances, including the senior CC secretaries. Between 1926 and 1928 there was an explosion of newspaper reports on reader response to party propaganda campaigns. For the party elite, this was a time of unnerving political and discursive instability. During this period the formation of a new opposition coalition within the party, the so-called Trotskii-Zinovev Opposition, overlapped with the 1926 belt-tightening campaign, a war scare in 1927, unrest at Moscow factories, and increasingly clear indications of peasant hostility to the regime. Fear that their grip on power was slipping prompted Stalin and his allies to monitor carefully the mood of the populace, using intelligence reports and the reader letters provided by the newspapers.

Reader letters and intelligence reports revealed great popular anger at the power and privileges of the party elite, even among rank-and-file Communist activists. They also demonstrated that many readers of the press did not understand or did not respond to the press's explanations of the need for material sacrifices to build socialism. If this was the dictatorship of the proletariat, many worker writers asked, why were real wages stagnant or dropping? And why were bosses still walking around in suits, addressing their employees as *ty* (the familiar, as opposed to the respectful, form of "you") and drawing high salaries?

But the letters also suggested a solution to these problems of propaganda reception. A substantial proportion of the press's audience, and especially the young male activists who made up the core of the party and Komsomol, were very susceptible to scapegoating. They were quite ready to blame the party opposition, the kulaks, corrupt middle-level management, and amorphous "class enemies" for economic difficulties. By the late 1920s party leaders, in response to this revelation, would intensify their use of scapegoating to "explain" economic difficulties and vent popular anger.

Belt Tightening and Resentment of Bosses

In March 1926 Feliks Dzherzhinski, head of the Supreme Council on the Economy, launched a publicity effort in support of a new *rezhim ekonomii*, or belt-tightening campaign. Dzherzhinski and agitprop officials aimed to coordinate a massive drive to cut production costs in industry. Part of the drive was persuading factory workers to accept wage freezes, benefits cuts, and even firings. As the campaign developed, however, intelligence reports from several sources (reader letters, party agitators, OGPU informers) showed that it was confusing and angering workers and ordinary party activists. The press was not adequately explaining to the "laboring masses" the reasons for the squeeze on their wages or the need for sacrifices. In response, party agitprop officials emphasized the need to tailor the press's message to lower-level party activists and the peasants who were migrating to the cities in search of construction or industrial work. Soviet leaders considered the support of both these groups essential for their continued rule, for the activists did the party's hard spadework and the immigrating peasants were the novice members of the proletariat, new cadres for the party's "own" class. From the party's point of view, both groups' reception of the press was dangerously unstable.

During the winter of 1926–1927 M. Erlikh, the secretary of *The Worker Gazette* editorial staff and member of the paper's party cell bureau, forwarded several reader letters, intelligence reports, and articles personally to Stalin. These all had to do with worker discontent, especially in connection with the belt-tightening campaign. On November 8 Erlikh sent Stalin a letter from a forty-year-old cleaning lady with the family name of Nekriakova. Nekriakova complained that she couldn't feed herself, her sister, and her five children on her wages of forty-five rubles a month. She described her feelings of bitterness upon going to see the celebration of the ninth anniversary of the October Revolution while her children sat home hungry. "I think, how HAPPY I am that we've had nine years of the revolution, and I say, 'To hell with the revolution.' Look what they've done, the specialists live nicely, the administration lives nicely. They've got big salaries and benefits too. And if we the proletariat aren't educated we'll be put down just like before. Things are even worse under Soviet Power [than before]."[29] Other reports on the progress of the belt-tightening campaign also showed that workers were angered by the party's demands for sacrifice. In one June 1926 memo sent to Molotov, Sergei Gusev, head of the CC Press Department, noted that many worker correspondents were protesting "distortions" in the campaign, in particular the practice of economizing by cutting into workers' "material situation."[30]

With both peasants and workers feeling that the state was squeezing them, all kinds of expenditures reported in the press became suspect. One reader whose letter was included in a *Peasant Gazette* report to Molotov came up with a particularly ingenious "counterreading" of an article in the journal *Krasnaia niva (Red Field)*. The article triumphantly announced the construction of a monument to Lenin, but the reader, A. L. Trofimchuk of Kursk province, saw the construction as a waste of money:

> When Lenin was alive, he said, there is no need to build monuments to a revolutionary—he must create a monument to himself through his labors for the Worker-Peasant State. But these words, apparently, have been forgotten. And now that Lenin's dead they are building very expensive monuments to him, which require large quantities of money. Recently I read in the journal *Red Field* that work had begun on the construction of a monument to Ilich, the preparations for which alone will cost several "grand," as we say in the countryside.
>
> Involuntarily I ask myself: would Ilich have demanded such expenditures on himself, obviously not. The peasants say, what is this for, when our local mill is falling down for lack of funds to renovate it. Or the sugar factory, which they began to repair but then stopped and fired the workers. And aren't there many such factories in the USSR?[31]

Far more suspect than monument building were salary increases for technical specialists and administrators, especially when workers' salaries were dropping. In the fall of 1927 a lumberjack wrote in to the central newspaper *Batrak (Rural Day Laborer)* with a piece he titled "Things Are Nice for the Specialists, but Bad for Workers." The piece was included in a *Rural Day Laborer* report to Stalin and Molotov. "Everywhere we hear that only the specialists are getting raises, and there are none for the workers. What we don't know is why. Let's take for example, our own Vetchinskoe timber tract. Just a few days ago we got the labor contract to sign. There we see that they increased the specialists' salary, but as for the lumbermen, as their salaries had been 20 rubles, so they remained. We don't know whose fault this is, whether the union or the inspector is supposed to take care of it. And the lumbermen are up to their necks in work . . . but as for our wages, it's don't complain, you're getting plenty."[32]

In accordance with the policy established in 1923–1924 by the Workers' and Peasants' Inspectorate, the belt-tightening campaign was to include exposure of production inefficiencies and denunciation of incompetent or dishonest personnel. The objectives were to explain current economic difficulties, enforce discipline by exemplary punishment of a few malefactors, and promote vigilance against inefficiency and "wrecking." But caution was required in publishing denunciations of corruption. In a June 8, 1926, brief to Molotov on the progress of the propaganda campaign, Press Department head Sergei Gusev praised newspapers that balanced their coverage of "shortcomings" *(nedostatki)* with that of achievements. Too much self-congratulation might make workers wonder why their salaries weren't being raised, but too much self-flagellation also had undesirable consequences. Heavy publicity of incompetence and thievery could undermine the authority of both economic administrators and party, making workers reluctant to cooperate further in the belt-tightening campaign. Specifically, some workers began to bridle at purchasing further government bonds as part of the "industrialization loan" program. In the early summer of 1928, for example, a worker at Moscow's Printing Plant No. 16 refused to purchase a second round of bonds, saying, "The typographical workers won't give a kopeck for the Second Industrial Loan, as the Communist Party does not know how to administer the economy. I read in the newspaper about a case in which 15,000 rubles was initially budgeted for the construction of a building which eventually cost 400,000."[33]

Information about reader response to the 1926–1927 belt-tightening campaign revealed to central authorities a disquieting interpretive instability. Workers were not convinced that the sacrifices demanded of them were necessary, nor were they sure that the party and factory administrations were handling the economy competently. Agitprop officials had to navigate the narrow channel between the Scylla of "self-flattery" and the Charybdis of excessive criticism. Too much positive coverage and workers would demand higher salaries; too much denunciation and they might withhold financial and moral support from the state. Scapegoating proved to be the means of shooting the gap.

An Alliance of Workers and Peasants?

The keystone of NEP newspaper coverage was the concept of the *smychka*, the alliance of workers and peasants to defeat the bourgeoisie and build socialism. Although workers were definitely the senior partner in this alliance, coverage of the *smychka* was supposed to stimulate a spirit of shared struggle and mutual sacrifice. Workers, party leaders hoped, would participate in "patronage" organizations to aid the countryside and accept lower wages and longer working hours to produce low-cost industrial goods for sale to the peasantry. Peasants, in their turn, would support Soviet Power, pay the agricultural tax in kind, and sell their harvest to the state. In spite of hopes for cooperation and shared sacrifice, however, rural residents in 1926–1927 were expressing increasing resentment of worker privileges and the cities in general. Peasants were not convinced that Soviet Power was acting in their interests; on the contrary they felt put upon. Publicity of the *smychka* did not appear to be winning rural support. One measure of this was the widespread disenchantment with the agricultural tax, the cornerstone of the party's efforts to normalize relations with the peasantry during the NEP. In a 1926 study by *The Peasant Gazette* letter department of 1,295 letters dealing with the agricultural tax, 338 writers expressed dissatisfaction with the tax, whereas only 60 were satisfied with it.[34]

The peasants' sense that the agricultural tax was unfair reflected a more general feeling of victimization. Ivan Nikiforovich, of Saratov province, who identified himself as a "poor peasant and day laborer," wrote to *Rural Day Laborer* in September 1927 to voice his protest at the Communist Party's betrayal of the peasantry. "In the newspaper *The Siren* I have found out that many lords, princes and officers have been shot," he began. "That is good, it is high time those bastards were wiped out, but there is one thing which is not pretty—in the newspapers they sing a sweet song, sweeter than the nightingales, but as for action, there is nothing but oppression of the peasants." Nikiforovich complained that the party was off track, "far from Leninism." "Everywhere they've put in 'gentlemen' [gospoda], and they don't let the poor redneck peasant [bedniak muzhik] in anywhere, because they're afraid. . . . I wouldn't let these educated bastards' sons in anywhere, I'd teach only the workers and peasants. They trampled on us for 1,000 years, now we should trample them. We the poor peasants will be needed only when they declare war, then they'll need us, but right now they consider us dung."[35] Other letters to *Rural Day Laborer* in the same file with Nikiforovich's attacked the privileges of office workers in rural areas, as well as specialists. There were demands that the salaries of both administrators and specialists be cut. Typical headings for such letters included "Office Workers Get Benefits, but Laborers Don't," and "Office Workers in the Countryside Are Insured, but Laborers Aren't." All of these letters reached the CC leadership.[36]

In November 1926 Iakov Iakovlev, editor of *The Peasant Gazette*, forwarded to Molotov a peasant letter expressly rejecting all the talk of *smychka*. Iakovlev planned to run a reply to this letter in his newspaper, and apparently wanted Molotov's go-ahead. According to the writer, P. Koshelev from the village of Nikulin in Tver province, worker privileges and the low price of agricultural produce compared with industrial goods made a mockery of the *smychka*. There could be no real alliance between city and country until peasants' labor was valued equally with workers'. Koshelev complained that the revolution had done nothing to improve the peasants' lot, whereas "the worker's every need is taken care of, he gets a good salary, has a good apartment, easy work, these days he feels himself almost a lord." The peasant, he wrote, "drinks homebrew, while the worker drinks 40 proof and sometimes even cognac."[37]

Another writer, Iakov Buzytskii, a veteran of the Russo-Japanese War, questioned the sincerity of two key early NEP slogans—"Close the Scissors!," which referred to the need to eliminate the gap between prices for agricultural and industrial goods, and "Face to the Countryside!," which was a call for the party to cultivate peasant support and modernize Russian agriculture. "The only time you turn your face to the countryside," Buzytskii wrote to *The Peasant Gazette*, "is when it's time to collect the agricultural tax." He closed his letter with an implicit threat of peasant rebellion against Soviet Power: "Remember, comrades, the revolution is not over. The peasant is at a dead end, the bourgeoisie is not sleeping."[38]

Judging by Molotov's request for information about peasant attitudes toward the war scare, the Central Committee leadership was listening with anxiety for just this kind of threat. Buzytskii's missive reached the highest levels of the party leadership, along with hundreds of other peasant letters. Taken as a whole, the message of these letters was clear—Russia's peasants had not bought the party's rural policy or slogans. Many of them saw the *smychka* as a cynical hoax played on them for the benefit of the new ruling class, the workers. In their letters peasants zeroed in on a key contradiction in party propaganda, which boldly declared Soviet Power the "dictatorship of the proletariat" at the same time as it pushed the Alliance of Workers and Peasants.

Blaming the Opposition

By late 1927 intelligence reaching the Central Committee indicated that the population as a whole was not buying the party's major agitation campaigns. Reader interpretations of the newspapers were various and unstable, leading to discursive disorder unsettling to party leaders and agitprop officials. Rumors flew fast in the countryside, undermining the official presentation of news and party policy. The population's response to a major war scare in 1927, at least as recorded in official intelligence reports, created the impression among Soviet leaders that their state was in real danger of collapse from the combined effects of internal erosion and external pressure.[39] The success of the Soviet press's attempt to sell the agricultural tax and the *smychka* to peasants had been at best problematic. Moreover, the party appeared to be in danger of losing its bases of support among factory workers as a result of the belt-tightening campaign of 1926–1927. Many sectors of the working class thought the party was demanding unfair sacrifices of them while coddling specialists and factory administrators.

Reader letters to the newspapers along with other intelligence sources also suggested a way out of the problem of unstable interpretation of the press. Many sectors of the populace deeply resented the privileges accorded to other groups—peasants envied workers their apartments and social services, workers begrudged specialists and factory administrators their high salaries, ordinary subjects were furious at party members for their "bureaucratism" and privileges. To some extent the Bolsheviks themselves set up this situation by preaching equality and then practicing hierarchy. In a more direct fashion the Bolsheviks had fanned the flames of class conflict by publicizing the trials of corrupt or criminal officials, administrators, and specialists as a matter of policy. But whatever the causes of popular fury—and there were many others, including the privations, deprivations, and violence that attended the first ten years of Soviet Power—many Soviet subjects were ripe for a scapegoating campaign.

In the spring of 1926 two of Stalin's major political opponents, Leon Trotskii and Grigorii Zinovev, joined forces in an attempt to change the party's agrarian and industrial policies. The coalition's spokesmen argued that the party's agrarian policies under the NEP were allowing relatively wealthy peasants, the kulaks, to accumulate wealth and exploit their poorer neighbors. The relaxation of state controls on trade and the reduction of agricultural taxes, they argued, had opened up space for the development of a proto-capitalist class. The Opposition wished to change economic course to a "left" tack, taxing the peasants more heavily in order to fund industrialization, while at the same time providing relief for poorer peasants with tax exemptions and government loans. Opposition supporters also aimed to crack Stalin's control of the party executive apparatus and the state bureaucracy. They denounced the growing "bureaucratization" of government, claiming that under the pressure of Stalin's dictatorship the party was calcifying into a privileged caste of place holders more concerned with protecting their own perquisites than carrying on the revolution. In response the opposition proposed more democracy within the party and more control over bureaucrats by the "nonparty masses."[40]

The Soviet press carried out a well-coordinated campaign against this so-called Left Opposition from the summer of 1926 until early 1928 (the Opposition itself controlled no major newspapers after Stalin's winter 1925–1926 takeover of the Leningrad party organization, which Grigorii Zinovev had headed). The campaign focused around accusations that the Oppositionists were "schismatics" who rejected party discipline, and around other kinds of name-calling. Stalin and the journalists allied with him calumniated the Opposition leaders as "Mensheviks," "rotten liberals," and "wreckers of socialist construction," and mocked their offers of submission as "two-faced" and "pharisaical." Editors published reader letters that castigated the Opposition as "schismatics," traitors to "Lenin's sacred precepts," and saboteurs of the worker-peasant alliance.

As the campaign against the Opposition developed, party leaders and journalists monitored popular response closely. Newspapers saved files of reader letters on the Opposition and regularly included sections headed "On the Opposition" in their intelligence reports. These letters and reports revealed two potentially complementary trends. On the one hand many letter writers (about one-quarter of the total, according to my survey of one of *The Peasant Gazette*'s files of letters on the Opposition) somehow questioned the CC's line, expressing confusion about policy debates, desire for more information on the Opposition, desire for more party democracy, or outright support for Opposition views. Given that the authors were writing in to an official newspaper that had been running an anti-Opposition campaign for months, that they all signed their letters in spite of significant risk of police investigation, and that Bolshevik officials aimed to achieve monolithic support for their policies among "the laboring masses," this was a significant level of dissent. For party leaders it was a revelation of discursive chaos.[41]

On the other hand most letter writers supported the CC and voiced rage against the Opposition for undermining party unity at a critical point in the development of Soviet society. Within the latter group young male party and Komsomol activists were particularly vocal, demanding harsh punishment of Oppositionists and blaming them for all of the Soviet Union's woes. The more radical of these letters stayed one step ahead of the press: when the newspapers were talking about excluding Trotskii and Zinovev from the Central Committee in 1926, Komsomol members were calling for their exclusion from the party. In 1927 some rural Komsomol members corresponding with *The Peasant Gazette* were demanding execution of the Opposition leaders, a possibility the newspaper had never broached.[42] Whoever these youth were taking their cues from, it was not from the press (it could well have been from local officials and activists). Their angry letters, littered with the refrain of "enough babying of the Opposition!" suggested that there was a large cohort of young activists who would respond well to an even nastier press campaign than that of 1926–1928, one that would portray Stalin's opponents within the party as saboteurs, spies, and traitors deserving of execution. The readiness of most of the letter writers, and particularly the activists, to blame the Opposition for all the problems besetting the USSR suggested that the best way out of discursive chaos would be an intensification of scapegoating and denunciation of traitors and hidden class enemies.

The rage of the young rural Komsomol members was just one element in a broader compound of popular anger and distress. Sometimes this was directed against Oppositionists—according to *Peasant Gazette* correspondent A. Burenkoe, some people in his village "were saying right out that Trotskii's got to be thrown in jail and beaten good."[43] Some letters contained phrases that could not have been drawn from official propaganda of 1926–1928, but presaged the accusations against the "Trotskii-Zinovev United Center" at the great Moscow show trials of 1936–1938. F. V. Koplova, a woman from the Kursk area, wrote that the Opposition were "traitors to the people" *(izmennikov naroda)*.[44] A second letter, the name of whose author was illegible, called Trotskii a "wrecker" *(vreditel)*.[45] Vasilii Ivanovich Titov, of the village of Vorobevo, Tver province, declared that "there is no place in the family of the revolutionary people for schismatics."[46] These accusations went beyond official rhetoric in two directions. Bypassing the press's denunciations of the Oppositionists as traitors to the party or the proletariat, some writers instead charged them with betraying "the people," replacing the categories of class warfare with the rhetoric of populist resentment. Others took the accusation of "wrecker," applied previously to technical specialists suspected of sympathizing with the White opposition to the Bolsheviks, and attached it to the Oppositionists, who were still party members. These isolated rhetorical turns in the *Peasant Gazette* letters are signposts pointing the direction in which official discourse would go in the middle 1930s. They suggest that the rhetoric of the Moscow show trials of the 1930s fit with (and was meant to fit with) a preexisting vocabulary of populist resentment.

The populace as a whole was angry, frightened, and terribly uncertain about the future. Perhaps as a result of this fear and frustration, people hungered for information about the conflicts within the Soviet leadership. Perhaps also such news was a "sensation" analogous to the coverage of political scandals in bourgeois newspapers. Whatever the reason, attacks on the Opposition *sold newspapers.* During the years 1926–1928 people snapped up any newspaper edition carrying news about the struggle with the Opposition. In the summer of 1927 demand for *Pravda* took a sharp jump, which *Pravda* circulation chief Aleksandr Pismen attributed to the paper's frequent, copious coverage of the Opposition.[47] An OGPU intelligence report reaching the Central Committee's Secret Department in late November 1927 confirmed that demand for the paper was high, noting that "the appearance of the 'Discussion Page' [a section containing material on the Opposition] created such hot demand for *Pravda* that the price for one issue went up to one or two rubles."[48]

Through the safety valve of reader letters came the ominous hiss of fury at "bureaucratism" and the privileges enjoyed by the party elite. The "laboring masses" resented party members for their good salaries, their perquisites, and the petty despotism of their rule. Having a petition for housing denied, receiving wages late, being addressed by a bureaucrat in suit and tie with the familiar pronoun *ty*, rather than the formal and respectful *vy*—all of these frustrations and humiliations contributed to the popular anger against the party. Reader letters showed that Opposition leaders could be scapegoated for the "bureaucratism," corruption, and incompetence of local officials, and for the failure of official policy to alleviate the sufferings of the general population.

Readers of the Soviet newspapers responded in utterly divergent ways to the propaganda campaign against the Trotskii-Zinovev Opposition. Nobody was taking polls, so we have no way of quantifying that response. Yet we can draw certain conclusions from the reader letters that the regime collected and saved. So, presumably, could Stalin, Molotov, and the bureaucrats who staffed the Central Committee Department of Agitation and Propaganda. Reader letters revealed that the regime newspapers were *not* transmitting a single message to their audience, and that counterreadings and misreadings were not only possible, but common. They revealed that the population's reception of official propaganda was unstable. But they also demonstrated the mobilizing power of attacks on enemies within. Many activists would have applauded much nastier press campaigns and harsher punishments for the Opposition. Even among the nonparty populace, resentment of the party elite could be channeled and focused on Stalin's political opponents. Taken together with the popularity of news about the Opposition, the letters suggested a recipe for future campaigns against those who deviated from the "general line." Shrill and simple attacks on Oppositionists as traitors to the "people" *(narod)* would cut through the confusion of the rank-and-file Communist activists and provide a focus for popular anger against the party. The campaign would culminate in execution of the dissenters, which would both appease popular fury and frighten into silence those who might still read official propaganda critically.

Worker Response to the Shakhty Trial

On March 10, 1928, Soviet newspapers published news that the secret police (GPU) had uncovered a plot by engineers and technical specialists to sabotage production at the Shakhty coal mines in the Donbass. Historians have generally recognized the publicity around the putative plot and ensuing trial as the kick-off of a deliberate campaign to mobilize worker support with rhetoric of class war against specialists and kulaks.[49] As such it was both a continuation of the strategy of maintaining worker trust in Soviet Power by the prosecution of corrupt administrators *and* a quantum leap in the intensity of that prosecution. The CC leadership hoped to reinforce the party's proletarian support base by capitalizing on worker resentment of technical specialists and administrators. The announcement of the GPU's investigation at the Shakhty mines was followed closely by the Central Control Commission's April 1928 declaration of a "self-criticism" campaign giving workers and lower-level party cadres more freedom to criticize higher-ranking party officials and administrators.[50] The self-criticism or *samokritika* campaign put pressure on factory administrators and party/Soviet officials of a Rightist stamp who saw mass mobilization by activation of worker anger as a threat to labor discipline and production.

As in earlier press campaigns, party organizations monitored the population's response to the Shakhty affair closely. Of particular interest was the reaction of workers, for they were the most important targets of the publicity campaign. In late March 1928, the Moscow Party Committee's Information Department produced several intelligence reports on worker response to the discovery of the specialists' "plot." In mid-July the Information Department again assembled intelligence summaries on the Shakhty affair, this time on Moscow workers' reaction to the sentences that concluded the trial. Both sets of reports appear to have been based mostly on notes taken by lower-level party agitators working at Moscow factories. The reports revealed that publicity of the Shakhty affair had indeed aroused and mobilized the anger of factory workers against specialists and factory administrators. Not only did press coverage of the Shakhty affair tap into and focus workers' resentment, but it actually motivated them to take positive actions, such as purchasing larger quantities of government Industrial Loan bonds.

The initial announcement that "economic counterrevolution" had been unmasked in the Donbass sparked a wave of excitement and agitation among Moscow factory workers. An Information Department report dated March 23 described "great agitation" among workers at several Moscow factories, including two manufactories of construction materials. "During the lunch break there was group reading of the newspapers and conversations and arguments about these events. In some localities workers demanded that the party cell call an immediate session or meeting to discuss the question of the events in the Donbass. . . . Everywhere the workers are saying that the party, the labor unions, the managers and the GPU were late in uncovering the counterrevolutionary plot."[51]

The report went on to quote individual workers, many of whom viewed the prosecution of the "plotters" as a long-delayed confirmation of their own grievances against the factory administration. Some workers also saw the unmasking of the wreckers as a sweet, deserved retribution for the wrongs they had suffered at the hands of all kinds of authorities, from labor union officials to managers to party cell secretaries. One railroad employee said, "The sons-of-bitches screwed up our work for six years and no one paid any attention." Many workers seemed to be convinced that the party and GPU had willfully closed their eyes for years to the abuses and wrecking wrought by the specialists. A worker from the Stormy Petrel Factory complained, "It's always like that with us—the labor union and the party cell just drowse along until thunder strikes. And then all the bells start to clang." Another worker (at the New Dawn Factory) observed that "the Communists are not vigilant enough. They've got to put completely trustworthy Communists in managerial work."[52]

News of the Shakhty affair touched off demands for harsh punishment of the plotters, and for harsh measures against specialists in general. One worker opined that "it's essential to terrorize that 'public' [the specialists] a bit." According to reports from the Sokolnicheskii ward committee, the "vast majority" of workers in Sokolniki thought that "we must shoot all of them [the accused specialists] or else we'll have no peace." Nonparty workers at the Ilich Factory demanded harsh punishments of the Shakhty counterrevolutionaries, saying, "Ripping their heads off would be soft treatment." A transport worker suggested hanging, and workers at the Derbanevskii Chemical Factory demanded that the Shakhty specialists be shot without trial.[53]

At the conclusion of the Shakhty trial in July 1928 eleven of the fifty-three accused were sentenced to death, and five were actually executed. The Moscow Committee Information Department reported that the majority of workers were not satisfied with the sentences, that "at all enterprises conversations go on about how the sentences were weak, too soft, and that it was necessary to shoot more." As when the story of the Shakhty affair first broke, news of the sentences provoked lively discussions and arguments among Moscow workers. At the Frunze Factory "the main topic of conversation from the first thing in the morning throughout the workshops was the sentence in the

Shakhty trial." One city ward committee informed the Information Department that "at the largest enterprises of the ward a lively exchange of opinions among workers about the sentences is ongoing." The ward report offered a few sample comments to summarize worker reaction. "The sentences are weak. They should have shot at least twenty." "Was it worth so much effort to shoot only eleven persons? The trial itself cost quite a bit of money." At the Central Union of Cooperatives' printing plant a group of nonparty employees had taken the initiative to gather signatures on a petition for harsher sentences to the Central Executive Committee.[54]

Some workers thought the "softness" of the sentences reflected a judicial double standard that dictated heavier punishment for workers and lighter ones for specialists and intellectuals. "If my brother appeared before the bench as an accused person, they'd have shot him, but they spared the engineers," angrily commented one worker. Said another, "The sentence is soft. They shoot *us* for minor misdemeanors. Vyshinskii [the prosecutor] himself is a professor, he's for his own, why did they appoint him chairman of the court?" A third worker, from the Platinum Factory protested that "they shoot workers for trivial infractions, and spare the engineers."[55]

The Shakhty trial provoked in workers anger and an urgent sense that Soviet Power was under threat. At least in some cases it also motivated them to take positive action. An August 24, 1928, Information Department intelligence brief on worker response to the Second Industrial Loan campaign reported that the Shakhty trial had helped increase subscriptions. "The workers make a close connection between the bond issue and the Shakhty affair trial," wrote the author of the report. Under the heading "The Workers' Answer to the Shakhty Affair," this author noted "at the Duka Factory the workers themselves put forth the slogan, 'Our Answer to the Wreckers'" in connection with the loan campaign. At a money-printing facility some workers said that "after the Shakhty trial we resolved to ask the government for a bond issue, now we must carry through our side of the bargain." Other workers, at the Dorogomilovskii Factory, declared, "We will answer the Shakhty trial with a loan—that's the proletarian way."[56]

Moscow workers reacted to the Shakhty affair more or less as the party's agitprop planners must have hoped. News of the GPU investigation and trial effectively tapped worker resentment of specialists and factory administrators, reminding them that Soviet Power was on their side against the privileged "burgies" (*burzhui*) and in some cases even channeling their anger in constructive directions, such as subscriptions to the Second Industrial Loan. The Shakhty trial thus served a double purpose as mobilizer and safety valve for worker anger. Reports on workers' response to the affair present a picture of almost unanimous support of the party leadership's attack on technical specialists. In 1928 specialist baiting was one issue on which party and proletariat could agree.

Bolshevik Political Culture and Reader Response to the Press

By 1926–1927 a clear sense was emerging among upper-level Bolshevik officials that scapegoating and denunciation of hidden class enemies worked as a means of mobilizing activists and redirecting popular resentments. This was certainly the conviction of Stalin and many of his high-level supporters. Thus in June 1926 Stalin, in a letter to his right-hand man Molotov, suggested that simple charges of "schism" against the Trotskii-Zinovev Opposition would be a more effective propaganda ploy than detailed policy discussion. Stalin preferred the accusation of "schism" *(raskol)* "because the workers will understand this, for they value party unity and it will be a serious warning to other opposition-ists."[57] Nikolai Smirnov, editor-in-chief of the CC's *Worker Gazette* and a Stalin appointee, expressed a similar view of his worker audience in November 1926 in response to a CCC censure for publishing an excessively harsh cartoon of the Opposition leaders. "Not one worker reader of the newspaper will understand the (CCC's) formulation of 'harm done to the party by the caricature,' [but will] understand only that *The Worker Gazette* is somehow incorrect in its battle with the Opposition. . . . This resolution sharply lowers the authority of the newspaper. "[58] Smirnov insisted that only harsh attacks on the Opposition could uphold the credibility of *The Worker Gazette* with its worker readers. He shared Stalin's image of the worker audience as a mob that responded to images and emotions rather than reason.

Although higher-ranking party members generally acknowledged that workers responded with enthusiasm to harsh denunciation of oppositionists and class enemies, many believed this could be a danger-ous political tactic if taken too far (or if not controlled tightly enough by the party CC). Whereas hard-liners advocated simple, emotional appeals that would mobilize the "laboring masses" on the side of Stalin and the CC majority (agitation), moderate advocates of "enlightenment" journalism (propaganda) urged journalists to reason with readers and provided nuanced "illumination" *(osveshchenie)* of contested issues. Moderates supported the enlightenment approach not out of a commitment to pluralism, but out of faith that rational discussion would reveal the correctness of party policies. They also believed that the party's mission was to educate the masses, to coax them into "political consciousness."

Worries about excessively harsh denunciation of corrupt officials and class enemies hidden within the state apparatus were woven throughout party propaganda discussions in the 1920s and early 1930s. Thus when CC Press Department chief Sergei Gusev addressed the March 1927 meeting of the journalists' professional union, he stressed the difference between "healthy" and "unhealthy" criticism. He attacked *The Worker Gazette* for excessively nasty caricatures of Opposition leaders and described the undesirable effects of such caricatures on "barely conscious workers." Seeing such a caricature, Gusev claimed, the worker who lacked political consciousness would say, "There's the fat exploiter, there's the enemy that sucks our blood, that robs us." In Gusev's view portraying *any* party member, oppositionist or not, as an exploiter might give workers the wrong idea. Conference delegates seconded Gusev, charging hard-liners with "a chase after sensations."[59] One delegate from *Pravda* (Landau) characterized worker response to exposés of corrupt officials. "The worker reads, and he thinks, I am good, I am ideal, I am the proletariat, I am building socialism, and meanwhile the bosses are making a comeback [in the form of the party apparatus]."[60] Excessively harsh exposés, in the view of enlightenment advocates, played on workers' worst instincts, undermined party/state authority, and were analogous to the sensationalistic scandalmongering of the bourgeois press.

Many Bolshevik journalists and officials were fully aware that the party press made use of scapegoating to influence popular mood. An excellent example of this comes out of archival documentation related to the summer 1930 attack by *Komsomolskaia pravda* and the Moscow RKI on the Moscow Fruit and Vegetable Cooperative Union (Soiuzplodoovoshch). In a press campaign that ran throughout July 1930 *Komsomolskaia pravda* accused officials of the Cooperative Union of sabotaging the supply of produce to the Moscow populace. Problems with the provision of produce in Moscow were the subject of long-standing worker complaints and the campaign scape-goated Cooperative Union officials for shortages. On July 30 *Komsomolskaia pravda* reported that the director of the Cooperative Union, Bezdezhskii, was issued a censure by the RKI's Moscow court and banned from holding supervisory posts in the future.[61]

Bezdezhskii appealed the RKI decision to the party CCC in August. His appeal was an unusually frank account of the mechanics of a scape-goating campaign. "The central press campaign illuminating the issue of provisioning the cities with vegetables . . . ," Bezdezhskii wrote, "has taken a turn which is not entirely correct. Trials are organized one after the other. The organization and its employees are characterized as wreckers and bureaucrats who are impeding the business of provision-ing the workers." Bezdezhskii described what he believed were the real reasons for the produce shortage, which included May and June frosts, a shortage of qualified personnel at the Cooperative Union, lack of refrigerator cars, and the refusal of some officials in South Ukraine, the North Caucasus, and the Transcaucasus to export vegetables from their regions. Instead of rational discussion of these problems, he claimed, the press had engaged in "slander." As a result, Moscow workers had turned against the cooperative officials. Near the end of his appeal Bezdezhskii concluded that "the question, obviously, is not of me personally. . . . I put the question [to the Control Commission] now: if dumping dirt all over me, as director of the Cooperative Union, is necessary for the revolution, if it is in the interests of the party at this particular moment, then I have no objections to the decision (of the Moscow RKI court)." In other words, Bezdezhskii was aware that party leaders deliberately set up scapegoats to take the blame for problems of worker living standards, even if the accused were not guilty.[62]

Journalists, propaganda officials, and party leaders, then, were aware of the uses and abuses of sensational exposés of enemies hidden within the party/state apparatus. They understood that such denunciations had the potential to mobilize popular (worker) anger but also to under-mine authority. Some advocates of an enlightenment approach even charged that sensational exposés pandered to the worst instincts of "backward" workers. Nonetheless, the simple and vicious approach ultimately came to dominate Bolshevik discourse.

Undoubtedly Marxist and Leninist ideology, particularly Marx's understanding of history as the unfolding of class warfare and Lenin's avant-gardism, contributed to the development of a militaristic and militant Bolshevik culture and to the deliberate use of scapegoating tactics to manipulate popular moods. So, too, did the militarization of the party during the Civil War years. But the assumptions and tastes of the many hundreds of thousands of young Russian men, mostly "manual laborers," recruited by the party after 1924 certainly helped put paid to the enlightenment orientation of official NEP culture and decisively influenced the development of a Stalinist culture based around antirational militance, glorification of toughness and violence, and scapegoating.

~ *II*

THE CREATION OF MASS JOURNALISM AND SOCIALIST REALISM

~ 4

The Creation of Mass Journalism

In the middle years of the New Economic Policy (NEP) era, young, radical Soviet journalists at mass worker and Komsomol newspapers created the new forms of journalism that came to dominate the Soviet press during the Stalin era. Responding to Central Committee (CC) directives to cooperate in the 1926 belt-tightening campaign to raise industrial productivity, newspapermen created original journalistic genres that were aimed at monitoring and facilitating production; denouncing incompetence, slacking and sabotage; and generally advancing the progress of industry. These new journalistic forms, which included the coverage of "socialist competitions" between enterprises and "production reviews" in which newspapermen went onto the shop floor to seek out and correct production bottlenecks, were part of the organizing and denunciatory functions of the Soviet press.

As younger Bolshevik journalists who had gained their newspaper work experience under Soviet Power replaced Old Bolshevik editors and non-Bolshevik veterans of the prerevolutionary press, the tone and content of individual Soviet newspapers and the press as a whole shifted in the direction of mass journalism. During the self-criticism campaign of 1928–1929 the Central Committee transferred mass journalists into key positions at central newspapers. There ensued an intense struggle, with newspapermen defending more conventional journalism. Although disciplined by the Central Committee in the fall of 1929 for publishing denunciations of higher-level officials without permission from above, mass journalists were victorious in this struggle. In a revolution that echoed through the pages of Soviet newspapers right down to the end of the USSR, they converted most of the popular press to their style of news coverage, dedicated to mobilizing society for efficient production rather than supplying the populace with information, edification, or entertainment.

The mass journalists' mantra was a single sentence about the functions of the revolutionary press taken from Lenin's 1901 article "Where to Begin." In making the argument for the publication of a socialist newspaper with nationwide distribution, Lenin said that such a paper "is not only a collective propagandist and a collective agitator, it is also a collective organizer." Lenin meant that setting up the distribution of the paper would require organizing a national network of Social Democratic activists, a network that could provide the party's leaders with information and aid in "the organization of various revolutionary actions."[1] Although the mass journalists of the middle and late 1920s took the slogan of the newspaper as "collective organizer" for their own, Lenin's original formulation had nothing to do with mobilizing society for production and everything to do with the organizational problems of an underground political party. It was not until September 1918, when he published a short article in *Pravda* titled "On the Character of Our Newspapers," that Lenin suggested that Bolshevik newspapers might have a role in organizing society for industrial production. According to Peter Kenez, the article called for less policy debate in the press and more coverage of the concrete work of production, of successful and unsuccessful factories. The press was supposed to facilitate economic growth and the construction of Communism by singling out examples of good work and exposing incompetence and slacking at the point of production. In later years Lenin continued to show an interest in focusing the Soviet press on problems of production rather than politics. In December 1920, for example, he proposed to a Central Committee Plenum that both *Pravda* and *Izvestiia* be turned into "production instead of political organs."[2]

Soviet journalists did not make Lenin's vision of a press oriented toward control and organization of production real in his lifetime. In later years Soviet historians sought to trace the origins of socialist competitions and other techniques of mass mobilization for production back to the Civil War era,[3] but the newspaper press did not come into its own as organizer and auditor of production until the party's belt-tightening campaign of 1926.[4] During the Civil War period and the first years of the NEP, press organs of all sorts ran occasional coverage of "Volunteer Saturdays" *(subbotniki)* and production contests *(konkursy)* between enterprises. But newspapermen did not organize these events; they simply reported on them. Nor did they unmask the incompetent or dishonest "concrete bearers of evil" who obstructed production. Their stories were typical wartime exhortations of the populace to contribute their energy to the military effort.[5]

The institutional base for mass journalism as well as the self-criticism campaign of 1928–1929 was built in the first years of the NEP. The decision by CC agitation-and-propaganda (agitprop) officials in the winter of 1921–1922 to set up mass worker papers as part of the new differentiated press network established one pillar of the base on which mass journalism would rest.[6] The organization of a worker correspondents' movement (1923–1924) dedicated to the exposure of administrative incompetence and malfeasance in factories and the state apparatus set up a second. And the party's encouragement of wall newspapers, workplace broadsheets on which worker correspondents could offer suggestions or criticism to management, set up a third.

One of the functions that Agitprop Department officials hoped the mass worker newspapers and the worker correspondents' movement would fulfill was that of denunciation of malefactors within the state, party, and industrial apparatuses. The vision of a Soviet press that would monitor the bureaucracies and expose abuses appeared during the Civil War in Lenin's article "On the Character of Our Newspapers" and in the resolutions of the Eighth Party Congress, which met in March 1919.[7] With the end of the Civil War newspapermen began strenuous efforts to recruit volunteer correspondents to check up on bureaucratic work and production.

In the first years of the NEP the CC Agitprop Department exercised little effective control over the worker and village correspondents' movements. Labor union and mass newspapers demanded many different tasks from worker correspondents and evolved various methods of recruitment and supervision. Some correspondents were elected by their labor union committees, others were appointed by a party, Komsomol, or labor union organization, and still others were self-selected. Expectations for correspondents also varied. At some papers, such as *Shveinik (Seamster)*, the organ of the garment workers' labor union, correspondents were expected simply to provide editors with poetry, short stories, memoirs, notes on union activities, and information on contract negotiations. At others editors expected correspondents to unmask corrupt or incompetent administrators, recruit subscribers to the paper, and organize reading circles, lectures, and

"Newspaper Corners." *The Worker Gazette*, the CC's mass worker newspaper, demanded the most of its correspondents, specifically asking that they gather information on the moods of workers and "organize public opinion" in the interests of proletariat and party. Editors instructed correspondents about tasks and topics for discussion on the pages of the newspapers and through pamphlets, roving instructors, and occasional conferences.[8]

The central mass worker newspapers *Worker Moscow* and *The Worker Gazette* laid particular emphasis on denunciation and unmasking of corrupt or incompetent administrators. In 1924–1925 both papers institutionalized these functions by establishing "Investigative Bureaus" *(Biuro rassledovaniia)* at their editorial offices. At these bureaus newspaper employees sorted denunciatory letters from worker correspondents and forwarded them to appropriate authorities, such as the provincial prosecutor's office, the party Control Commissions, or the Workers' and Peasants' Inspectorate (RKI).

Like the mass newspapers, Komsomol papers and journals were also committed to building up a correspondents' movement, in their case one of "youth correspondents." Provincial youth newspapers and the central Komsomol journal *Young Leninist* had been publishing letters from youth correspondents at least as early as 1924. A February 12, 1925, circular to provincial Komsomol committees from the Komsomol Central Committee's Press Department chief, M. Zorkii, described the work of a typical youth correspondent circle organized at the main repair shops for the Moscow-Kursk railroad. Of the 305 master mechanics young enough to be eligible for Komsomol membership, 204 belonged to the youth organization. The correspondents' circle had twenty-eight members, seventeen of them Komsomols. The youth correspondents wrote to a number of newspapers, but most often to their own wall newspaper or *Worker Moscow*. The chairman of the wall newspaper's editorial board recruited correspondents, and until recently individual workshops had also elected them. The latter practice, however, had been stopped because those elected rarely wrote to the paper. The circle met once a week. Two members of the enterprise's Komsomol cell bureau were supposed to supervise its work, but they rarely attended meetings. The editing of the paper was up to the correspondents themselves, with conflicts between them settled by vote. Most youths who belonged to correspondents' circles, the report concluded, wanted to become Komsomol members and get their correspondence published.[9]

The Komsomol correspondents' movement began a rapid expansion after *Komsomolskaia pravda*, the organization's first nationwide newspaper, began publication in May 1925. The Komsomol Press Department's March 1925 prospectus for the new paper was very conservative. *Komsomolskaia pravda* was to be a "leading political organ" targeting university students and Komsomol leaders, not youth in general or even the entire Komsomol membership.[10] But in August 1925, after only two months of publication, the Komsomol Central Committee replaced *Komsomolskaia pravda*'s chief editor, A. Slepkov. The new editor, Taras Kostrov, transformed the paper into a mass organ, aimed at the mass of uneducated activists rather than elite university students. In the coming years *Komsomolskaia pravda* exercised a decisive influence on the evolution of Soviet journalism.

Kostrov was a very young man with an impeccable revolutionary pedigree. The son of a member of the People's Will revolutionary organization, Kostrov was born in 1901 in Chita, where his parents were in exile, but grew up in Odessa. As a child he met the prominent Social Democrats Giorgii Plekhanov and Vera Zasulich and read Marxist and revolutionary literature, including Lenin's works. Arrested for demonstrating against Russian involvement in World War I, Kostrov was evidently active in the Odessa revolutionary movement even before 1917. He joined the Bolshevik Party in 1919 and edited the underground newspaper *Odesskii kommunist (Odessa Communist)* during the period when Odessa was under White occupation. After the Civil War Kostrov did party work in Lugansk (the Donbass area), Kiev, and Kharkov. The Komsomol Central Committee called him to Moscow in late 1924, probably in connection with a conference organized by the Press Department to recruit provincial newspapermen for work in the central Komsomol press.[11]

Under Kostrov's direction *Komsomolskaia pravda* underwent a rapid metamorphosis. In the fall of 1925 he presented a revised blueprint for the paper to the Komsomol Central Committee. He proposed to turn *Komsomolskaia pravda* into a mass newspaper devoted to organizing youth correspondents, creating factory wall newspapers that would intervene actively in production, and targeting the lowest level of Komsomol activists.[12] After the change in direction, *Komsomolskaia pravda* became one of the leading newspapers in the development of the correspondents' movement, mass journalism, and the denunciatory function of the press.

The worker and youth correspondents' movement, the mass worker newspapers, and the Komsomol press were incubators for the mass journalists who came to dominate the Soviet press between 1928 and

1930. Most mass journalists got their early training in newspaper work not at the state journalism schools but as worker/youth correspondents. They were often young workers recruited into the correspondents' movement "straight from the bench," or boys from other humble backgrounds, the sons of village schoolteachers, photographers, clerks, and the like. The activities of the early correspondents' movement differed from later mass journalism in that they did not involve direct intervention in production by the newspaper. Correspondents might expose corruption in the state apparatus or "shortcomings" in production, or they might organize meetings to promote subscriptions to the newspapers, but regular staff journalists did not get involved in events on the shop floor. In their insistence that the press monitor the "achievements and shortcomings" of the state bureaucracy and the economy, however, agitprop bureaucrats and editors were edging toward the notion that newspapers should themselves take action to create achievements and correct shortcomings. And by promoting the correspondents' movement, Komsomol leaders and party agitprop officials were creating an institutional base for such intervention.

Reporters, Information Flow, and Mass Journalism

The development of mass journalism was not just the result of orders from party leaders. The new journalistic methods solved production problems for editors and reporters. In fact, the development of the first "production reviews" in the first months of 1926 coincided with a vigorous debate among journalists and agitprop officials in Moscow and the Ukrainian capital of Kharkov about the future role of the reporter in the Soviet press. At the center of the debate were linked problems of information shortage and news production. According to contemporary sources, the Soviet reporter was being converted into a mere "courier" as state institutions and enterprises tightened their control over information. Reporters at Moscow newspapers often did not (or were not allowed to) attend the official meetings and conferences that they were supposed to cover, but depended instead on after-the-fact accounts, protocols, or stenographic reports prepared by the Press Bureaus (the equivalent of a public affairs office or public relations liaison) of the participating institution or institutions. All the reporter had to do was pick up the documents at the Press Bureau's window, take them back to the editorial offices, and perhaps edit them. Under these conditions, it was unclear that newspapers needed reporters any longer.

But it was also unclear how editors might find, or create, interesting news. The protocols and stenographic reports prepared by the Press Bureaus were dull, stereotyped, and repetitive. Mass journalism developed in part as a solution to these difficulties. The newspapermen who pioneered production reviews and socialist competitions sought not only to fulfill the party leaders' demands that they participate in raising productivity and mobilize the worker/peasant correspondent "armies," but also to find an alternative way to use their reporters and generate news in an information-scarce environment.[13]

Although a Politburo commission had considered ways of breaking up the informational logjams created by the Press Bureaus in 1923–1924, the issue did not become a live one for working journalists until the second half of 1925.[14] In June of that year the journalists' labor union organ *Zhurnalist (Journalist)* as well as newspapers in Kharkov and Moscow took up the issue. One of the earliest and most controversial volleys in the debate was an article by I. Alekseev, editor of the Kharkov newspaper *Proletarii*, titled simply, "Toward a Discussion about the Reporter." In this piece, which he ran in his own newspaper, Alekseev argued that reporters had become superfluous. Most of their functions could be fulfilled by "a responsible courier" picking up documents prepared by Press Bureaus. Although some of Alekseev's opponents in Moscow, notably Sergei Ingulov, later accused him of advocating the abolition of reporting as a profession, his article actually argued the need to redefine reportorial work. Worker-peasant correspondents, Alekseev assumed, were the basic agents monitoring the state apparatus for corruption and incompetence, but reporters might find a limited role following up on their denunciations and complaints. However, to justify their position in the editorial apparatus, reporters were going to have to seek out new, creative work methods.[15]

Journalist began running discussions of the role of the reporter in its June/July 1925 issue, as part of a series of debates sponsored by the Moscow House of the Press's *(Dom pechati)* Association for Newspaper Culture. Discussions and debates about the role of the reporter continued for about a year in *Journalist* and at the House of the Press. Although the participants often cast their comments in the form of arguments, they concurred on the most important points. The reporter, they claimed, had been converted into a "courier" by the Press Bureaus' control over access to state institutions, and by his own lack of initiative.[16] Held in contempt by most officials, he found it nearly impossible to obtain interviews. Editors provided reporters with little or no guidance or support. Yet the reporters had also failed to seek alternatives to the Press Bureaus and other bureaucratic sources of information, and so bore some responsibility for their own predicament. If they were going to preserve their jobs, they needed to bypass the Press Bureaus, overcome their own passivity, and seek news right on the shop floor or in the fields. One obvious, immediately available resource for reporters in carrying out this task was the newspapers' worker-peasant correspondents.

Reporters themselves blamed the Press Bureaus for blocking their access to senior officials, conferences, and meetings.[17] In 1925–1926 *Journalist* and the CC instructional journal *Red Press* published a series of anecdotes about reporters' grueling efforts to make contact with senior sources. On the Reporter's Page of *Journalist*'s February 1926 issue a reporter at *The Siren* described an assignment to get a statement from an important trust director, characterized by his department chief as a "demi-Commissar." Initially refused access, the reporter spent days hanging around in the foyer of the "demi-Commissar's" building until he was able to slip into his office by posing as a foreign correspondent.[18] Even a reporter from the central party organ *Pravda*, the most prestigious newspaper in the USSR, was unable to get an interview with the provincial party secretary or newspaper editor during a one-week stay in Briansk.[19]

But reporters and editors also shared responsibility for the poor, clichéd quality of domestic news in Soviet papers. In the first days of 1926 there occurred a series of incidents at Moscow newspapers that demonstrated reporters' failure to get out of the editorial offices and their reliance on schematic story types. One Moscow newspaper ran a story describing the funeral of a prominent engineer, complete with an account of weeping workers carrying the coffin, on the day of the actual ceremony. The mourners, *Journalist* noted ironically, were able to read about the funeral as they walked in procession toward the cemetery. A second paper published a piece about an old peasant riding an "agit-plane" in the town of Sebezh. Upon returning to earth, the peasant assured a waiting crowd that there was no God up there. But this story, like the funeral article, was prewritten. The agit-plane had never taken off because of mechanical problems.[20]

The prewritten pieces about the funeral and the agit-plane's flight were symptomatic of the reliance of both editors and reporters on standard forms for different kinds of stories. Mikhail Koltsov, the prominent Soviet feuilletonist who recounted these anecdotes, compared the standard story forms to a press room's stock cuts for illustrations, called *klishe* in Russian. Thus, Koltsov wrote, there was a clichéd form for a funeral story, for a demonstration story, for a formal ceremony, for a show trial, and so on. The widespread printing of prewritten stories proved the existence of these "clichéd stories." Both editors and reporters collaborated in their production, taking "the line of least resistance."[21]

At the Association for Newspaper Culture meetings reporters frequently complained of a lack of attention from editors, right down to the level of the department heads, their direct bosses. There was a "wall," they claimed between the editorial staff and the reporters. One commentator in *Journalist* bemoaned the "unenviable" place of the reporter in the editorial offices in this way: "In reality the reporter is a mere executor of orders. The department heads, who almost without exceptions have never reported and know nothing of the job, pay no attention to him. The department head does not know which reporter is attached to which institution, and often gives assignments which are either out-and-out impossible or inappropriate for the present moment. Let's not even talk about the editor—he has no time for reporters. There are no production meetings scheduled so the reporter has no place where he can express his doubts and difficulties and no one with whom he can share his experience."[22]

One reason head editors paid little attention to reporters was that they were simply too busy to do so. At the Moscow and central newspapers in the 1920s head editors were generally Old Bolsheviks with commitments to multiple posts in the state apparatus, as well as to party work. In Notebook and The Reporter's Page, regular departments in *Journalist*, the editor was portrayed as a distant, distracted figure so overwhelmed by party commitments that he had no time to guide his subordinates or seriously examine their articles. Some editors did not know the names of all their staff. Frequently the editor left the newspaper offices early because he had a lecture to deliver or some party meeting to attend. One Notebook told of an unnamed Moscow editor who worked on the province party and Executive Committees and belonged to the All-Union Central Executive Committee as well. Because he usually had to speak at workers' meetings and other public events in the afternoons and evenings, this man arrived for work very early in the morning to write the day's editorial. Another editor complained that he was often up until three or four in the morning at party functions and back at the editorial offices by seven. Bukharin, the editor of *Pravda*, was described as hiding in the guards' booth outside the newspaper offices so as not to be disturbed while he scribbled an editorial on an envelope.[23]

To fill the newspaper, overloaded editors depended on stenographic reports of party leaders' speeches, resolutions, directives, and other official documents that required little or no editing.[24] Press Bureaus were more than happy to provide such canned material. Mezhericher, a writer from *The Worker Gazette*, blamed the Soviet newspapers' inability to find exemplary workers and peasants to present to the "broad masses" on the reporters' lack of initiative and dependence on the Press Bureaus, which did no more than "collect protocols and summary reports."[25] But busy editors may also have preferred the Press Bureaus' material, which was uncontroversial, easy to edit, and did not require reporters to exercise their often meager literary skills.

A second reason for poor relations between editors and reporters was the latter group's low cultural status. Intellectuals in prerevolutionary Russia had long denigrated the commercialism of the mass press, despised the corruption of reporters who took bribes in exchange for favorable coverage, and dismissed writing for the commercial press as a vulgar sellout.[26] Bolsheviks and other Russian socialists tended to share the intelligentsia's disdain for reporters and for the "yellow," "boulevard" journalism they produced. These attitudes carried over into the postrevolutionary years, when reporters were habitually denigrated as "yellow journalists" and "sensation chasers." In the Bolshevik mind, the word "reporter" conjured up an image of the bourgeois newspaperman catering to the "philistine" tastes of déclassé urban masses for "pornographic" stories of the sexual adventures and luxurious lives of the rich and famous.[27] These attitudes made the reporter's work more difficult not just in the editorial offices, but also at the state institutions where he went to gather information. Apparatchiks feared reporters' capacity to damage their institution while at the same time despising them. Distrust and derision infected their relations with lower-ranking newspapermen. One reporter from *Pravda*, Dimin, lamented official distrust of the newspapers in general at a House of the Press discussion: "Institutional distrust of the reporter and the newspaper harms work, and the responsibility for this lies with the directors of the institutions. Three quarters of us [reporters] have never met face to face the directors of the institutions we serve."[28]

State officials often denigrated reporters as "grubbers after a few rubles," a phrase referring to the frequent financial deals between journalist and source. It was not infrequent for official sources to demand an "honorarium" for the information they provided. According to a reporter at *The Worker Gazette*, the director of an unnamed state institution who refused to give an interview without such an "honorarium" cited previous instances in which writers for *Izvestiia* and *Economic Life* had paid him for material.[29] Another reporter who participated in the House of the Press discussions, Kaufman, explained that Press Bureau personnel were aware that even regular staff reporters were paid mostly by the line and expected a cut of their earnings. To make reporters more independent of this kind of corruption, participants in the House of the Press meetings repeatedly recommended that they be paid set salaries, or at least that their base salary be raised.[30]

When Press Bureaus or their parent institutions wanted a piece published, they could offer a reporter a straightforward bribe, or pressure him through connections with his newspapers' editors. Iakushev, an *Izvestiia* reporter and prerevolutionary veteran, lamented that the Press Bureaus marked even the dullest material "must print." If the reporter did not make sure that this material was published, the Press Bureau staff would cut him off from further information.[31] Through connections with editors, Press Bureaus and their parent institutions also exercised a veto over critical material, according to *Evening Moscow* reporter Sukhanov. If a reporter handed in a piece critical of a specific organization, his department head would call up the organization to clear it with staff there.[32] A later commentator in *Journalist* (early 1927) described the Press Bureaus as the materialization of "the community of interest" between newspaper editors and state officials. Reporters were the wild card in this situation, the potential disrupters of that "community of interest," and the Press Bureaus were designed to control them.[33]

The special province of the reporter in early Soviet newspapers was the Chronicle section, a holdover from the Chronicle sections of the big prerevolutionary urban newspapers such as *Moskovskii listok (The Moscow News Sheet)* and *The Russian Word*. Chronicle sections (sometimes also labeled Happenings) traditionally had carried news of fires, crimes, accidents, and other unusual events, as well as public-service-related announcements about gallery openings, the arrival of foreign delegations, open hearings on controversial issues, and the like. Some reporters complained that Soviet editors were so cautious about running "yellow" items in the Chronicle that they had squeezed all interest out of the section.[34]

Central Committee pressure to devote more space to specific slogans and party agitprop campaigns forced editorial staff to find material that fit within specific "agit-morals." In response to this pressure, and to the taboo on "yellowism," Soviet Information Department heads often inserted a monotonous compilation of facts that fit one of these centrally mandated "agit-morals."[35] In 1923 a commentator in *Journalist* gave one example of the practice, a piece in *The Worker Gazette* titled, "Labor Safety Still Inadequate," which consisted of a summary list of worker correspondents' complaints about unsafe conditions in their workplaces. "From the factory Kramator Comrade So-and-So informs us. . . . Comrade X from Vyksy writes about a similar problem. . . . Things are even worse at the factory Aviation Equipment." This was hardly stuff to grab readers' attention.[36]

One feuilletonist used an imaginary dialogue between a reporter and an editor to show how the pressure to fit stories to the CC's schedule of "agit-morals" affected the day-to-day routine of the editorial offices. The conversation exemplifies the way in which dull Press Bureau material that fit within the framework of official propaganda campaigns tended to displace the more sensational "Chronicle" items about fires, accidents, scandals, and crime.

(Reporter): The fire brigade was on the way. But the horses couldn't make it—they were staggering. The firemen left them behind and ran on alone. They reached the fire long before their equipment. The problem was that the horses were dying of hunger.

(Department Editor): No, Comrade, we can't print that.

But it's fact, a true story.

Even so.

Well, what do you want then?

Socialist Construction.

We don't have any "Socialist Construction"! All we've got are protocols, conferences, agendas!

Fine. Print them.[37]

The taboo against sensationalism was connected with prejudice against reporters, and both contributed to the increasing predominance of dull, bureaucratic material in the Soviet press. Throughout the NEP era it was precisely those newspapers with the liveliest, least official Chronicle departments that retained the largest numbers of reporters from the prerevolutionary era. These were also the papers that came under the heaviest attack for boulevardism and yellow journalism. *Evening Moscow*, Leningrad's *Evening Red Gazette*, and *Izvestiia* until 1926 were the most conspicuous of these. A 1930 Central Control

Commission (CCC) report on *Evening Moscow*'s staff identified four reporters and writers who had worked for the prerevolutionary newspapers *Odesskie novosti (Odessa News)*, *Odesskaia pochta (Odessa Post)*, and *Odesskie izvestiia (Odessa Herald)*.[38] According to A. Kliachkin, who reported on the cinema for *Evening Red Gazette* beginning in 1924, several reporters from the prerevolutionary Petersburg press worked at that paper's City Information Department.[39] Both *Evening Moscow* and *Evening Red Gazette* came in for very harsh criticism from agitprop officials and journalists at other newspapers. In the April 1926 edition of *Journalist*, for example, V. Verner, an editor from the central cooperative newspaper *Cooperative Life*, launched a vituperative attack on *Evening Red Gazette*, calling it "a boulevard newspaper," and "a newspaper for people of the past[40] and people without a future." According to Verner *Evening Red Gazette* 's stock in trade was murder trials, reports on the market for precious stones, prostitution, "abortions, violence, a 16 year old boy and his 17 year old girl lover, two women and one man, two men and one woman, etc., etc., and 'special methods for the restoration of sexual function.'" Its audience consisted of idle members of the intelligentsia, "people of the past," women without productive work, déclassé lower-class youth "under the influence of the streets and the NEP." In short, a thoroughly unsavory newspaper.[41]

Izvestiia never came under the kind of attack that the evening newspapers did. However, its editors did fret about the continued employment of a large number of reporters from I. D. Sytin's prerevolutionary newspaper *Russian Word*. Ivan Gronskii, an editor at *Izvestiia* from the summer of 1925, writes that *Russian Word* 's entire Moscow Information department had transferred to the newspaper, complete with department head Konstantin Matveevich Danilenko. Gronskii claims that on his first day of work at *Izvestiia*, head editor Ivan Skvortsov-Stepanov told him that their number one priority was phasing out politically unreliable nonparty journalists, especially Danilenko's reporters.[42] Skvortsov-Stepanov, who was also new to *Izvestiia*, had been brought in to make staff cuts, clean up the paper's finances, organize better coordination between different news departments, and ensure the newspaper's political reliability.[43] Under these circumstances the Moscow Information Department, packed with veterans of the bourgeois press who produced old-style Chronicle items, was a natural target for cuts. Between August and December 1926 Skvortsov-Stepanov merged Moscow Information with the all-Union news department, fired most of the reporters, and brought in a whole new cohort of department editors.[44] Simultaneously, *Izvestiia* made its first real experiment in mass journalism, setting up an Investigative Bureau on November 1.[45] These steps changed the appearance and content of the newspaper, as the Moscow "Chronicle" was replaced by reports on reader letters.

Between the editors' and officials' view that lazy reporters and sensation-seeking "hack chroniclers" were responsible for the poor quality of Soviet domestic news, and the reporters' opinion that the Press Bureaus were at fault, the reporters' position seems more plausible. Soviet institutions were developing barriers against the outflow of information, among them the Press Bureaus. In part this was a reaction to the regime's deliberate and extensive use of denunciation as a tool of governance. For market competition and a formal system of checks and balances within the state apparatus, the Bolsheviks had substituted surveillance from above and denunciation from below. Through these two mechanisms the party leadership hoped to keep incompetence and corruption in check. The natural reaction of state institutions was to try to dam the flow of information. N. Valevskii, a commentator published in the March 1926 issue of *Journalist*, summarized the process well when he wrote that "our institutions have dug in behind the barrier of their Press Bureaus against Vladimir Ilich's motto: 'Exterminate the unfit.'"[46]

In his work *The Origins of the Stalinist Political System*, Graeme Gill argues that the combination of party-sanctioned denunciation from below, or self-criticism, and central appointment of officials from above resulted in the development of "family groups." These were "localised power cliques" that through tight networks of personal relationships strove to defend themselves by suppressing criticism from below and controlling the flow of information to the center. Gill writes that "if local control was sufficiently tight and the network included all of those with separate institutional channels to the centre, the local elite could hope to impose a sort of 'conspiracy of silence' on events in the area." Central intervention could thus be prevented.[47] Representatives of the central press who traveled to the provinces often faced obstructionism from such local "family groups" desperate to maintain their control over information flow in and out of their provincial fiefdoms. The proliferation of the Press Bureaus seems to have been a different reaction to the same combination of denunciation from below, represented by worker-peasant correspondents, and surveillance from above, represented by the press. The reaction was different from the formation of family groups in that it was an institutional formation rather than a personal network. However, family groups and Press Bureaus belonged to the same genus of defenses against criticism from below and surveillance from above.

The discussions at the House of the Press were not mere debates for the sake of debating. Inside the editorial offices newspapermen really were worrying about the future role of the reporter and finding ways to generate news that went beyond the parroting of institutional communiqués. At a July 14, 1926, general meeting of the party cell at *The Worker Gazette*, Communist employees of the newspaper discussed reportorial work, the isolation of reporters from party members and editors, and the need to find new ways of covering economic and production news. After a presentation on "work among nonparty journalists," a lively conversation ensued. Semen Narinian, a young reporter who had begun his career one year before at *Komsomolskaia pravda*, asserted that because editors did not include reporters in discussions of their plans for the newspaper, the latter fell into a pattern of writing according to stereotyped formats: "The reporters already know the clichéd forms acceptable to editors. They write according to templates. If you brought them into discussions of [your] plans, into discussions of the work of their departments, they would liven up their work."[48] Afonin, another cell member, explained that "the nonparty journalists are complaining that they are seen as bureaucrats and dismissed. They adjust themselves to the tastes of the editorial staff. In this way, the nonparty journalists among us remain politically illiterate."[49]

Immediately after the discussion of the reporters' place at the newspaper, the cell moved on to consider an "informational circular" from the Moscow Committee of the party. Among the topics touched on by the letter was the necessity of more coverage of economics and production. M. Erlikh, the editorial board secretary and the paper's liaison with the Central Committee leadership, picked up this theme, expanding upon the need to "show more of the growth of our economic construction."[50] Here, at a *Worker Gazette* party cell meeting in July 1926, concerns about the role of the reporter converged with central instructions to find new ways of covering production and economic news.

In 1925–1926 editors and agitprop officials saw a problem with the quality of domestic news coverage, which was disintegrating into a heap of official protocols, directives, stenographic reports, and institutional communiqués. The alternative represented by the old school of prerevolutionary reporters—reports on fires, accidents, crimes, trials, and society scandals—was not acceptable. The regime needed a new kind of local, domestic news that would show the laboring masses how ordinary people like them were engaged in the battle to build a socialist society. Through this new kind of news the "black hands"—the tillers and manual laborers—would speak, criticizing their bosses when they were corrupt or incompetent, and expressing their commitment to building socialism. The party leadership expected the young men and women entering journalism to create this kind of news for them, although they had no specific directions for how it might be done. The journalists themselves would have to figure that out. And for young journalists it must have been clear that the future lay with the mass journalism demanded by their bosses, and not with the Press Bureaus or the pre-revolutionary reporters.

Belt Tightening and Organizing Production

The belt-tightening campaign of 1926, aimed at cutting production costs in industry, provided the impetus for the intensive development of "mass methods" of journalism. The CC Press Department initiated the newspaper publicity campaign in early 1926, arranging for Feliks Dzerzhinskii, chairman of the Supreme Council on the Economy (VSNKh), to speak on belt tightening before a meeting of Moscow newspaper editors. Dzerzhinskii called on newspapermen to aid enterprise managers *(khoziaistvenniki)* in the improvement of productivity and to put the managers themselves "under the microscope" (literally, *pod stekliannyi kolpak*, or "under the glass bell") to ensure that they made efficient use of state funds.[51] Circulars were sent out to local party Press Departments and newspapers giving general instructions on running the campaign. *Red Press* ran CC Press Department instructions and regular evaluations of individual papers' coverage of belt tightening.[52]

The Trade and Industrial Gazette, the organ of VSNKh and of industrial management in general, was the first newspaper to take up the campaign, on February 21, 1926.[53] Following the example of recent campaigns against supply shortages, production stoppages, and absenteeism, the newspaper drew on reports by its provincial correspondents and interviews with high-ranking officials from banking and industrial trusts. The interviews were constructed to publicize the measures taken by managers to cut costs, such as giving up their personal autos provided by the trust, eliminating excess paperwork, and cutting the funding for workers' clubs. On February 24 the paper ran on page one the Supreme Council on the Economy directive that ordered managers to cut production costs.[54] As part of the early publicity for the campaign, *The Trade and Industrial Gazette* brought in Dzerzhinskii. In a March 2 lead editorial, Dzerzhinskii called on newspapermen "not just to mobilize our managers, to demand from them the implementation of measures, but to organize the monitoring of the reality of these measures, the real achievement of actual ... economies." Dzerzhinskii wanted the newspapers to mobilize ordinary factory workers to participate in the campaign, not just run interviews with managers.[55]

Picking up on Dzerzhinskii's complaints about the press's excessive reliance on higher-ranking sources, the central trade union organ *Labor* criticized *The Trade and Industrial Gazette* (ironically the organ of the Supreme Council on the Economy, Dzerzhinskii's commissariat) for focusing almost exclusively on management. *Labor* complained that *The Trade and Industrial Gazette* based its reports almost entirely on interviews with trust chairmen, board members, and factory managers. It spoke, in short, with the voice of management, and tended to blame blue-collar workers for the supposedly inflated costs of production. Around the time of the beginning of the belt-tightening campaign, for instance, *The Trade and Industrial Gazette* ran pieces complaining that technical specialists were overloaded with work and that worker absenteeism, commitment to labor union activism, and expenditures on workers' clubs were mostly to blame for high overhead costs.[56] *Labor* criticized *The Trade and Industrial Gazette* for overemphasizing problems of labor discipline and ignoring management responsibility for inflating production costs.[57] The problem was finding a way to give workers a voice in the campaign to raise productivity and lower costs. After all, Soviet Power claimed to be "the dictatorship of the proletariat."

From the earliest phases of the belt-tightening campaign the Central Committee's Press Department prodded newspapers to find ways to mobilize workers and give them a voice. In an early spring speech to a meeting of the Moscow section of the journalists' labor union section (SRP), CC Press Department chairman Sergei Gusev called upon the press to uncover management waste and rid administrators and directors of their "lordly ways," by exposing them to the "court of worker and peasant public opinion." To investigate and denounce management corruption and incompetence, Gusev instructed the newspapers to use "their great army of worker and peasant correspondents."[58] Beyond this general advice, Gusev expected newspapermen to find their own way in creating new forms of organizing journalism that would raise productivity.[59]

In May, Aleksei Ivanovich Kapustin, the editor of the Tver province party newspaper *Tverskaia pravda*, took up this challenge. After an extended discussion of ways to promote the belt-tightening campaign, *Tverskaia pravda*'s journalists initiated a series of audits of local factories that they called "*obshchestvennyi* production reviews." The adjective *obshchestvennyi* signified that all of official Soviet society would partici-pate. Before beginning the first review, of a small leather manufactory employing around two hundred operatives, the newspaper's staff had their plan of action approved by the local party committee, the province Council on the Economy, the factory's party cell, and the factory labor union committee. The review itself began with the publication of fac-tory director Timofeev's views on cost-cutting and a call to the factory's worker correspondents to respond. Next a *Tverskaia pravda* reporter roamed the factory with a sketch artist in tow, talking to blue-collar workers, foremen, and mechanics about the production process and ways it might be improved. At this stage of the campaign, according to an account by a *Tverskaia pravda* journalist, "politically backward" workers scoffed at the possibility that management would take their proposals seriously. "Politically conscious" workers, on the other hand, made a number of cost-cutting proposals, such as a campaign against drunkenness on the job. In all the paper gathered forty-two cost-cutting proposals and published letters from fifty-six workers.[60]

Tverskaia pravda published the workers' suggestions and comments on them by the factory director and the chairman of the provincial Council on the Economy. According to *Tverskaia pravda*'s account of the campaign, the publication of their proposals gave the workers confidence that management would have to take them seriously. Along with the dialogue between administration and employees about cost-cutting, the newspaper ran caricatures, portraits, and profiles of work-ers at the leather factory. After two weeks of such coverage, spanning eight issues of the paper in early July 1926, *Tverskaia pravda* called a "production meeting" to summarize and implement the review's results. One hundred twenty-five workers attended the first day of the two-day meeting, in which the director and workers debated which cost-cutting proposals to introduce at the factory. In the end the direc-tor agreed to implement twenty-four of the proposals, all of them approved by the local party committee, the party cell, the factory labor union committee, and the factory administration. *Tverskaia pravda* promised the workers to return after a month or two to be sure these suggestions were being put into practice.[61]

Soon after concluding the production review at the leather factory, Kapustin undertook several larger reviews, at an electrical power station, the First of May textile factory, and the Proletarian Woman textile combine. Coverage of the latter production review appeared in thirty-five issues of the paper, and *Tverskaia pravda* received about 1,900 letters from workers making suggestions for streamlining production.[62]

The Tver editor and his newspaper had been attracting attention with organizing journalism and high-quality local coverage for years. Kapustin, a typesetter and twenty-year veteran of the prerevolutionary Petersburg typographical industry, became editor of *Tverskaia pravda* in 1919 and as of 1926 had already enjoyed an unusually long seven-year tenure as editor of a single newspaper. During this period his paper built up a reputation as one of the leading provincial mass worker organs in the USSR. In 1923–1924 Kapustin organized a competition among Tver consumer cooperatives for best shop, best salesperson, best cashier, and so on, basing his final judgment on the letters, petitions, and proposals of ordinary consumers. The goal was to stimulate cooperatives to provide consumers with better supplies and service. Kapustin's cooperative competition won plaudits at the Central Cooperative Union, and elsewhere in official circles.[63] A November 1924 evaluation of provincial Russian newspapers by the Central Committee's Press Subdepartment called *Tverskaia pravda* "one of the best newspapers in the Republic. It is lively and has wide coverage of local, all-Republic, and world events. Its basic material is concentrated on local life. Totally literate and disciplined. Materials are extremely varied and its shortcomings incidental."[64]

From the point of view of factory management and party leaders concerned with maintaining order and discipline in the workplace, Kapustin's new mass journalism had the advantage of giving workers a voice, but in a carefully controlled environment. The entire review process was monitored by factory administration, local economic officials, labor union officials, and the relevant party organizations. When factory directors or labor union committees obstructed a review, Kapustin relied on province party officials to override their objections and discipline them. His "*obshchestvennyi* production reviews" depended on the support of the local party organization to counterbalance possible resistance from factory administrations, trusts, or the economic bureaucracy. Thus, they did not violate CC rules barring local or provincial newspapers from criticizing party committees at their own level in the administrative hierarchy.[65] Although the production review offered workers a voice, it was only to offer concrete suggestions on production processes and perhaps to criticize individual factory directors, not to attack labor policy as a whole or higher authorities.

Tverskaia pravda's communal production review also offered an opportune solution to the party's difficulties in managing the worker correspondents' movement. The movement had by 1926 run itself into a cul-de-sac, at least in the opinion of the party leaders in charge. Nikolai Bukharin announced this in a May 1926 speech to the Third All-Union Conference of Worker-Peasant Correspondents, and Sergei Ingulov followed up with a June 1926 article in *Journalist*. Both Bukharin and Ingulov expressed their concern that members of hostile social groups, in particular kulaks, priests, and politically "backward" peasant migrants to the cities, were infiltrating the correspondents' movement. In rural areas, they claimed, there was the danger of a wholesale takeover of peasant correspondents' circles by openly anti-Soviet kulaks and their allies. In the cities new peasant immigrants taking jobs in industry and construction brought with them "petty bourgeois" ideas, infecting other workers with their lack of political and labor discipline. In the letters written by worker correspondents, Bukharin claimed, the petty bourgeois ideology of the new arrivals from the countryside was reflected in "an inappropriate sharpness of tone with respect to managers and labor union officers," overly enthusiastic denunciation of superiors, failure to recognize the real achievements of Soviet industry, attacks on specialists, and "the covering up of negative aspects of the workers' own production work." To a degree that party leaders were not comfortable with, the worker and peasant correspondents' movement had become a forum for criticism of Soviet Power and existing labor relations. Bukharin and Ingulov understood this criticism as a result of social changes that were causing the party leadership as a whole much anxiety, namely the immigration of peasants to the cities (a consequence of industrial growth) and the layering out of village society into kulaks and poor peasants (supposedly under way in the countryside as a result of NEP's liberal trade policies). Yet Bukharin and Ingulov were at cross purposes with Sergei Gusev, the Press Department chief, who in May 1926 was actually working to mobilize worker correspondents to audit and criticize upper-level management. The party leadership, desiring at once to institutionalize some form of worker *kontrol* ("monitoring" or "auditing") over administration *and* to limit criticism of authorities from below, was obviously in a dilemma.

What was the solution? Tighter party control of worker/peasant correspondents, answered both Bukharin and Ingulov. Previous party policy, as formulated in June 1925 by Orgburo decree, was a compromise between supporters of complete party control and advocates of limited organizational autonomy for the movement, led by Bukharin and Lenin's sister Mariia Ulianova. Party committees would guide the worker correspondents' movement through Communists who worked on newspaper staffs or volunteered to serve on the editorial boards of wall newspapers, but without issuing direct instructions to the correspondents. At the May 1926 conference of worker-peasant correspondents both Ingulov and Bukharin argued that provincial party committee Press Departments should take a much more active role in supervising the worker-peasant correspondents' circles.[66]

An August 1926 CC decree followed Bukharin and Ingulov's proposals in broad outline. The decree insisted on stronger direction of the correspondents' movement by grassroots party organizations. The CC called on party cells to hear regular reports from Communists involved in the work of circles and wall newspapers. The cells were to include instruction of the correspondents on their regular agenda for the supervision of "local civic organizations." Although the editorial boards of wall newspapers were to be elected by correspondents themselves, Communists involved in the movement were expected to exercise their "ideological influence" to secure the choice of the "most active, politically disciplined, authoritative worker-peasant correspondents." In addition local party organizations would appoint the head editors of all print newspapers, including low-circulation workplace organs (*mnogotirazhki*). Following the recommendations of Ingulov's June article in *Journalist*, the CC ordered newspaper editors to appoint Communists with extensive experience in "organizational/civic work" to head their worker-peasant correspondents' departments.[67]

Yet here, too, party leaders appear to have been at cross purposes. Even as the CC moved to strengthen local party organizations' control over wall newspapers, the party's Central Control Commission (CCC) was taking steps to increase the autonomy and independence of action of the entire worker correspondents' movement. An early 1926 CCC circular ordered the RKI to bring worker correspondents directly into their investigations of the state apparatus. Local offices of the RKI were each to appoint one employee to maintain contact with local worker correspondents *through the local newspaper's Department of Worker Life.*[68] If implemented, this decree would tend to increase the freedom of action of worker correspondents and their wall newspapers, by putting them into contact with alternative centers of authority. Depending on the local political situation, attacks on provincial party bosses from below would be facilitated.

The reality on the ground in early 1926 was that most factory wall newspapers functioned as the organs of party, Komsomol, or labor union committees. According to worker correspondents writing in to *Worker Moscow*'s correspondents' journal, *Put rabselkora (The Worker/Peasant Correspondent's Road)*, local party or Komsomol cell bureaus appointed the editors of most wall newspapers and directly supervised their work. Money for the wall newspaper often came from labor union committee Cultural Commissions, which also handled factory libraries, excursions, the management of lectures and theatricals at worker clubs, and the like.[69] Frequently the wall newspaper itself was called "organ of the party/Komsomol cell of the so-and-so factory." Not only were a high percentage of so-called worker correspondents actually white-collar office workers,[70] but many wrote to the newspaper as representatives of their factory, labor union committee, or party organization rather than as individual members of the correspondents' movement.[71] The CCC circular on linking local Control Commissions with worker correspondents threatened this status quo by opening up a channel through which correspondents could criticize their own party or union organization.

Tverskaia pravda's production review campaign in the summer of 1926 was an answer not just to the broad question of how to mobilize workers and offer them a voice in the discussion of cost-cutting measures, but to the more specific problem of how to supervise worker correspondents and coordinate their activities with party organizations and the newspapers. At smaller enterprises, such as the leather factory first reviewed, reporters were in direct contact with workers on the shop floor, enabling them both to solicit and screen suggestions for rationalizing production (i.e., cutting costs). At larger factories, *Tverskaia pravda* set up a "mobile editorial office" where several newspapermen provided "guidance and instruction" for worker correspondents and editors of enterprise wall newspapers.[72] The latter then explained the production review to the workers and solicited their suggestions and opinions. In all cases the workers' proposals were subject to review by the province party committee, labor unions, and the local Council on the Economy before final submission to the factory management. In sum, the newspaper-coordinated community production review embodied precisely the kind of tight control over worker correspondents that the party's leading Agitprop and Press Department officials were looking for in the summer of 1926.

Because it offered solutions to urgent problems of mass mobilization, Kapustin's "Under the Microscope" campaign won the favor of important figures in the CC Press Department and the *Pravda* editorial offices. Sergei Gusev and Mariia Ulianova supported Kapustin and publicized the new methods of journalism he was developing. On March 11, 1927, *Pravda* published an article by Gusev on *Tverskaia pravda*'s experience organizing factory production reviews.[73] This piece was followed by articles in *Red Press* (March 1927), *Journalist* (December 1927), and *Worker-Peasant Correspondent* (April 1928), the last authored by Ulianova.[74] The promotion and coverage of production reviews would become a central part of the new-style mass journalism of the First Five-Year Plan period.

Between 1927 and 1932 the Central Committee promoted a number of journalists from *Tverskaia pravda* and the Tver party agitprop apparatus to important positions in the central press, particularly at *Pravda*. Kapustin himself was made assistant editor of *Worker Moscow* in 1928, but almost immediately transferred to *Pravda* at the request of Mariia Ulianova.[75] In the following three years Kapustin would serve as head of *Pravda*'s Worker Life department and assistant head of the Economics department.[76] During his tenure at *Pravda* Kapustin not only organized production reviews, socialist competitions, and "roving editorial offices," but represented the newspaper at sessions of the CC Department of Agitation, Propaganda and the Press (APPO, the successor to the Agitprop Department).[77] Petr Nikolaevich Pospelov, who was on the editorial staff of *Pravda* beginning in 1931, had served in Tver as editor of a labor union newspaper and chief of the province Agitprop Department between 1920 and 1924 before moving on to the position of "instructor" in the Central Committee Agitprop Department. In the 1940s Pospelov would become head editor of *Pravda*.[78] Vasilii Ivanovich Khodakov, who had been a Komsomol organizer and provincial agitprop official in Tver (1926), where he came into contact with Kapustin, went on to edit various Crimean newspapers and serve as a "roving correspondent" for *Pravda* in the 1930s.[79] Ivan Riabov, a reporter for *Pravda*'s Agriculture Department starting in 1929, and a member of the newspaper party cell's bureau, began his journalistic career at *Tverskaia pravda* and the Tver Komsomol newspaper, which he had edited. Like Kapustin, Riabov moved on to work for *Worker Moscow*, and then *Pravda*.[80]

Other cadres from Tver went to *Komsomolskaia pravda* and *Kooperativnaia zhizn (Cooperative Life)*, the organ of the Central Cooperative Union during the first years of the First Five-Year Plan. Andrei Troitskii, appointed head editor of *Komsomolskaia pravda* by the Central Committee Orgburo in March 1930 after a rapid succession of purges at the newspaper, began his career as secretary of the Tver province Komsomol Committee in 1920.[81] Denis Liakhovets, a reporter who worked at *Cooperative Life* beginning in August 1927, had worked at *Tverskaia pravda* after a stint as a student at the State Institute of Journalism in Moscow. At *Tverskaia pravda* Liakhovets headed the Department of Party Life until September 1925, served as secretary of the editorial board until January 1926, and then became chief of the Information Department. He was most likely involved in *Tverskaia pravda*'s production reviews of the summer of 1926. At *Cooperative Life* Liakhovets headed a group of young reporters who attacked the paper's senior administrators and strove to introduce new mass methods of journalism.[82]

Tverskaia pravda was not the only site where mass journalism developed, nor was the production review the only technique of mass journalism. About the same time Kapustin and his "school" at *Tverskaia pravda* were creating the production review, Komsomol organizations and journalists in the Urals region, the Donbass, Moscow, and Leningrad were engineering new forms of mass journalism. Like the production review, these were responses to the CC's insistence that newspapers exercise closer control over worker/peasant correspondents and that all "civic organizations" take a more active role in promoting productivity.[83] These forms of work all involved the newspaper intervening directly in production, organizing some type of rationalizing or production-raising activity, and reporting on it. The first "shock brigades" of elite young workers dedicated to increasing productivity, for example, were organized in 1926–1927 in Moscow, Leningrad, the Urals region, and the Donbass. To cite one instance, in late 1926 worker correspondents for a wall newspaper on the Moscow-Kursk Railroad organized a "full utilization brigade," which collected 1,089 rubles' worth of scrap metal for use in pouring new ball bearings.[84] *Komsomolskaia pravda* and the Leningrad Komsomol organ *Changing of the Guard* covered the activities of a number of such brigades. In the fall of 1926 both papers also began publicizing production competitions between factories and individual workers. One of the earliest forms these took was contests for "best young worker" (these foreshadowed the designation of highly productive operatives as "shock workers" in the early 1930s and the great Stakhanovite campaigns of the middle and late 1930s).[85] By November 1927 the Komsomol CC Secretariat was regularly instructing provincial newspaper editors to undertake more "organizational-mass work, including production competitions and reviews."[86] *Komsomolskaia pravda* went on to sponsor the first "mobile editorial offices" in which journalists visited a factory or construction site with a railroad car containing a fully equipped print shop and editorial facilities. The reporters would organize socialist competitions, production reviews, and other production events, and publish a newspaper on the spot. They also reported on their activities in *Komsomolskaia pravda*. The newspaper, in short, had manufactured its own news from the point of production. Other central newspapers, including *Izvestiia* quickly set up their own mobile editorial offices (see illustrations for photographs of *Komsomolskaia pravda* mobile editorial offices in the early 1930s).

The CC's *Worker Gazette* also got into the business of mass journalism. In the summer of 1927 the newspaper organized a socialist competition for highest productivity between coal mines in the Donbass, Siberia, the Urals, and the Moscow area. The campaign was dubbed "The Newspaper's Battle for Coal." The editors dispatched teams of journalists to the participating mines to arrange the details of the competition and report on it.[87]

Another important site where newspapermen developed mass journalism was the Urals region party organ *Uralskii rabochii (The Urals Worker)*, a mass worker paper that had been praised by the CC Agitprop Department as early as 1923.[88] Prompted by directives from the CC and the Supreme Council on the Economy, *The Urals Worker*'s coverage of industry and "worker life" in 1926–1927 moved steadily in the direction of organizing production. The progression demonstrates how the party leadership's concern with mobilizing workers from below to raise productivity motivated the creation of mass journalism. The chronology of changes at the newspaper also shows that *The Urals Worker* undertook direct intervention on the shop floor only after CC Press Department Director Sergei Gusev's March 1927 *Pravda* article endorsing *Tverskaia pravda*'s "production reviews."

The formal kick-off of the belt-tightening campaign in *The Urals Worker* came on March 5, 1926, when the paper published a Telegraph Agency of the Soviet Union (TASS) story on Dzerzhinskii's interview with representatives of the central press on its front page. The editors ran the story under headings such as "Liquidate All Unnecessary Expenditures," "Thrift Is the Party's Most Important Directive," and "Press and Proletarian Society to the Aid of the Managers."[89] *The Urals Worker*'s initial approach to the belt-tightening campaign was conservative and focused on management's demands that workers raise productivity. Under the heading "For Economy and Thrift," the paper published interviews with trust board members, factory directors, and Commissariat of Trade officials in which they enumerated the steps taken to cut production costs and echoed central rhetoric about the importance of raising productivity.[90]

Then, on April 23, after about one month of such coverage, the paper ran a self-critical front-page article titled "Overcoming the Formal Approach (On Some Results of the Campaign for Belt Tightening)." This piece laid out the standard rationale for belt tightening—the USSR had to industrialize without "enslaving" itself to foreign capital, so thrift was necessary to aid the internal accumulation of capital. Participation of all sectors of Soviet society was necessary for effective economizing, but the press's coverage of the belt-tightening campaign to date had been "bureaucratic." In bold type the newspaper explained what this meant: "general judgments in published articles and interviews with managers and directors of institutions are dominating over the coverage of concrete facts and measures for thrift." *The Urals Worker* then criticized its own implementation of the campaign for focusing on interviews with managers and officials. In the future the press's task would be "bringing the broadest strata of workers, peasants, and office workers" into the campaign. The problem to date, according to this article's author, was fear of "compromising" any higher-ups. The solution was "merciless denunciation of all disorders, abnormalities and crimes."[91]

From internal evidence, this article appears to have been motivated by a second Dzerzhinskii presentation to the Moscow press attacking the "bureaucratism" of the belt-tightening campaign to date.[92] This kind of a push from the center may have been necessary to overcome the resistance of provincial officials who feared criticism from below and to ensure coverage of belt tightening from the shop floor. Official transcripts of the Urals region party committee plenum of March 1926, for example, reveal an ongoing conflict over the role of *The Urals Worker* in promoting worker correspondents' criticism of management from below. On one side of the debate were committee secretary Rumiantsev and his deputy Shipov (probably the director of the regional committee's Press Department). These two advocated turning *The Urals Worker* into a "leading" newspaper for the provincial party and Soviet elite, attacked excessive denunciation of management from below, and implied that they wished to fire *Urals Worker* editor Viktor I. Filov. They appear to have been nervous about a possible newspaper-led campaign against local factory managers and officialdom.[93] Editor Filov, who addressed the plenum in reply, opposed any change in *The Urals Worker*'s status, arguing that the Urals Party organization needed a regional mass newspaper to connect with the "average worker." The party, he claimed, ought to be paying *more*, not *less* attention to the worker correspondents' movement.[94]

Renewed CC and VSNKh pressure to turn up the fires under the press's denunciatory function catalyzed changes in *The Urals Worker*'s coverage of industry and "Workers' Life." Approximately one month after Dzerzhinskii's criticism of the belt-tightening campaign for bureaucratism, the newspaper began running a series of interviews with workers on the shop floor under the headings "For Economy and Thrift," and "Our Interviews with the Workers."[95] In these interviews workers criticized inefficient production procedures and suggested ways to improve them and save raw materials such as ore and flax. Then, in the summer of 1927, *The Urals Worker* reported on the activities of "shock brigades" of Komsomol members dedicated to rationalizing production and on Komsomol-sponsored factory contests for "best young worker."[96] It was also in the summer of 1927 that the newspaper's massive campaign for the "Exchange of Experience" between workers at different factories began. In the latter campaign *The Urals Worker* newspapermen interviewed workers from different factories about their methods of economizing. From August until November 1927 the Exchange of Experience *(pereklichka)* section ran regularly in the paper. At the beginning of the campaign the interviews were arranged on the page so as to simulate a live "Production Meeting on the Newspaper's Pages."[97]

The timing of the first instances of full-blown mass journalism (meaning the organization of contests, production reviews, or exchanges of experience by the newspaper, rather than individual inter-views with workers) at *The Urals Worker* and *The Worker Gazette* makes it probable that Sergei Gusev's March 1927 endorsement of *Tverskaia pravda*'s work in *Pravda* lay behind them. At both papers newspapermen began organizing and covering shop-floor events in the summer of 1927, months after Gusev's article appeared. As a reading of *The Urals Worker* shows, however, in 1926 the center's belt-tightening campaign was already pushing mass worker newspapers besides *Tverskaia pravda* toward reporting from the shop floor.

Like *Tverskaia pravda*, newspapers in the areas where production competitions and worker "shock brigades" first appeared in 1926–1927 became a source of cadres for key positions in the central press during the period of the Cultural Revolution and the "renewed assault of socialism" (1928–1930). These papers included *The Urals Worker* and the Sverdlovsk Komsomol paper *Na smenu (On Guard)*. The influx of cadres from Sverdlovsk newspapers was most likely connected with the February 1929 appointment of A. N. Gusev, the head of the Urals regional Agitprop Department, to the post of assistant head of the Central Committee Agitprop Department. Gusev went on to head the Newspaper Sector of the Agitprop Department beginning in October 1929 (replacing Sergei Ingulov).[98] Another veteran of the Ural regional agitprop apparatus, F. A. Mikhailov, editor of the Urals *Peasant Gazette* in 1926–1927 and *The Urals Worker* in early 1928 as well as former head of the regional party committee's Press Section, worked as assistant editor of *Poor Peasant* during the First Five-Year Plan. Mikhailov also edited *Poor Peasant*'s successor, *Selsko-khoziaistvennyi rabochii (Agricultural Worker)*. In 1931 he held a post in the Central Committee's Culture and Propaganda Department as a newspaper reviewer and instructor.[99]

Many other newspapermen from the Sverdlovsk Party organization followed Gusev and Mikhailov to Moscow. In March 1930 the CC Org-buro appointed *Urals Worker* editor Filov to the editorship of the CC's *Worker Gazette* and D. G. Tumarkin, also from the Sverdlovsk party organization, to the editorship of *Labor*.[100] Filov's former assistant editor at *The Urals Worker*, A. Tsekher, was already assistant editor of *The Worker Gazette*, having been transferred to the post in November 1929.[101] Iosif Stanevskii, an organizer in *The Urals Worker*'s Department of Mass Work, was transferred to *Komsomolskaia pravda* in January 1931, where he became a member of the editorial board and head of the Department of Organization and Mass Work.[102] In March 1930 the Orgburo appointed V. M. Bubekin, a former editor of *On Guard*, to serve as assistant editor and head of the Information Department at *Komsomolskaia pravda*.[103] In the summer of 1932 Bubekin would become head editor of *Komsomolskaia pravda*.[104] While working at the central Komsomol organ, he brought in a number of young journalists who had worked under him at *On Guard* to serve as reporters and correspondents.[105]

A third source of journalistic and agitprop cadres for the center during the Cultural Revolution and First Five-Year Plan was the Donbass region, in particular the regional paper *Luganskaia pravda* and the youth correspondents' circles organized by *Komsomolskaia pravda*. Iurii

Zhukov, who would serve as head editor at *Komsomolskaia pravda* and *Pravda* in the 1940s and 1950s, began his career in 1927 or 1928 at *Luganskaia pravda*.[106] The head editor of *Luganskaia pravda* at this time, the Old Bolshevik and former mechanic Mikhail Davydovich Garin, was transferred to *Pravda* by the Orgburo in November 1929.[107] Boris Gorbatov, who grew up in a miners' town in the Donbass and also worked at *Luganskaia pravda* together with Zhukov and Garin, moved on to cover the start-up of the first furnaces at the Magnitogorsk steel mills.[108]

In addition to the senior editors who rotated through positions at *Luganskaia pravda* before going on to jobs in the central press, an entire cohort of young mass journalists got their start as members or organizers of youth correspondent circles in Lugansk and other Donbass towns. During the Cultural Revolution *Komsomolskaia pravda* cultivated a special relationship with youth correspondents in the Donbass, eventually promoting a number of them to positions as reporters, essayists, and organizers at the newspaper's Moscow offices. Vasilii Turov and Mikhail Semikolenov began their journalistic careers as youth correspondents in the Donbass, and Aleksei Abramenkov, although from the Moscow area, did his first work for *Komsomolskaia pravda* as a youth correspondent organizer there.[109]

With the exception of Tver, a textile city, the sites where mass journalism emerged in 1926–1927 were heavy industrial and mining centers where the Bolshevik regime was focusing investment, cadres, and political effort. As the Soviet leadership felt its way through the confusion and ambiguities of the NEP era, centers of heavy industry became not just focuses for Bolshevik energy and investment, but sacred amphitheaters wherein the elite—young Bolshevik working-class cadres—played out a ritualized battle to industrialize the Soviet Union. Even before the period of the First Five-Year Plan, the Urals and the Donbass, along with specific industrial enterprises such as the Krasnyi putilov and Krasnyi treugolnik factories in Leningrad and certain factories around Dnepropetrovsk and Kharkov, had become ritual battlegrounds where workers and party could play out the central struggle of history, as envisioned in Marxist-Leninist theory. The ambiguities of NEP Russia were banished so that the proletariat, the avant-garde and driving force of modern history, could storm the heights of the future without interference from disordered crowds of peasants, traders, and intellectuals clogging the attack routes. On one level mass journalism was an attempt by newspapermen to create news and pick up concrete quality-control functions in factories and mines, but at

another level the "raids," "reviews," and "socialist competitions" organized by the press were all skirmishes in the grand battle to capture the
heights of communism. Mass journalists saw themselves as warriors
leading the advance. This was the self-image that they took into the
Cultural Revolution. This was the metaphor that became the core of a
new Bolshevik self-understanding during the First Five-Year Plan.[110]

Mass Journalists and the Bolsheviks' Social Revolution

The newspapermen who pioneered mass journalism were part of a
gigantic social revolution deliberately created by the Bolshevik Party in
the 1920s and early 1930s. Throughout this period the party recruited
workers and others from among the laboring masses, providing
them with preferred access to goods, educational opportunities, and
white-collar jobs. Many of these new party members had experienced
disruption of their families, displacement, and violence during the revolutionary years, and the party earned their militant loyalty by providing
them power, a measure of stability, and a channel for social advancement. By the early 1930s young men of working-class and other humble
origins dominated the party/state apparatus in the USSR. Although
Communist journalists were more educated and somewhat less working
class than party members as a whole, they still shared many experiences
and assumptions with them. They were well qualified to write for both
rank-and-file Communists and Soviet officialdom.

During the so-called Cultural Revolution, a period of attacks by
young Communist militants on established institutions running from
1928 to 1931, young Bolshevik mass journalists took over Soviet newspapers in Moscow and the provinces. In a series of purges they worked
together with the CC executive apparatus to fire Old Bolshevik editors
who opposed Stalin's new policy course (collectivization) and many
lower-ranking nonparty newspaper staff members. This revolution can
be traced in purge records, biographies of individual journalists, and
statistics on the Soviet journalistic profession. It was inextricably tied up
with newspapers' adoption of mass journalistic methods, which in turn
was part of the retargeting of the press at the new Soviet elite.[111] The
mass journalistic revolution and the retargeting of the Soviet press were
thus part of the larger social revolution made by the Bolshevik leadership in the 1920s and early 1930s.

Archival data provides a fairly detailed picture of the journalistic
profession at the time of the mass journalists' takeover of the press. At

the State Archive of the Russian Federation (GARF) there are stored the results of the journalists' labor union's survey of its members in the last months of 1929. At this time the SRP included most editorial staff employees at Soviet newspapers, excluding labor union organs and some of the provincial press. The SRP survey covered 4,998 persons, or around three-quarters of all union members. It provides excellent data on patterns of occupational stratification, age distribution, party membership, social origins, and educational background for Soviet journalists of the time.[112]

Most SRP members were writers or editors. Counting those working for the Departments of Mass Work, who solicited, sorted, read, and edited reader letters, just over 70 percent of the SRP's membership was engaged in writing or editorial work above the level of copy editing.[113] More than half of SRP members were under thirty years old, and 87.4 percent were forty or younger. Almost three-quarters of the section members were men (74.7 percent). Among the various occupational groups represented, women dominated only in the low-status job of copy editor. Only about 10 percent of writers and editors were women.[114] Party members and candidate members made up approximately one-third of total union membership, much higher than in the general population or even in many Soviet institutions. Among editors (not including copy editors) the percentage of Communists was very high—73.4 percent, or almost three-quarters. By 1929, then, the upper levels of Soviet journalism were dominated by young male Communists.[115]

According to official data, the Communist fraction of the SRP was far less proletarian than the Communist Party as a whole (33.9 percent proletarian as opposed to 61.4 percent). But supplementing official data with other evidence suggests that most Communist journalists were still of relatively humble, if not worker, origins. To begin with, many of the "white-collar" positions held by SRP members before entering newspaper work were not elite, but low-status and low-paying jobs. For example, editor and writer A. Tararukhin worked as a village schoolteacher before entering journalism, feuilletonist and editor Lev Sosnovskii as a pharmacist's assistant, and *Komsomolskaia pravda* correspondent Tovii Karelshtein as a courier and cashier. In addition, many "white-collar" parents of journalists also held low-status, poorly paid jobs such as freelance photographer (*Komsomolskaia pravda* correspondent David Novoplianskii's father), elementary schoolteacher (*Pravda* foreign correspondent Aleksei Kozhen's mother), or railway clerk (*Red Star* editor David Ortenberg's father).[116] Communist journalists, whether categorized by the party as "worker," "peasant," or "white collar," generally had humble social origins. As a result most of them understood the social and cultural milieu of the ordinary party activist.[117]

According to the SRP's 1929 survey, its members were quite highly educated compared with the population at large and even the party membership. A total of 98 to 99 percent of members in all occupational groups had completed secondary school, and 13 percent had finished university. The SRP statistics, however, did not show just how spotty and schematic most journalists' education was. Only 6.8 percent of SRP members had any specialized education in journalism.[118] In much of the secondary and higher education system, basic literacy, numeracy, and Marxism-Leninism dominated. Many newspaper staff members with "higher education" had never been full-time students but rather part-time attendees of party political education programs or the evening programs sponsored by various newspapers and Moscow's House of the Press. In short, the educational gap between young Communist journalists and ordinary party members was not as wide as SRP statistics suggested.[119]

The mass journalists' takeover of the press in 1928–1930 involved intense strife along multiple lines of fracture. There were battles between Communist and nonparty journalists, but also among editorial office Communists, most obviously between young mass journalists and senior Old Bolshevik editors, many of whom had an "enlightenment" orientation toward newspaper work. The SRP's data reveal two very important divisions among Communist journalists that helped to shape these conflicts. First, younger journalists as a group were far more proletarian than their seniors. This was the result of the party's efforts to bring more workers into white-collar positions, including in journalism. Throughout the 1920s the percentage of former workers among novice Communist journalists increased. By 1929 more than half of all Communists entering journalism were ex-proletarians. Many of the most militant mass journalists came from this cohort of young ex-factory workers.[120]

Another major split was between Communists on the editorial staffs and Communists in the Departments of Mass Work. More than 95 percent of head editors were Communists, as were just over 60 percent of department heads. It was of course party policy to put Communists in editorial positions, so it is not surprising that most editors were party members. There were relatively fewer Communists among print shop

Taras Kostrov, editor of *Komsomolskaia pravda*, 1925–1928. Source: *Komsomolskaia pravda*.

foremen and copy editors (17.4 percent), the two typographical occupations within the SRP, or among reporters (35.2 percent). Printing and reporting were both low-status jobs. Party affiliation, in other words, corresponded to the occupational hierarchy at newspaper offices—Communists held the prestigious management positions, whereas non-party members mostly stood on the lowest rungs of the ladder.[121]

The Departments of Mass Work were the exception to this rule. In the early 1920s the duties later handled by these departments, such as

Staff of *Komsomolskaia pravda*'s mobile editorial office at the Urals Machine Factory, 1933. Iurii Zhukov, who will become a leading Soviet journalist of the 1940s and 1950s, is the tall man standing behind and slightly to the left of Rosa Zhukova, his wife and the only woman in the picture. Source: *Komsomolskaia pravda*.

instructing worker-peasant correspondents and processing reader letters, were low status. But as the CC began demanding more coverage of mass journalistic events, editors created Departments of Mass Work to organize these events and to handle reader correspondence. The prestige of the departments rose and they became the elevator up from the ground floor for ambitious young Communist newspapermen. During the Cultural Revolution the Departments of Mass Work increased their power and the scope of their work greatly, as their members led workplace insurrections against Old Bolshevik editors and nonparty staff. These departments, together with Departments of Party Life, were the launching pads for mass journalists' takeover of the central press. Roughly speaking, one can identify the Communists in the Departments of Mass Work with the new cohort of proletarian journalists entering newspaper work in the mid-to-late 1920s, and with the advocates of mass journalism.[122]

Communist reporters and organizers for the Departments of Mass Work were in an unstable and ambiguous position. They did not belong

Mass journalist Igor Maleev at work at the Odessa Komsomol newspaper *Young Guard*, 1924–1925. Maleev, a protegé of Taras Kostrov, went on to work in Moscow at *Komsomolskaia pravda* and *The Worker Gazette*. The sign behind him says "Department of Worker Life." Source: *Komsomolskaia pravda*.

to the editorial or literary elite, but they hoped for advancement. As Communists, they could make their voices heard in more important forums than nonparty members. They had access to authority. Moreover, many of them had "clean" class origins and felt righteous and invulnerable on these grounds. It was these men who were in the best position to lead insurrections against senior editors and purges of nonparty staff. They were also the most likely candidates for promotion when these purges opened up senior editorial and literary positions.

The domination of Communists in the Departments of Mass Work, together with the huge influx of former workers into journalism in the years 1928–1929, both suggest that a new cohort of young party newspapermen of proletarian and other humble origins was emerging at the end of the 1920s. These men (to repeat, most journalists were male) found their way into jobs at Soviet central newspapers via two routes. Some newspapers promoted a few printers or other blue-collar employees to office positions as clerks, secretaries, worker-peasant correspondent instructors, or reporters as part of the party's *vydvizhenie* ("moving up") program of moving workers into white-collar jobs. This

Moisei Chernenko of *Komsomolskaia pravda* (right) working with Best Machinist Kolesnichenko (center) and his assistant Prokhorenko at mobile editorial office at Iasinovataia Station, 1933. Source: *Komsomolskaia pravda*.

arrangement almost never worked out.[123] Most people with blue-collar work experience who succeeded as journalists in the central press were actually moved up by provincial or local newspapers. Typically, a young factory worker might join the Komsomol, get involved in his workshop wall newspaper, move up from there to writing for his factory or ward newspaper, then to sending "notes" to the city or province organ. The city or provincial newspaper might then hire him as a regular staff correspondent or reporter if he wrote well and/or had the right connections in the local party apparatus. From a large city paper the Central Committee Press Department might promote a young writer into a position at a Moscow newspaper. Most of the journalists of worker background who secured literary or editorial positions at central papers had previously been regular staff writers for provincial papers or local Moscow papers.[124]

To summarize, the development of Stalinist culture in the newspapers was integrally linked to the social revolution made by the party leadership in the 1920s and early 1930s. The drastic changes in the language, content, and presentation of central Soviet newspapers during the

Staff of *Komsomolskaia pravda* at Magnitogorsk construction site in front of the railcar containing their mobile editorial office and print shop, 1931. In center, seventh from right, is Demian Bednyi, Stalin's "court poet." Source: *Komsomolskaia pravda*.

Cultural Revolution was associated with the increasing influence of a new cohort of young Communist journalists sponsored by the CC executive apparatus. In some cases these journalists actually took control of their newspapers; in others they pressured their superiors to adopt new methods. The new journalism they championed aimed to mobilize rank-and-file party activists to carry out the party agenda. Precisely because they shared so much with the rank-and-file—they were young men of humble origins who were committed to and benefited from the party—the mass journalists understood their audience well.

Mass Journalists' Experiences and Their Commitment to the Party

Leninist regimes came to power in poor, predominantly agrarian countries. In addition, these countries generally went through periods of intense disruption because of civil war, decolonization, and/or outside

Correspondent Moisei Chernenko and two other *Komsomolskaia pravda* staff in front of mobile editorial office at unidentified site, 1932. Source: *Komsomolskaia pravda*.

invasion at the time of the revolution. In Russia the disruption and violence that preceded and accompanied the Communist seizure of power fortified individual members' commitment to the party, strengthened their ethic of heroism and self-sacrifice, and reinforced their readiness to use violence against suspected class enemies after victory. To understand young mass journalists' identification with the party and its goals, and to understand the forms of journalism they created, we need to know something of their aspirations, their education, their family background, and the social and economic circumstances in which they grew to adulthood.

As a group young Soviet journalists in the 1920s were hard bitten, ambitious, and insecure. The majority of them came from impoverished family backgrounds. As children growing up in the era of World War I, the Civil War, and collectivization, many experienced horrific violence, displacement, and flight from armies. As a result of the violence and the epidemics that accompanied it, a high proportion of Soviet journalists of the 1920s lost their fathers in childhood or early adolescence. Those young newspapermen who made it to the Moscow and important provincial newspapers were the hard-driving survivors of the catastrophes of 1914–1921 and later, collectivization. They sought power, social status, and education. The party was able to take advantage of these strivings by providing preferred access to higher education and jobs. In fact, in a situation of violence and deprivation, the party offered itself as the sole source of professional advancement, education, material well-being, national rejuvenation, and vision for the future. For many of these journalists the party seems to have served as a kind of surrogate father. Little wonder that ambitious young men of the lower classes were drawn to it, made their careers within it, and came to identify with it. And little wonder that many of these men were disposed toward brutality and bullying.[125]

One typical young newspaperman was A. Tararukhin, in 1930 a night editor at the organ of the railway workers' union, *The Siren*, in Moscow, and an active participant in the purges that "Communized" the editorial staff and brought the newspaper under Stalin's control. In connection with the fall 1930 purge at *The Siren* Tararukhin wrote a detailed autobiography, which remains in the files of the party's CCC. Tararukin was born in 1896 into the family of a landless peasant who made his living as a day laborer, cobbler, and stove repairman in the Don region of the Ukraine. His mother was illiterate. He attended a local church primary school, and then a two-year *uchilishche*, or technical school. From the age of twelve he helped with his father's work while going to school. At sixteen he could no longer continue his schooling because of a lack of money, and began working full time for his father. But Tararukhin persisted in his dream of getting an education, and in 1914 placed first in entrance exams for a local teacher-training school run by the Orthodox church. He paid for his first year of schooling there by hauling mortar with his father during the summer, and then received a scholarship. In 1918 he graduated and became a teacher.[126]

One of the themes of Tararukhin's early life was conflict with local Cossacks, a privileged caste of landowners who received special treatment from the state in exchange for military service. The Cossacks looked down on the poorer Russian peasants. In his autobiographical statement to the CCC, Tararukhin wrote about how, when he was a child, drunk Cossacks frequently broke into his house, demanding money for alcohol. If they did not receive it, they would beat his father and sometimes Tararukhin himself. "The word *muzhik* [redneck peasant] was a gross insult among the Cossacks. We were constantly subject to bullying," Tararukhin wrote. The conflicts with the Cossacks helped to decide Tararukhin's political alignment in 1917, against local landlords and for socialist revolutionaries. To a man from a landless peasant family such as Tararukhin, the party and the revolutionaries in general presented themselves as an outside counterforce to the Cossacks and the oppression of local landlords.[127] In his 1930 statement Tararukhin said that in 1917, "I had only the most confused idea of what the party was. The political question was easily decided—there were the wealthy landholders (bogachi), the atamans [Cossack chieftains], and the poor peasants, and the outsiders. I was from among the poor peasants, and so it followed that I should be with the poor peasants, with the outsiders."[128]

In 1918 Tararukhin began work as a teacher in a village in Danilov province, also in the Don region. With the Civil War under way, Tararukhin was not receiving a salary, and the village had to provide him with food. He worked with the new village soviet, and displayed particular zeal as an antireligious activist, burning books from the local church's library. The book burning and the confiscation of the church library earned him the enmity of some local peasants as well as the priest, the deacon, and the church elder. When the White Cossacks occupied the village where he was teaching in June 1919, there were dire consequences.[129] The Cossacks arrested Tararukhin immediately, probably on the basis of the priest's denunciation. At the petition of his father and the director of the teacher-training school where he'd studied, Tararukhin was released, agreeing not to leave the village and to appear before the occupying ataman once a week. For reasons that are unclear, but may have had to do with fear of retribution against his family, Tararukhin did not violate this bond.[130]

On November 4, 1919, as the Red Army approached the village, Cossacks and local policemen rounded up Tararukhin and about seventy other persons suspected of Bolshevik sympathies and drove them south across the steppe. During this trek, which lasted at least two weeks, Cossack troops stripped the prisoners of their footwear, their bags, and their warm clothes. It was now winter, and cold rain fell constantly. "I could barely drag myself over the ground," Tararukhin wrote later. "My neighbors Starostin and Kovalev dragged me between them . . . I lost strength, then consciousness." Tararukhin was eventually left by the Cossack guards in a pile of bodies at a rural train station. It is not clear how the bodies came to be there, although Tararukhin does mention that a typhus epidemic was just hitting the area. In 1930 Tararukhin did not remember this episode clearly, but he did recall waking, crawling out from the pile of bodies, seeing other heaps of corpses around the station, staggering away, and seeking shelter in a small hut on the fringes of the village.[131]

In February 1920, only weeks after his ordeal, Tararukhin was accepted into the party without any preparatory period of candidacy "because I had done my candidacy under White torture." In the ensuing months he gave himself over to party work entirely, helping to organize armed detachments that were requisitioning grain from local peasants, doing agitprop work, publishing a newspaper and political bulletins, turning a monastery into a secular orphanage ("a children's home"), and fighting "with a rifle in my hands" against contingents of Whites still operating in the area. Of these months, Tararukhin especially recalled the lack of sleep and the need to carry a rifle constantly. Local party cadres were engaged primarily in confiscating grain from peasants and battling "bandits," both of which involved frequent combat.[132]

Tararukhin went on to survive two attempts to expel him from the party, first as "an alien element" (a teacher), and then for supposedly plagiarizing a speech by Commissar of Enlightenment Anatolii Lunacharskii in one of his newspaper articles. He served on the regional party committee, edited the local newspaper *Red Word*, wrote for the Russian Telegraph Agency (ROSTA), and worked as a party agitator. In January 1922 Tararukhin traveled to Moscow as a delegate to the Third Congress of Press Workers. He eventually made a career at Stalingrad and then Moscow newspapers.[133]

In the fall of 1930, while working as a night editor at *The Siren*, Tararukhin was denounced during a purge of the newspaper's party organization. Although formally charged with collaborating with the old "opportunist" leadership of the construction workers' labor union while at the union's newspaper *Postroika (Construction)* in 1928, obstructing the transfer of reporters to set salaries, and opposing collectivization, Tararukhin's real sins seem to have been his cost-cutting measures and staff cuts at *The Siren*. His chief attackers were printers and lower-level editorial office personnel. Tararukhin, who saw himself as a faithful servant of the party, responded to the attacks with fury, hurt, and bewilderment. In his autobiographical statement to the CCC, he grieved that he had been "libeled" and "thrown overboard." "This is political death," he wrote, "and I cannot live outside the party. . . . it follows that I cannot continue to exist physically either. . . . the years of the revolution tempered me, but the libel has passed all bounds, I am writing to ask that you defend me." Tararukhin displayed a sense of frustration and even despair at being idle and excluded from party work "during a time of the most important construction."[134]

Tararukin's desperate attachment to the party makes sense in context. At stake in the purgewas not only professional advancement, but opportunities to live in the larger cities, and access to health care and special cooperatives that sold higher-quality goods. In a time of scarcity and social disruption, the party had deliberately eliminated other sources of advancement and material support for newsmen and aspiring intellectuals of all sorts. Having leveled, as it were, the social landscape, Bolshevik leaders were now using state resources to create a new elite. The fierce commitment of many new members to the party was equaled by the bitterness of those who were excluded.

⁓ BETWEEN 1922 AND 1929 party leaders and Agitprop officials created a new journalistic elite by channeling the educational and career aspirations of ordinary Russian youth. They were able to tap into and direct a social revolution already under way, in which Russian children from humble families sought education and advancement. By setting itself up as the sole source of social mobility, moral purpose, and material well-being. the party won intense commitment from many of its cadres. For large numbers of Communist newspapermen the party was a refuge in a time of intense social disruption and violence. For the many who lost their fathers at a young age, it may even have served as a kind of surrogate parent. The party leadership's special relationship with its cadres, however, was set up at the expense of the rest of society, which was isolated from political power and denied access to resources. The widening gap between the party and the "nonparty masses" was *the* central social fact of Soviet life in the middle and later 1920s. The need to deny this contradiction of the Bolsheviks' egalitarian rhetoric and justify their new privileges probably contributed, if only unconsciously, to young party journalists' self-righteousness and strident insistence on bringing newspapers "closer to the masses."

~ 5

Mass Journalists, "Cultural Revolution," and the Retargeting of Soviet Newspapers

Between 1928 and 1930 mass journalistic language and stories took over the central press. At many newspapers, including *Pravda*, this change was caused directly by mass journalists taking over the editorial offices and leading purges of nonparty, Old Bolshevik, and enlightenment-oriented editors and writers. The Central Committee (CC) executive apparatus, controlled by Stalin, catalyzed this process by promoting mass journalists to posts at the central papers and issuing repeated orders to the press to adopt their methods. The CC's transformation of the press had dual purposes. First Stalin and the CC secretaries allied with him aimed to wrest control of all press organs from Rightists who might question forced collectivization or rapid rates of industrial growth. The most prominent Rightist was Nikolai Bukharin, head editor of *Pravda*. Second, as part of mobilizing to carry out the new program, CC agitation-and-propaganda (agitprop) officials aimed to retarget the entire central press at ordinary party activists and "green" workers coming into factory production from the countryside. They believed mass journalism, with its military language and presentation of labor as a heroic epic, was the best method for reaching these audiences.

For two decades the dominant paradigm for describing the offensives undertaken by militant young Communists against their superiors in many fields of culture during the First Five-Year Plan has been "Cultural Revolution." The paradigm as elaborated in the 1978 anthology *Cultural Revolution in Russia, 1928–1931* actually included two distinct dynamics—the young Communists' uprising and the accession to ideological hegemony of "utopian" Marxist theories in diverse cultural fields, including law, history, and economics. Contributors to *Cultural Revolution* described a similar trajectory in different fields, from New Economic Policy (NEP) moderation to rising utopianism during the First Five-Year Plan, followed finally by retreat (part of the larger "Great Retreat" postulated by Nicholas Timasheff) and often repression of the radical Marxists. They questioned to what extent the momentum for the Cultural Revolution came from the party leadership ("from above"), the party rank and file ("from below"), or quarrels within the professions (also "from below"). Sheila Fitzpatrick, editor of the volume, also stressed the *vydvizhenie* or promotion of young workers into white-collar positions through preferential promotions and admission to higher education. This promotion, she argued, generated substantial social support (i.e., support from below) for the party and its "new course."[1]

I take the term "Cultural Revolution" to refer to young Communists' attacks on their superiors and their supposedly Marxist cultural agendas in the period 1928–1931. In the case of Soviet newspapers, then, the young Communist militants were the mass journalists, and the cultural agenda was consisted of their new methods of producing news. In the case of journalism I would emphasize, as Michael David-Fox does in his work on early Soviet higher education, that the *institutional bases* for the Cultural Revolution of 1928–1931 were laid quite early in the NEP era.[2] In the press these were the worker/peasant correspondents' movement, the so-called mass newspapers, and workplace broadsheets and newsletters *(stengazety* and *mnogotirazhki)*. I would also argue that the *social and cultural bases* for the uprising of 1928–1931 were laid during the NEP, at least in the case of journalism. The young Communist activists who were the target audience of mass journalism, after all, were recruited into the party in the NEP years. And the methods and language of mass journalism developed during those years as newspapermen experimented with ways to reach and mobilize those activists without resort to taboo "bourgeois sensationalism."

Looked at from the perspectives both of immediate causes and longer-term context, the Cultural Revolution in the newspapers was created largely from above, by party leaders. Bolshevik leaders of all orientations, from Trotskii to Bukharin, agreed in the early 1920s on the need to recruit large number of proletarians into the party, and they did so. They agreed on the need to connect with "the masses," and the activists in particular, by organizing a worker/peasant correspondents' movement and establishing mass newspapers. The decision to run the 1926 belt-tightening campaign, and to order newspapers to participate, came from the highest levels of the Bolshevik leadership. In response journalists at provincial mass newspapers created the specific forms of mass journalism. CC secretaries Stalin, Kaganovich, and Molotov, operating through the CC Agitprop Department, Orgburo and Secretariat, made the decision to undertake collectivization and industrialization, to attack the Right, and to launch an ideological and cultural offensive in late 1927. Officials in the CC executive apparatus allied with Stalin ignited the conflagration of 1928–1931 by promoting mass journalists into the central press, ordering newspapers to adopt mass journalistic methods, promoting *samokritika*, or "self-criticism," insisting that newspapermen demonstrate party loyalty, running purges and cost-cutting campaigns at editorial offices, and using personal connections to arrange workplace attacks on Stalin's Rightist political opponents.

This study examines the Cultural Revolution from the perspectives of the CC secretaries, Agitprop Department officials, and Soviet newspapermen. Perhaps because of source limitations scholars have neglected these perspectives for decades, focusing instead on conflict and accommodation between the party and the nonparty intelligentsia. Yet the initiatives of the party leaders, the agitprop officials, and the Communist newspapermen were arguably the most important forces in the shaping of Bolshevik culture. Taken together these groups controlled the cultural priorities of the party/state, including funding decisions. They set the general tasks for the mass party press, which included organs that reached millions of readers. This was several orders of magnitude larger than the readership of the intellectual and theoretical journals that feature prominently in most works on cultural revolution and the origins of Stalinist culture. The propaganda priorities and decisions of party leaders mattered, and they mattered more than those of any other agents of cultural production.

It is common sense, however, that Stalin, the other CC secretaries, and CC propaganda officials were not gods capable of creating an entire culture from nothing. They set the tasks for culture and suggested certain directions. Direct producers of culture, including the mass journalists, created the concrete solutions to these tasks, and they did so using available artifacts—the language of the Civil War newspapers, the practices of the worker/peasant correspondents' movement, and so on. This was one kind of input "from below" into Bolshevik (and by extension, Stalinist) culture. Another kind came from the reading preferences of young Communists and Komsomols as revealed in their letters and in reader studies. For example, widespread resentment of the privileges of bourgeois specialists and party officials was expressed in the preference for scapegoating and denunciation of class enemies. The self-criticism campaign of 1928–1929 aimed, among other things, to tap that resentment through the publicity of events such as the Shakhty trial of March 1928. The frustration and resentment of many ordinary Communists and many nonparty Soviet subjects in 1928 were real. CC initiatives aimed to mobilize and manipulate that anger.

Analysis of the CC executive's priorities for agitation and propaganda suggests a simplified periodization for the history of early Soviet culture. Rather than the three-period schema of "NEP pluralism/First Five-Year Plan utopianism/Great Retreat" I suggest a two-period framework of "NEP mass enlightenment project/culture as mobilization." For the agitprop apparatus the transition from the NEP to the First Five-Year Plan in culture was characterized not by the end of some commitment to pluralism but by a shift in agitprop priorities from mass enlightenment of the populace to mobilization of activists. In the next three chapters I demonstrate that the priorities of agitprop officials and newspapermen during the First Five-Year Plan were not utopian but pragmatic. Above all they involved mobilizing party activists to fulfill the Plan using class resentments, military metaphors, and militant rhetoric. This was *already* a retreat from NEP positions, in that the newspapers devoted less energy to remaking the masses' collective psyche. It was also a retreat in that the new mass journalism aimed to mobilize activists using preexisting resentments and preferences for tales of battle and adventure. I contend that the Great Retreat in party agitprop began in 1928–1929, with the shift to the large, but quite pragmatic, task of mobilizing activists by appealing to their hostility toward class enemies and their need for a heroic identity. By 1930 top agitprop officials and CC secretaries were already talking about using the "romance" and "pathos" of socialist construction to mobilize activists. This was a move taken straight out of the Komsomol agitprop playbook, and it led directly into the official formulation of socialist realism, the keystone of high Stalinist culture.[3]

Preparations for the Central Committee's Cultural Offensive

In April 1928 the Central Committee declared a self-criticism campaign, an invitation for party and Komsomol activists to denounce corrupt bosses and bureaucrats. This declaration opened up space for debate and criticism of lower-level authorities in the press and at party and labor union meetings. Combined with the March trial of bourgeois specialists accused of sabotaging production at the Shakhty coal mines in Ukraine, the call for self-criticism was the signal for a full-scale Communist offensive against Rightists, doubters, and temporizers. The mass journalists' takeover of the central press was part of this offensive.

Central Committee planning for the cultural part of this offensive began in the winter of 1927–1928, probably not coincidentally at the same time as a sharp drop in government grain procurements prompted Stalin and his allies to order harsh punitive measures against peasants suspected of "speculation." The cultural offensive and the Stalinist attack on the peasantry thus took shape simultaneously. On October 3, 1927, the CC issued a resolution instructing party committees to ensure more coverage of party life and ideological issues and less of financial and economic news. The resolution also instructed the CC Press and Agitprop departments to work up a new plan of Communist education for newspapermen, thus signaling that journalists could no longer be politically neutral "bourgeois specialists." They would have to serve as active promoters of the party's agenda.[4]

About the same time as the CC resolution on the Communization of the press, CC officials began working up proposals to revise the supervision of the newspaper network. The central figure in planning the reform seems to have been Nikolai Smirnov, deputy director of the CC Press Department and former editor of *The Worker Gazette* (as discussed in Chapter 1 Smirnov had been Stalin's personal choice to edit *The Worker Gazette* in 1922). As editor of the latter paper, he was of course one of the pioneers of mass journalism. Smirnov's goals were to concentrate the efforts of the CC press apparatus on ideological and political guidance of the newspapers, to ensure more publicity of the CC's own work, in particular its new policy toward the peasants, and to change the criteria for CC evaluation of Soviet newspapers from "professional" (layout and writing style) to "ideological" (sticking to the party line, publicizing CC policies). Overall he aimed to strengthen the CC's ability to set the agenda for the Soviet press. In pursuit of these goals the CC Orgburo in early 1928 approved Smirnov's initiatives to set up a CC Press Office that would run regular meetings with editors and to merge the CC Agitprop and Press departments. On May 3, 1928, the Politburo appointed an entirely new leadership for the reorganized Agitprop Department. The stage was set for the CC's offensive on "the cultural front." A. I. Krinitskii, new head of the department, promptly undertook a series of fierce attacks on the Commissariat of Enlightenment's "soft" policies in education. Sergei Ingulov, deputy director of Agitprop and head of the reorganized Newspaper Section, promoted the self-criticism campaign, encouraging newspapermen to denounce "class enemies" and corrupt officials. Both men maintained close ties with mass journalists at the central newspapers.[5]

Purges and the Mass Journalists' Takeover of the Newspapers

The mass journalists' revolution was not a single discrete event, but rather an extended conflict played out in a series of purges and promotions that ran from the fall of 1927 well into 1930. It began with CC transfers of mass journalists from the provinces into the central press (summer–fall 1927) and the October 1927 CC resolution calling for the "Communization" of journalism. The resolution, which mandated a more ideological, CC-centered approach to news, also insisted that newspapermen receive a more "Communist" education, and that they behave not as neutral bourgeois specialists, but as active promoters of the party's agenda.[6] These CC moves coincided with a general purge of Left Oppositionists (supporters of Leon Trotskii, Grigorii Zinovev, and Lev Kamenev) from the party. The self-criticism campaign announced by the CC in April 1928 then opened up higher officials, particularly those inclined to the Right (i.e., supporters of Nikolai Bukharin and opponents of coercive measures against the peasants), to attacks from below at their workplaces and in the press. Mass journalists used the self-criticism campaign to assault senior editors, including prominent Rightists in the central press (including Bukharin and Ulianova at *Pravda*).[7] The self-criticism campaign developed into an attack directed by Stalin and his allies in the CC on the Rightist Moscow party leadership and the labor union leadership. During the fall 1928 purge of the Rightist leadership of the Moscow party organization, mass journalists with close ties to the Stalin-dominated CC took over effective control of *Pravda* and other Moscow newspapers. In the winter of 1928–1929 the Stalinist leadership attacked labor union leaders and took control of the Central Council of Labor Unions. Finally, in April 1929 the Sixteenth Party Conference fired Rightist leaders Bukharin, Mikhail Tomskii (head of the Central Council of Labor Unions), and A. I. Rykov from their senior posts and ordered the first general purge of the party since 1921. The conference also mandated that a purge of nonparty employees of all Soviet institutions should follow the party purge. The party and nonparty purges that began throughout the Soviet press in late 1929 targeted nonparty journalists and Communists perceived as insufficiently militant. Issues of *Journalist* from early 1930 explicitly linked the Communization of the newspapers with the adoption of mass journalistic techniques.[8]

This chapter describes in detail the transition from NEP moderation to mass journalism at *Pravda* and *Izvestiia*, the two most important central Soviet newspapers. But insurrections by young Communist newspapermen and purges of veteran journalists accompanied the transition to mass journalism at many other newspapers, both central and provincial. Three examples are *Cooperative Life, Evening Moscow*, and *The Siren*. At *Cooperative Life*, the flagship organ of the Central Cooperative Union, young mass journalists assigned to the newspaper by the CC between August 1927 and February 1928 led an insurrection against older senior editors. The rebellion culminated with the CC Secretariat firing the paper's head editor in July 1928.[9] At *Evening Moscow*, too, an insurrection and purge facilitated the transition to mass journalism. In December 1929 the CC Secretariat appointed S. A. Volodin editor-in-chief of *Evening Moscow*. Volodin, a militant mass journalist and veteran of the CC's mass worker paper, *The Worker Gazette*, presumably had a mandate to introduce mass journalism at the paper. His appointment was followed by a purge of non-Communist journalists from the editorial offices.[10] At *The Siren*, organ of the railway workers' labor union, purges accompanied Stalin's attack on the union leadership. Between May 1928 and November 1930 *The Siren* went through multiple changes of editors and a series of purges. According to Sergei Ingulov and A. Tararukhin, night editor and an active supporter of Stalin's attack on the old labor union leadership, the purges were aimed at increasing the proportion of Communists on the staff, getting rid of the "longtime residents" who supported the old railway union Central Committee, and "making the newspaper more militant."[11]

Editorial Conflict and Mass Journalism at *Pravda*, 1928–1929

At *Pravda*, debates about mass journalism intersected with Stalin's campaign to remove Nikolai Bukharin and his "pupils" from the editorial staff. Well before Bukharin's opposition to the decision to force industrial growth rates came out into the open in May 1928, Stalin was using the CC executive apparatus to limit his influence at the paper. The first step was to balance Bukharin's protegés on the editorial board with editors who supported Stalin. On January 26, 1928, the Politburo approved a resolution accepting Bukharin's own plan for reorganizing the *Pravda* editorial staff. Probably under pressure from Stalin and other CC secretaries to balance his own supporters on the editorial board, Bukharin agreed to co-opt Krinitskii, K. S. Karpinskii, a former editor of *The Worker Gazette*, and A. Bubnov, a Stalin supporter and head of the Red Army's Political Directorate (PUR).[12] Only two weeks later, on February 9, the Politburo brought Emelian Iaroslavskii, prominent party figure and head of the CCC, onto the *Pravda* board. According to reports reaching Leon Trotskii in the summer of 1928 Iaroslavskii had been placed on the board to keep an eye on Bukharin. Possibly Stalin wanted a more "authoritative" figure than Krinitskii or Bubnov to counterbalance his opponent.[13]

In the summer of 1928 Stalin and his allies in the Politburo took further steps to undermine Bukharin at *Pravda*. On June 26, 1928, they proposed to him yet another reconstitution of the editorial board. On August 8, presumably as the result of this second reorganization, the Politburo confirmed the appointments to the board of G. Krumin, formerly head editor of *Economic Life*, and M. A. Savelev, formerly head editor of *The Trade and Industrial Gazette*. After this reorganization the only member of the "Bukharin school" left at *Pravda* was Dmitri Maretskii. The other "pupils," V. N. Astrov, A. N. Slepkov, and E. V. Tseitlin, were removed from the board.[14] Bukharin continued in his official capacity as head editor, and Mariia Ulianova, Lenin's younger sister and a Bukharin supporter, held on to her post as editorial staff secretary.

The result of the editorial staff changes was uncertainty about who would make what decisions on content. On September 20, 1928, Krumin sent a memo to the other editorial board members (Maretskii, Ulianova, Iaroslavskii, and Savelev, but curiously, not Bukharin himself) regarding the problem of "processing articles." To ensure that all members of the board participated in content decisions, Krumin proposed a complex scheme that included maintaining rolling lists of all articles proposed for publication, their origins, their current location in the editing apparatus, and who had seen them.[15] In fact, however, Bukharin's people were gradually being squeezed out of the decision-making process, and the result was continuing confusion about who was in charge. Sometime soon after February 10, 1929, Bukharin ally

Dmitrii Maretskii complained to the editorial board about changes made by other board members to one of his lead editorials. According to Maretskii these changes were made without his authorization. This incident, he claimed, was part of a larger "policy on the part of several editorial board members of isolating the lead editor of the Central Organ and member of the Politburo Comrade Bukharin." In response new board member Savelev drafted a resolution denying all of Maretskii's charges.[16]

In September 1928, five months earlier elections for a new party cell bureau had put Bukharin's opponents firmly in control of the paper's party organization. According to an ex post facto account in the July 9, 1929, edition of *Pravda*'s in-house newspaper, *Pravdist*, the bureau election took place at the height of the CC's struggle against Bukharin's Right Deviation. They were part of the follow-up to a July 1928 plenary session of the CC that had promulgated the slogans of "an unflinching Bolshevik line," industrialization, crushing of the class enemy, and "socialist reconstruction of agriculture," that is, collectivization. *Pravdist* said that "comrades were elected to the bureau who could guarantee the implementation of the party line against Trotskyite ideology and the Right Deviation." The electors had rejected certain unnamed senior editors, who although they enjoyed positions of power at *Pravda*, "were vacillating." Presumably some of Bukharin's supporters were removed from the party cell bureau at this time.[17]

The most important result of the September 1928 elections was the elevation of Leonid Kovalev to the post of bureau secretary, head of the *Pravda* party organization. Kovalev, a personal friend of Stalin's wife, Nadezhda Allilueva, was one of the dictator's key contacts at *Pravda*, instrumental in helping to wrest control of the paper from Bukharin and Ulianova. In September 1929 Stalin would laud Kovalev's services as head of *Pravda*'s Party Department, writing that "he has done a pretty good job of putting it [the department] together in spite of . . . Ulianova's opposition."[18] Kovalev's increasing power at *Pravda* had consequences for the official cultural line of the party as well as for politics. Ulianova and Bukharin were principal proponents of the NEP mass enlightenment project and prime movers in the early development of the worker-peasant correspondents' movement. Stalin's undermining of their positions at *Pravda* also meant the beginning of the end for mass enlightenment and the notion of dialogue between party and masses.

As early as the spring of 1928 Kovalev was the key contact inside the paper for the CC executive apparatus. In 1928–1929 he was *Pravda*'s only representative at meetings of the CC Orgburo and Secretariat, where most of the Central Committee's important business was transacted.[19] Through the new chief of the CC Newspaper Section, Sergei Ingulov, Kovalev controlled staff appointments at the paper,[20] and through direct channels of communication with the Secretariat and Stalin himself, he exercised a strong influence on news content and coverage. Kovalev was involved in efforts to make *Pravda* reflect the agenda of the CC executive apparatus more closely and to open up information channels that bypassed Bukharin. In February 1928, while still only deputy chief of the paper's Party Department, Kovalev proposed giving *Pravda* direct access to the CC's departments, rather than channeling news on CC activities through the CC Information Department and the official CC publication, *Izvestiia TsK*. Kovalev proposed to put the Party Department in direct contact with high CC officials, and to allow Party Department journalists to attend CC department and special commission meetings. The proposal, which was approved by Stalin in a handwritten note to other Secretariat members, allowed the *Pravda* Party Department editors to get around Bukharin and exercise control over content in collaboration with high-level CC officials.[21] Later in 1928 Kovalev, together with Ingulov, drafted a proposal to revamp the *Pravda* Party Department so as to give more coverage to internal CC activities and local party organizations. The CC Secretariat approved this proposal on December 14, 1928.[22]

Aleksei Kapustin, the former editor of *Tverskaia pravda* and founder of mass journalism, was another key leader in the Stalinists' takeover of the editorial offices. According to a June 1929 article in *Pravdist*, his department, Worker Life, was in fact controlling *Pravda*'s national news agenda.[23] Like Kovalev, Kapustin had good connections inside the CC Agitprop Department and attended its sessions.[24] Judging by his public insistence in the spring of 1929 that *Pravda* attack Bukharin's Right Deviation more harshly, Kapustin was also a strong Stalin supporter.[25]

Within the *Pravda* organization debates about mass journalism received a strong impulse from Kovalev's appointment of a new party production commission, which was supposed to review the organization of the news departments, improve labor discipline, and rationalize production.[26] Kovalev used the production commission to promote the mass journalists' agenda. He also used *Pravda*'s in-house newspaper, *Pravdist*, which he edited after October 1928.[27]

Beginning in the fall of 1928 mass journalists recently promoted to positions at *Pravda* took on newspaper veterans and leading feuille-tonists such as Mikhail Koltsov in debates about the future of the Soviet press. The mass journalists, based in the Party, Worker Life, and Mass Work departments, advocated expanded coverage from the shop floor, the organization by newspapermen of production reviews and socialist competitions, and the structuring of news coverage around party slogans. All this was to be at the expense of other departments where veterans of *Pravda* from the Civil War years dominated, including National News, International News, Court Chronicle, and the Bureau of Investigation.

Shortages of paper made the battle to define "news" a nasty one. Because of newsprint shortages, the CC Orgburo ordered *Pravda* to reduce the size of its weekday edition from eight to six pages in January 1928.[28] In January 1929 lack of paper forced *Pravda*'s editors to cut the paper down to four pages per edition. The contraction of space in the newspaper intensified struggles between departments to place their own news. In December 1928 *Pravdist* ran a lead article suggesting that space be saved by cutting short foreign and domestic news items (from the Chronicle) and ending the practice of printing full transcripts of party leaders' speeches. The author suggested that systematic coverage of news from five to six of the most important factories and construction projects in the USSR would be superior to bits and pieces of the Chronicle. News from these sites, where workers and Bolshevik cadres were literally building socialism, was more significant than trivial crime reports from provincial cities. As the *Pravdist* article demonstrated, the paper shortage forced newspapermen to consider carefully what kind of news should have priority. Someone's stories had to be cut.[29]

Debates about mass journalism peaked between November 1928 and July 1929. They were facilitated by initiatives from the CC, and ultimately, from Stalin. In late 1928 the Central Committee launched a "Face to Production" campaign inside the labor union movement. CC executives' goal was to turn the unions into instruments for raising production. In response officials of the journalists' union, the journalists' labor union section (SRP), ordered their own "Face to Production" campaign at the newspapers in January 1929. As part of the campaign the union's Central Bureau set up a Press Cabinet headed by Mikhail Gus, a prominent SRP official, former newspaperman, and author of a major study of Soviet newspaper language. The Cabinet published a newsletter, "The Beauties of Style," and sponsored debates at the *Pravda* editorial offices and the Moscow Press Club about newspaper language, mass journalism, and self-criticism. Press Cabinet-sponsored events were among the most important forums for discussion of the transition to mass journalism throughout 1929.[30]

The most vocal mass journalists at *Pravda* were the writers Bulyzhnik and Tanin, who specialized in reporting socialist competitions, production reviews, and exchanges of experience *(pereklichki)* from factory shop floors.[31] Judging from their news coverage, both worked for the Department of Mass Work. In late December 1928, Bulyzhnik began a crusade to reorganize all of *Pravda*'s news coverage into "shock campaigns" that would promote party slogans. In a December 29 piece written for *Pravdist*, he taxed *Pravda* journalists with "negligence" in the selection of articles and toleration of "random news, just one thing after another," urging them to take up "campaigning, organizing activities." The entire newspaper, Bulyzhnik argued, ought to be organized around a limited number of ongoing agitprop campaigns. Bulyzhnik pointed to the mass journalism of *Komsomolskaia pravda* and *The Worker Gazette* as positive examples for *Pravda* to follow. To emphasize his point, he even compared *Pravda* unfavorably to *Evening Moscow*, notorious for sensationalism and a neutral tone. Even *Evening Moscow*, he wrote, "battles for the organization of winter resorts [for workers] and for finding the best way to clean the streets." *Pravda*, in contrast, did very little organizing, and there was no coordination of agitprop campaigns between departments. Only individual mass journalists, including Aleksei Kapustin, organized campaigns.[32]

Bulyzhnik's article excited heated debate at *Pravda*. Mikhail Gus replied to him in *Pravdist*, arguing that the best way to propagandize the masses was through carefully selected "daily facts," and criticizing Soviet newspapers for inability "to deal with facts, to use them properly and exhaustively." Gus's emphasis on facts signaled that he was defending Chronicle and Information departments against the onslaught of Bulyzhnik and his "campaign school."[33]

Gus was an outsider at *Pravda*, but some journalists within the editorial offices also opposed Bulyzhnik. On January 5, 1929, E. Loginova, writing in *Pravdist*, attacked "screeching campaigns" and "screeching impulsive attacks." Loginova explicitly opposed the "screechiness" of *Komsomolskaia pravda*, and she endorsed the NEP schema for a press differentiated by target audience. Rather than imitating the mass newspapers, she contended, *Pravda* needed to fulfill its role as "leading party organ" and run more "serious" coverage.[34]

Kovalev and N. Naumov, head of the paper's Komsomol cell and editor in the Party Department, supported Bulyzhnik in this debate.[35]

Although they opposed too much "shouting" and denied that the entire newspaper had to be devoted to shock campaigns, Kovalev and Naumov affirmed that campaigns were "the highest form" of journalism and ought to be "the main form of daily newspaper work." In a January 12, 1929, article in *Pravdist* Kovalev backed campaign-style mass journalism, spelled out its principal function as issuing orders to party cadres, and suggested ways to increase its appeal to mass readers. The ideal campaign, he wrote, should avoid abstract sloganeering, include concrete stories from daily life, and use a variety of different journalistic genres, from wire service reports to reader letters. Like Bulyzhnik, Kovalev insisted that various departments of the newspaper should coordinate their coverage around a single set of party slogans.[36]

Debate about mass journalism and "information" continued in *Pravdist* and at Moscow's Press Club until the summer of 1929, culminating in a purge and reorganization of the *Pravda* editorial offices. Mass journalists, led by Kovalev, Tanin, Bulyzhnik, and Naumov, continued to attack the "calm" presentation of news, advocating instead "live militant work," "sallies" into factories, and "short shock headlines." Their arguments clearly linked the organization of workplace events such as socialist competitions with the use of militant shock language.[37] They argued successfully for shifting the scene of the most important front-page news from foreign countries to the factories and construction sites of the Soviet Union.[38] They even launched an attack on the feuilleton, in Soviet journalism usually a humorous or satirical commentary on daily life, often from the writer's own experience. Some of *Pravda*'s biggest names in the late 1920s were feuilletonists, including Mikhail Koltsov, David Landau, and David Zaslavskii. In February and March 1929 mass journalist Bulyzhnik savaged these writers on the pages of *Pravdist*, complaining that their stories, based around incidents such as a jewelry theft or a brawl at a local cafeteria, were frivolous and divorced from the real concerns of the laboring masses. Like other newspapermen, Bulyzhnik insisted, feuilletonists had to learn to integrate their coverage into shock campaigns and focus their stories around "the sharpest problems of our day," and most especially industrialization. In other words Koltsov and company had to stick more closely to the topics designated by the CC Agitprop Department.[39]

The mass journalists' attacks were directed against specific departments and specific factions in the *Pravda* editorial offices. *Pravdist*, for example, attacked the Department of Juridical Consultation and Courts for running too much politically "neutral" material and publishing the Court Chronicle, a compilation of random crimes, thefts, and incidents of domestic violence. *Pravdist* also repeatedly excoriated the Department of Domestic News and its chief N. M. Rabinovich for depending on Chronicle items from the capitals and neglecting coverage of the provinces, "economic construction" (factories and construction sites), and "the struggle with bureaucratism."[40] Rabinovich supposedly did not publicize party slogans or organize "the worker/peasant masses around party tasks."[41] The Department of International Life, headed by David Abramovich Ikhok, also came in for heavy criticism. According to *Pravdist* Ikhok spent too much space on Chamberlain, Churchill, the League of Nations, the Little Entente, and the Big Entente. *Pravdist* argued that less space ought to be devoted to international news and "the behind-the scenes maneuvers" of diplomats, and more to exclusively Soviet topics such as collective farms, industrialization, and the progress of state grain procurements.[42] Both Rabinovich and Ikhok were longtime protegés of Ulianova, who remained secretary of the editorial offices until the summer of 1929. Ulianova had brought them on board during the Civil War, and stayed in touch with both by letter as late as 1935. *Pravdist*'s attacks on these men and their departments, presumably approved by Kovalev, were not just part of the debate about the direction of Soviet journalism. They were also part of Stalin's campaign to squeeze Ulianova, Bukharin, and their supporters out of *Pravda*.[43]

In late 1928 *Pravda* had three departments that handled reader letters, the Bureau of Investigation, the Workers and Peasants' Inspectorate Page, and the Department of Mass Journalism. Under Kovalev *Pravdist* began a series of articles attacking the first two departments for failure to process letters expeditiously, lack of "connection with the masses," and poor selection of correspondence for publication.[44] The point of these attacks became clear in early January 1929, when A. Romanovskii, head of the Department of Mass Work, wrote a piece for *Pravdist* arguing for handing over *all* letter-processing functions at *Pravda* to his section. Romanovskii promised to file all letters by theme and geographic provenance and answer every one.[45] The Department of Mass Work was the mass journalists' bailiwick, involved in organizing worker/peasant correspondents and production events. In late January or early February the editorial office production commission, headed by Kovalev and charged with cutting editorial staff costs, decided that the Department of Mass Work would process all correspondence and the other two departments would be shut down.[46]

The absorption of all letter-processing functions into the Department of Mass Work was not only aggrandizement of the mass journalists' position in the editorial offices, but also a commitment to a particular method of preparing reader correspondence for publication. Journalists working for the Inspectorate Page or Bureau of Investigation depended mostly on culling unsolicited correspondence to find publishable letters. Mass journalists referred to this as "spontaneity" *(stikhiinost)* and "drift" *(samotek)*, two of the most derogatory words in the Bolshevik lexicon. At the Department of Mass Work, on the other hand, "organizers" and "instructors" went into factories, collective farms, and other enterprises to solicit letters about specific topics. In this manner they "organized public opinion." This is not to say that readers stopped sending individual unsolicited complaints or denunciations, or that newspapers and prosecutorial organs stopped investigating them. But increasingly, *published* letters were solicited beforehand by journalists gathering material for particular propaganda campaigns.

In April 1929 Aleksei Kapustin, the founder of mass journalism, former editor of *Tverskaia pravda,* and now head of *Pravda's* Department of Worker Life, spelled out the advantages of soliciting collective letters from workers or others. Kapustin first noted the increase in *Pravda's* publication of such letters between 1928 and 1929. He explained that *Pravda's* journalists relied increasingly on such collective letters because of their "political quality . . . and organizational meaning." By composing the letter himself or at least "instructing" the authors, the journalist guaranteed that it would convey the proper political message. By getting many workers, collective farmers, or party cadres to sign, he effectively created the impression of mass support for party policies. Kapustin was still intensely concerned with controlling the worker and village correspondents' movement and generating appropriate letters, just as he had been when he organized the first production review in the spring of 1926.[47]

More and more, mass journalists tended to solicit worker signatures on collective letters. These were generally declarations of loyalty to Soviet Power and the party, oaths to fulfill certain production goals (as in a socialist competition), or paeans to party leaders. In the military image of Soviet society presented by the press during the First Five-Year Plan these collective letters figured as the bulletins from "loyal soldiers" at the production "front." The closing down of *Pravda's* Bureau of Investigation and Workers and Peasants Inspectorate Page was part of the trend toward such collective letters.

In the summer of 1929 mass journalists consolidated their control of

Pravda's editorial offices, as the Politburo replaced head editor Nikolai Bukharin with a three-man editorial bureau. Bukharin's firing coincided with a purge of the paper's party organization and a major reorganization of the editorial offices directed by Kovalev's production commission. In the last week of July 1929 the new editorial bureau approved the production commission's recommendation to merge the Rural Department, the Department of Worker Life, and the Department of Domestic News into a single Department of National (literally "Internal") Life.[48] It seems likely that the chief of the new department was Aleksei Kapustin, for in the weeks just before the reorganization, *Pravdist* had repeatedly suggested that Rabinovich, the chief of the Department of Domestic News, be purged and his department merged with Kapustin's Department of Worker Life.[49]

Together with the Department of Mass Work's absorption of the Inspectorate Page and the Bureau of Investigation, the merger of the three national news departments meant that more space would be devoted to mass journalism, and more resources would be available to mass journalists. *Pravda* would follow the path described by Bulyzhnik, Tanin, Kovalev, Naumov, and other mass journalists in the debates of 1928–1929. Its news would be more "political," organized almost entirely around party slogans. *Pravda*'s journalists would eschew the mere "registration of facts" and go out instead to the fields, the construction sites, and the factories to "organize public opinion" by soliciting collective letters and organizing news events such as socialist competitions. They would take a properly martial tone, rejecting the neutral language of wire service reports and the Chronicle. Above all they would seek to mobilize *Pravda*'s audience, the rank-and-file party activists, to carry out the tasks designated by the CC.

In the summer 1929 purge Kovalev and his allies removed most of the remaining veterans of the Bukharin-Ulianova years at *Pravda*. On July 17, 1929, Grigorii Filipchenko, proletarian poet and sometime *Pravda* employee, wrote to Ulianova, his friend and patroness since the Civil War years, describing conditions at the editorial offices. Ulianova was staying at a sanatorium, having apparently suffered a nervous breakdown as a result of the relentless Stalinist attacks on her at *Pravda*. "The purge commission," Filipchenko wrote, "has assigned all the old *Pravda* employees to leave and take up work at various places all over the Soviet Union." He gave a harrowing description of the ostracism and humiliation that the Stalinist mass journalists heaped on the remaining veterans. "Life is one big insult, they are crushing me . . . it is impossible to defend oneself. One can say nothing: they distort it all, twist it until it is unrecognizable, until it has the opposite meaning. . . . I will find work somewhere [else]. I can't stand it here. Quarrels are already breaking out among the victors, it's very tense."[50]

With the ascension of the Stalinists at the editorial offices, the imperative to mobilize activists to carry out the First Five-Year plan replaced the gradualist mass enlightenment project. The Stalinist mass journalists brought with them a new martial language and new methods for presenting Soviet society as an army following the commands of the party leaders. It is a great irony that the new journalistic language and techniques developed as part of the very mass enlightenment project that mass journalists rejected. Ulianova and Bukharin were two of the early advocates of a strong, well-organized worker/peasant correspondents' movement, yet in large part, veterans of that movement were the ones who overthrew them.

Ivan Gronskii and the Transition to Mass Journalism at *Izvestiia*

At *Pravda* the transition to mass journalism was a revolution, with violent debates between the mass journalists and the advocates of "information." At *Izvestiia*, however, senior editors acting in cooperation with the Central Committee apparatus managed the changeover, restraining militant mass journalists who advocated purges of nonparty staff. The shift to mass journalism was also more gradual than at *Pravda*. The newspaper began to take on a "mass" aspect in the spring of 1929, with imperative headlines, more military vocabulary, and more coverage of industrialization and collectivization. The transition period continued through 1931.

One important difference between *Izvestiia* and *Pravda* was the political alignment of its editors. In 1928–1929 Nikolai Bukharin at *Pravda* opposed Stalin, whereas the senior *Izvestiia* editors supported him. In 1927, even before the open outbreak of hostilities between Stalin and the Right Opposition, Ivan Gronskii, then second-in-command at *Izvestiia*, confronted Bukharin and his associates Maretskii and A. Slepkov in a debate about economic development at the Institute of Red Professors.[51] In his memoirs Gronskii claims to have been in daily telephone contact with Stalin throughout the 1928–1929 party political crisis, consulting with him about news coverage, the political situation, and Trotskyite activity in the editorial offices.[52]

Management style also helped to make the transition to mass

journalism less turbulent at *Izvestiia*. Gronskii, who became de facto editor-in-chief at *Izvestiia* in early 1928, proved adept at controlling his staff with a mixture of intimidation and conciliation. In the workplace he was disposed toward discipline and restraint, as opposed to vituperative self-criticism and denunciation. After an initial purge of the *Izvestiia* offices in the winter of 1926–1927, Gronskii resisted firing staff members.

Gronskii's "conservatism" was also reinforced by *Izvestiia*'s place within the Soviet press network. The central state newspaper, *Izvestiia* was generally understood by both editors and readers to be less "political" than *Pravda*, the central party organ.[53] Its target audience was educated city dwellers—professionals, engineers, government administrators, and the like. *Izvestiia* had more scope than party papers to present news of crime and accidents, science stories, theater reviews, and other nonpolitical items. Thanks to *Izvestiia*'s special place in the Soviet news network, to his own managerial skills, and to his connection with Stalin, Gronskii was able to keep rebellious young Communist reporters at his newspaper under control in 1928–1932 and manage a gradual transition to mass journalism.

Throughout his tenure at *Izvestiia* Gronskii had the support of the "class of 1926," the journalists who had come to the paper in the wake of the 1925 financial scandal and the resulting firings. Gronskii himself was a member of this class, along with a number of other writers and editors, including S. Raevskii, A. Starchakov, Ia. Selikh, L. Liam, G. Ryklin, M. Zhivov, A. Garri, A. Agranovskii, and E. Gnedin. Many of these men were recent graduates of the Institute of Red Professors.[54] They formed the backbone of the *Izvestiia* editorial staff until 1934, when Bukharin replaced Gronskii as editor-in-chief.

A shifting coalition of militant Communist writers, printers, and clerical staff contested Gronskii's authority at *Izvestiia*. Among those who challenged him regularly were the feuilletonists B. Levin and G. Lvovich. Both were mass journalists suspicious of Gronskii's "liberalism" toward nonparty staff and pursuit of sensational stories (Arctic expeditions, rescues, disasters, automobile races, and the like). In the summer of 1931 G. Krumin, newly appointed editor-in-chief, mobilized disgruntled staff in an attempt to dislodge Gronskii, but failed. Using the rhetoric of party discipline, his connection with Stalin, and his record as a promoter of mass journalism, Gronskii fended Krumin off and eventually had him transferred from *Izvestiia*.

Gronskii, a Civil War veteran and recent graduate of the Institute of

Red Professors, arrived at *Izvestiia* in June 1925. Nominally he was subordinate to editor-in-chief Ivan Skvortsov-Stepanov, but in fact he ran the paper. Skvortsov-Stepanov might be away from the office for months at a time, as in early 1926 when he went to Leningrad to manage the purge of Zinovev supporters from that city's press. Gronskii's first major task at *Izvestiia*, according to his memoirs, was to cleanse the editorial staff of about fifteen prerevolutionary reporters left over from *The Russian Word*, all of them working in the Moscow news department. In the winter of 1926–1927 he purged the veterans, gutting the Moscow department and promoting the concentration of "informational" news in the USSR department, staffed by fellow class of '26 members Starchakov and Zhivov. As a result national news fitting the Central Committee's agitprop agenda began to replace miscellaneous urban news.

Changes in the thematic organization of news also accompanied a second purge at *Izvestiia* in late 1927. The editors decided to shift from the organization of news items by location (sections headed "Kharkov," "Leningrad," "the Urals," etc.), to arrangement by "shock themes" designated by the Central Committee Agitprop Department ("Grain Procurements," "Labor Discipline," "Elections to the Soviets"). Under Gronskii's direction, then, the increasing "Communization" of *Izvestiia*'s staff was linked with growing subordination to the Central Committee's agitprop agenda.[55]

In the first months of 1929, almost one year after the beginning of the Central Committee's self-criticism campaign, *Izvestiia* editors and writers began to make the newspaper's headlines more militant. They abandoned neutral titles such as "Entering the Second Quarter [of the fiscal year]" or "Health Care in Five Years" for imperative phrases and shock vocabulary. At the same time the editors began discussing the possibility of reorganizing the letters department, the Bureau of Investigation. After a routine report on the bureau's work on February 6, 1929, a number of senior journalists spoke up with criticisms. Gronskii and some of his editorial board colleagues taxed the bureau with passivity, contending that *Izvestiia* needed to publish more of its material. The bureau needed to coordinate the letters it published with ongoing party campaigns and use "roving Communist correspondents" to "seek out the weak points of our (socialist) construction" and organize letter writing campaigns.

The harshest criticism of the bureau came from Lvovich and another writer by the name of Ivanov. Lvovich argued that under the existing system of passively receiving letters, "the most part of the complaints reaching the bureau come from class alien elements—kulaks, artisans, priests." To combat this tendency, the bureau had to make an active effort to correspond with workers. Ivanov chimed in that "even thieves" wrote in to the bureau. Lvovich and Ivanov were pointing to the "public mood" problem discussed in Chapters 3 and 4, namely the flood of complaints, denunciations, and critical comments sent in to the newspapers. This flood appeared to threaten the bases of party propaganda work. It required both an explanation and an active response. The explanation, in the view of Lvovich and Ivanov, was that "class alien elements" were writing in. The proper response was to organize friendly classes (the proletariat, poor peasants) to write in with politically correct letters. Essentially Lvovich and Ivanov took the same line as Aleksei Kapustin at *Pravda*—letter departments needed to "organize public opinion."[56]

Izvestiia's transition to mass journalism accelerated in August 1929, as an editorial commission headed by Gronskii reviewed the work of the newspaper's various departments. In a self-evaluation submitted to the commission, editors of the Soviet Construction section suggested important changes in their department's priorities, including more news about the role of local soviets in industrialization and collectivization, more coverage of the provinces, and more use of material from local correspondents. The department would send its own staff to the provinces to recruit correspondents and maintain regular communication with them through "instructional letters" explaining what themes to write about. It would broaden its thematic content from specifically "soviet" topics such as the redrawing of county *(raion)* boundaries to major Central Committee propaganda campaigns such as the promotion of grain procurements, the expansion of sown area, and the elimination of illiteracy. The editors proposed to model their department on *Pravda*'s Party Department, now leading the mass journalistic revolution in the Soviet central press. They referred to the department's new role as "political propagandist and *organizer of the masses* around the soviets."[57]

The Gronskii commission also reviewed the work of the Information Department. Its report criticized the department editors for failing to cultivate ties with "party-Soviet *obshchestvennost* (official society)," and ordered it to make "direct connection with the masses," propagate "the experience of the localities," and put "hot issues" on its agenda. The department was to recruit worker/peasant correspondents at large industrial enterprises, construction sites, and collective farms.

Correspondents were preferably to be activists working "directly in production," "sufficiently qualified and politically developed" to fit their own experiences into the larger frameworks of party agitprop campaigns.[58]

During the winter of 1929–1930 *Izvestiia*'s adoption of mass journalistic methods proceeded apace. On December 1, the editorial board ordered the Information Department to send *all* of its reporters and writers out to industrial sites and collective farms to cover "the life of the enterprises and their lower-level production cells."[59] At an early December general meeting, the newspaper's party members approved a resolution that affirmed the need for "organizational-leadership work" rather than mere "reflection of what is," thus endorsing the most fundamental principle of mass journalism. The resolution also promised that *Izvestiia* would "disseminate the experience of our great construction sites in a timely fashion and find new forms to present material."[60] Between January and March 1930 editors organized and dispatched several "brigades" of *Izvestiia* correspondents to cover the spring sowing campaign in the Middle Volga region. Imitating the work of *Komsomolskaia pravda* at Leningrad factories, two of the *Izvestiia* brigades set up mobile editorial offices that published newspapers for local distribution.[61] Also early that year *Izvestiia* dispatched writers to important factory construction sites in the provinces, such as Stalingrad's Tractor Factory. Later that summer, on Gronskii's initiative, the newspaper introduced a new department, called For the Fulfillment of the Economic Plan.[62]

The impetus for *Izvestiia*'s adoption of mass journalistic methods seems to have come from the CC executive apparatus. There was plenty of direct contact between Central Committee officials and *Izvestiia* editors. Gronskii was in regular contact with Stalin by telephone throughout this period. *Izvestiia* department heads routinely attended briefings at the CC Agitprop Department offices, and the editorial board paid attention to CC directives.[63] At a March 1, 1930, editorial board meeting devoted to coverage of the spring sowing campaign, editor P. G. Baranchikov complained that *Izvestiia* still had not fully implemented "the Central Committee's resolution on reforming our work."[64] Baranchikov was probably referring to a Central Committee circular of January 25, 1930, which instructed a number of newspapers, including *Izvestiia*, to introduce "a special department of operational reports on the achievements and shortcomings of factories, mines, trusts, railroads, enterprises of the sea and river merchant marine, state farms, and collective farms."[65]

Gronskii avoided a full-scale purge of the *Izvestiia* staff after 1926, but the transition to mass journalism was nonetheless difficult. The paper could not shake its reputation inside the party as "apolitical," soft line, a mere "registrar of facts." As the radical rhetoric of the "Cultural Revolution" and the First Five-Year Plan reached a crescendo, the future for young journalists seemed to lie at more militant papers such as *Komsomolskaia pravda*. As a result many writers left *Izvestiia* in the spring of 1930.[66]

Other problems were associated with the actual practice of mass journalism. By April 1930 the cost of sending journalists to the provinces, communicating with them by telephone or telegraph, paying their living expenses, and setting up mobile editorial offices forced the editors to consider cuts in the newspaper's correspondent network. By the summer it was also evident that in the rush to send writers out to the provinces, no one had bothered to work out just what the new methods of "brigade work" entailed, or to instruct the writers in them. Many of the journalists had no idea how they were supposed to go about organizing brigades of local correspondents. So they made up fake brigades, writing pieces for the newspaper themselves and then collecting signatures on them from workers or collective farmers. In some cases journalists did not even go to the trouble of collecting signatures, but forged them.[67]

The fabrication of brigades by *Izvestiia* writers demonstrates how, in response to central demands for news of ordinary work experience and proletarian "heroes of socialist construction" Soviet journalists created what Jeffrey Brooks has called a "hyperreality." This was a particular optimistic "public vision of the world" characteristic not just of Stalinist press coverage, but also of socialist realist literature. Under pressure from the center to produce news of heroes from field and shop floor, and without much time or guidance, some *Izvestiia* writers just made up their stories. Brooks views the creation of the socialist realist "hyperreality" as the result of a complex interaction between upper-level officials and journalists. The *Izvestiia* story confirms his hypothesis and indicates that the hyperreality was ultimately generated by CC demands for a certain kind of news.[68]

The summer of 1930 began a new round of conflict at the *Izvestiia* editorial offices, threatening Gronskii's leadership of the paper. The CC transferred G. I. Krumin from the *Pravda* editorial board to the post of *Izvestiia* editor-in-chief just as disagreements about the "excesses" of collectivization divided editors and journalists at the latter paper.[69] On top of all this the Sixteenth Party Congress's endorsement of brigade methods of work generated renewed efforts to adopt the techniques of mass journalism.[70] Against this background Krumin tried to wrest control of *Izvestiia* from Gronskii by mobilizing preexisting hostility against him, playing on the militants' sense that he was soft on the peasantry, uncommitted to mass work, and opposed to self-criticism.

Immediately upon arrival at *Izvestiia*, Krumin appointed a commission to draft a plan for reorganizing the editorial offices (July 22, 1930). The commission included two Gronskii allies (the editors Baranchikov and Selikh) and at least one of his critics, the young Communist reporter Mezhlumian.[71] On August 31 commission chairperson Liia Polonskaia and Krumin presented the commission's reorganization plan to a closed meeting of *Izvestiia*'s party members. They argued for an extensive Communization of the staff and for a reorganization of the editorial staff departments. Krumin and Polonskaia proposed that *all* of the paper's news departments, rather than just the Information Department, begin organizing brigades of writers and worker/peasant correspondents. Mass work would be expanded and the handling of news and information accelerated and streamlined so as to ensure its efficient transmission to the populace. All newspaper departments had to learn to fit their news material into party propaganda campaigns and transmit that news rapidly.[72]

Krumin's proposed reorganization of the editorial office set off the most serious battles at *Izvestiia* since the 1926–1927 purges. Gronskii's opponents, including the mass journalists Lvovich and Levin, rallied to support the new head editor. For about nine months, until April 1931, *Izvestiia* was thrown into turmoil. Krumin's allies attacked Gronskii for failure to purge politically unreliable staff members, promote proletarians to editorial office jobs, or develop mass work. They charged that under Gronskii *Izvestiia* had not sustained contacts with provincial correspondents or published exposés of "rot" in the bureaucracy. The dispute spilled over into larger political issues, as Krumin's supporters criticized Gronskii and the class of 1926 for supposedly expressing doubts about forced collectivization. Ultimately, however, Gronskii was able to use his connection with Stalin to secure Krumin's removal. His allies in the *Izvestiia* party organization then disciplined his remaining opponents on charges of Trotskyism.[73]

In spite of editorial conflict both Gronskii and Krumin expanded mass journalism at *Izvestiia* throughout this period. In the late summer and fall of 1930 *Izvestiia* was once again dispatching correspondents' brigades to the Middle Volga region, this time to report on the harvest.[74] In March 1931 *Izvestiia* journalists were trying to take on planning and coordination functions in the economy, mediating a dispute between managers supervising the construction of the Cheliabinsk Tractor Factory and the steel trust Stalmost over the latter's late delivery of construction materials.[75]

There was a clear mandate from above for all of this. In April 1931 the Central Committee's issue of a directive on the supervision of the worker/peasant correspondents' movement gave a renewed impetus to mass work at *Izvestiia* and other Soviet newspapers. The directive called for worker/peasants correspondents to focus on solving concrete problems of production (the mechanization of coal quarrying, for instance), publicizing positive achievements, and denouncing the regime's political enemies. Newspapers and local party committees were to strengthen supervision of the correspondents through the appointment of more "instructors" and the formation of combined brigades of experienced journalists and correspondents.[76] In response to this directive *Izvestiia* editors implemented the Krumin/Polonskaia proposal for expanding mass work to all departments. They also ordered the expansion of the newspaper's worker correspondent network in provincial factories, the establishment of "organic ties" with enterprise wall newspapers, and increased supervision of correspondents through regular instructional meetings, individual correspondence, and printed circulars.[77]

The April 1931 directive on the worker/peasant correspondents' movement reflected CC agitprop officials' increased concern with showing the "positive achievements" of the ordinary men and women working to industrialize the USSR. *Izvestiia* editors followed the CC's new direction. In late June 1931 they passed a resolution prescribing a new face for *Izvestiia*'s news and literary journal, *Krasnaia niva (Red Field)*. Finding fault with *Red Field* for its "dry and stereotyped" summary of domestic news and its unorganized, "weak . . . sentimental" coverage of foreign news, the editors decided to transform it into a "genuine militant organ of socialist construction." This meant the journal "should consider one of its most pressing tasks a visit in literary form to various detachments of socialist construction, and also systematically present literary portraits of the heroes of the Five Year Plan." In pursuit of these goals *Red Field* needed to solicit contributions from "proletarian writers and strike workers."[78] The *Izvestiia* editors' decision to transform *Red Field* foreshadowed the next episode in Gronskii's professional life—his involvement in the creation of socialist realism, an officially sanctioned literary genre that would "show the heroes of socialist construction."

The End of Reader Studies

In 1929–1930 party agitprop specialists intent on mobilizing Soviet society to fulfill the First Five-Year Plan put an end to rigorous studies of reader response to the newspapers. They argued that the press's primary function was to issue orders and that reader reception was "subjective," whereas the party line embodied absolute truth. In place of reader studies based on anonymous questionnaires, Soviet agitprop officials and newspapermen adopted the mass journalists' alternative, reader conferences. Pioneered in the mid-1920s by The State Publishing House (GIZ), and mass newspapers trying to sell subscriptions, the reader conference usually began with a formal presentation, either a public reading or a lecture by a journalist. Readers attending the conference would then comment on the book or newspaper under discussion. Because the comments were made in a large public forum, the conference was not an effective way to gauge readers' private response to print materials. In most cases propagandists used the conferences to educate readers in the "correct" response through the preliminary presentation and verbal feedback on their comments. Newspapers ran them also to sell subscriptions. Reader conferences were thus an excellent means of "organizing public opinion," and CC Agitprop officials in 1928–1929 encouraged publishers to set up as many as possible.[79]

Why did the reader study based on anonymous questionnaires disappear? In 1928 the mass journalists' trumpeting of their slogan "Closer to the Masses" actually prompted a new wave of such studies, including efforts at *Pravda* and *Worker Moscow*.[80] But in 1930 an ideological sea change washed reader studies away. Under the pressure of the First Five-Year Plan mobilization, party theorists transformed Bolsheviks' self-image. They abandoned the view, common during the NEP years, of the party as a technician of history, manipulating a complex social system and coaxing the reluctant masses toward socialist enlightenment. Instead, they portrayed the party and particularly the Central Committee leaders as the prime movers of history, issuing commandments like the Old Testament God. This change owed much to mass journalists' relentless exaltation of "organization" over the educational and informational functions of journalism. Stalin and his compatriots issued orders and cadres obeyed—thus would socialism be achieved. Under these assumptions, reader studies were obviously superfluous.

Zhurnalist (Journalist), organ of the journalists' professional union and, unofficially, of the CC Agitprop Department, opened the assault on reader studies in March 1930. The attack was led by M. Bochacher, a prominent advocate of mass journalism who had reported in *Journalist* favorably on the "mass methods" employed by Baku's Komsomol organ *Vyshka (The Derrick)*. The elimination of reader studies was linked with the rise of mass journalism from the beginning. The core of Bochacher's argument was that the newspaper was "an objective reality," whereas reader response was "subjective," fickle, and hence not worthy of scientific study. Frivolous writers of fiction might cater to their audience's philistine tastes, but newspapers ought to be more serious. The study of reader response, Bochacher wrote, "brings us into the subjective sphere of 'subjective projections' of tastes, interests, and fashions." Trying to adjust the newspaper to those tastes and interests was tantamount to "pluralism," acknowledging the validity of alternative worldviews. Bochacher's argument was quite confused, but behind it there lay the idea that Marxist theory gave journalists such a precise and true picture of "social relations" that there was no need to supplement it with empirical studies. Doing empirical studies implied that Marxist theories of history and society might be incomplete and thus constituted a threat to the party's authority.[81]

In his article Bochacher attacked Mikhail Gus and two other advocates of reader studies, V. Kuzmichev and N. Rubakin. According to Vadim Volkov, Kuzmichev and Rubakin theorized reading as an "active process whereby meaning was constructed through the reader's projection of certain individual and group mental dispositions." The idea that readers' reception of print material might be out of the author's control threatened the whole notion of propaganda with the possibility of unstable, multiple meanings. It also undermined the concept of "enlightenment," the idea that Soviet propaganda simply had to shine the light of Marxist theory through the confused and chaotic darkness of culture to illuminate "reality."[82]

Mikhail Gus published a rejoinder to Bochacher's attack in the same issue of *Journalist*. The only "objective" reality, he argued, was to be found in the dialectical *relationship* between newspaper and reader. This was the object of reader studies. Gus denied that the newspaper was a one-way conveyor belt of the party's message to the masses. Although the party was the "primary producer" of the newspaper, the masses themselves participated in production directly by writing to the editors and indirectly through political activity. Gus tried to historicize the relationship between party and proletariat, claiming in effect that Bolshevik ideology was a historically conditioned outcome of the interaction between the two. It was progressive in the sense that the alliance was determining the shape of the next great era of world history, but it was not absolute truth.[83] Gus's ideas were clearly more Marxist than Bochacher's (they were also more coherent), but as the party approached the Great Break its members were not in the mood for subtle, dialectical arguments. The party's job was to lead the masses through crisis to socialism, and the press was to disseminate the leaders' orders. There was no time or patience for the slow evolution of party and masses as complex "subject/objects."

A drumbeat of attacks on Gus and Kuzmichev followed Bochacher's piece in *Journalist*. In the journal's March 15 issue V. Kugel criticized Kuzmichev's new book, *The Organization of Public Opinion*, for recommending that Soviet newspapermen study the new American "science" of public relations. The role of the press in bourgeois society, Kugel contended, was to sell false consciousness—the bourgeois worldview—to the working class. But in the USSR newspapers taught workers and peasants their real class interests. Thus bourgeois public relations amounted to a catalog of tricks, whereas Soviet propaganda presented the truth. In Kugel's account, Soviet journalists did not need trickery, nor did they need reader studies to tell them how to appeal to their audience. The truth was simple.[84]

The attacks continued with reviews of two of Gus's new books, *Information in the Newspaper*, and *Problems of Newspaper Studies*. In April a student at the State Institute of Journalism (GIZh), P. Cherepenin, published a barbed evaluation of the first work. *Information in the Newspaper*, Cherepenin claimed, undervalued the organizational function of the press, choosing instead to concentrate on education *(vospitanie)*. At this particular moment, as the party began the drive to industrialize the USSR, Cherepenin argued, the newspapers' role as "organizer of the masses around the party, around concrete slogans," was of paramount importance. He also challenged Gus's proposition that militant, agitational slogans were inherently superficial. "What is wrong," he asked, "with the formulation of ideas in slogans?"[85]

Two months later, in June, B. Reznikov reviewed *Problems of Newspaper Studies*, a collection of articles edited by Gus. Reznikov focused on the individual contributions by Gus and Kuzmichev. He criticized Gus for differentiating between the proletariat (the "object" of the party's propaganda) and the party (the "subject" that created the propaganda). In reality, Reznikov asserted, the party and proletariat were one. To state otherwise was to make the proletariat into a passive object of the party's manipulation, rather than an evolving, self-realizing subject. Reznikov's arguments obviated the need for reader studies. The party and proletariat were identical, therefore the party did not need to seek knowledge about the proletariat.[86]

In the summer of 1930 debates about newspaper studies culminated in a dispute about pedagogical methods at the State Institute of Journalism. The result was the defeat and purge of advocates of reader studies and "information" (as opposed to agitation). The most prominent victims were Gus and A. Kurs, an instructor at the institute and former editor of *Journalist* and the Siberian newspaper *Sovetskaia sibir (Soviet Siberia)*. Kurs had recently proposed a revised three-year curriculum for GIZh that would emphasize reporting, information-processing skills, and reader studies. Like Gus, he believed that Soviet journalists had much to learn from the bourgeois press, especially in America. Among Gus's and Kurs's prominent opponents was Viktor Filov, former editor of *The Urals Worker*, mass journalist, and now head editor of the CC's *Worker Gazette*. Filov accused Kurs in particular of advocating "apolitical" and "technical" pedagogy, undervaluing courses in Marxism, and overvaluing the experience of the bourgeois press.[87]

Komsomolskaia pravda, a longtime opponent of Gus's "theory of information," supported mass journalists at GIZh in the spring and summer of 1930 with articles denouncing Kurs and other "Right Opportunist" proponents of "the bourgeois theory of newspaper studies." Pedagogical questions were not all that was at stake in these attacks. The Komsomol organ also charged Gus, Kurs, and other GIZh instructors with sympathy for the Right Deviation and doubts about collectivization. In the summer of 1930 GIZh was reorganized and renamed the *Communist* Institute of Journalism, or KIZh. In October the GPU (the secret police) accused Kurs and other instructors at the institute of connections with Syrtsov and Lominadze, two prominent party members under investigation for Rightist sympathies and opposition to forced collectivization. The CCC expelled Kurs from the party, and he lost his position at the Institute of Journalism. Gus apparently also lost his teaching job about this time. Agitprop officials "honored" both men by naming a new deviation after them—"the

Gus-Kurs Deviation" in newspaper studies. With this label, party bureaucrats and mass journalists marked off a new orthodoxy in journalism studies, an orthodoxy that excluded neutral presentation of information, reader studies, and the differentiation of newspapers by target audience.[88]

In a time of crisis, when party leaders thought they needed to send their cadres the most unequivocal, direct messages possible, the NEP project of gradually enlightening the masses was collapsing. Reader studies disappeared with the collapse. Increasingly, agitprop specialists accepted a set of simple (and often contradictory) assumptions about their newspapers. The press's primary job was to convey party orders to its own cadres and the nonparty masses through militant sloganeering. It was not for the cadres or the masses to wonder about the correctness or consequences of the party's instructions. As Stalin was fond of saying, the Soviet press was not a "discussion club." Readers and journalists both could rest assured that the newspapers reflected "objective reality." The party, as avant-garde of the working class, knew the true class interests of the proletariat and expressed them through the press. Precisely because the party *was* the proletariat, there was no need to interrogate workers' reading comprehension with reader studies. The party *already knew* the true interests of the proletarians. Those workers who questioned that knowledge simply displayed their "backward" political consciousness.

Mass journalists such as Bochacher and Filov led the assault on reader studies and its practitioners, most prominently Gus. They connected reader studies to the neutral presentation of information and the educational function of the press. Their attack, however, resonated outside journalistic circles. It was part of a larger ideological shift connected with the collapse of the NEP mass enlightenment project, namely the removal of the party from *within* history, and its establishment as History itself. From being a contingent object of underlying historical forces, the party became the primary moving subject of History. During the NEP era, party theoreticians had pondered the relationship between party and proletariat as a complex historical and sociological problem. They saw the party's rise to power as contingent upon deeper social and economic forces. Thus, for Kuzmichev and Gus, the party might be the primary progressive actor in the world, a surfer riding the forward wave of history, but that did not ensure that party leaders knew much about the currents and winds that moved them forward. Hence the need for study of social relations, including reader reception of the party press. But in the new narrative, the party itself *became* the moving force of History with a capital "H." Because they were the embodiment of the social forces pushing History forward, party leaders had no need for empirical study of society. Under these assumptions, it no more made sense to question the direction taken by the party than it did to question the course and amplitude of an ocean wave.

The Central Committee Retargets the Press

The appointment of mass journalists to key positions in the central press was part of a drive by the CC Agitprop Department to retarget the newspapers. Once Stalin and his allies in the CC had made the very risky decision for collectivization and rapid industrialization, they needed to reinforce the weakest blocks in the Bolshevik support base. In their view these were new recruits to the party and the masses of "green" workers newly arrived from the countryside. In the winter of 1927–1928 party agitprop officials began retargeting the press at these groups, mostly through the promotion of agitation, mass journalism, and the shock campaign. The long-term effect was to homogenize high-circulation Soviet newspapers and weaken the differentiation of the press by target audience.

In changing the orientation of the press, the Soviet leaders responded to a social revolution that they themselves were making "from above." Between 1924 and 1933 the Communist Party recruited millions of new members, increasing in size from less than half-a-million members to 3.5 million. The "Lenin Enrollment" of 1924–1925 alone brought 200,000 new "workers from the bench" into the party.[89] The working class also expanded rapidly as the USSR industrialized after 1926. According to official figures the number of industrial workers in the Soviet Union grew from just over 2.3 million in 1926 to almost 8 million in 1937. Most of the new workers came from the countryside, and the Bolshevik leaders were deeply suspicious of their "backward peasant mentality."[90] In similar fashion they worried about the "political illiteracy" and ideological unreliability of new party members.

The unreliability of newly recruited workers and politically illiterate party activists had been a major concern of the party leadership since 1926. Early on, party leaders focused their attention on the penetration of the worker correspondents' movement by hostile or ignorant workers newly arrived from the countryside. Nikolai Bukharin, in his speech to the Third All-Union Conference of Worker/Village Correspondents in May 1926, cautioned that "the influx of new strata of workers into production will undoubtedly be reflected in the worker/village correspondents movement, that petty bourgeois of the city and the countryside will undoubtedly seek to express their 'ideals' [while] masquerading as worker/peasant correspondents." To demonstrate that this was already happening, Bukharin read an excerpt from a hostile letter complaining of excessive party restraints on correspondents' freedom of expression.[91] Sergei Ingulov incorporated Bukharin's warning into his June 1926 lead editorial in *Journalist*, and CC secretaries repeated it in an August 1926 resolution calling for tighter supervision of the correspondents' movement.[92]

Apart from class contamination of the correspondents' movement, journalists and agitprop officials also worried about adjusting the press to reach "green" workers. During the March 1927 plenum of the journalists' union Central Bureau, Sergei Gusev, then head of the CC Press Department, warned that even so-called mass worker newspapers were too complex, "both in language and in composition" to reach "the mass of new workers, who especially need daily political tutoring." Gusev called for the creation of a cheap "popular mass newspaper to serve the new strata of workers." In general, he said, mass newspapers needed to work harder to exorcise the peasant moods of "backward groups" of the proletariat—to defuse demands for a repeal of the agricultural tax in kind, for example, and discredit the concept of an independent "Peasant Union."[93]

The resolutions of the Fifteenth Party Congress, which met in December 1927, noted the need to improve propaganda both for green party workers and new party recruits. They warned that the growth of the Soviet economy was sharpening class contradictions, forcing desperate "private-capitalist layers of the city and countryside" to greater efforts to propagandize "backward strata among artisans and craftsmen, peasants and workers." To break the influence of the "private-capitalist" social groups on backward peasants and workers, the party had to "intensify the struggle on ideological and cultural fronts." The congress also noted the imperative of "Leninist unity and proletarian discipline in the party's ranks, along with continuous work to raise members' ideological-theoretical and cultural levels," especially in view of the influx of workers into the party during the 1927 October Levy of new Communists.[94]

Between July 1928 and May 1931 CC agitprop officials made a series of decisions with the overall aim of retargeting the press at green workers and politically illiterate party activists. The project seems to have begun after the reorganization and merger of the CC Agitprop and Press Departments in the spring of 1928. On July 28, Sergei Ingulov, recently appointed head of the Agitprop Department's Newspaper Section, submitted a plan to the CC Secretariat for a major conference of newspaper editors from all over the USSR. Ingulov noted that this would be the first national conference of editors since 1925. He proposed to discuss the newly instituted self-criticism campaign (see the next chapter), coverage of collectivization and grain procurements, the training of new cadres of newspapermen, the financing of the press, and reaching *"the backward and new strata of workers and women workers."* In Ingulov's view all of these items were part of the party's new agitprop offensive connected with industrialization.[95]

Also in July 1928 the Agitprop Department drafted, and the CC Secretariat approved, a plan to publish a new "mass critical-bibliographical journal" aimed at middle-level party agitators, university students, and "the broad stratum of Soviet activists." According to the Agitprop Department report on the plan, existing literary/bibliographical journals served a very narrow intelligentsia readership, but were beyond the comprehension of the average reader. The new journal's chief task would be "to struggle mercilessly with distortions of the Leninist-Marxist line" in literature, guide readers' choice of books, and combat their illiteracy and ignorance. In December the plan was implemented with the founding of *Literaturnaia gazeta*, the official journal of the Soviet Writers' Union.[96]

Another move in the retargeting of the press was the CC Secretariat's April 1929 resolution "On the Newspaper *Poor Peasant*." During the Civil War *Poor Peasant* had been the CC's newspaper for ordinary peasants, but when *The Peasant Gazette* began publication in late 1923, it was retargeted at rural officialdom. Now the Secretariat ordered the paper to revive its earlier mass approach. In the resolution, drafted by Sergei Ingulov, the Secretariat commanded *Poor Peasant* to give more coverage to collectivization and kulak opposition to Soviet Power, to simplify its language to make it more accessible to the ordinary peasant, and to undertake more mass work, such as reader conferences and instructional meetings with peasant correspondents. Ingulov's unpublished report to the Secretariat indicated that the goal was to make *Poor Peasant* more accessible to village Communist activists and not just rural officials.[97]

Although some Bolshevik officials inveighed against the "abstract character," clichés, and repetitiveness of mass journalism's shock campaigns,[98] these were the party's tools of choice for reaching backward activists and workers. Ingulov made this clear in a summer 1928 report to the CC Orgburo evaluating the press's use of mass work. According to this report two core tasks of mass journalism were to "attract the most backward and passive laboring strata into civic-political life" and "activate local party, soviet, labor union, and official *[obshchestvenni]* organizations." Ingulov also mentioned mobilizing "the masses around core political slogans and economic campaigns" and encouraging them to offer constructive criticism of management. In short, the purpose of mass journalism was to organize lower-level party activists to carry out CC-designated tasks and pull backward workers and peasants into the party's sphere of influence.[99]

In his evaluation of the press's performance, Ingulov praised the work of the provincial newspapers that had pioneered mass journalism, especially *Tverskaia pravda, The Urals Worker, Luganskaia pravda,* and *Komsomolskaia pravda.*[100] This suggests that the CC's promotion of mass journalists from these organs into the central press was part of a conscious project to retarget the central newspapers. They were the source of the new methods agitprop officials demanded to mobilize activists, and they were the source of the cadres who knew those methods.

In the winter of 1929–1930 CC officials began a much more thorough overhaul of the Soviet press network than previously attempted. The twin imperatives of saving paper and refocusing the press on activists and green workers motivated the reform, which continued through 1932. The CC channeled resources toward mass newspapers and away from specialist publications, periodicals attached to minor institutions (the "institutional press"), and evening newspapers. The differentiation between newspapers by peasant and worker audience was watered down as the CC merged many provincial peasant papers with their worker counterparts. Some organs oriented toward more educated, white-collar readers were converted into mass newspapers (*Izvestiia,* for example, and the teachers' union organ *The Teacher's Gazette*), and others were closed (*Poor Peasant* and *The Industrial and Trade Gazette*).[101]

The first round of consolidation occurred in December 1929 and January 1930. In those months the CC Orgburo merged the central financial economic organs *Economic Life* (organ of the Council on Labor and Defense), *The Industrial and Trade Gazette* (organ of the Supreme Council on the Economy), and *The Transport Gazette* (organ of the Commissariat of Communications and Transportation) into a single publication, *Industrialization*, attached to the Supreme Council on the Economy. The CC also closed the evening newspaper *Evening Kiev*, and cut paper supply norms for other evening papers in Moscow, Leningrad, and Odessa by between 50 and 60 percent.[102] It shut down or reduced paper supplies to more than 100 specialty organs, ranging from *Natural Sciences in the Schools* to *State Insurance Bulletin*. In nineteen provinces mass peasant newspapers were folded into the main party organs, which were generally designated as mass worker papers.[103] The central cooperative press also took a hit. Two of the three central cooperative organs, *The Consumer Association* and *Cooperative Life*, were merged, and the third, *Rural Cooperatives*, was handed over to *The Peasant Gazette*.[104] A second, more extended, round of consolidation took place between May 1931 and January 1932 and involved the closure of 172 specialty journals, the consolidation of another 78 into only 32 publications, and major cuts in the labor union press.[105]

The most prominent casualty of the 1931–1932 consolidation was the CC's mass worker paper *The Worker Gazette*. With *Pravda*'s transformation into a mass organ for lower-level party activists *The Worker Gazette* lost its function in the CC press network. Given the limited supply of newsprint, the CC could not afford audience duplication between *Pravda* and *The Worker Gazette*. In January 1932 the Politburo closed down the latter paper.[106]

The commission that debated *The Worker Gazette*'s fate, chaired by Culture and Propaganda Department head Aleksandr Stetskii, produced a report that contained a succinct account of the retargeting of the Soviet press. According to this report the actual effect of reorganizing the newspaper network had been to target party activists *almost exclusively* and to slight green workers. "In recent years," it said, "there have been fundamental changes both in the newspaper network and in the [social] composition of the workers. In the newspaper network as it presently exists there is no newspaper that is truly and completely targeted at THE BROAD MASSES OF WORKER READERS. Simultaneously THE MASS OF WORKER READERS WHO ARE POORLY PREPARED POLITICALLY IS INCREASING, all new cadres are pouring into the ranks of the working class." Judging by Stetskii's report, then, by mid-1931 the Soviet newspaper network was aimed mostly at party activists.[107]

Between 1930 and 1932, the CC shifted newsprint and financial resources to periodicals serving party activists and, to a lesser extent, green workers. Periodicals serving urban white-collar readers, professionals, specialists, academics, and bureaucrats were cut in size or even closed down. Many peasant newspapers were also shut down, as were some labor union organs. The mass press became more and more homogeneous. Increasingly it spoke with the voice of central party officials, rather than middle-level state institutions (trusts, commissariats, labor unions, professional organizations). The consolidation of the newspaper network was part of the same overall process that transformed *Pravda, Izvestiia,* and other central newspapers into mass worker organs aimed at party activists.

The retargeting of the newspaper network was an attempt to mobilize available resources for the highest-priority tasks during a great crisis. Party leaders understood that forced collectivization and measures to raise productivity in industry would alienate both peasants and workers. Their first priority in this situation was to ensure the loyalty and reliability of their own cadres, the party rank-and-file. For the moment the CC put on hold the task of propagandizing the masses. They would make the Great Break without peasant or even working-class support, relying on coercion and Communists' loyalty to the party.

Emergency mobilization for specific tasks meant depriving the general population of attention and resources. This dynamic pervaded the Soviet system during the First Five-Year Plan. It applied not just to the energies of propagandists but also to material resources, and it linked purely "intellectual" production with material production. The newsprint shortage demonstrates the connection. In a time of crisis the limits on newsprint supplies forced journalists to cut lower-priority news, such as Chronicle items, out of the papers. It also forced them to channel available paper into production for the most important audience, party and Komsomol members. Indeed, party leaders considered getting newspapers to the grassroots activists so important that they deprived the general population of paper for other uses, such as wrapping, writing, and hygiene. Between 1924 and 1932 an increasing proportion of Soviet paper production went into newsprint and so-called cultural paper in general (newsprint, book paper, writing paper). By 1932 about one-third by weight of *all* Soviet paper production was in newsprint (see Table 4). During this same period the USSR eliminated paper imports entirely. All of this meant proportionally less paper available for packing, cleaning, rolling cigarettes, or using in the toilet. It demonstrates the extraordinarily high priority that the CC assigned to propaganda in general, and to propaganda aimed at activists in particular.

Table 4. Production of newsprint and "cultural paper" as a percentage of total
paper production (thousands of tons), 1924–1932

Year	Paper production	"Cultural paper"	Newsprint
1924–25	191.6	40.7%	6.0%
1925–26	228.4	35.5%	2.5%
1926–27	260.0	32.8%	0.0%
1928–29	384.0	52.1%	23.4%
1929–30	470.0	63.4%	30.4%
1931	497.0	64.3%	32.0%
1932	471.2	58.8%	32.5%

Sources: V. A. Veinova, *Bumazhnaia promyshlennost SSSR, 1917–1957 gg.* (Moscow: Goslesbumizdat, 1958), 97; GARF, f. 5566, op. 3, d. 4, l. 39; RTsKhIDNI, f. 17, op. 114, d. 315, ll. 50–57; d. 338, l. 3.

Concern with securing a political base during a fluid social and economic revolution made from above by party leaders motivated the retargeting of the mass press. Even as they moved to recruit millions of proletarians into the party and draw tens of millions of peasants into the cities Bolsheviks worried that these massive social shifts would undermine their previous support base among veteran workers. New arrivals in the party and the factories, they feared, would contaminate Marxist-Leninist ideology with "petty bourgeois" and "peasant" attitudes. The Bolsheviks solution was to focus the high-circulation newspapers on new party recruits and green workers. At all levels of the party agitprop apparatus and Soviet journalism there was remarkable consensus on the need to retool the press to reach these "backward" groups (although there was disagreement about the right way to go about it).

The creation of mass journalism and the retargeting of the newspaper network were collaborative efforts in which CC officials set up general problems of agitation and propaganda for solution by journalists. Party leaders provided overall guidance, but the newspapermen themselves created the solutions—the socialist competitions, the production reviews, the Komsomol "raids." This in turn suggests that the new forms of journalism that portrayed ordinary Communists as heroes of industrialization had real appeal for party cadres. After all, the young journalists who created them were themselves from the party rank and file. Seen from this angle the rise of mass journalism and of high

Stalinist culture as a whole looks less like a one-sided imposition by Stalin and a small group of high-level agitprop officials than a collaboration between party leaders and their new cadres. It was a product *of* the party leadership's "revolution from above," but *by* party officials and mass journalists.

~ 6

The Central Committee and Self-Criticism, 1928–1929

A CENTRAL THRUST OF the Central Committee's (CC's) cultural offensive of 1928–1929 was the "self-criticism" campaign initiated in April 1928. In that month a joint plenary meeting of the CC and the Central Control Commission (CCC) called for the mobilization of ordinary workers and party activists for intensified criticism of factory management and Soviet institutions. This was in the immediate aftermath of the trial of bourgeois specialists (in this case engineers) accused of sabotaging production at the Shakhty coal mines in the Donbass. The term "self-criticism" *(samokritika)* did not refer to individual confession, as in the Chinese Cultural Revolution, but to the denunciation of corrupt or incompetent state employees by co-workers or journalists—the party/state system criticizing itself. The stated purpose of the 1928–1929 self-criticism campaign was to raise "class vigilance" against Shakhty-type sabotage, weed out corruption and inefficiency from the state apparatus, and make local party organizations more accountable both to central authorities and to "the nonparty masses." Judging from the denunciations and exposés published in the central press in the succeeding months, party leaders (in particular those allied with Stalin) intended the campaign to signal an end to New Economic Policy (NEP) era collaboration between Communist officials and private traders. They also aimed to harness labor unions to the drive for "labor discipline," and punish Rightist party officials who opposed forced collectivization and accelerated industrialization. The self-criticism campaign was thus one phase of Stalin's revolution from above, in which party officials attempted to use militant young Communist journalists and activists against doubters, shirkers, and supposed saboteurs in the state bureaucracy.

The main difficulty of the campaign was upholding party discipline and containing the anarchistic enthusiasm of the young militants. Mass journalism had two sides—aggressive exposure of "rot" in the party/state apparatus and the organization of shop-floor events designed to raise productivity. Throughout 1928 and 1929 Stalin, the other CC secretaries, and the leadership of the party's CCC struggled to rein in the press's most aggressive attacks while still using mass journalists to bully their political rivals and retarget the newspapers. In September 1929, having defeated the Right Deviation, they initiated a dramatic purge of militant newspaper editors. The victorious Stalinist leaders (Stalin, Kaganovich, Molotov, and Ordzhonikidze, to name the most prominent) thus signaled their determination to control self-criticism and discipline the mass journalists.

Debates about the proper role and limits of criticism in Soviet society went back to the beginning of the NEP era. At that time the journalists' labor union section had endorsed wide-ranging freedom of criticism for party newspapers and their worker/peasant correspondents. The section's Third Conference did this even as the Central Committee Orgburo passed a secret resolution that effectively barred press organs from criticizing party committees at the same or higher level in the administrative hierarchy.[1] During the belt-tightening campaign of 1926–1927 the issue of criticism heated up again as party officials encouraged the press to monitor production and expose inefficiency and corruption. Journalists questioned whether criticism of management improved productivity by mobilizing worker enthusiasm or reduced it by undermining labor discipline. Party leaders strove to sort constructive criticism from denunciations based on personal animus or disruptive impulse. They also tried to prevent "suppression of criticism" by local party officials.

After 1925 the proliferation of wall newspapers, the increasingly tight links between worker correspondents' circles and the Workers' and Peasants' Inspectorate (RKI), and the Komsomol's establishment of brigades of activists (the "Light Cavalry") who investigated bureaucratic malfeasance set up the institutional base for the self-criticism campaign of 1928–1929. Also, as discussed in Chapter 5, the Agitprop (agitation-and-propaganda) Department was reorganized in the winter of 1927–1928. As part of the restructuring the CC Agitprop and Press Departments abandoned close supervision of the local press, a move that may have opened the dam for an uncontrolled wave of denunciation in the provinces. Simultaneously, the new Agitprop Department leadership, A. I. Krinitskii and Sergei Ingulov, encouraged denunciations and unmasking of corrupt officials.[2]

After the April 1928 Central Committee/Central Control Commission plenum, party leaders' public statements about the self-criticism campaign followed two lines. At a mid-April speech to Moscow Komsomol activists on the results of the plenum, Stalin emphasized self-criticism's function as a tool for enforcing party discipline, heightening working-class vigilance against class enemies, and preparing workers "for the business of governing the country." Stalin opened his speech by noting the "businesslike character" of the plenum, the absence of oppositionists obstructing efficient work, and the overall lack of conflicts (draki) among delegates. He set up a distinction between "counterrevolutionary self-criticism," which questioned Central Committee policy decisions and aimed at undermining Soviet/party rule, and constructive criticism aimed at monitoring the apparatus's fulfillment of central decisions and improving Soviet institutions. Needless to say, Stalin encouraged the latter but swore to stamp out the former. Healthy, constructive criticism, he asserted, helped correct problems in the functioning of the state apparatus and fostered "the political culture of the working class." Stalin hoped "to develop in [the working class] the sense of being master of the country, to facilitate the working class's education in the business of governing the country." In spite of the success of the Revolution, the working class still did not have the "cultural strength" to govern. Properly controlled self-criticism would serve as a school in the "habits and ability to manage the country . . . the economy . . . industry." In Stalin's account, then, self-criticism was a tightly supervised "school" for the "tutelage" (vospitanie) of the working class and a finely tuned tool for surveillance and the enforcement of discipline.[3]

In contrast to Stalin's emphasis on discipline, the rooting out of opposition, and "tutelage," Nikolai Bukharin's focus was on "intra-party democracy." In a speech to Moscow Komsomol activists, Bukharin decried the lack of "democracy" within the party, asserting that the Shakhty Affair would not have been possible if there were "real democracy within the party." If there were real openness and discussion within the party, if there were true freedom of criticism, vigilant workers would have exposed the Shakhty plotters long before they did real damage. At the opening of the Fifteenth Conference of the Moscow province Komsomol in the last week of April 1928 Komsomol CC secretary Aleksandr Kosarev and *Komsomolskaia pravda* editor Taras Kostrov echoed the themes of Bukharin's speech. Kosarev called for a massive mobilization of Komsomol and party activists for "an attack on all fronts of our socialist construction," and Kostrov insisted that "democracy" was essential for the proper functioning of party and Komsomol cells. "The speech of a cell member at a cell meeting against a bureau decision," Kostrov said, "is not a violation of discipline, but rather of 'mutual self-protection' *[krugovaia poruka]*. It is a good thing when such mutual self-protection is violated." Under the slogan of "self-criticism," then, Kostrov and Bukharin were advocating freedom of policy discussion within the party, whereas Stalin promoted the monitoring of the state apparatus's fulfillment of central orders.[4]

Whatever the leadership's intentions for the campaign, the April Plenum's endorsement of self-criticism set off a firestorm of attacks on local party organizations in the central press. *Komsomolskaia pravda* and *The Worker Gazette* led the way, with *Pravda* and some of the provincial mass newspapers following close behind. Between March 1928 and September 1929 one exposé of provincial corruption and mismanagement followed another. Press attacks on party officials in Smolensk, Vladimir, Tver, Tula, Riazan, Baku, Astrakhan, Leningrad, and other districts were followed in most cases by judicial, GPU (secret police) or party disciplinary action against offenders. Militant journalists also attacked all-Union organizations, including labor unions, the Institute of Marxism-Leninism, and the Union of Atheists *(Soiuz bezbozhnikov)*. As self-criticism engulfed one institution after another, top party officials struggled to clear fire lanes that would limit damage without actually extinguishing the campaign itself.

The Worker Gazette and the Limits of Self-Criticism

The Worker Gazette was one of the pioneers of mass journalism, a mass worker newspaper targeted at rank-and-file factory operatives. But mass journalism, as already noted, was Janus-faced. Mass journalists such as Kapustin worked in tight coordination with local officials to promote production, whereas others, such as Kostrov undertook unauthorized exposés of corruption high up in the party hierarchy. *The Worker Gazette*, like *Komsomolskaia pravda*, had a reputation for particularly scathing exposés and caricatures of party officials who had fallen from favor. Within the editorial offices there was a long-running debate about the "negative" side of mass journalism—denunciation and self-criticism. What should the limits of public criticism in the USSR be? Was criticism "from below" necessary as a check on party and state authorities? What were the risks of mobilizing the anger of the "laboring masses" against authority?

Between the summer of 1928 and the fall of 1929 militant advocates of self-criticism struggled with moderates to dominate the newspaper's editorial offices. Among the moderates were Feliks Kon, an Old Bolshevik appointed head editor by the CC in November 1928, Olga Spandarian, editor of the children's journal *Murzilka*, Elena Akhmanova, head of the newspaper's Soviet News Subsection, and Ganetskaia, head of the paper's Party Department. Apart from Kon, all of these editors were women and two, Spandarian and Ganetskaia, were wives of Old Bolsheviks. All of these moderates approached the problem of self-criticism and denunciation with caution. They were acutely aware that inflaming popular anger was a game that might burn innocent victims and cause unexpected collateral damage. Arrayed against the moderate faction was a group of young party militants, including Iogan Altman, a Komsomol leader and head of *The Worker Gazette*'s Department of Party Life, S. Volodin, a former *Pravda* reporter who headed the party cell, M. Erlikh, chief of the Information Department, and Chernia, a member of the party cell bureau.

The Worker Gazette had a longtime reputation for aggressive denunciations of corrupt party officials and Oppositionists. The paper's writers jumped into the self-criticism campaign with zest. In July and early August 1928 *The Worker Gazette*, together with *Labor*, began running a series of articles exposing alleged disorders within the Vladimir party organization. Coverage was continuous and highly critical, including a regular section sarcastically headed "Review of Vladimir's 'Achievements.'" Party activists in the province were portrayed as drunks, shysters, and sexual debauchees. The Vladimir party secretary, I. Rumiantsev, demanded an investigation of the case by the CCC and also protested the newspapers' campaign to Stalin and Molotov. In its August 13, 1928, finding on the case, the CCC called the newspaper editors' decision to cover the "shortcomings" in the Vladimir organization correct, but noted their "political error" in publishing pieces that were "exaggerated and distorted" and of a "screeching sensational character." The CCC, in other words, intervened to moderate the tone of *The Worker Gazette*'s denunciations. The Central Committee Secretariat later downgraded the CCC's finding of a "political error" to a simple "error." Nonetheless the party leaders seem to have been fed up with *The Worker Gazette*'s obstreperousness, for they removed K. Maltsev from the head editorial post immediately after this incident.[5]

In the third week of November 1928 the Central Committee transferred Old Bolshevik Feliks Kon from his job as head editor of the Red Army newspaper *Red Star* to the head editorship of *The Worker Gazette*. Kon brought a raft of *Red Star* newspapermen with him, and he came with a mandate to tone down *The Worker Gazette* and bring militant advocates of self-criticism under control. In his first meeting with the party cell bureau, on November 20, Kon warned that *The Worker Gazette* journalists had forgotten that their newspaper was an organ of the CC, accusing them of "a chase after sensations." "We must struggle with the polemical tone taken [by the newspaper]," he asserted. Kon also said the newspaper would aim for a more highly cultured audience, "workers with high qualifications and a part of the party membership." *The Worker Gazette* had to become "a small *Pravda*," with more sophisticated coverage of politics and economics for party members. "The Information Department," he griped, "is limping, it chases after novelties, after sensations, and overlooks the life of factories and workshops." In discussion Elena Akhmanova offered Kon a strong endorsement, citing CCC Presidium member Solts's comment that *The Worker Gazette* "represented the 'yellow press.'" Volodin objected to Kon's comments. He contended that turning *The Worker Gazette* into "a small *Pravda*" meant betraying the newspaper's basic assignment as a mass workers' newspaper. Volodin's comment was the opening round in a duel with Kon that went on for almost a year.[6]

At the general party cell meeting the next day, Kon reiterated his warnings against sensationalism, urging journalists to check their facts more carefully before publishing denunciations and exposés. "We should take a businesslike approach to our materials, and not chase after 'color.'" Kon argued for positive organizing mass journalism, but against overzealous criticism. He endorsed more coverage of workers' movements abroad by the International News Department, and urged the Party Department to do more reporting on "worker activists." He also cautioned the Information Department reporters to give up their "chase after sensations" and present more "workers' chronicle" and other coverage supposedly of interest to "the factory operatives."[7]

There were a number of objections to Kon's speech from the floor. Volodin asserted that *The Worker Gazette* must remain "militant," and chided Kon that no matter how carefully journalists checked their facts some mistakes would always be made. S. Miasov, a reporter and Komsomol member who would later become a prominent advocate of mass journalism in *Journalist*, objected to Kon's criticism of reporters. He argued that a new kind of reporter had come into existence who was ready to participate in party propaganda campaigns and join the "editorial family" as a "full member with equal rights."[8]

The militance of *Worker Gazette*'s younger writers led to charges of "Trotskyism" against some and the intervention of the secret police. The first victim was Igor Maleev, a protegé of Taras Kostrov who came with him from Odessa to Moscow. Maleev was arrested in October 1928, about the same time Kostrov was fired from the editorship of *Komsomolskaia pravda*.[9] Then, in late January or early February 1929 Komsomol cell secretary Torchinskii was arrested by the GPU and charged with collaborating with Trotskyites and storing opposition literature in his apartment. On February 7, 1929, Iogan Altman informed a party meeting of Torchinskii's arrest, warning that "we must maintain personal relationships within the framework of healthy distrust, of comradely self-criticism." The meeting voted to exclude Torchinskii from the party and Komsomol.[10]

At *The Worker Gazette* the purge of party unreliables got under way earlier than at other newspapers, perhaps because of the "left" disorders among the Komsomol members. Between late March and late May 1929 a commission of head editor Feliks Kon, Olga Spandarian, and Ganetskaia, all moderates on self-criticism issues, organized and ran the purge. In addition to evaluating members' fulfillment of their assigned party work and their attendance at party meetings, the purge commission solicited comments about Communists from nonparty employees. The question of soliciting denunciations "from below" was a vexed one. The relatively moderate purge commission members chose to bring into the purge process only labor union activists, keeping rank-and-file employees out. Some party cell members, including Erlikh, objected, calling for the editorial office wall newspaper to "sound the alarm to the masses" and put out a box for denunciations from nonparty members. In response Elena Akhmanova accused Erlikh of wanting to create a "St. Bartholomew's Massacre," a nightmare of uncontrolled denunciation by angry lower-level workers (the reference was to a massacre of Protestants in sixteenth-century France). Here as at other times a clear distinction emerged between advocates of vigorous, unlimited self-criticism and moderates who feared the dangers of such a move.[11]

Party cell records do not show all of the purge results, but the purge commission did reprimand two cell members, Iastrebov and Plotkin, for failure to carry out their party assignments. A third journalist, Chernia, was questioned by the commission about his former Trotskyite sympathies and a denunciation from the management in his apartment building. Chernia escaped, however, without disciplinary action.[12]

Immediately after the conclusion of the party purge, the increasingly intense campaign against Nikolai Bukharin, A. I. Rykov, and the Right Opposition provided militants in the editorial offices with a chance to counterattack the moderates. At a June 14 party meeting Altman, Chernia, Plotkin, and one Dogmarov, a journalist hired by Altman, criticized Party Department head and moderate Ganetskaia for Rightist sympathies. Supposedly Ganetskaia had expressed doubt that Bukharin, Rykov, and their allies had really formed an antiparty faction. She also got into trouble for an incident several months old in which she questioned Altman's assertion that the Right was against self-criticism. In the face of these accusations Ganetskaia was defensive, but continued to assert that "Bukharin is not Zinovev" and "I still cannot believe that Bukharin would take the road of factional struggle." Akhmanova spoke up in Ganetskaia's defense, saying that she shared her pain at "losing Bukharin."[13]

The attack by Altman and others on Ganetskaia signaled the militants' ascendancy at *The Worker Gazette*. Throughout the summer the newspaper appears to have been run by Volodin and other radicals. Volodin and Information Department head Erlikh urged the editorial office wall newspaper *The Paper Clip* to "sharpen" its attacks on the administration (especially head editor Kon).[14] To Kon's intense anger, party cell members tried to dictate his hiring and firing decisions.[15] With regard to the newspaper's content, Volodin and other militants pursued an agenda of mass journalism and aggressive criticism of "bureaucratism" in Soviet institutions, especially the labor unions. The Bureaus of Worker/Peasant Correspondence and Investigation were merged with the Technical Secretariat in a single Department of Mass Work.[16]

Volodin and the other militants seem to have been unaware of their perilous standing with the CC leadership. CC attention was drawn to *The Worker Gazette* organization by a letter from a reporter, Lapinskii, who denounced the party cell leadership for attacking the senior editors and practically wresting control of the newspaper from them.[17] Not only were the militants savaging the CC's appointee to the head editorship, Kon, but they were also engaging in "sensational" assaults on various labor union organizations. In early September Volodin himself approved a series of pieces denouncing the Central Committee of the miners' union, a series that did not have the approval of party CC officials.[18] Within two weeks the Secretariat fired him as part of a much broader crackdown on excessively militant mass journalists.

Komsomolskaia pravda and Self-Criticism

Komsomolskaia pravda under Taras Kostrov was known for its "sensationalistic" attacks on official institutions, and these intensified as the self-criticism campaign took off. Within weeks the paper was in trouble with top party authorities. On June 26, 1928, Stalin published in *Pravda* a reprimand to *Komsomolskaia pravda* and other papers, "Against the Vulgarization of the Slogan of Self-Criticism." The party, he wrote, did not need all kinds of self-criticism, but only self-criticism that "raises the working class's level of culture, develops its militant spirit, strengthens its faith in victory, . . . helps it become the genuine master of the country."

> Some say that once we have self-criticism, we don't need *labor discipline*, we can quit work and busy ourselves with chatter about anything. . . . This is not self-criticism, but an insult to the working class. Self-criticism is necessary not for the undermining of labor discipline, but for its *strengthening*, in order to make labor discipline *conscious*, able to maintain itself against petty bourgeois laxness.

> Others say that once we have self-criticism, leadership is no longer demanded, it is possible to leave the wheel and let "things take their natural course." This is not self-criticism, but a disgrace. Self-criticism is necessary not to weaken leadership, but to strengthen it.[19]

Stalin admonished *Komsomolskaia pravda* not to "turn criticism into a *sport*, a striving for *sensation.* " He criticized the paper in particular for a caricature of the leadership of the Central Council of Labor Unions (VTsSPS), which it had run recently. Such coverage served no purpose other than "to make the philistine chuckle." The Komsomol's "Light Cavalry," Stalin warned, was in danger of turning into the "Frivolous Cavalry."[20]

Komsomolskaia pravda editors and the Komsomol CC were quite ready to defend themselves against Stalin's criticisms. On July 17 the Komsomol CC Bureau met and approved a letter to Stalin. The bureau denied Stalin's charges of sensationalism, putting the caricature of labor union leaders in the context of *Komsomolskaia pravda's* ongoing dispute with the Council of Labor Unions and the Commissariat of Labor over the reserving of a set percentage of factory job openings each year for new adolescent workers *(broni podrostkov)*. *Komsomolskaia pravda* and the Komsomol leadership objected to proposed cuts in the percentage of reserved positions. The bureau's letter to Stalin defended *Komsomolskaia pravda's* "principled position" on the issue and accused the labor union leadership of "not knowing where Marxism ends and Fordism begins." *Labor* (the organ of the Council of Labor Unions), the letter complained, had used Stalin's phrases against *Komsomolskaia pravda*. By attacking *Komsomolskaia pravda* and its "Light Cavalry" publicly, Stalin had undermined their campaign against "bureaucratism."[21]

In late November 1928 the Politburo decided to remove head editor Kostrov, holding him responsible for "incorrect, and at times simply untrue characterizations of the Right Deviation" and "conciliatory tendencies toward the Left Deviation" in the newspaper's coverage.[22] The removal appears to have had a double trigger. In September, Kostrov, along with V. V. Lominadze and L. A. Shatskin, both senior Komsomol officials, was involved in a confrontation with CC secretary Molotov at the Institute of Red Professors. The Komsomols demanded the right to name the leaders of the Right Deviation in print—Molotov refused to allow them to do so.[23] *Komsomolskaia pravda's* loud campaign against labor union bureaucratism (intended to discredit the labor union movement before its Eighth All-Union Congress) also played a role in Kostrov's dismissal. Although this campaign converged with attacks by Stalin's allies on the central union leadership,[24] *Komsomolskaia pravda* editors were probably offended by their hectoring insistence that the labor unions were failing to protect ordinary workers, especially young workers, from management abuses. In the first half of November, during the lead-up to the Eighth Congress of Labor Unions, *Komsomolskaia pravda* repeatedly stressed the need to protect workers' salary gains, pay apprentices according to the regular wage scale, expand in-service training, and improve working conditions and workplace safety.[25] The paper also ran pieces directly attacking Soviet managers for exploiting labor, such as a November 14 article that ran under banner headlines proclaiming "Labor Contracts Are Not for Them/Many Managers Violate Labor Contracts/Hundreds of Clauses Are Dead Letters."[26] *Komsomolskaia pravda's* repeated direct assaults on management flouted Stalin's June warning against turning self-criticism into "a tool for slandering our managers and other officials."[27] No doubt this was the background for the accusations of Left sympathies against the paper's editors.

The response of the Komsomol CC and *Komsomolskaia pravda* editors to Kostrov's removal was remarkably obstreperous. The Komsomol CC Bureau passed a resolution rejecting the Politburo's assertion that the *Komsomolskaia pravda* editorial board was deviating from "the party's general line," and calling on it to review Kostrov's dismissal. Simultaneously Kostrov's colleagues on the *Komsomolskaia pravda* editorial board, I. Bobryshev, D. Bukhartsev, Iakov Ilin, and M. Charov, tendered their resignations in a letter to the Politburo. The editors denied that they had ever shown "conciliatory tendencies toward the Left Deviation" or published "an incorrect . . . characterization of the Right Deviation." They backed up their assertion that they had always supported the party's general line with quotations from *Komsomolskaia pravda*, even comparing these with Stalin's words on the same issues. The four editors also reminded the Politburo of their services "in the struggle with the labor unions." Since the summer of 1927, they wrote, *Komsomolskaia pravda* had battled the unions on issues of protecting laboring youth. During the preparation for the Eighth Congress of Labor Unions the paper had attacked union bureaucratism in the same terms as other important central organs and Molotov himself. The *Komsomolskaia pravda* editors concluded by stating their intention to resign their positions in protest of the Politburo's censure.[28]

On December 1, three days after its initial meeting to deal with the Politburo's censure of *Komsomolskaia pravda*, the Komsomol CC Bureau convened again. This time it passed a motion "noting" the Politburo resolution, but not endorsing it. Bureau members tied six to six on a vote to deny the charges of "a conciliatory tendency toward the Left Deviation" at *Komsomolskaia pravda*. They voted unanimously, however, not to accept the resignations of the remaining four editorial board members, and they nominated one, Bobryshev, as their candidate to replace Kostrov as head editor. Rather than initiating a full-scale purge of *Komsomolskaia pravda* editors, a move that might well have pleased party leaders, the bureau chose to maintain the entire editorial staff intact, implicitly endorsing the newspaper's political line to date.[29] On December 12 the bureau did finally vote to approve the Politburo censure and ordered *Komsomolskaia pravda* to publish its text. The bureau also, however, confirmed Bobryshev, Ilin, Bukhartsev, and Charov as the newspaper's new editorial board.[30]

Kostrov's removal did not resolve the tensions between the CC leadership and *Komsomolskaia pravda,* nor did it moderate the Komsomol paper's tone. The paper continued to run exposés of labor unions, provincial party organizations, and other Soviet institutions. To cite four examples, in February 1929 *Komsomolskaia pravda* journalists accused labor unions of encouraging absenteeism and drunkenness at the Dnepr dam construction project, and in March they attacked critics at the national Academy of Arts as "reactionary idealists." In May they assailed the Moscow province committee of the union of sales personnel *(Soiuz sovtorgsluzhashchikh)* for ignoring complaints from their membership.[31] Then in June they undertook an assault on the Union of Atheists *(Soiuz bezbozhnikov),* which occasioned an intervention by Emelian Iaroslavskii and the party's CCC.

Komsomolskaia pravda ran regular antireligious campaigns around major religious holidays (especially Christmas and Easter), encouraging Komsomol members to participate in alternative atheist celebrations at workers' clubs, in cinemas, and on the street. The paper also egged members on to harass participants in religious ceremonies.[32] In early June 1929, the newspaper expanded its attacks to include the party's own Union of Atheists, accusing the organization of taking too soft a line against religion. Insofar as these attacks had a pragmatic goal, it appears to have been expanding the Komsomol's influence over antireligious activities and displacing the Union of Atheists. At the All-Union Congress of Atheists that June, Komsomol delegates openly confronted the union leadership in a debate over proper techniques of antireligious propaganda.

The Komsomol's hatchet men in the attack on the Union of Atheists were *Komsomolskaia pravda* editorial board member D. Bukhartsev and the writer M. Galaktionov. Bukhartsev and Galaktionov charged the union with neglect of grassroots organizational work in factories and villages, failure to participate in the Easter antireligious campaign, and ideological "conciliationism" *(primirenchestvo).* Under the latter charge, the *Komsomolskaia pravda* journalists included accusations that Union propaganda literature portrayed religion as a progressive force (in descriptions of Christian sectarian activity in labor union organization, for example). They also charged that the union viewed religion merely as "a survival of the old world" rather than "a weapon" in the hands of active class enemies of Soviet Power. Because the union leaders saw religion as a "survival," a kind of dark cloud of ignorance, they expected it to disperse naturally, and they opposed efforts to annihilate it because they feared these would alienate backward workers and peasants from the party. It was precisely an "annihilation" of religion that Bukhartsev and Galaktionov demanded. At the congress Komsomol delegates advocated "administrative measures" against religions (i.e., police action against religious celebrations), whereas union leaders argued for limiting antireligious action to the agitprop campaigns.[33]

As reported in *Komsomolskaia pravda*, debate at the Union Congress was very nasty. Anatolii Lunacharskii, the Commissar of Enlightenment and the quintessential soft-liner in the Bolshevik leadership, referred to Komsomol delegates as "Komsomol pups" *(Komsomolskie sobachenki)* after commentators in *Komsomolskaia pravda* criticized his presentation. Lunacharskii had portrayed Russian sectarianism as a late-coming "Reformation" that was working a positive spiritual revolution among Russian peasants.[34] When *Komsomolskaia pravda* editor Bukhartsev spoke to the congress, delegates from the Union of Atheists interrupted him, demanding his removal from the floor.[35]

Emelian Iaroslavskii, chairman of the CCC, delivered the congress's closing speech. In keeping with the CCC's overall commitment to controlling criticism, Iaroslavskii came down hard on the Komsomol militants, citing Stalin's article against the "vulgarization" of self-criticism. He also noted that Bukhartsev and Galaktionov were in opposition to the Thirteenth Party Congress's resolution restricting antireligious propaganda to the dissemination of "materialist explanations of natural phenomena and social life" (May 1924). Iaroslavskii also criticized the Komsomol spokesmen for not offering concrete suggestions for the improvement of antireligious propaganda and for their use of "anarchist phrases." Further, he confronted them with quotations from Lenin and Engels about the foolishness of alienating lower-class believers with gratuitous attacks on religion.[36]

With Iaroslavskii's intervention and the conclusion of the congress, *Komsomolskaia pravda* abruptly abandoned its assault on the Union of Atheists. In the fourth week of September the paper published a single article repeating criticisms of the union for neglecting grassroots activism, but otherwise the campaign ceased.[37] In the case of the Union of Atheists, as in *The Worker Gazette*'s attacks on the Vladimir Party organization, intervention by "moderates" based at the party CCC halted loud denunciatory campaigns by central mass newspapers. Iaroslavskii in particular seems to have been concerned with controlling rhetorical excesses and attacks on higher-level party institutions. But his actions often ran counter to those of the CC Agitprop Department, which generally encouraged aggressive criticism by the press. The contrast between Iaroslavskii's CCC and the Agitprop Department typified one of the most important dilemmas faced by the entire party leadership—how to use the newspapers to monitor the bureaucracy without undermining Communist authority as a whole.

Conflicting Signals on Self-Criticism

Agitprop Department officials, particularly department head Krinitskii and Ingulov, his deputy and head of the Newspaper Section, were much more supportive of denunciation and self-criticism than the CCC under Iaroslavskii. In two summer 1928 reports to the CC Orgburo, Ingulov emphasized the need to protect worker/peasant correspondents from censorship by local party organizations.[38] Labor unions, Ingulov claimed, were failing to fulfill their duty to defend worker correspondents against harassment and persecution.[39] He praised newspapers that engaged in aggressive denunciation, endorsed "the development of self-criticism from below," and stressed the danger of "a conciliatory attitude" among correspondents to incompetence and corruption in everyday work.[40]

The handling of accusations against the Tver party organization by *Tverskaia pravda* demonstrated Agitprop Department officials' readiness to support self-criticism. In January and February 1929 *Tverskaia pravda* ran a series of articles, picked up by *Pravda*, charging leading members of the Tver party organization with alcoholism, "suppression of self-criticism," and collaboration with "alien elements" (former landowners, merchants, and kulaks). *Tverskaia pravda* also charged that some officials were using personal connections to gain acquittals from province court judges. On March 7, 1929, a combined session of the province's party committee bureau and Control Commission Presidium considered the charges and ruled against *Tverskaia pravda*. Delegates took disciplinary action against court employees, but reprimanded the newspaper for its "sensational, demagogic spirit" and declared most of the charges false. They fired head editor Shafranskii.[41]

On April 5, 1929, the party CCC confirmed the Tver verdict, but also reprimanded the province party organization for inadequate supervision of the press. At the CCC session, however, CC Agitprop Department head Krinitskii defended Shafranskii, making charges of serious corruption inside the Tver party organization. On May 10 he wrote a letter to Iaroslavskii and CC secretary Lazar Kaganovich, protesting the CCC's support for the Tver party committee's "one-sided decision" and calling Shafranskii's firing "incorrect."[42] The Tver case demonstrated the policy split between the CCC and the Agitprop Department on issues of self-criticism. Whereas Iaroslavskii and his colleagues at the CCC tended to be skeptical of denunciations, Krinitskii and other Agitprop officials tended to believe them. The CCC protected local officials, but the Agitprop Department encouraged attacks on them.

Stalin, Molotov, and Kaganovich, the leading CC secretaries, generally stood with the CCC on issues of criticism. They tended to be tougher on self-criticism and militant journalists than the Agitprop Department. A November 1928 case involving the Donbass newspaper *Luganskaia pravda* and the Dnepropetrovsk organ *Zvezda (The Star)* demonstrates the point. Like cases of excessively militant self-criticism at *The Worker Gazette*, *Komsomolskaia pravda*, and *Tverskaia pravda*, the *Luganskaia pravda* incident illustrated how the newspapers that pleased central officials with their pioneering of mass journalistic techniques also annoyed them with their insubordination and militance.

The incident arose from exchanges of production experience conducted in Donbass coal mines and Dnepropetrovsk metallurgical factories by *Luganskaia pravda* and *The Star* respectively. In early November the two papers began publishing the workers' suggestions for improving production. On November 9 editors took the unusual step of addressing a number of worker proposals directly to the upcoming plenary session of the party CC. That day *Luganskaia pravda* ran on page one the headline "Our Proposals to the Central Committee Plenum," while *The Star* proclaimed, "Two of the greatest party organizations of the Ukraine, Dnepropetrovsk and Lugansk, on the pages of *Luganskaia pravda* and *The Star* place before the plenum a number of urgent tasks in the strengthening of metal production and the mining of coal." Among the proposals to the CC plenum were supplying the Dnepropetrovsk factories with more electrical power, approving the construction of a special machine-building factory, reopening a recently closed metallurgical factory, and introducing a three-shift system to the Donbass mines. The newspapers thus lobbied simultaneously for increased central investment in local industry and the intensification of labor.[43]

The verb *predlozhit* used by both *The Star* and *Luganskaia pravda* in their "appeal" *(obrashchenie)* to the CC had a more imperative ring than its English translation "to propose," especially in the Bolshevik political context. CC officials themselves used it as a synonym for "to instruct" or "to order" in communications with lower-level party and Soviet organizations. The newspapers' headlines had a demanding and presumptuous tone. The body of their texts addressed to the plenum had an even more imperative shading. *Luganskaia pravda*, for example, admonished the CC that "these proposals should be implemented in the shortest possible period of time—we suggest *[predlagaem]* no later than January 1." The imperative nature of these "proposals" was made explicit in a telegram released to TASS (Telegraph Agency of the Soviet Union) and all Ukrainian newspapers by RATAU, the Ukrainian Republic wire service, which said that *Luganskaia pravda* and *The Star* "have placed their *demands* before the Central Committee Plenum in the name of the miners of Lugansk and the metal workers of Dnepropetrovsk." Worried TASS employees forwarded this report to the Central Committee Agitprop Department, which halted publication.[44]

Luganskaia pravda and *The Star* had violated the top-down direction of self-criticism by directing their proposals *upward* to higher-level party organs rather than laterally to their own party committees or downward. Agitprop head Krinitskii recommended that the CC Secretariat censure the editors and issue a warning to the Ukrainian CC and the Lugansk and Dnepropetrovk regional party committees of the unacceptability of addressing demands to the CC plenum. The Ukrainian CC would consider the workers' proposals and carry out "explanatory work" in Lugansk and Dnepropetrovsk to help workers understand the two newspapers' mistakes and the proper role of the press in socialist construction. But when the CC Secretariat met to consider the Agitprop Department's recommendations on November 26, 1928, its members took a significantly harder line than Krinitskii had recommended. They fired the editors of *Luganskaia pravda* and *The Star*, censured the secretaries of the Lugansk and Dnepropetrovsk regional committees, ordered the Ukrainian CCC to "correct the unacceptable mistakes" of both papers, and instructed the Agitprop Department to place an article in *Pravda* reprimanding the papers.[45]

Nearly all central officials would have considered that press "demands" of the CC were unacceptable, but there was a significant difference in tolerance for militant self-criticism between the Central Committee secretaries and the officials of the Agitprop Department. Where Ingulov and Krinitskii wanted to give a light spanking to the *Luganskaia pravda* and *Star* editors, the CC secretaries fired them, sending a message to the entire Soviet press that the Central Committee would not tolerate insubordination. At the conclusion of the self-criticism campaign in September 1929 this difference would result in the firing of Ingulov and Krinitskii from the Agitprop Department.

The End of the Self-Criticism Campaign

In spite of increasingly frequent signals that top Central Committee leaders desired more coverage of positive achievements and less denunciation of "shortcomings" and "rotten spots" (gnoiniki),[46] mass newspapers continued to attack provincial party organizations, labor unions, and other Soviet institutions through the summer of 1929. Some of these attacks undoubtedly had central sanction; others did not. One of the most publicized provincial "rotten spots" was Astrakhan. There, officials of the province Financial Department were accused of accepting bribes in exchange for favorable treatment of local fishing cooperatives and private fish merchants.[47] Coverage of the trial of "the Astrakhan wreckers," which ran regularly in Pravda and Komsomolskaia pravda in August and September of 1929, reinforced the message that the New Economic Policy was over and party officials could no longer collaborate with local traders.

In late August 1929 mass journalists at Pravda, having just succeeded in taking over the newspaper, made a fateful decision to hunt even bigger prey, namely the Leningrad province party committee. Coverage in Pravda began on September 1, in the Party Department headed by Leonid Kovalev. The department's story picked up on local worker correspondents' accusations that officials of Sevzaptorg (the Northwest Regional Trading Cooperative), a Leningrad consumer cooperative, had engaged in illegal dealings with private merchants, selling them construction materials below market price and borrowing large sums of money from them. In 1928 three members of the Sevzaptorg party cell denounced these dealings in the cooperative's wall newspaper. All were immediately fired or forced to quit. According to Pravda, they spent the next year trying to get a hearing from Leningrad newspapers, the regional Control Commission, and their neighborhood party committee. One of them, Migush, killed himself after being shouted down at a party cell meeting by the Sevzaptorg chairman and abused as a "charlatan" and "a bastard." In an article on the incident Leningradskaia pravda then smeared Migush as psychologically unstable and an alcoholic.[48]

Pravda accused Leningradskaia pravda and the province Control Commission of suppressing self-criticism and ignoring evidence of corruption at Sevzaptorg and other cooperatives. The Leningrad party organization's response to the denunciation was swift—the party committee's bureau appointed a commission to investigate disorders at

Sevzaptorg and other cooperatives, instructed the ward *(raion)* party committees and the press to "develop self-criticism," and ordered an investigation of the local party committee. On September 3 *Pravda* reported that numerous factory party committees, one of them at the huge Red Putilov arms works, had passed resolutions endorsing its criticisms of the Leningrad organization. Also on September 3 the militant Leningrad Komsomol paper *Changing of the Guard,* which had provided *Pravda* with some of the initial information on the Sevzaptorg disorders, joined the central organ's condemnation of "suppression of self-criticism" in Leningrad. Leningrad's main party newspaper, *Leningradskaia pravda,* remained in a defensive stance, asserting that some of the accusations against local party officials were "mistakes."[49]

In the following week the campaign against disorders in the Leningrad organization expanded in the central press and in Leningrad itself. *Komsomolskaia pravda* joined the attack on September 6, accusing *Leningradskaia pravda* of "a conciliatory attitude toward the Right Deviation." The wave of unrest "from below" rolled on, as many factory and ward party cells passed resolutions criticizing the regional leadership and calling for "a review of the highest branches of the Soviet apparatus in Leningrad." On September 7 the Leningrad regional party committee met in plenary session to discuss the *Pravda* charges. After an opening address by committee secretary Sergei Kirov, the plenum resolved to replace the leadership of the ward party organization involved in the Sevzaptorg case and reorganize the regional Control Commission. The party committee also approved the reports of the three commissions investigating disorders at the cooperatives.[50]

On September 9, 1929, a plenary session of the Leningrad regional Control Commission convened to elect a new Presidium. After the election (in which several leading officials were removed), the plenum set up six commissions to investigate newspaper charges against Leningrad cooperatives, trusts, and banks. By this time *Leningradskaia pravda* and the Leningrad evening newspaper had abandoned their earlier defensive stance and gone on a denunciatory rampage against regional officials. Then, in an ominous hint that a real denunciatory St. Bartholomew's Massacre might be in the offing, on September 13–14 *Pravda* and *Komsomolskaia pravda* both reported that the GPU had uncovered "a gigantic wrecking organization on the dimensions of Shakhty" at Leningrad shipyards.[51]

Party leaders at the highest level were alarmed at the unrest triggered by *Pravda*'s exposé of Sevzaptorg. Already on September 11 Emelian

Iaroslavskii, who was now on the *Pravda* editorial board, attempted to blunt criticism of the Leningrad organization in a commentary that ran on page two of the central party organ. Iaroslavskii praised the Leningrad regional committee for the steps it had taken to correct problems in local party work. Although he affirmed the importance of close attention to worker correspondent denunciations, Iaroslavskii devoted most of his editorial to warnings against "obvious excesses," "anarchic self-criticism" (*stikhiinaia samokritika*), and "exaggerations based on unchecked facts" in press coverage. He singled out *Leningradskaia pravda*'s September 7 edition for publishing unfounded accusations against local party organizations, cautioning party committees that "supervision of the press is weakening." The press must not be allowed "to oppose itself to party organs." Iaroslavskii was clearly trying to cut off further large-scale attacks on the Leningrad organization.[52]

Stalin, who was at the Black Sea resort of Sochi on a one-month vacation at this time, was worried about *Pravda*'s criticism of the Leningrad organization, which had not been cleared with him or other Central Committee secretaries. He also lacked confidence in Iaroslavskii's ability to handle the situation. On September 9 he wrote to Molotov in Moscow that "it is no good that Iaroslavskii has begun to set himself up . . . as the de facto head editor of *Pravda*. This is dangerous and harmful for business, as along with all of his other mediocre qualities he is weak in the area of *political leadership* (he loves to *float along* on the waves of the 'masses' moods)." In other words, Iaroslavskii was too ready to give militants in the editorial offices their head. Stalin also claimed to suspect that his old political opponent Grigorii Zinovev was behind the attacks on the Leningrad organization. Zinovev, he believed, had it in for the Leningrad leaders Sergei Kirov and N. P. Komarov, who had replaced him at the head of the city party organization after the 1926 purge of Left Oppositionists.[53]

On September 13, Stalin again wrote to Molotov (and also to new CCC chairman Sergo Ordzhonikidze) about the Leningrad situation:

> The attack on the Leningrad leadership in *Pravda*. . . was a gross error. . . . Someone (that is, an enemy of the party) wanted to make it look as if the Leningrad authorities were against the correction of shortcomings (which is *untrue!*), as if they were *obstructing* self-criticism and *did not accept it* (which is *untrue!*). And the bunglers at *Pravda* let them get away with it. And they created a huge stink, to the amusement of those hostile to the party. They forgot

that the Leningrad organization is not the *Sochi* or the *Astrakhan* or the *Baku* organization [three other party organizations that had come under public attack during the self-criticism campaign]. They forgot that a blow at the leadership of the Leningrad organization, which provides reliable support to the Central Committee, is a blow at the Central Committee's own heart . . . *The Central Committee's mistake* was for a single minute *to remove its hands from the wheel* with regard to the *Pravda* editorial bureau, forgetting that there, in the bureau, sits the self-criticism "sportsman" comrade Iaroslavskii, who possesses the happy talent of not being able to see anything further than the tip of his nose.

The same thing must be said about *Komsomolskaia pravda* and the local organs of the press.

Let the Central Committee Secretariat *once again take the wheel in its hands*, let it reassert control over *Pravda* and *Komsomolskaia pravda*, let it *change the tone and spirit* of self-criticism in those newspapers—and then all will be well.[54]

Stalin's reference to Iaroslavskii as a "self-criticism *sportsman*" recalled both Iaroslavskii's active role as an adjudicator of "criticism" cases and Stalin's own earlier polemic against self-criticism as "sport." Stalin wanted to halt the "sport"—the militant, even sensationalist denunciations of high-level party officials—and he was sure that Iaroslavskii lacked the firmness of character needed to do that. He was also infuriated by what he perceived as Iaroslavskii's blindness to the political implications of the self-criticism cases he adjudicated.

Stalin's September 13 letter set in train disciplinary action against mass journalists. Sometime between September 13 and 22 the CCC called in Leonid Kovalev and the other members of the *Pravda* editorial board (Krumin, N. N. Popov, and Iaroslavskii) for a dressing down. Molotov and Ordzhonikidze both attended. According to Stalin's wife, Nadezhda Sergeevna Allilueva, who described the session in a letter to her husband, Krumin attempted to place all the blame for the Leningrad coverage on Kovalev. When the latter tried to give his version of events, Ordzhonikidze cut him off, "smashing his fist on the table in 'traditional' fashion, and started to shout, how long will Kovalev's intrigues *(Kovalevshchina)* continue at *Pravda*, the CCC will not tolerate it, and so on in the same spirit." Allilueva also reported (her version of the meeting came personally from Kovalev) that "Molotov announced that *Pravda*'s Party Department was not carrying out the Central Committee's line and was in general going beyond the party line in self-criticism." Also during this time period Agitprop Department chief Krinitskii attended a meeting of the *Pravda* editorial board and gave a speech in which he accused Kovalev of being a Zinovevite.[55]

According to Allilueva, Kovalev had in fact cleared the Leningrad materials with Popov and Iaroslavskii before publication. (A. I. Mariinskii, CC agitprop instructor, in a September 16 explanatory letter to Ordzhonikidze, also claimed that Iaroslavskii had approved the materials.)[56] But neither Popov nor Iaroslavskii had told him to clear the materials with Molotov, as they should have. Thus, Allilueva believed, the other *Pravda* editorial bureau members bore as much responsibility for the Leningrad "mistake" as Kovalev, who was being scapegoated. On Krumin's initiative the *Pravda* editors had already passed a resolution ordering Kovalev's firing, a move they had no legal authority to make. As Allilueva pointed out, only the Central Committee Organizational Department (Orgotdel) could remove *Pravda* editors from their posts. Kovalev, who appears to have been a personal friend of Allilueva's, had appealed to her to intervene in his defense. Allilueva in turn appealed to Stalin to intervene: "Don't be angry with me, but seriously, I am extremely sorry for Kovalev. . . . It is unacceptable to deal with such a [good] worker in this way."[57]

On the evening of September 22 the CC Secretariat called in many senior Soviet editors and agitprop officials for a meeting that Feliks Kon described to *The Worker Gazette* party cell on the following day. Kon had received a phone summons to the CC at 10:00 P.M. The late-night meeting made a fearful impression on the editor, who was obviously still shaken as he convened *The Worker Gazette* cell the next day:

> KON: (Last night) I . . . was at a secret session of the Central Committee, where the question of a number of press organs was discussed. As a member of the Central Control Commission, I was allowed in. The mood was extremely tense—they were smashing one editorial board after another.
>
> VOLODIN: Please don't discuss secret matters, just tell us what you're allowed to.
>
> KON: I know what can be spoken about and what is forbidden. . . . They fired comrade Kovalev, the head of the *[Pravda]* Party Department. And they fired the editor of *Worker Moscow* too.

They censured the Ukrainian newspapers. They smashed TASS for complete inability to present material from worker life. They fired one newsman after another for absence of a political line and for being politically alien. . . .

. . . This was the atmosphere and the situation in which the question of VOLODIN was decided. [58]

Kon went on to describe how the CC secretaries had issued a severe reprimand to the writer Mezhericher of *The Worker Gazette* and fired Volodin for publishing denunciatory material on the miners' labor union leadership without approval from higher authorities. This move Kon characterized as "a most serious, huge political error." When Kon had tried to speak up in defense of *The Worker Gazette*, Molotov had cut him off. When CC Agitprop Department head Krinitskii began to defend Volodin, Molotov had "shouted at him, didn't let him speak, announced that Krinitskii was responsible for 'Ingulov's intrigues' *[Ingulovshchina]*."[59]

In the meantime Stalin, who had ordered the Secretariat to "once again take the wheel" of the press, and who had practically accused Kovalev of being an Oppositionist in his letters to Molotov and Ordzhonikidze, now warned against making the *Pravda* party secretary "the scapegoat." In a September 22 telegram to Molotov, probably intended to reach him before the big Secretariat session, Stalin suggested that the question of Kovalev's firing from *Pravda* be postponed as "it is incorrect to turn Kovalev into the scapegoat. The main responsibility remains with the editorial bureau. It is not necessary to remove Kovalev from the Department of Party Life: he has done a pretty good job of putting it together in spite of Krumin's inertia and Ulianova's opposition." On September 23 Stalin wrote a letter to Ordzhonikidze along the same lines, noting also that Kovalev was "an absolutely disciplined member of the party" who would not have published the Leningrad materials without showing them to the editorial bureau members.[60]

Stalin's new solicitude for Kovalev, whom he had in barely veiled terms accused of being a Zinovevite Oppositionist in earlier communications, probably had several motivations. He did not wish to let Iaroslavskii, Popov, and Krumin completely off the hook for the Leningrad "mistake," nor did he want to disrupt work at *Pravda* during a time of turmoil by removing one of the paper's key editors. He also may have wished to leave the situation ambiguous until he returned to

Moscow and resolved it himself. Or, as an able politician he may have decided to keep his hand concealed until the last moment, to keep his personal preferences private. At any rate, his intervention saved Kovalev's job for the moment. On September 27 Ordzhonikidze informed him that "we haven't yet touched Kovalev, although he has committed a mass of idiotic errors. I agree with you that the supervisors of *Pravda* are more responsible than Kovalev, and that someone inside the Central Committee apparatus is even more responsible."[61]

By "someone inside the Central Committee apparatus" Ordzhonikidze apparently meant Ingulov and/or Krinitskii. In the next month both these CC officials would be called upon to justify their encouragement of "excesses" in self-criticism before the CCC. On October 15, 1929, Ingulov wrote a letter explaining his conduct to Ordzhonikidze. The letter suggested that he himself actually bore a fair burden of responsibility for the Leningrad "mistake." Ingulov reported that just before a Secretariat or Orgburo session in late August he had had a conversation with *Pravda*'s Kovalev, in which the latter had mentioned the materials implicating Leningrad party officials. Ingulov had replied that A. P. Mariinskii (an instructor for the CC Agitprop Department) had just returned from an investigative trip to Leningrad, where he had the impression of ongoing "suppression of self-criticism." Ingulov claimed not to have actually given his approval for publication of the materials, but Kovalev must have interpreted his comments as a green light.[62]

Documents attached to Ingulov's letter strongly suggested that Ingulov, Krinitskii, and Mariinskii had cooperated with Kovalev in setting off the "wave of self-criticism" in Leningrad. They included Mariinskii's report to Krinitskii on his August 1929 trip to Leningrad, which described widespread "suppression of self-criticism" in the city. According to Mariinskii, rank-and-file worker correspondents, newspaper editors, and regional party committee secretaries all agreed that the Leningrad press lacked "boldness" in self-criticism and that many party officials were hostile to self-criticism. The regional Control Commission generally forbade publication of denunciatory material and its chairman, Desov, was "an enemy of self-criticism." Communist journalists at the Leningrad evening paper *Red Gazette* and worker correspondents at the Red Triangle and Red Putilov factories griped to Mariinskii about "suppression." Local officials of the Control Commission, they said, demanded that journalists clear all denunciatory material with them before publication.[63]

After Mariinskii's investigation, CC Agitprop Department officials apparently encouraged *Red Gazette* to join *Pravda* in an all-out attack on high Leningrad officials. At a meeting at the newspaper's editorial offices just before his departure for Moscow, Mariinskii supposedly told journalists that the regional Control Commission was "thick with Soviet workers who opposed self-criticism," especially commission chairman Desov and Executive Committee secretary N. P. Komarov. "The Komarov group," he was quoted as saying, ". . . must be exposed." In his defense, Mariinskii wrote to Ordzhonikidze that "I have no idea of what [political] relations are like within the Leningrad leadership." He had simply done his duty to advance self-criticism in Leningrad. This "apolitical" stance was precisely the "sporting" attitude toward self-criticism, the "seeing no further than the end of his nose" that infuriated Stalin.[64]

Upon Mariinskii's return to the Central Committee, the Agitprop Department immediately summoned *Red Gazette* editor Chagin to Moscow and let him know that they expected more self-critical activity from his newspaper. The date was September 3, two days after *Pravda*'s initial publication on the Leningrad affair. At a meeting with Chagin Agitprop officials Krinitskii, Ingulov, and Mariinskii, as well as mass journalists from *Pravda*, including Aleksei Kapustin, criticized *Red Gazette* for failing to recruit worker correspondents, ignoring their letters, covering up incidents of suppression of self-criticism by the regional Control Commission, and neglecting "mass work" in favor of trivial, "philistine," and even "pornographic" denunciations. Political charges were also made against the paper, of conciliating the Right Deviation. Chagin and other *Red Gazette* journalists must have emerged from this meeting, and from the party cell session at Leningrad where Mariinskii spoke, convinced that central authorities wanted an all-out assault on the highest levels of the Leningrad organization.[65]

According to an after-the-fact account by A. I. Stetskii, head of the CC Agitprop Department from January 1930 onward, after *Pravda*'s September 1 article on the Leningrad organization, "an absolutely astounding picture unfolded at *Red Gazette*. In the course of a few days the newspaper's apparatus [lower-ranking journalists, that is] took over its management, which had been shaken and had shown inability to lead under the circumstances of criticism from the Central Organ *[Pravda]*. Not only *Red Gazette*, but also *Leningradskaia pravda* proved unprepared to cope with the broad wave of self-criticism that roared in." The mass journalists appear to have seized editorial control during Chagin's absence in Moscow. Under the leadership of militant journalists like one "Gordon," the assistant editor of *Red Gazette*'s Chronicle section, both papers began publishing exposés of numerous supposed "rotten spots" in the Leningrad organization.[66]

The picture that emerges from the Leningrad "mistake," then, is one of an attack on a prominent party organization loosely coordinated by Kovalev at *Pravda* and Agitprop officials Ingulov, Krinitskii, and Mariinskii with the acquiescence of Iaroslavskii on the *Pravda* editorial bureau. As Amy Knight has pointed out, there was tension within the Leningrad organization between the "Old Leningraders" Komarov (head of the Leningrad Executive Committee) and Desov (chief of the city's Control Commission) on one side and party secretary Kirov and his associates on the other. Kirov had taken over the city organization in 1926 and had brought with him from Baku a large cohort of associates, including Chagin, editor of *Red Gazette*. Mariinskii seems to have plugged into preexisting resentment of the "Old Leningraders" among Kirov's people when he promoted self-criticism in Leningrad. Kirov and Chagin themselves, however, apparently opposed an all-out attack on Komarov and Desov. Knight suggests that Stalin had precipitated the attack on Leningrad with a word to Kovalev, but there is no evidence for this. Stalin's angry reaction to the assault, moreover, suggests that it took him by surprise.[67]

Stalin, Molotov, and Kaganovich, who were not informed of the upcoming campaign beforehand, were outraged and intervened to shut down the campaign, and indeed, to redefine self-criticism for the entire press. On October 8, 1929, *Pravda*'s Party Department ran a long article by moderate Mikhail Gus admonishing newspapers not to take "a superficial approach to their work, to their material ('campaignism,' know-it-all-ism, inability and lack of desire to bring the matter to a successful conclusion)." Gus quoted Molotov as saying that newspapers needed to criticize their own work more, to turn the spotlight of self-criticism on themselves. He criticized the papers for "an absence of political restraint and cold-bloodedness," their "simultaneous inclination toward an emotional tone and semi-Trotskyite generalization," sensational exposés of innocent officials, and "hurried generalizations without any base." He accused them of "the sensational blowing up of 'rotten spots,' loud generalized accusations, hysterical screeches, 'Left' excesses . . . inadequate party discipline, and an inclination to generalize incorrectly from the facts." Gus singled out *Red Gazette*, *The Baku Worker*, and *The Urals Worker* for criticism.[68]

Journalist joined the chorus of condemnation against excesses in criticism. In the journal's October 15 issue Ingulov, perhaps as an act of penance, ran an article decrying "self-criticism which plays into the hands of class enemies." Ingulov criticized the same newspapers as Gus and warned overenthusiastic mass journalists against "petty bourgeois, semi-Trotskyite radicalism."[69] On November 1 the lead editorial called for a middle road on "self-criticism," avoiding "suppression" and "over-generalizations" simultaneously. This piece instructed journalists to remember that the editor and only the editor ran the newspaper— "attempts to interfere in the editor's competence, to replace him with party, labor union or Komsomol organizations, to share power with him, are not in the tiniest degree acceptable."[70] The writer clearly wanted to put an end to editorial office insurrections such as had occurred at *Red Gazette*.

Within the confines of their party cell meetings, if not in the press, mass journalists at central papers greeted news of the Central Committee crackdown with a mixture of disbelief and defiance. At *The Worker Gazette*, mass journalists who had been in conflict with moderate head editor Feliks Kon since late 1928 continued to insist that their own line on self-criticism was correct. When Kon, at the September 23–24 party cell meeting, attempted to use the September 22 Secretariat session as a stick to beat down resistance to his authority in the editorial offices, militant Communist journalists resisted.

In his presentation to the party cell on the CC's new line on self-criticism, Kon emphasized the Secretariat's decision to fire Volodin, who had been challenging his authority at the newspaper since the previous winter. According to Kon, "Volodin has tried to 'show' [me] how to run the newspaper, how to fire up self-criticism 'boldly.'" At this point the transcript of the meeting records an interruption, as one of the cell members commented, "And he did show you." Kon replied, "And he lost his head." He continued, "From this it is essential to draw conclusions. Perhaps Volodin's punishment is too harsh, but once the Central Committee has decided, there can be no further discussion or debate." Volodin had "taken an incorrect tone," Kon told his audience, so that "the newspaper overstepped its bounds." "We must be more careful with what we place in the newspaper," he warned. "One must not publish material that has not been fully checked."[71]

In the ensuing discussion militant Communist journalists hastened to defend Volodin and forestall any restoration of power to moder-ates punished in the summer purges (Akhmanova and Ganetskaia). Chernia, the writer who had once lost his voting rights for "Trotskyite" activities, granted that "we must accept the Central Committee resolution and guide ourselves by it," but qualified this with the proviso that "there are . . . people, who want to give the CC decision a false interpretation, to use it for their own personal goals. We will not allow this. The newspaper's line has been correct, even if comrade Kon denies this." Since Volodin had gained authority in the editorial offices, Chernia thought, the newspaper "has been militant, Bolshevik."[72] Other journalists echoed Chernia's comments. Some seem to have found it hard to believe that the CC would reject their methods. One Zaitsev noted that although the paper had to abide by the CC decision, Kon himself had admitted that Volodin's "political line was correct," which was cause for "great moral satisfaction." Erlikh, secretary of the editorial board, praised Volodin and *The Worker Gazette* for mobilizing "the genuine proletarian enthusiasm of the masses against distortions of the party line," and for denouncing disorders at a number of party and Soviet institutions. Iogan Altman, the cell propagandist, called Volodin's mistake "a complete anomaly" (*sovershenno sluchaino*) and praised his work.[73]

The mood of *The Worker Gazette* party cell on September 23–24 was defiant. At the conclusion of the discussion, members passed a resolution on Volodin's firing that bordered on insubordination to the Central Committee. Although recognizing the paper's "mistake" in publishing the materials on the miners' union, the cell also denied that the CC's decision meant "the overturn of self-criticism" or constituted a censure of *The Worker Gazette's* work as whole. *The Worker Gazette's* journalists should continue to take the line of militant self-criticism that had guided the paper since the summer purge of moderates in the editorial staff.[74]

In the ensuing months there was a purge of high-ranking mass journalists in the central press. On January 1, 1930, the Politburo finally removed Kovalev (and probably Naumov as well) from the *Pravda* editorial staff, at Stalin's instance.[75] Volodin had already been fired from *The Worker Gazette*. In late September or early October 1929 *Komsomolskaia pravda's* in-house paper *Gazetnaia nedelia (Newspaper Week)*, reported "a change in the leadership."[76] Sometime during this period the old editorial board of Bukhartsev, Bobryshev, and Ilin was purged (the fourth, Charov, retained his position), to be replaced by A. N. Troitskii from Tver and a cohort of Komsomol journalists from the Urals.[77] Other, more "moderate," editors were removed from their jobs for failure to keep restive mass journalists under control, most notably Feliks Kon at *The Worker Gazette* and Chagin, the editor of Leningrad's *Red Gazette*.[78]

Even the purged mass journalists remained, however, the straying sons of the party rather than its enemies. Most of the militants fired from major positions in the central press in 1929 continued their careers at other major Soviet publications. Volodin of *The Worker Gazette* went on to edit *Evening Moscow* in 1930; Kovalev became head editor of *Worker Moscow*. Taras Kostrov, fired from *Komsomolskaia pravda* in 1928, moved on to be editor of the Komsomol literary journal *Young Guard* in 1929 and assistant editor of the journal *Beyond the Border* in 1930 (he died of tuberculosis on September 18, 1930).[79] Bobryshev was head editor of the central journal *Our Achievements* from 1934 to 1936, and Bukhartsev served on the journal's editorial board after 1932. *Pravda*'s Naumov moved on to become head editor of the central Agitprop journal *Sputnik agitatora (The Agitator's Companion)* in January 1931.[80]

After the Leningrad "mistake" the CC secretaries also removed Krinitskii and Ingulov from their posts in the Agitprop Department for failure to control the self-criticism campaign, replacing them with A. I. Stetskii and A. N. Gusev respectively. Together with the personnel changes, the Agitprop Department was also reorganized (as part of a larger reorganization of the CC). On November 22, 1929, the Secretariat approved a plan that split Agitprop into two departments. The Department of Culture and Propaganda was to handle the press, "popular enlightenment" (meaning education), "propaganda and education of party members," and university education. The Department of Agitation and Mass Campaigns was to supervise coordinated agitprop campaigns of all kinds—socialist competitions, belt tightening, collectivization, grain procurements. In discussion of the proposal Stetskii and other lower-level agitprop officials expressed trepidation about putting management of the press, literature, movies, and radio in a separate department from "mass campaigns," but Kaganovich and Stalin defended the plan.[81]

On January 16, 1930, the Central Committee's Orgburo met to consider the question of the future direction of the Soviet press. CC secretaries Molotov and Kaganovich, Stalin's two most important lieutenants at this time, were present, together with senior agitprop officials. The meeting marked a decisive change in course for Soviet newspapers, from coverage of "Shadows"—denunciation and exposés of corruption—to coverage of "Light"—the achievements of Soviet Power and the heroism of rank-and-file Bolshevik cadres building socialism. It also marked the retargeting of the press at ordinary workers and lower-ranking party activists.

The final draft resolutions approved by the Orgburo (drafted by A. N. Gusev) lauded the press's work in denouncing the Right Deviation and ordered newspapers to continue exposing its errors. They set three priority tasks for newspapers—educating party activists in "theoretical questions" of Leninism and the "general party line," promoting industrial productivity and industrialization, and reaching "the masses of collectivized peasants" with the party's message. The resolutions also criticized the press for failure to popularize "the most important decisions of the party" among workers. Newspapers were no longer to publicize policy debates or "sensational" scandals, but to enforce the "general party line," convey the party leaders' decisions and ideological mandates into activists, and mobilize the populace for industrialization.[82]

In discussion of the press's performance at the January 16 session, Kaganovich and Molotov emphasized the imperatives of denouncing *political* deviations, covering more positive achievements, and shifting self-criticism from attacks on administrators to enforcement of "labor discipline" among workers. Kaganovich criticized the press's nearly exclusive focus on negative phenomena and lack of coverage of achievements: "Criticizing, educating people, the newspapers should at the same time organize them. They should educate the masses, organize them, and one can educate only by presenting various positive phenomena together with the negative. . . . We have so many positive achievements in the area of industrialization of the country, various innovations at factories, the adoption of the conveyor system, the use of coal-cutting machines in the Donbass and etc. Here we have concrete achievements. . . . We need pathos, but that is not enough, we need the presentation of concrete facts." Kaganovich singled out *Komsomolskaia pravda* as an example of a newspaper that had overstepped the proper bounds of self-criticism, saying that the purge of the newspaper's editorial office had uncovered "open Trotskyites, and covert ones, and semi-Trotskyites, and now all of that rot will be cleaned out." "Left" excesses in criticism would not be tolerated.[83]

Molotov admonished the newspapers not to undermine the work of industrial managers with baseless attacks. "And isn't it the case," he asked rhetorically, "that the managers know the business of management better than newspapermen, and isn't it the case that one learns better to manage and supervise on the production site, from live people who know what they're doing, than from newspapermen, even if they graduated from the Institute of Red Professors?" Both Molotov and

Kaganovich praised the press's coverage of shock brigades, but complained that many "backward" workers "had an ironic attitude to shock workers, there is no discipline in enterprises, there is no unified supervision, there is no organizational base, there is much laxness." The press's job was not to show all workers in a good light, but to enforce labor discipline, and to criticize those who undermined shock work and resisted the introduction of "shock brigades." In general, newspapers needed to be more friendly to management, to publish articles by managers, and so on. This was the final reversal of central officials' encouragement of publicity for the voices of ordinary workers at the outset of the 1926 belt-tightening campaign.[84]

Having driven their political enemies, both Left and Right, from the field, Stalin and his lieutenants were now disturbed by the disorder wrought by the self-criticism campaign. In the winter of 1929–1930 they moved to put a stop to unbridled denunciation and publicity of "shortcomings." They attempted to redirect press criticism from management to "backward" workers who were undermining productivity and labor discipline. They encouraged more publicity for the positive achievements of Soviet Power, especially in industry, at the same time that they insisted on merciless denunciation of those the CC designated as political enemies. The new slogan was discipline, both in politics and in the workplace.[85] Party activists and proletarians were "to close ranks" around their commanders in the Central Committee. The CC's new emphasis on careful checking of facts before publication meant the effective reinstitution of the ban on criticism of local party organizations without permission from above.

Within months of the January 16, 1930, Orgburo session Soviet agitprop officials were discussing ways to extend the press's new focus on positive achievements into literature, to produce a new fiction that would "show the heroes of socialist construction." This discussion ultimately led to the designation of an official Soviet literary genre, "socialist realism." As the next chapter shows, the formulation of socialist realism owed much to mass journalism and mass journalists.

~ 7

Mass Journalism, "Soviet Sensations," and Socialist Realism

AT THE JANUARY 16, 1930, session of the Orgburo described in the previous chapter Kaganovich, Molotov, and Agitprop (agitation-and-propaganda) Department officials charted a new course for the newspapers, insisting on more coverage of "achievements," fewer attacks on management, and more emphasis on labor discipline. The party leaders wanted the press to turn self-criticism on "backward workers" who shirked or came to work drunk, and away from management. But they also wanted the newspapers to encourage workers with stories of the accomplishments of model "advanced workers" in shock brigades and socialist competitions. This chapter shows how coverage of "achievements" and of "advanced workers" spilled over into literature, influencing the development of socialist realism.

Within two months of the Orgburo's January 16, 1930, session, Agitprop Department chief Stetskii, chief *rapporteur* for that meeting, drafted a CC resolution on literature that called for the creation of a new fiction targeted at the masses. This new literature was supposed to "represent the processes of the socialist reconstruction of the city and the countryside, the remaking of the proletariat and the peasantry in the transition period, the new directions of human relations, improvements in daily life, the class struggle of the world proletariat." Stetskii's draft also called for the unification of all genuinely "proletarian" writers in a single writers' union and the silencing of "fellow traveler" authors who would not make a full commitment to Soviet Power.[1] It harked back to the January Orgburo session on the press with its call to create a literature for the masses and show the achievements of the Soviet proletariat. It was also the CC's first step in the organization of a single monolithic writers' union and its formulation of an officially approved genre of mass literature, socialist realism.

In several respects mass journalism served as a model for the "proletarian literature" and socialist realism[2] of the early to mid-1930s, and especially for the so-called "production novel" (Valentin Kataev's *Time, Forward!*, Fedor Gladkov's *Energy*, Mariia Shaginian's *Hydrocentral*, Ilya Ehrenburg's *The Second Day*, Iurii Krymov's *The Tanker Derbent*).[3] The socialist realist novels of the 1930s followed mass journalism in placing the center of action on the shop floor, the construction site, or the collective farm, and in publicizing the heroic accomplishments of ordinary workers (in the early 1930s workers with extraordinary production records were known as "shock workers"; in the later 1930s they were "Stakhanovites"). At the center of many 1930s production novels (*Time, Forward!* and *The Tanker Derbent*, for example) was a socialist competition, the quintessential mass journalistic event. Like mass journalism, socialist realism presented ordinary industrial labor as an epic battle, and showed how participation in that battle transfigured the individual, making him or her into a true socialist. Like mass journalism, socialist realism was an attempt to galvanize and mobilize rank-and-file party activists without resorting to "bourgeois sensationalism."

Writers of production novels, such as Valentin Kataev, emulated mass journalists by going out to construction sites and factories on the periphery to gather material for their works and actively participate in "socialist construction." Indeed, Erica Wolf has recently demonstrated that Kataev based the major characters and events of the well-known production novel *Time, Forward!* on actual people and events at the giant Magnitogorsk steel complex, many of them covered in the local and central press.[4]

Scholarship on socialist realism has covered a range of themes. Katerina Clark and Boris Groys, for example, challenge earlier narratives of Stalinist oppression of the intelligentsia by exploring the collaboration of avant-garde artists and writers with the Soviet state in the formulation of socialist realism.[5] Clark and Gregory Carleton investigate the parallels between medieval European literary works and socialist realism, in particular the fuzziness of genre boundaries and the iconology of the saint/"positive hero."[6] Evgenii Dobrenko argues that socialist realism was a deliberate attempt to adjust literature to the middle-brow tastes of the ordinary Soviet reader, and that it had genuine mass appeal.[7] In *On Socialist Realism* Andrei Sinyavsky describes socialist realism as a spiritual system based on the limitless promise of a Communist future.[8] Sheila Fitzpatrick has examined the ways in which socialist realism and the ideal of "culturedness" legitimized the privileges of the new Soviet elite of the 1930s.[9]

To the extent that they address the historical development of socialist realism and its formulation as an official literary doctrine, scholars of Soviet literature situate it amidst the welter of disputes between various elite literary groupings competing for the party's favor in the 1920s.[10] But it is also productive to explore how the concrete problems faced by the party/Komsomol propaganda apparatus shaped the development of the genre. Rather than focus on debates among the literary elites and the problem of the uneasy partnership between the Soviet leadership and nonparty intellectuals, this chapter looks at discussions of propaganda policy within the party and the Komsomol and the interwoven development of Soviet journalism and Soviet literature. To the extent that I cover the *writers'* discourse on literature and authorship, I emphasize an underlying consensus about what mass literature *ought to be* that had developed by 1930 among most literary groups with pretensions to state support.

Sex, Hooliganism, and the Search for a Substitute for "Boulevard Sensationalism"

Throughout the New Economic Policy (NEP) era, journalists and fiction writers engaged in parallel, sometimes intersecting searches for mass genres that would appeal to ordinary readers without crossing the line into "yellow sensationalism" or "pornography." This search was overseen by party and Komsomol propagandists who wanted to enlist both literature and the mass press in the business of mobilizing ordinary party cadres, many of them semiliterate. The locus of experimentation, and the source of innovation in this search, was the Komsomol press and the Komsomol CC's Agitprop Department. Compared with the more conservative, even puritanical officials of the party's Agitprop Department, Komsomol editors and Agitprop bureaucrats were more willing to experiment with borderline genres, such as the "sensationalist" adventure tale. From the experimentation of the 1920s socialist realism, mass journalism, and "Soviet sensations" would emerge to dominate Soviet fiction and newspapers in the 1930s. In the process Soviet writers incorporated into their work certain elements of "sensational" bourgeois literature, such as the portrayal of the swashbuckling hero of Western adventure stories,[11] while dropping others, such as sexuality and "yellow" exposés of "hooliganism" and the criminal underworld.

From the earliest months of the NEP, party agitprop officials were concerned with eliminating bourgeois sensationalism from the press and from literature.[12] Although private and cooperative presses were the focus of the party's concern with boulevard sensationalism in 1921–1923, by the later years of the NEP era it was the regime's own Komsomol newspapers that were worrying top officials by publishing romance stories and detailed coverage of bizarre crimes. Komsomol newspapermen, at the forefront of the mass journalism movement, were also innovators in the coverage of hooliganism and the exploration of relations between the sexes. There were multiple reasons for the Komsomol press's readiness to test Bolshevik taboos in these areas. As Eric Naiman has demonstrated, party and Komsomol leaders in late 1925 were beginning a campaign to establish control over everyday behavior. They expected newspapers to participate in this campaign by exposing and condemning hooliganism.[13] In addition, the editors and writers at the Komsomol papers were aggressive and even reckless— they enjoyed tweaking the noses of more senior authorities. And higher-level party leaders allowed the Komsomol journalists greater latitude to experiment because of the Komsomol's special, high-priority mission—selling the party's message to youth. Young people generally had less disposable income than adults, so Komsomol newspapers had to be both cheaper and more immediately appealing than regular party and Soviet papers. In 1926–1927, the peak period of "yellow sensationalism" in the Komsomol press, major Komsomol newspapers and journals were operating with very large deficits even as party agitprop officials cut their state subsidies. The financial squeeze combined with the low income of their target audience meant that the Komsomol papers had to increase their circulation to survive. Exposés of corrupt local officials and sensational coverage of gang rapes and other especially horrible crimes was one way to attract readers.[14]

The wave of taboo-testing, "yellow" news stories and fictional tales in 1926–1927 went much further than Central Control Commission (CCC) and Central Committee (CC) officials had ever planned. In particular, Bolshevik leaders perceived the subject of sex as dangerous because it pointed toward the destabilizing effects of individual desire at a time when the party wanted discipline, loyalty, and sacrifice from the entire population. So they cracked down on the presentation both of sexual issues and of underclass crime in the Soviet press. As it turned out, this crackdown spelled the near total elimination of sex and anarchistic lumpenproletarian violence from Soviet newspapers and literature. Debauchery and crime, hitherto recognized as endemic problems of the Russian working class (and attributed to "cultural backwardness" and deprivation) were pushed out to the periphery of news coverage and of Soviet society, being attributed mostly to "class enemies" or corrupt foreigners.[15]

In the novel, as in news coverage, hooliganism and sexual issues were substantially eliminated between the mid-years of the NEP and the early 1930s. Fedor Gladkov's 1925 novel *Cement,* one of the prototypes for socialist realism, portrays a fraught relationship between the male hero, the returned Red Army soldier and worker Gleb Chumalov, and his wife, Dasha. When Chumalov returns from the Civil War he finds that the Revolution has transformed Dasha. Rather than look after their daughter, Nurka, who now spends most of her time in a "Children's Home," Dasha works in the local party organization's Women's Department. In the course of the novel, Chumalov has to deal with Dasha's refusal to cook for him and her refusal of sex. He has to accept that while he was away fighting she slept with other men (as he slept with other women). Throughout the novel, and at its end, the question of Dasha and Gleb's future relations is left unanswered. Near the conclusion, Dasha tells Chumalov, "Love will always be love, Gleb, but it acquires a new form. Everything will come through and attain new forms, and then we shall know how to forge new links."[16] *Cement* takes seriously the collision between the "traditional" patriarchal culture of its working-class heroes and the egalitarian ideals of the revolution.

By contrast Valentin Kataev's *Time Forward!* (1932) does not present sex or gender relations as important problems. Sex does not figure in the novel at all. Relations between the sexes matter only insofar as they obstruct or facilitate the overriding task of constructing Magnitogorsk, the new steel-manufacturing city in the steppe. In the course of the novel, Ishchenko, the worker "brigadier" in charge of a shock brigade, is distracted from the big push to set a new twenty-four-hour record for pouring concrete when his wife goes into labor. Korneev, the sector superintendent, is distracted by his sweetheart's departure for Moscow. In both cases the heroes' task is to dispose as rapidly as possible of personal crisis and return to the work site ready to serve. At the novel's end the most important "positive hero," the engineer Margulies, becomes engaged to Shura Soldatova, head of the section art shop, almost as an afterthought. Margulies's and Soldatova's love is entirely sublimated to the larger task of accelerating production tempos and socialist construction.[17]

The issues of hooliganism and the cultural backwardness of the working class were also muted between the publication of Gladkov's *Cement* and Kataev's novel. In *Cement*, Badin, chairman of the local Executive Committee and a tough, disciplined Communist, rapes a woman party member in a drunken frenzy. The workers in Gladkov's book curse, spit, and beat their wives. They are impulsive and incapable of organizing themselves without direction from above. *Cement* includes an entire chapter, "The Worker's Club 'Komintern,'" devoted to showing how the workers' rowdy behavior and lack of discipline disrupt a meeting of the local party cell.[18] In *Time, Forward!*, however, only the kulak's son Sayenko, a class enemy, engages in hooliganistic behavior, and his vices are limited to gambling, drinking, and trading.[19] In accordance with explicit tenets of proletarian literature (and later, socialist realism) the narrative of *Time, Forward!* is an argument that participation in socialist construction inevitably transforms the backward masses into cultured, conscious, forward-thinking workers. In Gladkov's *Cement*, however, the problem of cultural backwardness is much more intractable. Indeed, the working-class Communists' accomplishments are often inextricably tied up with their backwardness and lack of culture.[20]

Party leaders such as Emelian Iaroslavskii at the CCC used their authority to excise sexuality and working-class hooliganism from Soviet literature and newspapers in the late 1920s. Under this pressure journalists and authors increasingly shied away from the problem of proletarian cultural backwardness and anarchy, preferring instead to impute "traditional" virtues to workers and put amoral or antisocial behavior down to alien class background or congenitally evil character. Commentators fell silent about possible conflicts between "traditional," "backward" Russian culture and revolutionary ideals. This growing evasiveness coincided with the party's abandonment of the NEP-era mass enlightenment project. Deep cultural problems were ignored, not confronted.

Heroes and Adventure Tales

Gladkov's *Cement* also exemplified another flirtation with a borderline "bourgeois" concession to popular taste—the adventure tale. As Katerina Clark points out in *Petersburg, Crucible of Cultural Revolution*,

Gleb Chumalov resembles Douglas Fairbanks, the 1920s film idol who frequently played the role of "the swashbuckler operating in exotic climes."[21] *Cement* is set in an unspecified, semitropical locale in the North Caucasus, by the shores of the Black Sea. After his exertions in the Civil War, Chumalov even has the beefcake physique of the male Hollywood star. When he rips his shirt off in a bid to impress the unruly workers at a meeting of the factory party cell, Gladkov writes, "By the light of the oil-lamp they could see his muscles, from neck to waist, moving flexibly under the skin, outlined by the shadows."[22] *Cement* also features battles with Cossack rebels, executions, and an unrequited romance between Chumalov and the secretary of the party cell's Women's Department, Polia Mekhova. Perhaps for these reasons Gladkov's work was generally one of the most requested Soviet novels in library surveys from the latter half of the 1920s.[23]

Agitprop officials in the mid-1920s were well aware of the popularity of adventure tales among Soviet readers, especially younger male readers. Surveys of reader preferences done by librarians and literacy activists repeatedly found a high demand for adventure/fantasy stories by authors such as Jack London, Mayne Reid (an American writer, author of such mid-nineteenth-century works as *The Scalp-Hunters*), Jules Verne, Rudyard Kipling, Bernhard Kellerman (the German author of the epic construction novel *The Tunnel*), A. Novikov-Priboi (author of a collection of sea adventure stories), and even James Fenimore Cooper. Jack London led nearly every readership survey conducted. Surveys also demonstrated the popularity among young men and boys of historical fiction, especially historical fiction dealing with military themes, such as Tolstoy's *War and Peace* and recent Civil War epics by Soviet authors, such as Fadeev's *The Rout.*[24]

During the NEP years officials in the upper levels of the party agitprop apparatus generally had a negative and condescending reaction to "hack-work" adventure tales by Verne, Reed, Kellerman, and their ilk. Even the Soviet authors of Civil War epics were sometimes accused of "excessive pathos." Old Bolshevik intellectuals were particularly prone to a snobbish view of popular literature, with its overdrawn heroes, its sentimental romances, and its "false pathos." At a July 2, 1928, Orgburo session devoted to consideration of a new CC resolution on "The Improvement of the Youth and Children's Press," for example, Old Bolsheviks Platon Kerzhentsev, S. V. Kosior, Nadezhda Krupskaia, and Anatolii Lunacharskii took turns trashing recent publications by the Komsomol of adventure literature and decrying *Komsomolskaia pravda*'s "chase after sensations." Central Committee agitprop officials were unhappy with the state of children's literature in general, and with the Komsomol's efforts to reach young rural activists. In his written report on youth literature Kerzhentsev, the vice-chief of the Agitprop Department, criticized "elements of detective stories, bare-faced 'adventurism' [*prikliuchenchestvo*], and pornography" in Komsomol literature.[25] Kerzhentsev also launched an attack on overplayed heroism and the use of street jargon in stories published by the Komsomol and the Young Pioneers.[26]

The consensus at this meeting was clearly in favor of more "serious" literature, such as popular scientific and technical books, political/sociological texts, and works on geography, other lands, and "internationalism" in general.[27] The discussants linked the poor quality of the Komsomol publishing house with the "chase after sensations" by *Komsomolskaia pravda* and other youth newspapers.[28] A particularly offensive aspect of the "chase after sensations" was specialist baiting and the shrill, hysterical denunciation of class enemies. In his oral comments Kerzhentsev made particular mention of a provincial Pioneer paper that had described the "hooliganism" and "naughtiness" of the "Children of the Shakhty Wreckers." He characterized the piece as having "a harmful and sensational character."[29] For the Old Bolsheviks present at this Orgburo session, sensationalism in the Komsomol newspapers was closely linked with the Komsomol publishing house's publication of "fantastic" exaggerated adventure tales. Both undermined "collective spirit" and political discipline at the same time as they promoted vulgarity, low culture, and boastfulness.

The locus of experimentation with Soviet adventure stories, Soviet heroism and romance, and Soviet sensations throughout the 1920s was in fact the Komsomol publishing and agitprop apparatus. Senior party officials, despite their grumbling about vulgarity and philistinism, gave the Komsomol latitude to innovate because they considered the task of propagandizing youth so important. When Stalinist leaders and literary figures set course toward the targeting of rank-and-file activists with tales of revolutionary heroism and adventure in 1930–1932, they took their bearings from the track followed earlier by the Komsomol. As early as April 1923 a plenum of the Komsomol Central Committee declared its readiness to use epic historical fiction (with Civil War or Revolutionary themes), "romance," and "fantasy" to reach young readers, especially the *massovik*, the rank-and-file Komsomol member/activist.[30] The CC Plenum's resolutions expressed the ongoing conundrum of party literature and journalism—how to achieve popularity without crossing the border into "boulevardism."

The resolutions stated that, "considering it necessary to use youth's preference for romance and fantasy in the capacity of the basic pivot in the creation of a new belles lettres, the Plenum cautions against deviation in the direction of boulevardism, crime stories, or blind imitation of old forms. The Komsomol book should not under any circumstances break [the norms of] compositional discipline and literary form in the pursuit of popularity."[31]

Throughout the 1920s Komsomol CC Agitprop officials promoted the use of the revolutionary epic and heroic adventure tales to draw Komsomol cadres into the tasks of socialist construction. A June 2, 1926, resolution of the Komsomol CC Bureau foreshadowed the party's literary program in the early 1930s by calling for the promotion of new writers from among worker and peasant youth, the production of historical epics of revolutionary heroism, and the portrayal of realistic heroes, the worker Komsomols who were completing the revolution. The resolution referred to the need to "acquaint the novice [Komsomol member] with the heroic struggle of the proletarian people, the party, and the Bolshevik underground, constantly using this as an educational tool of Komsomol work." Komsomol literature required more realistic heroes, and more realistic presentations of the daily life of Komsomol members.[32]

In 1928–1932 Komsomol literary policy, with its emphasis on adventure, revolutionary epic, and "pathos," converged with developments in journalism and party literary policy to motivate the formulation of socialist realism. As the *Young Guard* publishing house and the Komsomol newspapers continued to publish adventure tales, Civil War epics, and other tales of "revolutionary romance," mass journalists were shifting the site of breaking news from the offices of trusts, labor unions, and commissariats to the point of production. Top party officials and central newspaper editors, in particular Ivan Skvortsov-Stepanov and Ivan Gronskii at *Izvestiia*, were also working hard to lure Maksim Gorkii out of exile. Gorkii's return to the Soviet Union was in turn part of a larger effort on the part of the *Izvestiia* editors and some party agitprop officials to tone down the excesses of self-criticism and put more emphasis on publicizing the achievements of Soviet Power. Also at this time, a number of journalists, including Gronskii at *Izvestiia* and the *Komsomolskaia pravda* editors, were devoting increasing space in their newspapers to coverage of "Soviet sensations," the *real-life* adventures and heroism of Soviet pilots, athletes, and Arctic explorers. The total constellation of the high Stalinist literary scene—news reports of grandiose victories on the "industrialization front," novels portraying the adventures and feats of the worker and engineer heroes who were building socialism, and sensational coverage of record-breaking airplane flights and hair-raising Arctic rescues—was coming together.

Soviet Sensations

Among the central newspapers, *Izvestiia* and *Komsomolskaia pravda* were the most active in publicizing the adventures and feats of Soviet athletes, pilots, and explorers in the second half of the 1920s. There appears to have been no special mandate from the party CC's agitprop apparatus for such coverage—the newspapermen themselves pioneered it. In the case of *Komsomolskaia pravda*, the coverage fit well with Komsomol CC mandates to show the heroism of Bolshevik cadres and infect readers with "an intense emotionalism." At the time of *Komsomolskaia pravda*'s founding in May 1925, editors and Komsomol agitprop officials were determined to use readers' (especially male readers') interest in sports, technology, and exotic, faraway lands to draw them into "socialist construction." Soon after the newspaper's founding, Iakov Ilin, one of the newspaper's senior editors and a pioneer of mass journalism, hired Lev Barkhash, a sports reporter and former Russian 800-meter champion, away from *Pravda* to do reporting on sports. Barkhash had recently participated in a military ski trek from Arkhangelsk to Moscow, which he had also covered for *Pravda*. In many ways this trek foreshadowed 1930s Soviet press coverage of Arctic exploration, right down to the handing out of medals at its conclusion (Barkhash and his three companions, all Red Army officers, received the title of "Meritorious Skier"). At *Komsomolskaia pravda*, Barkhash wrote about "mass tourism," Komsomol paramilitary exercises, and his own mountain-climbing feats.[33]

The career of Evgenii Riabchikov, a prominent reporter on aviation for *Komsomolskaia pravda* and *Pravda*, demonstrates the direct link between Russian boys' enthusiasm for modern technology, the Komsomol's attempt to use that enthusiasm as a tool of mobilization, and the central press's coverage of the heroic feats of Soviet aviators under high Stalinism. In a short, unpublished memoir written during the 1970s Riabchikov described how his own youthful fascination with aeronautics propelled him into a journalistic career. As a Young Pioneer in 1923 Riabchikov helped to light signal fires in a cow field that guided the first official Aeroflot flight from Moscow to Nizhnyi Novgorod to a safe landing. "From that time," he writes in his memoir, "I had the aviation bug." First as the editor of a Pioneer wall newspaper and later as a writer for the Nizhnyi Novgorod Komsomol organ, *Lenin's Guard*, Riabchikov often wrote about airplanes and their pilots. His role in the establishment of an Air Club in Nizhnyi, in the organization of a series of local "agitation flights," and in fund-raising for the construction of *Pravda's* giant "agit-plane," the *Maksim Gorkii*, caught the attention of Efim Babushkin, head of *Komsomolskaia pravda's* Information Department after 1930. Some time in 1932 or 1933 Babushkin invited Riabchikov to work at the central Komsomol organ, where he covered record-setting flights by Soviet pilots Gromov, Filin, Spirin, Galyshev, and Valerii Chkalov.[34]

As *Komsomolskaia pravda* developed its coverage of sports, aviation, and paramilitary exercises, Ivan Gronskii at *Izvestiia* began to focus on Soviet exploration of the Arctic. In his memoirs Gronskii describes how in 1928 he decided to run an extensive campaign around efforts to rescue the crew of the Italian dirigible *Italia*, which had crashed in the Arctic. Gronskii made the decision himself and he also chose to agitate for the dispatch of Soviet ships to aid international rescue efforts. The latter move got him into trouble, for the Politburo had already resolved that the USSR could not afford to participate in the rescue. *Izvestiia's* publicity forced the Central Committee to order the icebreaker *Krasin* taken out of mothballs in Leningrad and sent to the area of the crash, along with a second icebreaker from Arkhangelsk. The expedition was costly, and Stalin was furious with Gronskii, claiming that he had "violated the usual norms for relations between the Central Committee and the newspapers."[35]

In the upshot it was the Soviet ships that finally picked up the downed Italians, generating a swell of positive international publicity. In spite of Stalin's reprimand, Gronskii was very proud of his role in promoting the rescue expedition. He basked in the attention *Izvestiia* received from foreign correspondents in Moscow, who besieged the editorial offices for information on the progress of the rescue. Gronskii, a dedicated Bolshevik who had written for *Pravda* even before the Revolution, paradoxically enjoyed the prestige and plaudits he had earned from the bourgeois press with his "sensation." In his memoirs, he wrote that, "the press of the entire world was abuzz with news of the great feats of the Soviet Union and its representatives."[36]

Like adventure novels and newspaper serials, coverage of real-life adventure was contentious. At *Izvestiia* itself some journalists questioned the editors' predilection for sensational Arctic rescue stories. In

November 1928, soon after the conclusion of the *Italia* epic, the newspaper's in-house publication *Rulon* ran an article by feuilletonist G. Lvovich, complaining that "sensationalistic" coverage of a food shortage on a Soviet expedition to Wrangel Island in the Arctic had displaced important political material from the pages of *Izvestiia*. Lvovich, a young Communist mass journalist who had frequent run-ins with Gronskii in the late 1920s and early 1930s, described how a reporter and his department editor agreed over lunch to publish material on the shortage of provisions.[37] At first the reporter worried that the story might not be suitable for a serious, leading paper such as *Izvestiia*, but the editor reassured him and told him to write it.[38]

The reporter and editor rapidly developed a campaign publicizing the plight of Wrangel Island's fifty inhabitants and demanding a rescue effort (shades of the *Italia* campaign). The government began to consider the possibility of sending an expedition to provision the island by steamship, icebreaker, or airplane. Other newspapers followed *Izvestiia*'s lead, agitating for a rescue operation.

Then, suddenly, the campaign disappeared from the press. According to Lvovich, it turned out that there was no provisions crisis on the island. The Soviet explorers and island inhabitants had food and supplies to last them another year or year and a half. Yet *Izvestiia* (and other papers) had wasted large amounts of money and space on this campaign over a period of several months. Lvovich concluded that "important political material had been put aside during this period, because there was no space, because the reader was being distracted with . . . the 'tragedy' on Wrangel Island. And if you talk to me about the 'sensations of the foreign press,' I would say that we are no slouches ourselves."[39]

I dub the new stories on Arctic exploration, aviation records, and athletic feats "Soviet sensations" following the after-the-fact usage of Soviet memoirists. In their memoirs both Gronskii and Iurii Zhukov, a *Komsomolskaia pravda* mass journalist who went on to edit *Pravda* after World War II, label these stories "sensations." Zhukov, like Gronskii, takes particular pride in recounting the putative amazement of correspondents for Western bourgeois newspapers at the grand feats of Soviet aviators and sportsmen. In a work written in 1964, when the Soviet space program was riding a wave of "firsts" (first satellite, first man in space, first space walk), Zhukov explicitly compares the cosmonauts' space voyages to the record-setting flights of Chkalov and others in the 1930s. He refers to the first space walk as "something we might have read about some time in fantasy novels," and to the space program's successes in general as "a sensation" and "a Russian surprise."

Clearly for Gronskii and Zhukov, both veterans of 1920s journalism, coverage of heroic flights and Arctic expeditions was an ideologically correct substitute for the less savory sensations of the bourgeois mass press. The *Italia* rescue, Barkhash's mountain climbing exploits, and Chkalov's record-setting flights were all Soviet sensations.[40]

Maksim Gorkii and *Our Achievements*

Another important episode in the creation of socialist realism and high Stalinist culture was the drive by a number of party leaders, agitprop officials, and journalists beginning in late 1927 for more coverage of "the Light," of the achievements and accomplishments of Soviet Power. The backers of more positive propaganda were exasperated by what they perceived as the excesses of self-criticism, the ceaseless exposés of corruption and incompetence in Soviet officialdom. They feared that self-criticism was discrediting the party as a whole among the general population. The advocates of more publicity for Soviet achievements included prominent feuilletonists such as Mikhail Koltsov at *Pravda*, editors such as Gronskii at *Izvestiia*, and agitprop officials such as Artem Khalatov (the head of GIZ, the state publishing house). In the Soviet leadership Emelian Iaroslavskii and Anatolii Lunacharskii (Commissar of Enlightenment) also supported more positive news coverage. In its early phase (from late 1927 into 1929) the push for more publicity of achievements was closely associated with the campaign to bring the Russian socialist author Maksim Gorkii home from exile in Italy.

Many senior Soviet leaders, editors and agitprop officials were involved in the campaign to lure Gorkii back from exile to the USSR. Among the most prominent were Gronskii and Skvortsov-Stepanov at *Izvestiia*, Konstantin Aleksandrovich Maltsev at *The Worker Gazette*, and Khalatov at the state publishing house. The impetus behind the campaign came from the highest levels of the Central Committee. Bolshevik leaders and agitprop officials hoped to use Gorkii's prestige in European socialist circles and his popularity in the USSR in their propaganda efforts. At the request of head editor Ivan Skvortsov-Stepanov, Gorkii began to write intermittently for *Izvestiia* toward the end of 1925. By 1927 he was also writing for *The Worker Gazette*. Also beginning in 1927 Skvortsov-Stepanov and Gronskii began providing Gorkii, who was heavily in debt, with material support sent through Soviet diplomatic channels. According to Gronskii's memoirs, Skvortsov-Stepanov was directly in touch with Stalin about

Gorkii's situation (Stalin was also receiving information about Gorkii through Soviet diplomats and secret agents). In 1927 Stalin arranged for Gorkii to receive "quite a significant sum of money" from the Soviet state in the form of honoraria and advances for books in preparation for publication. Soviet diplomats in Italy began to negotiate with Gorkii about a possible visit to the USSR, even as the Central Committee issued an instruction to newspapers and other propaganda organs to organize a massive public celebration of his sixtieth birthday. Khalatov began corresponding with Gorkii in October 1927 and was involved in arranging his first return visit to the Soviet Union. The push to persuade Gorkii to return to the Soviet Union was thus a huge campaign coordinated between Stalin, the editors of central Soviet newspapers, and the state publishing house, involving private flattery, public spectacle, publication of the author's works, and financial incentives. All of these had their effect on the debt-ridden and homesick author. In May 1928 Gorkii met prominent representatives of the Soviet press (including Gronskii, Mikhail Gus, and Khalatov) at the International Exposition of the Press in Koeln, Germany, and then traveled on to Moscow. Although this trip was only a visit (Gorkii would not return permanently to the USSR until 1932), it did mark Gorkii's reappearance as an active participant in the Soviet literary and publishing world.[41]

As Gorkii was drawn into the Soviet literary world once again in the winter of 1927–1928, he immediately became involved in efforts to develop more positive news coverage, and specifically for the publication of a new journal to be called *Nashi dostizheniia (Our Achievements)*.[42] The journal would include departments covering the achievements of Soviet Power in all fields of life, from technology, to industrial production, to agronomy, to women's liberation, to culture, to the material comfort of workers. The journal would integrate positive news from many different levels of life, from the most mundane details of housework to the most elevated cultural and scientific endeavors, under the general theme of "achievements and feats." According to Gorkii's proposal for the journal published in *The Worker Gazette*, its target audience would be rank-and-file activists *(rabotniki)* throughout the USSR. Gorkii touted the educational significance of the new journal. "Activists *[rabotniki]* scattered in the most remote corners of the country will get a more or less broad picture of the general work accomplished on the territory of the Soviet Union. The rapidity of the development of that work will be clear to him [*sic*] when he compares data from one issue with that from another. He will feel himself a more lively and valuable participant in the great joint project."[43]

During Gorkii's summer 1928 tour of the Soviet Union, Khalatov organized a formal meeting between him and top Soviet editors and officials to discuss publication of *Our Achievements* (June 9, 1928). Along with Gorkii and Khalatov, attendees included Emelian Iaroslavskii, Anatolii Lunacharskii, Mikhail Koltsov, and Ivan Skvortsov-Stepanov. Aleksandr Fadeev, a leader of the Russian Association of Proletarian Writers (RAPP) and future first secretary of the Soviet Writers' Union, was also there.[44] Nearly all of those present were Old Bolsheviks, and most supported Gorkii's proposal. From their comments a fairly clear picture emerged of a journal devoted to counterbalancing the excesses of self-criticism and mobilizing party activists with coverage of the achievements of Soviet Power. Fadeev observed that although looked at in isolation the proposal for *Our Achievements* might seem a prescription for false boastfulness, in the total context of the Soviet press, the journal was necessary. "A journal that would take note of the bright side," he noted, "would be extremely useful."[45] Fadeev anticipated the appeal of the journal for young activists (nineteen or twenty years of age), the generation that was attending "Worker Faculty" *(rabfak)* schools at the factories. By showing how young Soviet activists were constructing socialism with their own hands *Our Achievements* would awaken the enthusiasm of other young activists "for building the new and the beautiful."[46]

Early planning for *Our Achievements*, which began publication in late 1928, took a number of cues from mass journalism and simultaneously anticipated the development of socialist realism. Gorkii's general interest in covering industry and technology,[47] his specific interest in covering "worker-innovators" who streamlined production with their inventions, and his concern with counterbalancing negative self-criticism with positive coverage resembled the central concerns of Aleksei Kapustin when he created the production review.[48] The projected audience for *Our Achievements* was rank-and-file party and Komsomol activists, the same audience targeted by the mass newspapers and mass journalists. Gorkii's plan to use the achievements of individual workers and peasants to awaken the enthusiasm of ordinary Soviet activists for socialist construction anticipated socialist realism. So, too, did Lunacharskii's interest in finding a form of fiction that would galvanize activists. The proposed equation of workers' achievements with successes in the more elevated fields of culture, art, and science anticipated the entire field of high Stalinist literary culture, in which Chkalov's record-breaking flights, Aleksei Stakhanov's record-breaking coal-mining shifts, and the opening of a conference on the works of Russian satirist Saltykov-Shchedrin at a workers' club were all heroic feats of socialist construction. In early 1930 Kaganovich, Molotov, and Stalin picked up Gorkii's call for more coverage of "the good." Gorkii himself became a key player in the formulation of socialist realism as an official literary doctrine.

Planning for *Our Achievements* also demonstrated how participants from a variety of institutional settings, from the newspapers to the Commissariat of Enlightenment, were thinking about the same problems facing the party, chiefly about how to galvanize a new generation of young activists with a sense of revolutionary purpose and enthusiasm. The common problems faced by the party as a whole, and the common assumptions of party higher-ups about feasible solutions, were more important in shaping Stalinist culture and socialist realism than the admittedly vicious internecine warfare between institutions and literary cliques.

Mass Journalism and Socialist Realism

In 1928–1929 the Komsomol continued to be a locus of literary and journalistic innovation. Together with Khalatov of the state publishing house and editors from *Young Guard*, the *Komsomolskaia pravda* editors were deeply involved in formulating policy for a new literature that would mobilize the mass of young Komsomol activists. The Komsomol editors sought answers to the same central problems Maksim Gorkii attempted to deal with in *Our Achievements*—mobilizing young activists, finding the right balance between "the Light" and "the Shadows"—but they were more ready to appeal to their audience's liking for adventure, heroism, and fantasy, they were more interested in deploying military metaphor and memories of the Civil War to motivate cadres, and they were probably more aware than Gorkii of mass journalism's successes in generating news from the shop floor. During the first two years of the Cultural Revolution (1928–1929) Komsomol cultural bureaucrats and the *Komsomolskaia pravda* editors formulated many of the main tenets of what would become known as "proletarian writing" and later "socialist realism." The *Komsomolskaia pravda* editors Kostrov, Bobryshev, and Ilin in particular were a link between mass journalism and the development of socialist realism, for they were both pioneers of mass journalism and leaders in the formulation of literary policy.

During the Cultural Revolution of 1928–1931 the Komsomol's peculiar contribution was the presentation of the Revolution and Civil War as a metaphor for the struggle to fulfill the First Five-Year Plan. In Komsomol propaganda industrial production became a kind of replaying of the heroic battles of the Civil War. Taras Kostrov early discerned the possibility of regenerating revolutionary fervor among young activists by appealing to the heroism of the Civil War era. In an April 1928 speech to the Fifteenth Moscow Province Conference of the Komsomol, Kostrov referred to the need "to check the fortification of the main line of our trenches, in the factories, in the workshops, and in the villages," and in the lower levels of the entire Komsomol organization. Kostrov presented the factories and fields of the USSR, the points of production, as "the trenches" of the Civil War. He decried the apathy of some Komsomol members who thought their life in the Soviet Union was boring because the class war was over. In France and in Germany, these members whined, life was interesting—"there are hand-to-hand grapples with the class enemy, but here with us all is dull and lukewarm." Kostrov called these attitudes "Nonsense! Lies!" He urged Komsomol activists to struggle with religious sectarianism, anti-Semitism, *smenovekhovstvo* (the view of some moderate intellectuals that the pressure of political and economic realities would inevitably transform the Bolsheviks into pragmatic social democrats), and foreign capitalism. He exhorted them to answer such defeatist moods with "the stubborn work of [socialist] construction, with daily deeds." The Bolsheviks had to be well armed and ready when proletarians of other countries called on them for aid in making the world revolution, or when aggressive capitalist powers tried to "pierce our fortress." Then the workers and the peasants would once more take up their rifles. Kostrov was acutely aware of the need to counter defeatist moods and indifference among young activists, and he proposed to do so by presenting the effort to industrialize and arm the USSR, as well as the repression of internal class enemies, as a replaying of the Civil War. This awareness was reflected in *Komsomolskaia pravda's* news coverage and in the Komsomol cultural bureaucrats' push to develop a heroic mass literature that would mobilize activists.[49]

In 1928–1929 *Komsomolskaia pravda* editors worked closely with the Komsomol CC Bureau in setting policy for a new mass literature. The focus of their efforts was the mobilizational use of fiction. In early 1929 *Komsomolskaia pravda* and the state publishing house launched a joint endeavor to publish the works of a number of Soviet authors in higher print runs and cheaper editions than ever before. The list of works published included a number of novels that would later be identified as models for socialist realism, including Fadeev's *The Rout*, Furmanov's *Chapaev*, Serafimovich's *The Iron Flood*, and Panferov's *Brusskii*.[50] On April 6, 1929, the Komsomol CC Bureau met to discuss the new series and mass literature in general with Khalatov, CC Agitprop official D. Khanin, and the *Komsomolskaia pravda* editors.[51]

In his presentation (later published in a low print run edition of two hundred copies), Khalatov defined the task of "worker political literature" as "the mobilization of the masses around the most important tasks of socialist construction (industrialization, rationalization of industry, socialist reconstruction, agriculture)." According to Khalatov the Thirteenth Party Congress's call in 1924 for the creation of a new mass literature for workers, peasants, and Red Army soldiers had not been fulfilled. He cited approvingly several successful publication series, including GIZ's Cheap Classics Library and the Novel-Newspaper *(Roman gazeta)* published by the newspaper *Moskovskii rabochii (Moscow Worker)*. But these were only a beginning. Only 12 percent of all book titles published in the Russian Republic were fiction, the genre preferred by mass readers. And of these titles, an unacceptably high proportion dealt with "alien" themes such as humor, World War I, prerevolutionary Russia, life in the West, fantasy, adventure, and White emigrés. In the first half of 1929 less than 5 percent of published titles dealt with the modern worker. Khalatov concluded that neither the state publishing house nor the Komsomol publishing house *Young Guard* was making a sufficient effort to reach new Communist cadres, young workers recently arrived from the countryside, or seasonal construction workers. Instead their literary production was still oriented toward the intelligentsia and higher-ranking party officials. It is noteworthy that Khalatov shared mass journalists' concern with reaching rank-and-file activists and "green" workers newly arrived from the countryside.[52]

The most active discussant in the conversation that followed Khalatov's lecture was Iakov Ilin, the *Komsomolskaia pravda* editor involved in promoting both mass journalism and coverage of Soviet sensations in sports. Ilin laid out his vision for mass literature in some detail, urging Khalatov and the GIZ editors to hire mass journalists to produce the new literature. Mass journalism, he asserted could serve as a model for a new fiction, as well as for real-life sketches *(ocherki)* of the accomplishments of ordinary cadres in socialist construction. Like future theorists of socialist realism, Ilin insisted on integrated presentation of the entire process of socialist construction, including difficulties put up by internal class enemies and residues of petty bourgeois mentality in the psyches of the Communist activists themselves. He criticized Gorkii's *Our Achievements* for ignoring difficulties and for its excessively dry presentation, in particular its heavy use of statistics. A more lively, "literary" presentation of personal narratives, showing how individuals overcame internal and external difficulties, would have more appeal for the mass reader, Ilin argued. Authors of the new literature, he said, should imitate mass journalists by setting their stories at the point of production and by personally visiting the field or factory to gather material and get "closer to the masses." He also contended that the new mass literature had to show the future prospects of socialist construction. This insistence on finding and presenting the embryonic utopian future in the present also portended an important plank of the socialist realist platform.[53]

The minutes of a meeting of editors of the *Young Guard* publishing house held on June 30, 1929, show participants groping toward a way to popularize the First Five-Year Plan and the task of industrialization in a literary form using heroism, adventure, and Civil War derring-do. The editors discussed the need for "a new type of adventure literature" that would avoid the "primitiveness" of works by authors such as Mayne Reid. This literature should include novels and short stories with a focus on themes from daily life, on situations young readers would recognize from their own experience. The First Five-Year Plan had to be sold to youth as a great adventure. The publishing house also needed to put out more historical novels dealing with the Revolution and Civil War. The main *rapporteur* to the session, Uzin, made it clear that the adventure of the First Five-Year Plan would be equated with the adventure of the Civil War. In doing so he made use of the phrase "heroes of socialist construction," which would become a key slogan of "proletarian writing" and socialist realism in the early 1930s. "For the adolescent generation," Uzin said, "I suppose that the focus should be on short stories and novels that illuminate the life and daily experience of the younger generation, here and abroad, the heroes of our socialist construction and the Civil War. We do not have such literature." Several minutes after Uzin finished speaking, an editor from the Leningrad branch of the publishing house, Borshanskii, endorsed Gladkov's

Cement as an example of the kind of heroic, adventure literature Uzin wanted. What *Young Guard* needed was a *Cement* for the Five-Year Plan.[54] Valentin Kataev's *Time, Forward!*, written two years later, answered Borshanskii's demand precisely.

The 1929 discussions on mass literature within the Komsomol almost completely ignored literature for girls and young women. The implied target of the new literature was the young *male* activist. Cultural bureaucrats discussed it in terms of heroism, adventure, war novels, fantasy, and popularization of technology, themes that 1920s library studies associated almost exclusively with male readers. At the June 30 meeting of *Young Guard* editors, the Leningrad representative Borshanskii noted the "total absence of literature for Komsomol girls," but no other participant was even concerned enough to pick up on his observation. Borshanskii's comments and other Komsomol sources—library studies and CC Agitprop Department reports on Komsomol members' reading preferences—suggest the meaning of the silence. According to Borshanskii, female members were mostly interested in "family life" and in stories about groups of "girlfriends" "hanging out together." Komsomol Agitprop Department analyses from the mid-1920s reported in disdainful language that girls' reading interests were "significantly more narrow than boys'," that they preferred "books 'about love,' 'on a woman's duties,' 'novels,'" and that they loved to read stories that were "entertaining" or "made them cry." In the view of Komsomol officialdom, girls were interested in the constrained, trivial, and highly individual worlds of families and love relationships. Boys, on the contrary, liked to read about grand world-historical events and processes, about the revolution, about technology, about adventure.

The Agitprop Department reports probably reflected a real difference in distribution of reading tastes between boys and girls, but they also reflected the cultural predispositions and prejudices of the officials who produced them. As Anne Gorsuch points out in a recent *Slavic Review* article, party and Komsomol officials tended to see women as "backward," passive, private, and apolitical, and men as forward thinking, active, public, and political. Even those who deplored women's subordination reinforced the stereotypes by denigrating family life as slavery and private life as trivial and bourgeois. These predispositions extended to analyses of reading habits. Komsomol officials (including women) often asserted that whereas male members were doing "serious" political reading in the newspapers, females were interested only in frivolous love stories.[55] The "masculinization" of Soviet literature and newspapers was determined by deeply rooted cultural categories, but it was accelerated by the party/Komsomol's drive in the late 1920s to rejuvenate the membership's revolutionary élan. Revolution was associated in the minds of many party officials with the "masculine" characteristics of courage in battle, discipline, and public activism. The "masculinization" was also accelerated by the retargeting of the press and literature at rank-and-file activists, who were mostly young and male (and increasingly working class).

From the first days of 1930 CC secretaries (most importantly Lazar Kaganovich) and Agitprop/Kultprop chief A. I. Stetskii sought ways to mobilize activists using positive coverage of socialist construction. They picked up the thrust of Maksim Gorkii's *Our Achievements* project, but rather than Gorkii's dry, measured approach, they preferred the more agitational, emotional approach of the Komsomol newspapers and mass journalists. Instead of statistics, they wanted individual stories, Soviet sensations, and socialist competitions. Beginning in 1930 the party's Agitprop Department and the leaders of RAPP, the literary organization favored by CC leaders at the time, urged authors to model their fiction on mass journalism and exemplary literary works such as Gladkov's *Cement.* The reliance of the RAPP authors and CC officials on literary models developed by the Komsomol and mass journalists during the NEP years made sense, for both the Komsomol and the mass newspapers had been working to reach young rank-and-file activists, precisely the group the party leadership now wanted to motivate, mobilize, and discipline.

Beginning in the fall of 1929 *On Guard in Literature*, the organ of RAPP, advised fiction and literary sketch *(ocherk)* writers to model their work on mass journalism. In August 1929, for example, Iu. Libedinskii, a prominent RAPP member, author, and literary theorist, scolded Soviet authors that they were writing too little about factories and workers' daily life. Writers ought to show not just life as it currently existed, but also the embryonic future—"future prospects" and "the development of the working class."[56] Immediately following Libedinskii's piece, in the same issue, the editors ran an article exhorting authors to go to the factories and fields to collect live material for their literary works. Echoing one of the mass journalists' key slogans, this article called writers "not observers, but participants in socialist construction." The role of the writer was not just to register and understand reality, but to take part in shaping it, just as the mass journalists were not just informers but "organizers of socialist construction."[57] These pieces advocated practices close to those of mass journalism, in particular shifting the story site to the factory shop floor, making the main characters workers, and having the author visit the point of production to gather "live" material. The overall emphasis on participation and organization rather than passive observation and recording also recalled mass journalism.

Another key article was by Vladimir Petrovich Stavskii, a young fiction and sketch author from a working-class family who had begun his writing career as a reporter at *Molot (The Hammer)*, Rostov-na-Donu's main party newspaper. Stavskii's career progressed from mass journalism to socialist realism—he later became general secretary of the Soviet Writers' Union. In his August 1929 article Stavskii described how he went about collecting material for a new book on socialist competition. Although he initially spent only three days at the Tver railroad car factory where he planned to set his sketches, Stavskii soon realized that he needed more time. Ultimately he worked at the factory for a month and a half, focusing on coverage of the work of shock brigades. Picking up the Komsomol's literary rhetoric, Stavskii related how after reading the factory newspaper's coverage of the socialist competition with a factory in Kolomenskoe (Moscow region), he had been inspired to write the stories "of all the heroes of the production front." He urged writers to take a job at the factories where they gathered material, not just to wander from workshop to workshop passively taking notes. By working at the Tver factory for an extended period of time, Stavskii claimed, he had been able to chart the slow processes by which socialist competition transformed the political attitudes of older, "backward" workers, making them into "conscious" proletarians. He also had been able to uncover the hidden enemies of Soviet Power, men who appeared to be workers but were infected with residues of petty bourgeois ideology. Stavskii's emphasis on showing how the process of socialist construction and factory labor transformed worker consciousness, and his insistence on the need to show both the incipient future and the residues of the old bourgeois, and feudal worlds foreshadowed official formulations of socialist realism. So, too, did his enthusiasm for publicizing worker heroes.[58]

In December 1929 *On Guard in Literature* ordered local RAPP branch organizations to link up with the worker correspondents' movement, one of the central institutions of mass journalism. The journal lambasted the Tula Association of Proletarian Writers for its lack of contact with worker/peasant correspondents' circles.[59] In August 1930 another article, "On the Work of Lower Level Circles," picked up on the theme, decrying local RAPP branch members' "condescension" toward and lack of contact with worker correspondents' circles. Rather than going on fantastic flights of literary imagination, members of local RAPP circles ought to be focusing on real production and social processes at their own factories. Ties with factory wall newspapers and their worker correspondents' circles would facilitate the collection of concrete material about factory life—"the presentation of the (individual) person in connection with production."[60]

By September 1930 the RAPP leadership's promotion of contacts with worker correspondents' circles had passed over into advocacy of "worker patronage" (*rabochee shefstvo*) of local RAPP branches. An appeal published in the RAPP journal that month, supposedly from workers at a factory in Moscow called V. I. Lenin, noted literature's important role in transforming the consciousness of workers and raising their cultural level. The appeal called for a new literature that would show the lives and exploits of ordinary workers and that would be built on the base already laid by mass journalism, the coverage of shock brigades and socialist construction.[61] The "workers'" appeal included a list of the factories where proletarians were ready to undertake "patronage" over RAPP, including some with the most venerable revolutionary traditions (the Red Putilov arms works in Leningrad, Moscow's Hammer and Sickle factory, and the AMO automobile works). The workers were to evaluate the writers' works at mass meetings, helping them to develop a literary language accessible to the ordinary reader and cultivate new literary cadres among ordinary factory operatives. The appeal in *On Guard in Literature* pointed in the direction of a literature that would imitate mass journalism, right down to the organization of mass events and the gathering of material on the shop floor.[62]

In February and May 1930, articles in *On Guard in Literature* by Iu. Libedinskii and K. Driagin defined the proper setting, subject matter, and tone for the new proletarian literature. Proletarian writers should portray how workers grew toward political consciousness through their labor inside the "collective," that is, an entire factory. Sketches and novels, then, should focus on the life of an entire enterprise. Proletarian literature, Libedinskii wrote, should "represent factories and manufactories, showing the production collective, live, dialectically developing people, showing him [*sic*] in the Communist reconstruction of the world, the reconstruction of himself, and the creation of a new Communist person."[63] Driagin's May article emphasized the need for a return to the "lyric" style, the "emotional romanticism," and the "heroism" of literature of the period of War Communism and the Civil War (1918–1921), echoing at least seven years of discussion within the

Komsomol agitprop apparatus. The end of the NEP and the initiation of the great industrialization drive "demand their own heroism, their own pathos, and the grandiose successes of [economic] renewal create the same rapture, awaken the same enthusiasm, as the struggle with weapons in hand." Driagin noted specifically that the suspense and enthusiasm of socialist competition could serve as a kind of proxy for the wartime excitement of 1917–1921—"Literature should obviously once again be penetrated by pathos and tension, presenting socialist competition and its inspiring effect."[64]

In his article Libedinskii cited both Stavskii and Mikhail Fedorovich Chumandrin as paragons of the new proletarian literature. Stavskii, as already noted, began his career as a newspaperman. Chumandrin's career also linked the world of 1920s journalism and 1930s proletarian/socialist realist literature. Born in 1905, Chumandrin came from a working-class family. His father was a worker in a boiler-making factory *(kotelshchik)*. Chumandrin began to write as a worker correspondent for local newspapers, but by 1925 was publishing short stories. Libedinskii particularly praised Chumandrin for juxtaposing the methods used by Furmanov and others in the presentation of Civil War historical fiction to the factory setting in his 1928 work, *The Factory "Rabelais."* In June 1930 a second commentator in *On Guard in Literature*, S. Dinamov, praised Chumandrin for pioneering the Soviet "production genre," and for making the factory "his world."[65]

About this time the editors of *On Guard in Literature* opened up a discussion of the newspaper *ocherk* (sketch) and its relation to fiction literature. Articles on this theme that ran between May 1930 and November 1931 demonstrated the close and evolving relationship between mass journalism and proletarian literature. Discussion was initiated by a May 1930 article analyzing the differences between the *ocherk* and the feuilleton, a short satirical piece (both were nonfiction genres). The author, L. Korelik, attempted to draw a clear line between the two genres, although in fact the terms were sometimes used interchangeably in Soviet journalism. In Korelik's categorization, the feuilleton was an outmoded genre that relied on coincidental, atypical anecdotes and unusual, even grotesque facts ("Catfish Eats Baby" or a piece on fraudulent use of government loans for home construction titled "Flying House"). The feuilletonist could point to some social problem or distortion, but did not point the way toward solution of the problem. The feuilleton often had an ironic tone (Korelik cited Lev Sosnovskii, the prominent *Pravda* feuilletonist and Trotskii supporter), which confused semiliterate Soviet readers. The *ocherk*, in Korelik's account, combined party directives with concrete facts illustrating their implementation (or failure thereof). Because it was shorter than the feuilleton, the *ocherk* fit well under the numerous headlines and headings of the shock campaign. The *ocherkist* avoided irony and "anecdotal shadings," which would be difficult for the mass reader to comprehend. Korelik linked the recent development of the Soviet *ocherk* directly to mass journalism, describing how reporters sick of reporting only from VSNKh and the central commissariats went out to the factories and the countryside to gather material for their *ocherki*. The *ocherk*, he concluded, was the genre best fitted for the years of the Great Break because of its accessibility to general audiences, its organizational role (combining party directives with sketches from the point of production), and its siting of news in the factories and the fields.[66]

From September 1930, *On Guard in Literature* presented the newspaper *ocherk* about production/factory life as a "transitional genre to the novel and the short story" and even as a model for proletarian literature. In that month's issue of the journal M. Luzin argued against the "false opposition" of the *ocherk* to the fictional genres. Although the author of the *ocherk* lacked the space to do a detailed portrayal of individual psychology, the genres were otherwise similar. Luzin devoted much of his exposition to an assault on the Futurist literary group Left Literary Front (LEF) (the poet Vladimir Maiakovskii was one of LEF's founding members) and its theories of literature and journalism. LEF critics had consistently polemicized against romance, literary fabrication (*literaturnaia vydumka*), frivolous sentimentality, and decoration in fiction. Instead they espoused a severe, nearly ascetic devotion to "naked facts" and "the precise pinpointing of the fact" (*tochnaia fiksatsiia faktov*). Their model for presentation of the unadorned fact was the newspaper story.[67] As Luzin pointed out, the LEF theorists' understanding of newspaper work as "the precise pinpointing of the fact" was naive.[68] Indeed, at the same time as the Futurists were condemning *literaturnaia vydumka*, or "literary fabrication," mass journalists were using the word *vydumka*, or "fabrication" to describe how they put together their socialist competitions, production reviews, and other mass events.[69] LEF critics called for a strong, revolutionary cleaving to reality, however harsh, but they utterly failed to understand how news was *manufactured*. Mass journalists, on the other hand, were acutely aware of the imperative to fabricate news. Luzin observed LEF's confusion on the issue, and denied that the *ocherk* was simply "factual," whereas novels and short stories were "literary inventions." Good novelists and good newspapermen alike, Luzin argued, selected, sought out, or manufactured facts that revealed the underlying dialectical development of reality—the struggle of class against class, which would lead ultimately to the victory of the proletariat and the founding of a socialist utopia. Both novelists and newspapermen ought to show the concealed processes buried deep within the welter of random facts. Both had to find the seeds of the utopian future that lay under the dirt and dust of the present. Luzin's essay connected the mass journalists' discovery that one could *organize* events that showed the proletariat struggling to construct socialism with an insistence that literature reveal "the typical" in life, the social processes of class struggle and socialist construction, and the portents of a Communist future to be found in the socialist present.[70]

The discussion of the *ocherk* and its intermediate position between newspaper reportage and literature pointed toward a certain bleeding together of journalistic and fictional genres. The boundaries were breaking down. For several months already, literary critics in *On Guard in Literature* had been discussing fictional works and collections of nonfiction *ocherki* together without always differentiating between them.[71] Luzin's September 1930 article in *On Guard in Literature* blurred the boundaries between nonfiction literary sketch and fiction by evaluating several collections of *ocherki* in terms of criteria usually applied by Soviet critics to novels. Thus, Luzin compared Ivan Zhiga's *Dumy rabochikh, zaboty i dela (zapiski rabkora) (Workers' Thoughts, Their Concerns and Affairs [Notes of a Worker-Correspondent])* with Furmanov's *The Rebellion*. Where Furmanov's novel connected concrete events with the class struggle, the historical development of the proletariat, and dialectical materialism, Zhiga's sketches were "static," the workers were idealized, their "low cultural level" smoothed over, and the real problems and difficulties of socialist construction ignored. Instead of a factory, Zhiga had portrayed "a beautiful stage set" on which workers played roles. What new proletarian writers needed to do, Luzin asserted, was to show the process of socialist construction and the dialectical unfolding of history in all their complexity, portraying both the good and the bad in the working class and in individual workers. They needed to show how the work of building socialism *inevitably* transformed backward, uncultured workers into politically conscious, Communist, cultured proletarians. Luzin was applying the same evaluative criteria to nonfiction sketches as he did to works of fiction, and he was doing so consciously. At the conclusion of his article, he spoke of radical changes taking place in the traditional system of literary genres. These changes were connected with the radical transformation of Soviet society during the First Five-Year Plan.[72]

The breakdown of traditional genre boundaries in Soviet literature of the early 1930s has been remarked upon by Gregory Carleton. Carleton argues that in socialist realist literature "authenticity," "cultural legitimacy," and ultimately truth value depend not on a given piece of literature's generic status as history, memoir, newspaper report, or fiction, but rather on adherence to a system of transgeneric rhetorical structures and modes he dubs *topoi* (following Ernst Curtius, a scholar of medieval European literature). *Topoi* include such parallel dichotomies as socialism versus nonsocialism, order versus chaos, knowledge versus ignorance, health versus illness, or production versus waste. In socialist realism, Carleton argues, the most important criterion for including a voice in a text is not its generic status, but its "reification of a topos." Thus the 1933 collection of sketches *Belomorsko-baltiiskii kanal imeni Stalina (The 'Stalin' White Sea Canal)*, purportedly a history of the canal's construction, includes passages that are fictionlike in inserting the reader into the narrative ("Try and listen in to a conversation") and using "the emotive techniques found in narrative journalism and historical novels." This is because the criteria for historical truth are no longer "the markers of a history or documentary chronicle—continuity of narrative focus and tense, the logical combination of event and person, . . . the reliance on empirically verifiable sources"—but rather the reification of *topoi*. In Luzin's discussion of the *ocherk* we see this principle in action. Empiricism and "the objective fixation of fact" are not necessary or even desirable characteristic for the non-fiction newspaper *ocherk*. Luzin judges the *ocherk* according to the same criteria he uses to evaluate fictional works. Is the work set at a factory or other productive enterprise? Does it show the life of the entire production collective? Does it show how the dialectical unfolding of history (read "socialist construction") makes workers into class-conscious Bolsheviks? Does it pick out and spotlight "the typical" from amidst the welter of mere facts—the backward worker who exemplifies kulak obstruction of industrialization, the careerist party official? Does it reveal the deep currents of the social and economic processes driving the USSR toward socialism? To use Carleton's terminology, Luzin judges both fiction and nonfiction works by whether they "reify *topoi*."[73]

In Soviet literature of the 1930s, Carleton argues, "different discursive modes can and do serve the same rhetorical purpose, though each mode may be formally identified as history, fiction, or children's tale, for that matter." This is the key to understanding *why* genres began to bleed into one another in 1930–1931. Increasingly party officials and cultural bureaucrats wanted newspaper reports and "proletarian literature" (and other genres as well, such as history) to serve a single rhetorical purpose, namely the motivation and mobilization of rank-and-file party or Komsomol activists to participate in socialist construction. Literature *and* the newspapers were to hold up a kind of mirror to party cadres, but a transformative mirror that showed them as brave warriors on the central battleground of history. To make a maximum economy of effort, other narratives were almost totally banished from literature, no matter what the genre.[74]

The breakdown in genre boundaries, then, reflected the enforcement of a common rhetorical function. It was accompanied by a breakdown of the occupational boundaries between journalists and novelists. RAPP leaders and party agitprop officials were holding up mass journalism as an example for fiction writers to follow, and many mass journalists were able to cross over to the field of belles lettres. Thus, a number of mass journalists ended up actually producing proletarian literature and socialist realism. Carleton notes the case of Iakov Ilin, the *Komsomolskaia pravda* editor who wrote the novel *The Great Conveyor* and the series of nonfiction sketches, *People of the Stalingrad Tractor Factory*. Both works dealt with the building and start-up of the Stalingrad Tractor Factory and both incorporate the same *topoi*. Carleton writes although the two books were "generically distinct," contemporary Soviet critics accepted them as "functionally equivalent." "Though by definition one is fiction and the other is documentary, each is held to illuminate the referent with similar precision."[75] Another journalist who made the transition to fiction was Boris Gorbatov. Gorbatov began his career as a reporter for the Donbass newspaper *Vserossiiskaia kochegarka (All-Russian Stoker)* in 1922 at the age of fourteen and went on to write several novels in the 1930s while also serving as a *Pravda* correspondent.[76] Even Leonid Kovalev, former secretary of the *Pravda* party cell and champion of mass journalism, edited a collection of poems, memoirs, party leaders' speeches, and short literary sketches dedicated to the construction of the Moscow subway system (1935). This collection transgressed genre boundaries in a fashion similar to that described by Carleton in the case of *The 'Stalin' White Sea Canal*.[77]

Beginning in January 1931, commentators in *On Guard in Literature* renewed their pressure on novelists to imitate the practices of mass journalism. The leading editorial in the journal's first issue of 1931 called for "literary processing of concrete material on shock work and the growth of Communist labor."[78] Number four, in February, announced a public letter released by the RAPP Secretariat condemning fiction writers' "lordly condescension" toward "the small forms," such as the newspaper *ocherk*. The RAPP leadership appears to have been trying to draw the teeth of mass journalists at *Journalist* who had picked up the LEF argument that all belles lettres were obsolete—that mass journalism had replaced all of their useful social functions. The RAPP response was to urge imitation of mass journalism and the "short forms" while also maintaining that "long forms" of fiction could still do some things newspaper sketches could not, such as give detailed portrayals of the individual's psychological development.[79]

In the same February 1931 issue of *On Guard in Literature* Vladimir Stavskii and mass journalist Boris Galin ran articles that urged the melding in the newspaper *ocherk* of mass journalism's organizational thrust with the bourgeois adventure story and certain elements of proletarian literature. Galin, a correspondent for *Komsomolskaia pravda*, underlined the importance of the *ocherk*'s "organizational role." Stavskii wrote that the fiction and sketch writer, like the mass journalist, was "battling actively for the reforming of reality in a Communist shape." He praised Galin, Ilin and other newspapermen for writing *ocherki* based on their own "civic activities" on the factory shop floor, comparing them to night raiders in trench warfare. In a move that recalled the 1920s Komsomol enthusiasm for the bourgeois adventure novel, Stavskii urged the Soviet "sketch writer-warrior" to follow the example of T. E. Lawrence's memoir of his guerrilla war against Turkish forces in Arabia, *Revolt in the Desert*. Like Lawrence, the Soviet "*ocherkist-warrior*" should use his pen to fight for the interests of his class. Stavskii also urged sketch writers to use Soviet works of *fiction* as models, in particular Furmanov's *The Rebellion* and *Chapaev*. He praised Galin, Ilin, and others for embodying certain principles of fictional proletarian literature in their work—showing the class struggle, selecting "typical" facts that epitomized the "tendency of development and the essence of phenomena."[80]

In May 1931 *On Guard in Literature* reprinted a *Pravda* editorial of April 13 that defined the role and themes of proletarian literature almost exclusively in mass journalistic terms: organizing the masses, increasing productivity, and promoting socialist competitions.[81] In May 1931 *Pravda* announced the party leadership's endorsement of yet another element of Komsomol mass journalism—"showing the heroes of socialist construction." In a full-page spread headed "The Country Should Know Its Heroes," the paper ran profiles of shock workers at metallurgical works, textile factories, and railway yards. Each worker had received a state medal of some kind, either an Order of the Red Banner of Labor or an Order of Lenin. Photographs of the workers accompanied the short biographies.[82]

From *Pravda* the trope of "showing heroes" spread rapidly throughout the Soviet publishing world, unifying genres from newspaper reportage to novels to history. Already on May 4 the RAPP Secretariat had called for "the literary presentation of the heroes of the First Five-Year Plan." *On Guard in Literature* picked up the appeal in a June 1931 piece titled "For the Showing of the Heroes of Bolshevik Tempos." Echoing the rhetoric of Komsomol Agitprop Department officials in 1929 *On Guard in Literature* called for both newspapers and RAPP journals to "show the heroes of the First Five-Year Plan." The journal once again instructed RAPP branches to imitate a number of mass journalistic practices—to bring fiction writers "closer to production," "to show socialist labor at our enterprises," and to cultivate a new generation of proletarian authors from among worker correspondents and shock workers. In October 1931 Iu. Libedinskii announced that the new tasks of "capturing" the hero of labor on the printed page and showing "the process of formation of a new consciousness" had finally dissolved the boundaries between genres. In addition to the rhetoric of heroism, Libedinskii also picked up the Komsomol's use of the word *pafos* (pathos) to describe an emotionally charged narrative.[83]

In exhorting their members to "show the heroes of socialist construction" the RAPP leaders told them to follow the example set by newspapermen. In the summer of 1931 *On Guard in Literature* scolded literary journals for falling behind the newspapers in showing heroes. The RAPP organ recommended that the doyens of high literature follow the examples of *Worker Moscow* (now edited by Leonid Kovalev), *The Worker Gazette*, and *Komsomolskaia pravda* in profiling heroes. "The newspapers," *On Guard in Literature* commented, "have moved ahead in comparison with the journals. In many newspapers showing the heroes of the Five-Year Plan takes first place."[84]

The party leadership's endorsement of the campaign to "show the heroes of socialist construction" in mid-1931 was a turning point in the history of Soviet propaganda, journalism, and literature. This was the public manifestation of a decision-making process that had been going on within the Central Committee at least since the January 16, 1930, Orgburo session devoted to press coverage of industrialization.

Central Committee secretaries and top Agitprop officials jettisoned their stern disapproval of excessive pathos, romance, and grandiosity in literature and adopted the Komsomol's more emotional approach with its emphasis on heroism, Soviet sensations, and adventure. This move was connected with the leadership's sense that they had to find a way to galvanize the younger generation of party activists with revolutionary enthusiasm. It was also the beginning of a CC campaign to coordinate publications in belles lettres, history, and journalism around the mobilization of rank-and-file cadres, a campaign that co-opted and built on earlier efforts to reach ordinary activists by mass journalists, Komsomol agitprop officials, Maksim Gorkii, and pioneers of Soviet sensations such as Ivan Gronskii. In April 1931 RAPP "adopted" Maksim Gorkii, hailing his contributions to Soviet literature in lead articles in *On Guard in Literature*.[85] By September 1931 Gorkii was working with the CC Culture and Propaganda Department, the RAPP leadership, and mass-journalists-turned-authors such as M. Chumandrin on the production of a series on The History of Factories, a series aimed at capitalizing on the youth enthusiasm for heroic history identified by the Komsomol in the 1920s.[86] The goal, of course, was to mobilize youth and ignite their revolutionary fervor. The conscription of many kinds of fiction and nonfiction literature into the central task of mobilization accelerated the dissolution of genre boundaries already begun by mass journalists and RAPP critics.

In the minds of Aleksandr Stetskii, head of the CC Culture and Propaganda Department, and his bosses, mobilization of literature required the formation of a single writers' association. On April 23, 1932, the CC passed a resolution, "On the Reconstruction of Literary and Artistic Organizations," dissolving RAPP and ordering the CC Orgburo to organize a single unified Soviet Writers' Union. In other fields of the arts, too, monolithic, state-supervised unions were to be set up (such as in music and painting). The CC leadership's purpose was to attain maximal mobilization of writers and artists behind the tasks set by the party. In literature, the resolution aimed to achieve the long-discussed unification of all writers' organizations while chastising RAPP leaders for their unremitting hostility to nonparty "fellow travelers" and other authors not in their organization. This hostility, party leaders thought, was obstructing the push for unification and mobilization. Hence the resolution, rather than unifying all Soviet literary effort under RAPP's aegis, abolished RAPP and proposed to set up an alternative monolithic literary organization.[87]

A second part of the mobilization of writers was the designation of an official Central Committee-endorsed literary doctrine. The CC secretaries and their deputies were proceeding to the formulation of the doctrine of socialist realism even as they issued the Reconstruction resolution. Because of the dissolution of RAPP and the proclamation of a new literary doctrine, historians and critics have tended to overemphasize the discontinuity between RAPP/proletarian literature and the Writers' Union/socialist realism. However, there was not only much continuity in leading personnel between the two unions, but there was also continuity in doctrine. In April and May 1932 Ivan Gronskii, then head editor of *Izvestiia*, was a member of a five-man Politburo-appointed commission that sought to bring RAPP leaders quietly into the new Writers' Union (the other commission members were Stetskii and CC secretaries Stalin, Kaganovich, and Postyshev). In his memoirs Gronskii describes a seven-hour session of negotiations between the commission and the RAPP leadership in early May 1932. The main issues at stake were RAPP leaders' desire to have their own autonomous section within the writers' union and the name to be applied to the new unified literary doctrine (in the end RAPP caved on both points). RAPP wanted to use their own designation, "the RAPP dialectical-materialistic creative method," whereas the Politburo commission pushed for a new name. Gronskii makes it clear that what was at stake in the discussion of the new official literary method was mostly naming and not actual doctrine. In the end the RAPP leaders accepted a new name, "the creative method of socialist realism," which Gronskii claims he and Stalin had agreed upon before the meeting. A comparison of later socialist realist doctrine with 1930–1931 RAPP statements on "proletarian literature" shows that the change was one of labels, not substance. RAPP formulations from *On Guard in Literature* issues of 1930–1931, Ivan Gronskii's 1932 speech to the first meeting of the Organizational Committee for the new writers' union, the union statutes prepared in 1933–1934, and Andrei Zhdanov's speech to the First Congress of the Writers' Union in August 1934 specify similar parameters for the new Soviet literature. The writer had to present "the typical," "contemporary events in their revolutionary development," and he or she had to select those "facts" that showed the process of socialist construction and the coming to political consciousness of the proletariat. The writer's work ought to be optimistic and to depict the "success of socialist construction." It had to appeal to the new Soviet mass reader. The work should include a coloring of "revolutionary romanticism," and it should seek out the seed of the future in the labors of the present. Finally, the writer should set his work at factories, construction sites, and collective farms, showing the heroism of the ordinary men and women building socialism.[88]

Cross-checking the key people involved in formulating literary doctrine in 1932–1934 with this chapter's account of the relationship between Soviet journalism and literature allows us to trace the origins of the various elements of socialist realism. In several cases we end up in 1920s newspaper journalism. The notion of presenting the process of "revolutionary development" and the transformation of working-class consciousness was drawn from Soviet fiction authors of the 1920s, such as Gladkov and Furmanov. The call to depict the successes or "achievements" of Soviet Power came from Maksim Gorkii, Ivan Gronskii, and other writers and editors who had become concerned with the disruptive power of self-criticism in the late 1920s. Both Gorkii and Gronskii were intensely involved in formulating socialist realism as official doctrine in 1932–1933. The imperative to appeal to the mass reader (read "rank-and-file activist") began with mass journalists and Komsomol agitprop officials in the mid-1920s and was picked up by CC cultural bureaucrats, including Stetskii, by 1929. The concept of "revolutionary romanticism" first appeared inside the Komsomol, where agitprop officials and newspaper editors had been appealing to male youths' enthusiasm for adventure tales, epic historical fiction, and "Soviet sensations" since the early 1920s. The motto also owed something to Ivan Gronskii, one of the pioneers of the Soviet sensation at *Izvestiia* in the late 1920s. Last but not least, the siting of the new Soviet literature at the factory and the use of strike work and socialist competition as vehicles to present the "heroism of socialist construction" went back to mass journalists' initiatives to create news from the shop floor during the 1926 belt-tightening campaign. This influence can be traced personally through mass journalists who later became prominent Soviet writers and cultural bureaucrats, such as Vladimir Stavskii, Mikhail Chumandrin, and Iakov Ilin. Several specific characteristics of socialist realism (and especially of the production novel) can thus be traced back to mass journalistic origins. Taking a broader view, both socialist realist literature and mass journalism arose from the party and Komsomol's search for forms that would substitute for bourgeois sensationalism, have genuine popular appeal, and mobilize rank-and-file activists.

~ Conclusion

WHEN I FIRST BEGAN RESEARCHING this project in 1992–1993 I sought to define and explain the sharp change in the tone of Soviet central newspapers between the mid-1920s and the early 1930s. Over time I realized that I was studying something larger than just the newspapers. As I read the papers and the discussions and debates among Soviet journalists I began to see how the master narrative of Stalinist culture—the story of the epic battle to industrialize the USSR—emerged during the New Economic Policy (NEP) years. Spinning off this tale were some of the central tropes of Soviet discourse in the 1930s and later—the glorification of the worker-activist as hero, the omnipresence of hidden enemies of socialism who were sabotaging production, the presentation of industrial labor as combat, and the conviction that socialist labor in general and socialist competition in particular were the furnaces in which the party forged workers' political consciousness. I became convinced that NEP newspapers and NEP journalists played a leading role in the creation of official Stalinist culture.

Behind the transformation of Soviet newspapers at the end of the NEP and the development of Stalinist culture were a series of moves made by party leaders as far back as 1922. Among these were the decisions to create a proletarian Communist Party by mass recruitment of workers, to use denunciation from below to monitor the state apparatus, to undertake forced-draft industrialization, and to focus the print media almost exclusively on mobilizing party activists. Other, apparently less momentous decisions also played a role in the origins of Stalinist culture. The creation of mass worker newspapers, workplace wall newspapers,[1] and the worker-peasant correspondents' movement at the outset of the NEP laid the institutional basis for the development of mass journalism, and thus of important elements of Stalinist discourse. The CC's 1927 decision to "Communize" journalism and promote young Bolshevik newspapermen from provincial cities accelerated the adoption of socialist competition and other mass journalistic methods throughout the Soviet press.

But the decisions of the Central Committee (CC) secretaries and their subordinates could only set the framework for the project of cultural construction. For the newspapers, journalists were the most important creative agents. Journalists acted within the framework set by the CC, but they were also constrained by Bolshevik theories of agitation and propaganda, in particular by the taboos on bourgeois sensationalism and appeals to individual desire. During the NEP journalists strove to create genres that would really appeal to party and Komsomol activists without transgressing these boundaries.

In this quest newspapermen were also constrained by the cultural artifacts and techniques available to them. As pioneers in the fashioning of the first state socialist mass media, they had a limited range of examples from the past to draw on. There were the models of the prewar socialist presses in Europe and the prerevolutionary Bolshevik press, but these were largely irrelevant because they had operated from a position of political opposition, not domination. There were a few cryptic utterances of Lenin about the press, which were elevated to the status of axioms. There were the prerevolutionary "copeck" papers, cheap publications for the urban masses, but these were problematic because of their "yellowism." There were the examples of various prerevolutionary Russian publications aimed at enlightening the masses, such as the Tsarist government's publication for peasants, *The Village Herald*, and the books and pamphlets put out by the Tolstoyan publishing house *Posev* (Sowing the Seeds). Finally, there was the experience of the Civil War Soviet press in mobilizing the populace for war. That was all.

The culture (or perhaps I should say cultures) of the "black hands"— those Russians who made their living by manual labor—strongly influenced the development of official Stalinist culture.[2] Cultural transformation in NEP Russia was inextricably tied up with the Bolsheviks' social revolution (made from above, but nonetheless real). Party officials and journalists tried to make the newspapers appeal to the new

cohort of young male working-class party members. Using reader studies, information on popular mood, reader letters, and their own predilections (many young Soviet journalists were themselves of humble
origins) they shaped official culture to cater to masculine working-class
culture. By the First Five-Year Plan they had incorporated into the
newspapers and into literature resentment of bosses, paeans to the
heroism of "worker-warriors" on the "labor front," and glorification of
physical toughness and strong will as the ultimate virtues. Outsized
feats of production, Arctic adventure tales, and miraculous technological advances were the Soviet sensations journalists fed their audience in
the 1930s.

The Transformation of the Press and the Periodization of Soviet History

The dramatic change in the Bolshevik leadership's cultural priorities at
the end of the NEP suggests the need for a revision of Nicholas
Timasheff's well-known Great Retreat thesis, which has come into
question in recent years. In 1946 Timasheff, a sociologist, argued that
from 1935 or thereabouts Stalin reversed revolutionary policies in an
effort to stabilize Soviet society by appealing to traditional Russian
values. Among other developments he cited changes in family policy
(criminalizing abortion, making divorce more difficult), the return to a
more traditional school curriculum, and the official revival of Russian
nationalism. The most important challenge to Timasheff has come
from Stephen Kotkin, in his 1995 book *Magnetic Mountain*. Kotkin
argues that high Stalinist culture was not a retreat from the revolutionary project, but a logical, if improvised, extension of it. Recently Karen
Petrone has extended Kotkin's critique of the Great Retreat concept,
contending that policy changes in the mid-1930s were too complex to
be categorized as "retreat."[3]

With hindsight it now seems that Timasheff's thesis was far too
broad, and that the Soviet regime in the mid-1930s did not retreat from
earlier revolutionary positions in politics and economics. However, it is
undeniable that there were major cultural changes during these years.
What are we to make of the blossoming of Stalin's "cult of personality,"
the rehabilitation of Tsarist military heroes, the appearance of Soviet
"ladies bountiful" *(obshchestvennitsy)* among the Stalinist elite, or the
state-sponsored worship of Aleksandr Pushkin? One thing we can say is
that the turn from enlightenment to pragmatic mobilization of activists

in the First Five-Year Plan adumbrated these changes. From 1930 the Central Committee leaders used culture as a pragmatic tool of mobilization and within certain limits were willing to take whatever tack would motivate their cadres to act on party orders. If this meant spurning Bolshevik taboos on newspaper sensationalism or the publication of "boulevard" adventure stories, then so be it. And if this meant the revival of taboo Russian nationalism, then that, too, was acceptable.[4]

Newly available archival evidence clearly demonstrates that for party policy on newspapers and literature, the most important turning point was in the winter of 1929–1930. In January–February 1930 the two most important Central Committee bureaus for brass-tacks policy making, the Orgburo and Secretariat, set course for the creation of a new literature that would show the daily process of socialist construction and motivate party cadres by presenting the romance, pathos, and adventure of industrialization. This literature would be modeled in part on newspaper genres developed during the NEP. It became socialist realism, the centerpiece of high Stalinist culture.

In culture, as in politics and economics, then, the key breakpoint in Soviet history up to Stalin's death was the years of the First Five-Year Plan. The party leadership abandoned the difficult, even utopian task of fashioning the New Soviet Man and opted for pragmatic methods of mass mobilization. This was the fundamental change, and the so-called Great Retreat that began in the mid-1930s followed from it.

Soviet Newspapers and the Neotraditional Image of Leninist Societies: An Interpretation

In the world context Soviet newspapers of the First Five-Year Plan were sui generis. It is true that they drew on the same technologies as mass circulation newspapers elsewhere, including the rotary press and new techniques for reproducing photographs, and it is true that many newspapers worldwide were both state subsidized and state censored. But Soviet newspapers by 1930 were embedded in a system of political legitimation that was fundamentally new and unique. This made them different from other newspapers worldwide, including other official state organs.

In the introduction I contrasted the evolving Soviet system of agitation and propaganda with the contemporaneous elaboration in the United States of public relations as a "science" studied and practiced by professionals. Behind agitprop and public relations lay two entirely different systems of political legitimation. In the liberal democracies of "the West" the legitimacy of governments depended to a large extent on what Max Weber calls rational/legal authority. That is, state officials claimed authority and the populace as a whole accepted that authority based on the notion that they came to power and governed according to rational norms and rules.[5] Thus, some officials were chosen in elections supposedly organized according to a legally defined and fair system. Others were chosen based on educational and professional qualifications specified by legal or administrative documents. The relationship of public relations (PR) to the legitimacy of this system was indirect. Governments could use PR tools to present the whole system of authority as rational and fair, but of course opposition political candidates, private corporations, and individuals could also use them for their own goals.

By the end of the 1920s the authority of the Soviet party/state rested on entirely different ground from the rational/legal liberal state. The Soviet press, the direct monopoly agent of the government, presented the Communist Party as a heroic organization specially designated by History to lead the USSR, and ultimately humanity as a whole, into the socialist future. The most important audience for this presentation was the rank-and-file party cadres themselves. What the nonparty masses thought was of secondary concern. Political scientist Ken Jowitt argues that the legitimacy of the Soviet state at this time was based on charisma, albeit the "impersonal charisma" of the party itself. In Weber's classification of political legitimacy, charismatic authority flows from an individual's perceived "supernatural, superhuman, or at least specifically exceptional powers or qualities."[6] According to Jowitt, for party members the party became an "impersonal organizational hero" with a special, almost supernatural connection to History and the socialist future.[7]

Jowitt argues that to maintain the party's legitimacy with its rank-and-file members, Leninist leaders must designate a "social combat task," a heroic assignment connected with the forward march of History. Without such an overarching task, the extralegal powers and personal connections of local party officials are no more than corrupt patron-client networks. In the absence of world-historical struggle, party officials use their authority to enrich themselves, their friends, and their relatives, and to develop a regular network of clients loyal to and dependent on them. In Weberian terms, this is the "routinization of charisma." According to Jowitt the outcome of this routinization is a state grounded in a version of Weber's "traditional" authority. (Weber

defines traditional authority as based on the personal loyalty of retain-
ers to their master and the master's purported connection to longstand-
ing and sacred "rules and powers.") Jowitt labels the system of political
legitimation in mature Leninist regimes as "neotraditionalism." He
thus signals that it is an amalgam of traditional and rational/legal
authority, in which the former nonetheless dominates. To quote Jowitt,
"The (neotraditional) framework recognizes methodical economic
action but favors 'heroic' storming; values professionals but subordinates them to tribute-demanding apparatchik 'notables'; attempts to
upgrade contract as a mode of economic predictability, but debilitates
its institutional integrity with *blat* [exchange of bribes and favors]."[8]

It is important to recognize that the term "neotraditionalism" does
not refer to some recrudescence of Russian tradition in the sense of
folkways or long-practiced customs. It does not refer, for example, to
Nicholas Timasheff's Great Retreat. Nor does it refer to Moshe
Lewin's argument that traditional peasant mentalities contaminated
and ultimately distorted the Soviet modernization project.[9] It refers
instead to Weber's classification of legitimate political authority, in
which Jowitt's thinking is based. In Weber's terms, Jowitt claims,
authority in Leninist societies begins with the (impersonal) charisma of
the party and devolves into (neo)traditionalism. The reasons for this
devolution have as much to do with political structures and ideology as
they do with the influence of traditional peasant society on the state.
Jowitt does not dismiss the effect of traditional peasant mentalities on
the Leninist state, nor do I.[10] But in the neotraditionalist image[11] of
society they do not appear in the foreground.[12]

Jowitt's conception of legitimacy in Leninist societies accounts very
well for data on the development of the Soviet press network through
the early 1930s. Between 1926 and 1930 militant young Communist
newspapermen, agitation-and-propaganda (agitprop) officials, and the
Central Committee leadership allied with Stalin sought to revive the
revolutionary élan of the party by designating a new heroic combat task.
This was, of course, the industrialization of the USSR. Presenting
industrialization as an epic battle was supposed to end the malaise and
corruption of the NEP era, which many Communists saw as a concession to capitalism. Newspapermen created that presentation. In Jowitt's
terms, the transformation of the Soviet press in the second half of the
1920s was all about mobilizing activists for the new social combat task,
and it was central to strengthening the legitimacy of the party leadership with ordinary party members. Industrialization reconnected the

party with the forward march of history because it supposedly led to the socialist millennium. Thus, it regenerated the party's charismatic authority.

To return to recent interpretations of Soviet history discussed in the introduction: The neotraditional image of Leninist societies based in Max Weber's sociology has more explanatory power than the postmodern emphasis on an overarching "modernity" common to Leninist and liberal states. It explains the fundamental differences between modes of legitimate authority in each regime type. But it also explains other characteristics of Leninist regimes that the modernity paradigm cannot. The most important of these for this book's argument is the development of an estate or status group hierarchy.

Through most of its history the Soviet Union evolved steadily into a hierarchical society divided into a number of status groups or estates. These were groups with specific legal privileges and disabilities, different levels of access to information, and different levels of access to state goods. The party/state endeavored to control movement from one group to another, admittedly with mixed success. Examples of these status groups included Communists who held jobs controlled by CC appointment (the *nomenklatura*), collective farmers (who could not legally leave their farms without official permission until the 1970s), residents of closed cities, people holding residence permits for "in-demand" cities such as Moscow or Leningrad, employees of high-priority defense enterprises, and the various passport nationalities.[13] In the 1920s at least the most important status division in the minds of party leaders and the population at large seems to have been between active party and Communist Youth League members on the one hand (the *aktiv*) and the nonparty masses on the other.

Some scholars influenced by postmodern theories have tended to gloss over the importance of hierarchy in the Soviet Union and to deny the conflicts and different points of view that might be expected to accompany the stratification of any society. This derives largely from the immense power to mold the world that they ascribe to discourse. Thus Stephen Kotkin in *Magnetic Mountain* describes many examples of the status group hierarchy at Magnitogorsk but argues that the new state-sponsored culture had a relatively uniform effect on the population as a whole, making nearly everyone into true believers in the Stalinist version of socialism.[14] More recently Jochen Hellbeck has suggested that by the 1930s even ordinary Soviet subjects (nonactivists) "had internalized authority . . . (and) cast themselves as revolutionary selves." Hellbeck essentially denies that Soviet subjects could act autonomously, recognize their own self-interest, or understand the contradictions inherent in official Stalinist discourse. They could not think outside official categories.[15]

Claims that official discourse exerted almost total control over the consciousness of Soviet subjects ignore a growing body of evidence that even at the height of Stalinist repression in the 1930s many individuals mocked party agitprop talk, questioned the assumptions of state propaganda, and sometimes even challenged the authority of party/state officials openly.[16] In the 1920s, as this book has demonstrated, readers responded in wildly divergent ways to messages conveyed by the official press. Some applauded the party's persecution of class enemies and welcomed the coming socialist millennium, some questioned party policies that they did not understand, and others raged against the grotesque lies that they found in the press. These diverse responses in part reflected the development of Soviet status groups. Party members and would-be party members were much more likely than other groups to be captivated by official discourse. To create a new Communist identity for themselves and to rise in the party/state hierarchy they had to master its language and its claims. Nonparty members understood very well that they stood outside the charmed circle of *obshchestvennost* (official society), and that party members to one degree or another had special rights and privileges. Many grumbled about this and resented it; some stood up and protested. The very notion of the party as a heroic vanguard leading society to the millennium, which came to be the basis of Bolshevik legitimacy, excluded the nonparty masses. It also denied the sweeping egalitarian rhetoric of the February and October revolutions in Russia. It was not hard for nonparty members to recognize this and resent it. Nor did they have to couch their resentment in terms of support for capitalism and liberal democracy or even their own rational self-interest.[17] There were plenty of socialist discourses available from the prerevolutionary era for the articulation of resentment and dissent.

As the Soviet newspapers focused more tightly on inculcating in Communist activists a sense of their special heroic mission, they widened the status divisions of Soviet society. Moreover, as experts since Alex Inkeles have recognized, the party developed a layered system of agitation and propaganda, with different information and different messages available for different strata of the status hierarchy.[18] This book has argued that in the late 1920s the party leadership came to channel the bulk of its propaganda resources toward the rank-and-file party activists.[19] To summarize, the Soviet press and the whole agitprop system both reflected and reinforced the evolving status hierarchy of Soviet society.

In neotraditionalist terms the development of a highly stratified status society ultimately goes back to the charismatic basis for the party's authority. By the First Five-Year Plan, at least, party activists obeyed orders from their leaders in large part because they saw themselves as part of an elite warrior band battling to reach the socialist (and industrial) future. In combat conditions unquestioning obedience to orders is absolutely necessary, and so is the ability to distinguish clearly between friend and foe. Hence the strict discipline and *exclusivity* of the party. Jowitt argues that the party's exclusivity and its members' compulsive fear of "contamination" by opportunists and outright class enemies comes out of the transformative project at the core of the party's impersonal charisma. Leninist parties seeking to transform their societies necessarily generate great turbulence and social disorder. In these conditions party leaders and the rank-and-file come to value discipline and loyalty above all. As in elite military units members develop a contempt for and suspicion of the "civilian" (nonparty) outsiders.[20]

I believe that we need to view Leninist societies in general, and the USSR in particular, as radical alternatives to liberal democratic societies. Leninism and the Stalinist developmental model that grew out of it are best understood as a coherent alternative to the modernity of the wealthy liberal capitalist states. Stephen Kotkin suggests this approach in *Magnetic Mountain*, but in my opinion he does not take it in the body of his book, choosing instead to emphasize practices that the Soviet Union shared with liberal democratic states. In the end Kotkin characterizes the Soviet Union as the most extreme development of modernity and the modern welfare state—as a logical extension of, rather than a radical alternative to, the modern liberal state.[21] I prefer to view Soviet state and society as Alexander Gerschenkron did in his seminal work *Economic Backwardness in Historical Perspective*—as a distinct developmental path to a industrial modernity.[22] The Soviet state emerged as a functional substitute for the liberal capitalist path to modern industrial power. In place of the industrialized capitalist democracies' commitment to market economics, parliamentary politics, and individual freedom,[23] the Soviet Union substituted state control of the economy, the vanguard party, and centrally organized coercion. The goal, as Stalin asserted on many occasions, was to gain the power of a modern industrialized economy and surpass the economic and military strength of the liberal capitalist states.

In this alternative modernity the newspapers' most important function was not to entertain, make money, promote rational debate, or even sell the party's messages to the population at large. It was the mobilization of cadres to fulfill the social combat task of industrialization. As Jowitt's discussion makes clear, industrialization did not just strengthen the USSR's economy and international security, it also sustained the legitimacy of the party *among its members*. In their handling of the press, party leaders were first and foremost concerned with communicating their orders and motivating rank-and-file activists to implement them. For much of Soviet history the "public" that really mattered was the bureaucrats, scholarly and technical elites, and activists who made up *obshchestvennost*. By 1930 these were the primary target audience for Soviet newspapers. And with the exception of a few limited periods (World War II and the Thaw, for example), they remained so until the middle years of Mikhail Gorbachev's perestroika.

Appendix
Archival Sources
Notes
Acknowledgments
Index

Appendix:
Notes to Tables

Explanation of Tables 1 and 2

Issues of *Izvestiia* from Jan. 6, 14, 22, 30, Feb. 7, 15, and 23 of 1925 and 1933. I followed the same procedure for *Pravda*, except that the Feb. 23, 1925, issue was unavailable. In its place I used Feb. 22. By taking editions at eight-day intervals I included every day of the week in the survey.

Rows one and two (total space and total domestic space) do not include advertising.

Rows three through eight all refer to material related to campaigns in progress. I determined which these were by referring to the relevant issues of *Krasnaia pechat* and *Kommunisticheskaia revoliutsiia*, and to *Resheniia partii o pechati* (Moscow: Politizdat, 1941). Row four for 1925 is a minor exception to this rule. Here I counted all verbatim printings of party resolutions, as well as of speeches and lectures by party leaders, in both 1925 and 1933. In 1933 all of this material dealt directly with campaigns in progress. In 1925 a small percentage of it, mostly from local party organizations, did not. Thus, my total figure for percentage of domestic space devoted to campaigns in 1925 is somewhat exaggerated. The jump in space devoted to campaigns from 1925 to 1933 is actually larger than this survey shows.

Campaigns sanctioned by the Central Committee in January and February 1925 had as their goals celebrating the anniversary of Lenin's death and the Red Army holiday, raising productivity through the "scientific organization of labor," encouraging mass participation in elections for local and provincial soviets, strengthening the *smychka* between worker and peasant, forming an alliance between "poor" and "middle" peasants, publicizing the electrification of the countryside, and preparing for the spring sowing. In 1933 the campaigns in progress were the anniversary of Lenin's death, the Red Army holiday, and "socialist construction," by which was meant raising industrial production, building infrastructure (bridges, telephone network, electrical net), the promulgation of the Second Five-Year Plan, and increasing the harvest. The number of themes and slogans presented by the newspapers in 1933 was fewer than in 1925.

Row three refers to articles and commentary by editors or by party leaders, literati, or academics who wrote a piece expressly for the newspaper. Row four, "Directives . . .", refers to verbatim transcriptions of speeches or to the printing of resolutions, directives, and laws. This is the voice of the government speaking directly to the reader. In row five I included denunciations of failures or sabotage of campaign-related work, descriptions by correspondents "from the front" of work in progress, and reports of successes. The "loyal soldiers" of rows six and seven are the party activists, local leaders, Red Army soldiers, collective farmers, and factory workers building socialism at the ground level. The reports I counted in row six differ from worker-peasant correspondent letters in that they are signed collectively (not by an individual) and always include a commitment to fulfill the center's orders.

These numbers demonstrate that *Pravda* and *Izvestiia* relied increasingly on verbatim transcriptions of Central Committee (CC) and Central Control Commission (CCC) documents and leadership pronouncements to fill space (row four). They also show a dramatic jump in the percentage of space given to coverage of campaigns and slogans promulgated by the Central Committee. In connection with the monolithic campaign to build socialism, two essentially new forms of journalism appear in 1933—the collective letter of "loyal soldiers" committing themselves to carry out orders, and the greetings and congratulations of the leadership to these same "soldiers." Also notable is the paucity of worker/peasant correspondent letters.

Explanation of Table 3

Table 3 was constructed by first counting the total number of domestic headlines and headings in the same twenty-eight issues of *Pravda* and *Izvestiia* sampled for Tables 1 and 2 (see above). I then counted domestic headlines and headings containing *boevoi*, or "militant/ fighting" language, and computed their frequency as a percentage of all domestic headings (the "shock index"). Fighting language includes the use of command form, implied command form (*nuzhno, nado, dolzhen* constructions, as well as phrases such as *Gazetu—v derevniiu!*), vocabulary of war and struggle (*borba, front, pobedit*), and exclamation marks.

The central press in 1925 contained a far higher number of Chronicle items. These were summary descriptions of local events, such as a blizzard, a library opening, or a fire, no more than a paragraph or two long, always appearing toward the back of the paper. The large number of these items in 1925 plus the change from a six- or seven-page to a four-page format accounts for the big drop in the total number of headings between 1925 and 1933. I did not count Chronicle headings which were the same type size as the regular text, in 1925 or 1933.

I determined the shock index for *Krestianskaia gazeta* and *Rabochaia gazeta* using the same method as for *Pravda* and *Izvestiia*. For *Krestianskaia gazeta*, a weekly in 1925, I used the issues from Jan. 6, 13, 20, and 27, Feb. 3, Apr. 28, and May 5, 1925. For *Rabochaia gazeta* I had only one 1925 issue available, Feb. 25.

Pravda and *Izvestiia* both show a large jump in shock headlines over the period discussed in this paper. Their shock indexes in 1933 are almost identical to that of *Krestianskaia gazeta* in 1925. Given that in 1925 the peasant newspaper *Krestianskaia gazeta* had a much higher shock index than the "leading papers" (*Pravda* and *Izvestiia*), which were targeted at educated urban populations and "advanced" party members, I hypothesize that the shock index is inversely proportional to the sophistication of a newspaper's target audience. By 1933, then, *Pravda* and *Izvestiia* had been retargeted at a far less "politically conscious" and intellectually sophisticated audience—the new cohort of young male workers recruited into the party since 1924.

Archival Sources

State Archive of the Russian Federation
(GARF—Gosudarstvennyi arkhiv rossiiskoi federatsii).

Fond 1244. Archive of the *Izvestiia* editorial offices.
Fond 9613. Archive of the *Gudok* editorial offices.
Fond 5446. Archive of the Council of People's Commissars (Sovnarkom).
Fond 5566. Archive of the Press Workers' Labor Union Section (SRP).

Russian State Archive of Social and Political History
(RGASPI—Rossiiskii gosudarstvennyi archiv sotsialnoi i
politicheskoi istorii).

Fond 14. Mariia Ilichna Ulianova.
Fond 17. Opis 60. Central Committee Department of Agitation and Propaganda, 1922–1924.
Fond 17. Opis 85. CC Secret Department.
Fond 17. Opisi 112, 113, 114. CC Orgburo and Secretariat, 1922–1938.
Fond 17. Opis 120. Miscellaneous CC documents, 1922–1937.
Fond 89. Emelian Iaroslavskii.
Fond 610. Letter archive of *Rabochaia gazeta*.

Central State Archive of Socio-Political Movements of the City of Moscow (TsGAOD g. Moskvy—Tsentralnyi gosudarstvennyi arkhiv obshchestvennykh dvizhenii goroda Moskvy).

Fond 190. Party organization of *Rabochaia gazeta* publishing house and editorial staff, 1924–1931.

Fond 420. Party organization of *Izvestiia* publishing house and editorial staff.

Russian State Archive of the Economy (RGAE—Rossiiskii gosudarstvennyi arkhiv ekonomiki).

Fond 396. Letter archive of *Krestianskaia gazeta.*

Fond 7927. Committee on Press Affairs attached to Council of People's Commissars.

Center for the Preservation of Documents of Youth Organizations (TsKhDMO—Tsentr khraneniia dokumentov molodezhnykh organizatsii). Now merged with RGASPI.

Fond 1. Opis 3. Komsomol Central Committee Bureau.

Fond 1. Opis 23. Komsomol Central Committee Department of Agitation and Propaganda.

Russian State Archive of Literature and Art (RGALI—Rossiskii gosudarstvennyi arkhiv literatury i iskusstvo).

Fond 2164. Personal file of Grigorii Vinokur.

Notes

Introduction

1. This study deals only with Russian-language newspapers. The central Russian-language papers, particularly *Pravda* and *Izvestiia*, were recognized from the Civil War era forward as the "authoritative organs" of the Soviet leadership. They set the tone for the rest of the Soviet newspaper press. The numerous national minority newspapers followed the central Russian-language press, of course, but also conveyed distinct messages with different emphases. The national minority presses deserve separate studies by scholars who are able to rigorously compare and contrast them with the all-Union Russian-language newspapers.

2. I use the term "Stalinist culture" here to refer to every level of Soviet official culture from the operating procedures and discourse of party cell meetings to "high culture" such as belles lettres and operas. The different levels were inextricably linked. Sheila Fitzpatrick has shown, for example, that one of the central tropes of socialist realist literature, the imagining of the shining socialist future embryonic in the grimy, chaotic present, pervaded Soviet print media from children's books to provincial newspapers to belles lettres. See Sheila Fitzpatrick, "Becoming Cultured: Socialist Realism and the Representation of Privilege and Taste," in Fitzpatrick, *The Cultural Front: Power and Culture in Revolutionary Russia* (Ithaca: Cornell University Press, 1992), 216–237.

3. Peter Holquist points out that in late Imperial Russia much of educated Russian society favored state-led "enlightenment" of the peasantry (*Making War, Forging Revolution* [Cambridge: Harvard University Press, 2002], 46). Thus the NEP mass enlightenment project offered an opportunity for nonparty intellectuals and professionals to work together with the Bolshevik leadership in a common undertaking.

4. On the end of reader studies, see Jeffrey Brooks, "Studies of the Reader in the 1920s," *Russian History* 9, pts. 2–3, 1982: 187–202; and Chapter 6 of this book. Aleksandr Etkind, in *Eros nevozmozhnogo: Istoriia psikhoanaliza v Rossii*

(St. Petersburg: "Meduza," 1993), has described the 1920s as an epoch of "psychological and pedagogical experiments" brought to an abrupt end during the First Five-Year Plan (see especially pp. 218–219). On the shutdown of the party's Information Department, which compiled regular reports on popular mood, see Terry Martin, "'Registration' and 'Mood': OGPU Information Reports and the Soviet Surveillance System," forthcoming in *Cahiers du monde russe*.

5. On the production of culture approach, see Wendy Griswold, *Cultures and Societies in a Changing World* (Thousand Oaks: Pine Forge Press, 1994), especially 1–17. Griswold refers to the method simply as "the sociology of culture." For a fascinating example of the approach, see Michael Baxandall, *Painting and Experience in Fifteenth Century Italy: a Primer in the Social History of Pictorial Style* (Oxford: Clarendon Press, 1972). An excellent example of the production of culture approach in the field of Russian/Soviet studies is Jeffrey Brooks's work *When Russia Learned to Read* (Princeton: Princeton University Press, 1985).

6. On the recruitment of young working-class males into the party in the 1920s, see Sheila Fitzpatrick, *Education and Social Mobility in the Soviet Union, 1921–1934* (Cambridge: Cambridge University Press, 1979), 15–16; and T. H. Rigby, *Communist Party Membership in the USSR, 1917–1967* (Princeton: Princeton University Press, 1968).

7. See Roger Pethybridge, *The Social Prelude to Stalinism* (New York: St. Martin's Press, 1974) and Moshe Lewin, *The Making of the Soviet System* (New York: Pantheon Books, 1985). Lewin argues that various pressures, including the peasant mentality of the population as a whole, distorted prerevolutionary and early revolutionary Leninism, making it more statist, violent, and authoritarian (see *Making of the Soviet System*, 202–240). Sheila Fitzpatrick has argued that the conservative cultural tastes of both Bolshevik leaders and party rank-and-file contributed to the "embourgeoisement" of the new Stalinist elite in the 1930s. See Sheila Fitzpatrick, *Education and Social Mobility*, 249–254; and "Becoming Cultured: Socialist Realism and the Representation of Privilege and Taste," in Fitzpatrick, *The Cultural Front: Power and Culture in Revolutionary Russia* (Ithaca: Cornell University Press, 1992), 216–237.

8. See Michel Foucault, *Discipline and Punish* (New York: Vintage Books, 1979), especially 3–24 and 135–141.

9. Frank B. Farrell, *Subjectivity, Realism and Postmodernism:the Recovery of the World* (Cambridge: Cambridge University Press, 1996), 248–249, 269–272.

10. See Kate Brown, "Gridded Lives: Why Kazakhstan and Montana Are Nearly the Same Place," *American Historical Review* 106, no. 1 (February 2001): 17–48; and Yanni Kotsonis, "A Modern Paradox:Subject and Citizen in Nineteenth and Twentieth Century Russia," in David Hoffman and Yanni Kotsonis, eds., *Russian Modernity: Politics, Knowledge, Practice* (New York: St. Martin's Press, 2000), 5. Other important works espousing the "USSR as a case of modernity" thesis are David Hoffman, "European Modernity and Soviet Socialism," also in *Russian Modernity*, 245–260, Stephen Kotkin, *Magnetic Mountain* (Berkeley: University of California Press, 1995), and Peter Holquist, "'Information Is the Alpha and Omega of Our Work': Bolshevik Surveillance in Its Pan-European Context," *Journal of Modern History* 69, no. 3 (September 1997): 415–450. Holquist's article shows that

the production of reports on popular mood based on secret perlustration of private letters was practiced by most of the major combatant states of World War I, as well as by the Bolsheviks and their White opponents in the Russian Civil War. The article thus fits within the "shared modernity" thesis. However, in his *Making War, Forging Revolution*, Holquist argues that although wartime practices of state control in Imperial and Bolshevik Russia were parallel to and influenced by similar practices elsewhere in World War I Europe, the Bolsheviks continued their wartime mobilization after 1921 in a way that set their "revolutionary project . . . fundamentally apart from other European states" (288).

11. Holquist, "Information Is the Alpha and Omega of Our Work."

12. John P. Thompson, *The Media and Modernity: A Social Theory of the Media* (Stanford: Stanford University Press, 1995), 152–159; and Anthony Smith, *The Newspaper: An International History* (London: Thames and Hudson, 1979).

13. Smith, *The Newspaper.*

14. Edward Bernays, *Crystallizing Public Opinion* (Boston: Houghton and Mifflin, 1923).

1. Agitation, Propaganda, and the NEP Mass Enlightenment Project

1. Peter Kenez, *The Birth of the Propaganda State: Soviet Methods of Mass Mobilization, 1917–1929* (Cambridge: Cambridge University Press, 1985), 35–49.

2. RGASPI, f. 14, op. 1, d. 322, ll. 7–39.

3. Published and unpublished documents from the 1920s are full of complaints that GIZh simply did not produce enough graduates each year to reduce the shortage of journalists. See, for example, delegate Naritsyn's comments at the Third Plenum of the Section of Press Workers, January 1929 (State Archive of the Russian Federation [GARF] f. 5566, op. 6, d. 2, 26–28).

4. E. G. Golomb and E. M. Fingerit, *Rasprostranenie pechati v dorevoliutsionnoi Rossii i v Sovetskom soiuze* (Moscow: Izdatelstvo "Sviaz," 1967), 98–103.

5. Kenez, 44.

6. Anatolii Mironovich Danilevich, "Gazeta 'Izvestiia'. Stanovlenie. Tipologiia (1917–1927g.g.)" (Ph.D. diss., Moscow State University, 1978), 69–70; Ivan Gronskii, *Iz proshlogol. . . . Vospominaniia* (Moscow: "Izvestiia," 1991), 108–113. *Izvestiia* moved into a newly constructed editorial/typographical complex in June 1927.

7. See Matthew Lenoe, "Stalinist Mass Journalism and the Transformation of Soviet Newspapers, 1926–1932" (Ph.D. diss., University of Chicago, 1997), 436–622.

8. GARF, f. 1244, op. 1, d.31, l. 50.

9. Central State Archive of Social Movements of the City of Moscow (TsGAOD g. Moskvy), f. 190, op. 1, d. 1, ll. 103–104.

10. TsGAOD g. Moskvy, f. 420, op. 1, d. 56, l. 44.

11. GARF, f. 5566, op. 6, d. 27, ll. 4, 23, 26, 34.

12. TsGAOD g. Moskvy, f. 420, op. 1, d. 57, l. 9.

13. Jeffrey Brooks, "The Breakdown in Production and Distribution of Printed Material, 1917–1927," in Abbott Gleason, Peter Kenez, and Richard Stites, eds., *Bolshevik Culture: Experiment and Order in the Russian Revolution* (Bloomington: Indiana University Press, 1985), 151–174.

14. See Louise McReynolds, *The News Under Russia's Old Regime* (Princeton: Princeton University Press, 1991), 297–299; and Lenoe, "Stalinist Mass Journalism," 974–976.

15. Published scholarship on the history of the Soviet press through 1930 includes Kenez, *The Birth of the Propaganda State;* Jeffrey Brooks, *Thank You, Comrade Stalin* (Princeton: Princeton University Press, 2000); "The Breakdown in Production and Distribution of Printed Material, 1917–1927," in Gleason, et al., *Bolshevik Culture,*151–174; "Public and Private Values in the Soviet Press, 1921–1928," *Slavic Review* 48, no. 1 (Spring 1989): 16–35; and "Official Xenophobia and Popular Cosmopolitanism in Early Soviet Russia," *American Historical Review* 97, no. 5 (December 1992): 1431–1448. Two important dissertations written in the 1990s are Steven Coe, "Peasants, the State, and the Languages of NEP: The Rural Correspondents Movement in the Soviet Union, 1924–1928" (Ph.D. diss., University of Michigan–Ann Arbor, 1993), and Julie Kay Mueller, "A New Kind of Newspaper: The Origins and Development of a Soviet Institution, 1921–1928" (Ph.D. diss., University of California–Berkeley, 1992). Although they deal with diverse subjects and present different theses, the works cited above all describe a period of decentralization, journalistic autonomy, and civic activism by worker/peasant correspondents, followed by a tightening of central control in the last years of the NEP (1926–1927).

16. See, for example, K. Berezhnoi, *K istorii partiino-sovetskoi pechati* (Leningrad: Izdatelstvo Leningradskaia universiteta, 1956); R. A. Ivanova, *Partiinaia i sovetskaia pechat v gody vtoroi piatiletki* (Moscow: Izdatel'stvo Moskovskogo gosudarstvennogo universiteta, 1961); and A. L. Mishuris, *Partiino-sovetskaia pechat v period borby za stroitelstvo sotsializma* (Moscow: Izdatelstvo Moskovskogo gosudarstvennogo universiteta, 1964).

17. The Central Committee departments responsible for supervision of the press were the following: from 1922 to 1924 the Department of Agitation and Propaganda (Agitprop), from 1924 to 1927 the Press Department, from 1928 to 1929 the Newspaper Section of Agitprop, and from 1930 to 1938 the Department of Culture and Propaganda (Kultprop). Between 1922 and 1924 the Agitprop Department contained a Press Subdepartment *(Podotdel pechati)*.

18. The last three examples cited can all be found in *Krasnaia pechat,* Jan. 20, 1924.

19. See the 1922 Sovnarkom decree establishing Glavlit in RGASPI, f. 17, op. 113, d. 584, ll. 36–38, and Mueller, "A New Kind of Newspaper," 44–45. David Ortenberg described the ability of central newspaper editors to override censorship decisions *throughout* the NEP and Stalin eras, in an interview with author, Apr. 19, 1995, tape recording and notes, Moscow. Ortenberg, who began his journalistic career in the early 1920s, edited the Red Army central paper *Krasnaia zvezda*

during World War II. A. Kotlyar, a journalist who worked at Ukrainian newspapers from the Civil War years to 1936, notes the impotence of Glavlit censors vis-à-vis senior editors even at provincial nonparty papers (A. Kotlyar, *Newspapers in the USSR. Recollections and Observations of a Soviet Zhurnalist* [New York: East European Fund, Mimeographed Series No. 71, 1955), 4–5, 11. A. V. Blium (*Za kulisami "Ministerstva pravdy": Tainaia istoriia sovetskoi tsenzury, 1917–1929* [St. Petersburg: Izdat. "Gumanitarnoe agentstv," 1994]) claims based on CC Orgburo documentation from 1922 that the main motive for establishing Glavlit was controlling the private and cooperative publishing industry, which had been reinvigorated as the New Economic Policy lifted controls on private trade. According to Blium, supervision of party and state-owned publications was not the primary concern.

20. On Mar. 8, 1924, the CC Orgburo decided to call in editors of all central newspapers at least once a month for meetings at the Press Department. The purpose was to inform editors of the CC agenda (RGASPI, f. 17, op. 112, d. 522, l. 51). Even before this, however, agenda-setting meetings at the CC Agitprop Department were frequent. On May 19, 1922, representatives of the major central newspapers and "party writers" met with CC Agitprop officials to coordinate coverage of publicity around the trial of Socialist Revolutionary leaders for terrorism. For an example of direct agenda-setting by the Politburo, see the Mar. 28, 1928, directive ordering *Pravda* and *Izvestiia* to publish the resolutions of a meeting of Moscow engineering and technical personnel after an address by Valerian Kuibyshev, head of VSNKh (RGASPI, f. 17, op. 3, d. 679, l. 4). See also the Politburo's Apr. 3, 1928, order to *Pravda* to publish an article by M. I. Frumkin that the paper had previously rejected (RGASPI, f. 17, op. 3, d. 680, l. 3). For an example of an Orgburo/Secretariat session at which both *Pravda* and *Rabochaia gazeta* representatives were present, see RGASPI, f. 17, op. 113, d. 584, ll. 1–2.

21. For Skvortsov-Stepanov's attendance at Politburo meetings in early 1928, see RGASPI, f. 17, op. 3, dd. 678–679. For Kovalev's attendance at an Orgburo/Secretariat session, see RGASPI, f. 17, op. 113, d. 685, ll. 1–3. On Gronskii's phone contact with Stalin, see Gronskii, 133–135.

22. Complaints that the provincial press imitated the central papers too closely were a constant refrain in *Krasnaia pechat (KP)*. For some instances, see *KP*, no. 23, 1925 (November): 31; or nos. 17–18, 1926 (September): 22.

23. In a 1923 case frequent publication of articles speculating on the imminent collapse of the *chervonets*, the new Soviet hard currency, prompted the Central Committee Secretariat to issue a circular ordering all newspapers to eliminate such discussion and "take a definite line . . . directed towards support and strengthening of our policy of deeper penetration of the *chervonets* into the market and the winning of trust towards it" (RGASPI, f. 17, op. 112, d. 482, ll. 4, 13—Secretariat session of Sept. 21, 1923). In early 1926 the CC Press Department submitted a proposal to the Secretariat to issue a warning *(postavit na vid)* to editors and reporters at *Rabochaia gazeta, Komsomolskaia pravda*, and Leningrad's *Krasnaia gazeta* after these newspapers published news of the appointment of a new chairman for the Supreme Council on the National Economy, before the official announcement (RGASPI, f. 17, op. 85, d. 20, l. 5). On Nov. 10, 1926, the Central Control Commission censured *Rabochaia gazeta* for publishing a caricature of party Opposition

leaders titled "Around the Bottle" (see *Rabochaia gazeta* editor-in-chief Nikolai Smirnov's letter to the Central Committee Secretariat in RGASPI, f. 17, op. 85, d. 18, ll. 19–20).

24. GARF, f. 374s.ch., op. 27s., d. 23, ll. 40–44.

25. RGASPI, f. 17, op. 113, d. 592, ll. 88–107ob; op. 3, d. 683, l. 4.

26. On Aug. 8, 1928, the Politburo confirmed the appointments of two new editors at *Pravda*, G. Krumin and M. A. Savelev, and also approved the removal of Bukharin's protegés Astrov, Slepkov, and Tseitlin from their posts (RGASPI, f. 17, op. 3, d. 698, l. 7). For one instance of Secretariat confirmation of an editorial appointment at a provincial paper, see the Secretariat session of June 20, 1928, in RGASPI, f. 17, op. 113, d. 639, l. 17.

27. The Committee on Press Affairs was formally attached to Sovnarkom, the Council of People's Commissars. Decisions about subsidies and paper supplies for newspapers appear regularly in the Orgburo and Secretariat files of the central party archive (RGASPI). For a November 1923 Secretariat directive that the Commissariat of Finance provide *Rabochaia gazeta* with a 400,000 ruble loan on favorable terms (these were not the practically worthless Civil War rubles but the gold-standard rubles of the NEP), see RGASPI, f. 17, op. 112, d. 502, l. 111. For a report from Press Department Deputy Director Vasilevskii to CC Secretary Viacheslav Molotov on implementation of a Jan. 22, 1926, Orgburo order lowering paper rations for a number of newspapers, see RGASPI, f. 17, op. 85, d. 20, ll. 1–4. For an instance in which papers were punished by cuts in their paper supplies, see the Dec. 30, 1929, Orgburo session at which paper supplies for three of the Soviet Union's most important evening papers were cut (*Vecherniaia Moskva* of Moscow, *Krasnaia gazeta* of Leningrad, and *Vechernie izvestiia* of Odessa).

28. To cite two examples: a spring 1923 Press Subdepartment report on *Rabochaia gazeta* noted that it had been subsidized throughout 1922, sometimes to the tune of 15,000 (hard currency) rubles a month (RGASPI, f. 17, op. 60, d. 895, l. 38); money for *Izvestiia's* 1925 purchase of an offset printing press and other typographical equipment from abroad came from state hard currency reserves (RGASPI, f. 17, op. 85, d. 18, l. 228).

29. See, for example, Stephen F. Cohen, *Bukharin and the Bolshevik Revolution* (Oxford: Oxford University Press, 1980), 125.

30. Ibid., 126.

31. *Zhurnalist*, March/April 1923, 8.

32. Vladimir Shishkin, "Belye piatna istorii, ili tainy sovetskoi partokratii," *Posev*, no. 5, 1990 (September–October): 119–123.

33. Brooks, "Official Xenophobia and Popular Cosmopolitanism," 1435.

34. See M. A. K. Halliday, *Language, Context, and Text: Aspects of Language in a Social-Semiotic Perspective* (Oxford: Oxford University Press, 1985), 3–14, 38–39.

35. This concept of voice is built on Jeffrey Brooks's observation, already cited, that "the press accommodated many voices and several distinct discourses, each linked with types of authors and targeted audiences."

36. Kenez, 8.

37. On Lenin's views of the press's functions in society, see Mark Hopkins, *Mass Media in the Soviet Union* (New York: Pegasus, 1970), 57–60.

38. See Hopkins, 58, and footnote on p. 343. See also Russian social democrat P. Akselrod's 1896 pamphlet *Ob agitatsii* (Geneva: Izdatelstvo soiuza russkikh sotsialdemokratov, 1896), especially pp. 16–19.

39. Quoted in Kenez, 7.

40. *Bolshaia sovetskaia entsiklopediia*, Moscow, 1926–1940, s.v. "Propaganda" and "Agitatsiia."

41. *Kommunisticheskaia revoliutsiia*, no. 4, 1923 (Feb. 15): 5.

42. *Resheniia partii o pechati* (Moscow, Politizdat, 1941), 22.

43. Ibid., 56.

44. See, for example, "Vozrozhdenie golodavshego Povolzhia, *Izvestiia*, Jan. 8, 1924.

45. RGASPI, f. 17, op. 112, d. 261, ll. 13–24; d. 276, l. 12.

46. For the Feb. 2, 1924, CC Press Department circular, see RGASPI, f. 17, op. 60, d. 865, l. 3.

47. See reports filed with the Agitprop Department on the activities of different newspapers with their correspondents (1923) in RGASPI, f. 17, op. 60, dd. 907, 935.

48. Mueller, 266–271.

49. On Eremeev and Karpinskii's plan for *Rabochii*, see RGASPI, f. 17, op. 112, d. 325, ll. 20–21; op. 60, d. 849, ll. 148–149.

50. On the Central Committee's instructions to the *Rabochii* editors and their subsequent removal from the paper's staff, see RGASPI, f. 17, op. 112, d. 296, l. 3; d. 301, l. 2; d. 325, ll. 2, 20–22.

51. *Pravda*, May 5, 1923; May 9, 1923; I. Stalin, *Sochineniia* (Moscow: Gosudarstvennoe izdatelstvo politicheskoi literatury, 1946), 5:281–290.

52. On Shafir's recall from Georgia, see RGASPI, f. 17, op. 112, d. 323, ll. 172–173, 176ob. For a 1923 report on children's literature to the Agitprop Department, authored by Shafir, see RGASPI, f. 17, op. 60, d. 920. See also Iakov Shafir, "Chitatel 'Rabochei gazety' v tsifrakh," *KP*, no. 26, 1925 (December 1925): 37; *Gazeta i derevnia* (Moscow-Leningrad: Krasnaia nov, 1924); *Rabochaia gazeta i ee chitatel* (Moscow: Izdatelstvo "Rabochei gazety," 1926). For a summary description of some of Shafir's studies, see Jeffrey Brooks, "Studies of the Reader in the 1920s," *Russian History* 9, pts. 2–3 (1982): 187–202.

53. On the formation of the Moscow Linguistics Circle, its agenda in 1921–1924, and Vinokur's later participation (1927) in the Commission on the Language of the Press, sponsored by the journalists' labor union section (Sektsiia rabotnikov pechati), see Russian State of Archive Literature and Art (RGALI), f. 2164 (Vinokur's personal file), op. 1, dd. 1, 2, 9.

54. On early Soviet reader studies, see I. P. Lysakova, *Tip gazety i stil publikatsii. Opyt sotsiolingvisticheskogo issledovaniia* (Leningrad: Izdatelstvo Leningradskogo Universiteta, 1989), 5–10; Jeffrey Brooks, "Studies of the Reader in the 1920s,"

Russian History 9, pts. 2–3, 1982; M. Gus, Iu. Zagorianskii, and N. Kaganovich, *Iazyk gazety* (Moscow: "Rabotnik prosveshcheniia," 1926); Shafir, *Gazeta i derevnia* and "Chitatel 'Rabochei gazety'"; M. Charnyi, "O *Vechernei Moskve* i ee chitatel'," *Zhurnalist*, no. 10, 1929 (May 15): 310–311.

55. See, for example, a lecture by Slepkov, the first editor of *Komsomolskaia pravda*, reprinted in *Krasnaia pechat*, Sept. 10, 1925, 36–39. Also see Anatolii Lunacharskii's speech reprinted in *Zhurnalist*, no. 15, 1924 (October): 9–11.

56. On the prerevolutionary attitudes of the intelligentsia toward the popular press, see Chapter 5 of Jeffrey Brooks's *When Russia Learned to Read* (Princeton: Princeton University Press, 1985). M. Levidov, in *Zhurnalist*, no. 5, 1925 (May): 42, also rooted the disdain among Soviet journalists for "boulevardism" in the prejudices of the prerevolutionary intelligentsia.

57. *Zhurnalist*, no. 3, 1923 (January): 21–26.

58. *Zhurnalist*, no. 1, 1927 (January): 20.

59. *Zhurnalist*, no. 4, 1923 (February): 29.

60. *Zhurnalist*, no. 1, 1927 (January): 20. See also George C. Bastian, *Editing the Day's News* (New York: Macmillan, 1923), Chaps. 11 and 12.

61. See Semen Gershberg, *Rabota u nas takaia* (Moscow: Politizdat, 1971), 23; GARF, f. 374 s. ch., op. 27s., d. 1069, ll. 13–14.

62. On *Tverskaia pravda's* development of the "production review," see Gershberg, 22–24 and "Novaia forma gazetnoi raboty," *Pravda*, Mar. 11, 1927, 3. On early shock brigades and production contests organized by Komsomol newspapers, see L. S. Rogachevskaia, *Sotsialisticheskoe sorevnovanie v SSSR: istoricheskie ocherki, 1917–1970* (Moscow: Izdatelstvo "Nauka," 1977), 72–79. For the earliest *Uralskii rabochii* coverage of Komsomol shock brigades and production contests, see *Uralskii rabochii*, July 20, 1927, 2; and July 29, 1927, 4.

63. A. M. Selishchev, *Iazyk revoliutsionnoi epokhi* (Moscow: "Rabotnik prosveshcheniia," 1928), 28–29, 85–92.

64. Leon Trotskii, *Sochineniia*, vol. 17, pt. 2 (Moscow: Gosizdat, 1926), 132–135, 143–148.

65. See, for example, issues of *Die Rote Fahne*, organ of the Hamburg Workers' and Soldiers' Council during the abortive November–December 1918 Communist revolution in Germany.

66. *Kommunisticheskaia revoliutsiia*, no. 3, 1923 (February): 84–95.

67. Ibid., nos. 21–22, 1925 (November): 24. *Zhurnalist*, August/September 1925, 77–81, presented a very similar definition of the shock campaign.

68. *KP*, Jan. 23, 1924, 21.

69. *Zhurnalist*, no. 5, 1925 (May): 41–42. See also no. 4, 1923 (February): 55–56.

70. *Zhurnalist*, no. 21, 1929 (Nov. 1): 642–644. Ingulov actually seems to have written this piece as a kind of penance. In 1928–1929 Ingulov headed the CC Newspaper Section of the Department of Agitation and Propaganda, helping to orchestrate a massive shock campaign to promote industrialization. As a result of "excesses" in this campaign he was fired from his CC post by Stalin and the other CC leaders in October 1929. See Chapter 6.

71. *Krestianskaia gazeta*, Jan. 6, 13, 20, 27, and Feb. 3, Apr. 28, and May 5, 1925.

72. "We're Succeeding" and "We Must Reform Our Party Cell" are from *Krestianskaia gazeta*, Jan. 6, 1925. The "ardent greetings" headline is from Jan. 13, 1925.

2. Newspaper Distribution and the Emergence of Soviet Information Rationing

1. See E. G. Golomb and E. M. Fingerit, *Rasprostranenie pechati v dorevoliutsionnoi Rossii i v Sovetskom soiuze* (Moscow: Izdatelstvo "Sviaz'," 1967), Jeffrey Brooks, "The Breakdown in Production and Distribution of Printed Material, 1917–1927," in Abbot Gleason, Peter Kenez, and Richard Stites, eds., *Bolshevik Culture: Experiment and Order in the Russian Revolution* (Bloomington: Indiana University Press, 1985), 151–174, and Julie Kay Mueller, "A New Kind of Newspaper: The Origins and Development of a Soviet Institution, 1921–1928" (Ph.D. diss., University of California–Berkeley, 1992), especially Chapter 3 (71–110).

2. The term "status group" is one translation of Max Weber's term *Stände* (another common English translation is "estate") and I use it in the Weberian sense, namely to signify a social group defined by considerations of honor, certain legal and economic privileges, and service to a "patrimonial" leader. Weber opposes "status group" to class, a social group defined by its members' occupations, market relations, and wealth. Status groups in Weber's definition tend toward exclusivity (that is, their members tend to associate socially with and marry one another) but they need not be completely closed groups as "castes" are. Weber views "caste" as an extreme example of a status group. See Max Weber, *Economy and Society. An Outline of Interpetive Sociology* (Berkeley, 1978), vol. 1, 227–232, 246–254 and vol. 2, 932–937. See also Ken Jowitt, *New World Disorder: The Leninist Extinction* (Berkeley, 1992), 121–158 and Janos Kornai, *The Socialist System: The Political Economy of Communism* (Princeton, 1992), 49–61, 360–377.

3. See Mueller, 72, and RGAE, f.7927, op. 1, d. 55, l. 135.

4. On the free distribution of newspapers during the Civil War, see Mueller, 72, RGAE, f. 7927, op. 1, d. 55, l. 135, and Golomb and Fingerit, 89. On the series of decisions about press distribution and administration in the winter of 1921–1922, see Mueller, 45–48, *O partiinoi i sovetskoi pechati. Sbornik dokumentov* (Moscow, 1954), 248, RGASPI, f. 17, op. 60, d. 845, ll. 3, 144, op. 60, d. 848, l. 46, op. 112, d. 261, ll. 20–21, 25, and d. 276, l. 12.

5. RGASPI, f. 17, op. 60, d. 853, ll. 1–4ob, Mueller, 81–83.

6. RGASPI, f. 17, op. 60, d. 845, l. 39, d. 846, ll. 45–46, 75, d. 849, ll. 46–47.

7. For the order to party members to subscribe to *Pravda*, see *O partiinoi i sovetskoi pechati*, 249.

8. RGASPI, f. 17, op. 60, d. 846, l.45.

9. RGASPI, f. 17, op. 112, d. 323, l. 9.

10. RGASPI, f. 17, op. 112, d. 336, l. 8.

11. For a record of 150,000 gold-backed rubles in subsidies provided at CC order for *Rabochii(Worker)*, see RGASPI, f. 17, op. 112, d. 325, ll. 23–23ob. A spring 1923 Press Subdepartment report on the newspaper reported that it had been

subsidized throughout 1922, sometimes to the tune of 15,000 gold-backed rubles a month (RGASPI, f. 17, op. 60, d. 895, l. 38). An instance of Central Committee subsidization of *Bednota* occurred on March 1, 1922, when the Secretariat agreed to provide funds that would enable the newspaper to go from a two- to a four-page edition (RGASPI, f. 17, op. 112, d. 294, l., ll. 4, 27).

12. A second form of collective subscription, much less common at this time, involved a group of peasants who each contributed a small sum to subscribe to a single newspaper. In this book the term "collective subscriptions" refers to institutional subscriptions unless noted otherwise.

13. RGASPI, f. 17, op. 60, d. 845, l. 157. The figured quoted refers to 57 percent of the papers' circulation inside Petrograd.

14. Mueller, 77–78.

15. See TsGAOD g. Moskvy, f. 190, op. 1, d. 4, l. 86; GARF, f. 374s. ch., op. 28s., d. 3288, ll. 12–26, 69–69ob. See also RGASPI, f. 17, op. 113, d. 699, ll. 53–60ob.

16. RGASPI, f. 17, op. 60, d. 870, ll. 15–16.

17. Ibid., d. 870, ll. 19–25.

18. RGASPI, f. 17, op. 60, d. 892, ll. 8, 10–10ob, 11, 26ob, 29, 32. See also d. 906, ll. 14–26.

19. GARF, f. 5446, op. 6, d. 9, ll. 4–5. I am grateful to my colleague Jon Bone for not only pointing out this source to me, but for collecting the data on 1924–1925 subsidies to *Krestianskaia gazeta*.

20. TsKhDMO contains reports by provincial Komsomol papers to the Press Department from 1925–1928. Of those newspapers reporting on their financial situation, none was making a profit. See, for example, TsKhDMO, f. 1, op. 3, d. 737, l. 157–159.

21. TsKhDMO, f. 1, op. 3, d. 19, l. 125.

22. RGASPI, f. 17, op. 113, d. 699, l. 58.

23. TsKhDMO, f. 1, op. 23, d. 589, ll. 49, 70–73; d. 737, ll. 24, 29, 39. Also RGAE, f. 7927, op. 1, d. 223, ll. 19–20.

24. RGASPI, f. 17, op. 60, d. 906, ll. 2–5.

25. Ibid., op. 112, d. 505, ll. 21–24. *Vecherniaia Moskva* was first issued on December 3, 1923. The Orgburo apparently made the final decision for publication on November 30.

26. For a direct published reference to *Krestianskaia gazeta*'s payment of a 5 percent commission to correspondents in 1930, see *Zhurnalist*, no. 3 (February 1), 1930, 94.

27. RGASPI, f. 17, op. 60, d. 892, ll. 77–78. RGASPI, f. 17, op. 60, d. 875, l. 38; d. 907, 69–70.

28. RGASPI, f. 17, op. 60, d. 895, ll. 2, ll. 7–8; d. 935, ll. 26–29.

29. RGASPI, f. 17, op. 60, d. 935, ll. 26–29.

30. GARF, f. 374s.ch., op. 27s, d. 3288, ll. 13ob-14; A. Fain, "Otdel raspros-

traneniia izdatel'stva *'Krestianskaia gazeta,'*" *Gazetnoe khoziaistvo,* no. 6 (June), 1930: 8–10.

31. For December 1926 subscription and sales data, see RGASPI, f. 17, op. 85, d. 18, l. 315. For November 1923 print run and subscription data, see table in RGASPI, f. 17, op. 60, d. 875, l. 38. According to this table, *Pravda*'s gross print run in November 1923 was 80,000, *Rabochaia gazeta* 's 127,000, and *Rabochaia Moskva*'s 48,285. In November 1923 *Pravda* sold a total of 13,554 copies to collective subscribers. According to the table cited above in November 1923 there were 43,676 individual subscriptions to *Pravda* in Moscow and 7,486 street sales on average per day. If we assume that all 13,554 collective subscriptions were in Moscow, then the maximum possible percentage of collective subscription in Moscow is 20.9 percent. See also RGASPI, f. 17, op. 60, d. 907, ll. 69–70. For the circulation of *Gudok* in 1923 and 1924, see RGASPI, f. 17, op. 60, d. 869, l. 1.

32. See Matthew Lenoe, "Stalinist Mass Journalism and the Transformation of Soviet Newspapers, 1922–1932 (Ph.D. diss., University of Chicago, 1997), 1–21, 334–435, 623–748.

33. Anatolii Mironovich Danilevich, "Gazeta *'Izvestiia.'* Stanovlenie. Tipologiia (1917–1927 g.g.)," Ph.D. diss., Moscow State University, 1978, 106.

34. GARF, f. 374s.ch., op. 28s, d. 1450, ll. 9–10; TsGAOD g. Moskvy, f. 420, op. 1, d. 2, l. 64.

35. GARF, f. 374s.ch. op. 28s, d. 1450, l. 9ob.

36. Ibid., ll. 9ob-10; TsGAOD g. Moskvy, f. 420, op. 1, d. 2, l. 64.

37. GARF, f. 374s.ch., op. 28s, d. 1450, ll. 9–10; TsGAOD g. Moskvy, 1. 420, op. 1, d. 2, l. 64.

38. See, for example, a December 1928 petition from the Central Committee of the construction workers' labor union to the party CC Secretariat for increased subsidies for the union newspaper *Postroika(Construction)*. The authors justified their petition based on high circulation numbers and the supposed necessity of issuing the paper daily rather than three times a week to reach construction workers (RGASPI, f. 17, op. 113, d. 685, ll. 108–110).

39. GARF, f. 5566, op. 4, d. 4, l. 38.

40. RGASPI, f. 17, op. 85, d. 20, ll. 1–6. In his report to CC Secretary Molotov on measures taken to deal with the paper shortage, Vasilevskii, the deputy director of the Central Committee Press Department, wrote of "inflated print runs" as a general problem, not peculiar to *Izvestiia*. Golomb and Fingerit (105–106) also imply that the whole complex of problems uncovered at *Izvestiia*, from inflated print runs to unlimited credit for subscribers, afflicted much of the central Soviet press.

41. One suspects that these deductions were made automatically, given Pismen's talk of a transition to "voluntary and individual subscription," cited earlier.

42. RGAE, f. 7927, op. 1, d. 24, l. 137; GARF, f. 5566, op. 4, d. 4, l. 207.

43. RGAE, f. 7927, op. 1, d. 24, ll. 137–8, 144.

44. Ibid., l. 138 (see note 47).

45. RGASPI, f. 17, op. 113, d. 615, ll. 4–5, 152–160.

46. RGASPI, f. 17, op. 113, d. 715, ll. 67–72; d. 727, ll. 33–36.

47. RGASPI, f. 17, op. 113, d. 823, ll. 94–94ob; op. 114, d. 237, ll. 2, 51–54; d. 238, l. 2.

48. RGASPI, f. 17, op. 114, d. 761, ll. 143–45. For the *Trud* and Mikoian petitions, see ibid., d. 215, l. 3, and d. 221, l. 14.

49. See "Postanovlenie Sovnarkoma SSSR, 16 avgusta, 1930," in *Gazetnoe khoziaistvo*, nos. 8–9, 1930 (August/September): 38.

50. For *Pravda*'s first setting of control numbers for distribution agents in 1929, see *Gazetnoe khoziaistvo*, no. 5, 1930 (May): 33–34. Issues of *Gazetnoe khoziaistvo* from 1930 are replete with discussions of "control numbers," the necessity of extending them right down to individual plenipotentiaries at the party cell level, and the imperative to make sure that they were fulfilled. On the postal commissariat's payment of fines in the event of failure to fulfill control numbers, see the Council of People's decree in *Gazetnoe khoziaistvo*, nos. 8–9, 1930 (August/September): 38.

51. See RGASPI, f. 17, op. 114, d. 612, l. 5; d. 761, l. 142–144.

52. "Vrednaia filantropeia," *Pravda*, June 20, 1936, 6; RGASPI, f. 17, op. 114, d. 761, ll. 141–145; RGASPI, f. 17, op. 113, d. 823, ll. 95–96; "Rasprostranenie i dostavka pechati v sotssektore derevni," *Gazetnoe khoziaistvo*, no. 5, 1930 (May): 9–11; *Gazetnoe khoziaistvo*, no. 7, 1930 (July): 9–12, 25.

53. Elena A. Osokina, *Ierarkhiia potrebleniia: o zhizni liudei v usloviiakh stalinskogo snabzheniia, 1928–1935gg.* (Moscow, 1993).

54. Ibid., and RGASPI, f. 17, op. 114, d. 612, l. 5 (see note 56). On Soiuzpechat's 1932 takeover of administration of subscription recruitment and processing, see Golomb and Fingerit, 109.

55. RGASPI, f. 17, op. 114, d. 336, l. 109 and RGASPI, f. 17, op. 114, d. 761, l. 144.

56. RGASPI, f. 17, op. 114, d. 336, ll. 107–112; d. 365, ll. 220–224; d. 761, ll. 141–166.

57. Janos Kornai, *Contradictions and Dilemmas: Studies on the Socialist Economy and Society* (Cambridge, 1986), 12–14, 36–44.

58. Ibid., 41–42.

59. Ibid., 22–23. Here Kornai also discusses the firm's hoarding of "factors of production" given the easy availability of subsidies from the state and the tautness of the plan. It is quite likely that Soviet newspapers hoarded newsprint, but I have not uncovered concrete examples of this.

60. Ibid., 25–27.

61. Kornai connects shortage, bureaucratic coordination of the economy, and rationing in *The Socialist System: The Political Economy of Communism* (Princeton, 1992), 240–245, 365.

62. On the insularity of the party during its consolidation of political power, see Jowitt, 88–91. For an example of Stalin's advocating a mobilizing role for the mass press early in the NEP, see his 1923 debate with Sergei Ingulov discussed in Chapter 1. Note that when I claim Stalin advocated using the press to mobilize

cadres I am fudging his actual wording, which referred to mobilizing the "working masses." However, based on my own reading of Soviet debates about press function in the early 1920s this was usually code for mobilizing party activists among the workers.

63. Arkadii Gaev, "Kak 'Pravda' dokhodit do chitatelia," *Vestnik instituta po izucheniiu istorii i kultury SSSR*, no. 7 (October–December 1953): 48–58. Gaev's description of the Soviet press in this article and a previous one ("Kak delaetsia 'Pravda'," *Vestnik instituta po izucheniiu istorii i kultury SSSR*, no. 4 [January–March 1953]: 87–96) confirms much of my data. He appears to have had insider knowledge of the Soviet central press.

64. See, for example, issues of *Pravda, Leningradskaia pravda, Trud,* and *Radianska Ukraina* from May 8 to 11, 1952. On May 8 *Pravda* introduced three important topics that were *not* copied or followed up in the other papers through May 11. These were the necessity of providing better education, technical and political, for drivers and mechanics working with agricultural machinery, the failure of the newspaper *Stalingradskaia pravda* to properly cover the work of lower-level party organizations (from the *raion* committee down), and the importance of extending the working life of mining machinery. Articles on such topics told party cadres what campaigns the Central Committee was focused on and which party officials and organizations were in disgrace.

65. Alex Inkeles, *Public Opinion in Soviet Russia* (Cambridge, 1950) and Vladimir Shlapentokh, *Soviet Public Opinion and Ideology* (New York, 1986).

66. Kornai, *The Socialist System*, 360–385.

3. Reader Response and Its Impact on the Press

1. See letter from S. B. Uritskii, former editor of *Gudok*, to Iakov Iakovlev, editor of *Krestianskaia gazeta*, Feb. 2, 1924, in RGASPI, f. 17, op. 60, d. 892, ll. 21–22.

2. For *Krestianskaia gazeta* reports to the Central Committee, see RGASPI, f. 17, op. 85, d. 19, l. 137 and following. For a description of *Gudok* reports to the Central Committee of the railroad workers' trade union, see GARF, f. 9613, op. 2, d. 94, ll. 1–1ob. For *Pravda* and *Izvestiia* reports forwarded to the People's Commissariat of Agriculture, see hereafter RGAE, f. 7486, op. 37, especially d. 65. For reports to the Moscow Party Committee by *Uchitelskaia gazeta* and *Golos tekstilei*, see TsGAOD g. Moskvy, f. 3 op. 9, d. 81, ll. 107–136, 156.

3. On Molotov's 1927 request for a report on peasant attitudes to the threat of war, see RGASPI, f. 17, op. 85, d. 19, l. 174. The regular *Krestianskaia gazeta* reports forwarded to Stalin and Molotov can be found throughout delo 19. For an example of an individual reader letter forwarded to Stalin, see RGASPI, f. 17, op. 85, d. 19, l. 131.

4. On the importance of the newspaper press and the worker-peasant correspondents' movement in teaching activists official language, see Jeffrey Brooks, "Public and Private Values in the Soviet Press, 1921–1928," *Slavic Review* 48, no. 1 (1989): 16–35; Michael Gorham, "Tongue-tied Writers: The *Rabsel kor* Movement and the Voice of the 'New Intelligentsia' in Early Soviet Russia," *Russian Review* 55,

no. 3 (July 1996): 412–429; and Steven Coe, "Peasants, the State, and the Languages of NEP: The Rural Correspondents Movement in the Soviet Union, 1924–1928" (Ph.D. diss., University of Michigan, 1993).

5. L. Miakishev, "Anketnoe obsledovanie chitatelia," *Gazetnoe khoziaistvo,* no. 2, 1930 (February): 14.

6. *Pravdist,* June 22, 1929, 2.

7. "Anonimnaia anketa," *Gazetnaia nedelia,* no. 18, 1930 (Feb. 25): 3.

8. RGAE, f. 396, op. 3, d. 41, ll. 49–52.

9. Ibid.

10. On the *Worker Moscow* survey results, see B. Kamenskii, "Chitatel'skie massy pod mikroskopom. Zaprosy i trebovaniia chitatelia," *Zhurnalist,* no. 14, 1929 (July 15): 437–439. On *Rabochaia gazeta* audience preferences, see Iakov Shafir, "Preobladaiushchii chitatel skii interes," *Zhurnalist,* no. 2, 1926 (February): 27–28. On *Evening Moscow,* see M. Charnyi, "O *Vechernei Moskve* i ee chitatel'," *Zhurnalist,* no. 10, 1926 (October): 42–43.

11. TsKhDMO, f. 1, op. 23, d. 590, ll. 30–33.

12. TsKhDMO, f. 1, op. 23, d. 591, ll. 40–43.

13. RGASPI, f. 17, op. 113, d. 637, ll. 19–31.

14. One census of visitors to seventy-five libraries in Leningrad province showed that 60 percent were age eighteen and under. Libraries in Cheliabinsk and Gomel reported similar proportions of visitors eighteen and under (54 percent and 56.3 percent respectively). See TsKhDMO, f. 1, op. 23, d. 588, l. 37.

15. TsKhDMO, f. 1, op. 23, d. 588, ll. 41–45.

16. Ibid., ll. 42–43.

17. See Chapter 7.

18. See N. Frideva, "Chitatel kievskikh politprosvetskikh bibliotek v 1926/27 g.," *Krasnyi bibliotekar,* no. 2, 1928 (February): 51–65; and TsKhDMO, f. 1, op. 23, d. 588, ll. 37–39.

19. TsKhDMO, f. 1, op. 23, d. 588, ll. 52–53ob.

20. See materials on the summer 1928 CC Orgburo resolution on the youth and Komsomol press (RGASPI, f. 17, op. 113, d. 637, ll. 7–94) cited above. It is also worth noting that agitprop officials at all levels of the party and Komsomol apparatuses frequently admonished journalists, propagandists, and publishers to take account of reader studies and other forms of reader feedback in planning newspaper content. See, for instance, the Komsomol CC's Apr. 14, 1927, response to a report by the Komsomol Moscow City Committee's Press Department in TsKhDMO, f. 1, op. 23, d. 737, ll.1–4 and the party CC Orgburo's instructions to book publishers to intensify study of reader preferences through the study of reader letters, the organization of readers' conferences, the distribution of book manuscripts to workers and peasants for comment, etc. (RGASPI, f. 17, op. 113, d. 688, ll. 2, 107–117).

21. Peter Kenez, *The Birth of the Propaganda State: Soviet Methods of Mass Mobilization, 1917–1929* (New York: Cambridge University Press, 1985), 49.

22. For a description of such coverage during 1920 by *Kurskaia pravda,* the Kursk Party paper, see Ivan Gronskii, *Iz proshlogo ...Vospominaniia* (Moscow:

"Izvestiia," 1991), 90–91. See also Julie A. Cassiday, *The Enemy on Trial: Early Soviet Courts on Stage and Screen* (Dekalb: Northern Illinois Press, 2000). Cassiday traces the development of Bolshevik show trials as theatrical spectacle, stressing the indirect influence of Symbolist Viacheslav Ivanov's theories of drama on Soviet courtrooms. According to Cassiday, "theories of a revitalized theater capable of shaping the human spirit connected the poet-philosopher's modernist ambitions to the disturbing reality of the Stalinist show trial" (Cassiday, 189). Without discounting Cassiday's argument, I take a different approach, focusing on discussion of show trials within the party agitprop apparatus and the recognition by journalists and Communist officials that scapegoating as a means of venting popular anger *worked*.

23. GARF, f. 374s.ch., op. 27s, d. 23, ll. 59, 65.

24. Ibid., l. 7.

25. Ibid., ll. 7–9.

26. See, for example, the "Resolution on the Current Tasks of Komsomol Newspapers" approved by the North Caucasus Komsomol Secretariat on June 25, 1926 (TsKhDMO, f. 1, op. 23, d. 590, l. 88ob). The quote is from this document.

27. See Matthew Lenoe, "Stalinist Mass Journalism and the Transformation of Soviet Newspapers, 1922–1932" (Ph.D. diss., University of Chicago, 1997), 241–248.

28. "Sud po trudovym delam. Nevinnye mladentsy," *Trud*, Jan. 12, 1924, 4; "V zasten kakh fiktivnoi arteli," *Trud*, Jan. 18, 1924, 5.

29. RGASPI, f. 17, op. 85, d. 18, ll. 29–30.

30. RGASPI, f. 17, op. 85, d. 20, l. 57.

31. RGASPI, f. 17, op. 85, d. 19, l. 64.

32. RGASPI, f. 17, op. 85, d. 20, l. 143.

33. TsGAOD g. Moskvy, f. 3, op. 9, d. 79.

34. RGASPI, f. 17, op. 85, d. 19, l. 304. The study was done for the Central Committee.

35. RGASPI, f. 17, op. 85, d. 20, l. 126.

36. Ibid., ll. 155, 159–160.

37. RGASPI, f. 17, op. 85, d. 19, ll. 229–230.

38. Ibid., ll. 224–226.

39. RGASPI, f. 17, op. 85, d. 289, ll. 2–21; d. 19, ll. 140, 182, 188; RGAE, f. 396, op. 5, d. 169, l. 400.

40. For a detailed description of the Trotskii-Zinovev Opposition and an account of its struggle with Stalin, see Robert V. Daniels, *The Conscience of the Revolution. Communist Opposition in Soviet Russia* (New York: Simon and Schuster, 1969), 273–321.

41. See Matthew E. Lenoe, "Reader Response to the Soviet Press Campaign Against the Trotskii-Zinovev Opposition, 1926–1928," *Russian History* 24, nos. 1–2 (1997): 89–116.

42. See, for example, letters in RGAE, f. 396, op. 5, d. 169, ll. 93, 524–524ob, and RGASPI, f. 17, op. 85, d. 19, l. 193.

43. RGAE, f. 396, op. 5, d. 169, l. 520.

44. Ibid., l. 421.

45. Ibid., l. 376ob.

46. Ibid., l. 358.

47. GARF, f. 374s.ch., op. 27s., d. 1362, l. 32.

48. RGASPI, f. 17, op. 85, d. 207, l. 96.

49. See Sheila Fitzpatrick, "Cultural Revolution as Class War," in *Cultural Revolution in Russia, 1928–1931*, ed. Sheila Fitzpatrick (Bloomington: Indiana University Press, 1978), 10–12; and Hiroaki Kuromiya, *Stalin's Industrial Revolution* (Cambridge: Cambridge University Press, 1988), 15–17.

50. See Kuromiya, 36; and "Pechat i nashi plany," *Izvestiia*, May 4, 1929, 1.

51. TsGAOD g. Moskvy, f. 3, op. 9, d. 79, l. 40.

52. Ibid.

53. Ibid., 40ob, 41–42.

54. Ibid., 68ob, 69.

55. Ibid., 68ob, 69.

56. Ibid., 80ob–81. The claim that Shakhty increased worker loan subscriptions might seem far-fetched, but foreigners employed in Soviet factories in the 1930s observed that workers did believe that "wrecking" by foreign intelligence agents was everywhere. John Scott describes Magnitogorsk workers as "greatly impressed" by a play about the necessity of rooting out foreign spies (*Behind the Urals* [Bloomington: Indiana University Press, 1989], 203). See also Peter Francis, *I Worked in a Soviet Factory* (London: Jarrolds, 1939).

57. Stalin in a June 25, 1926, letter to Molotov, Rykov, Bukharin, and other CC allies ("other friends"). See L. Kosheleva, et al., eds., *Pisma I. V. Stalina V. M. Molotovu, 1925–1936 gg.* (Moscow: Rossiia Molodaia, 1995), 72–74.

58. RGASPI, f. 17, op. 85, d. 18, l. 17.

59. GARF, f. 5566, op. 4, d. 3, l. 16, 25.

60. Ibid., l. 42.

61. See *Komsomolskaia pravda*, July 2, 1930, 1, 3; July 3, 1930, 4; July 12, 1930, 4; July 13, 1930, 4; July 30, 1930, 4.

62. GARF, f. 374 s.ch., op. 27s., d. 1931, ll. 47ob–49ob.

4. The Creation of Mass Journalism

1. Peter Kenez, *The Birth of the Propaganda State. Soviet Methods of Mass Mobilization, 1917–1929* (Cambridge: Cambridge University Press, 1985), 25–26.

2. Ibid., 49. See also Semen Gershberg, *Rabota u nas takaia* (Moscow: Politizdat, 1971), 49.

3. See, for example, L. S. Rogachevskaia, *Sotsialisticheskoe sorevnovanie v SSSR: istoricheskie ocherki, 1917–1970* (Moscow: Izdatel stvo Nauka, 1977), 39–47.

4. Julie Kay Mueller points out the importance of the year 1926 in her 1994 paper "The Russian Press during NEP: The Transformation of a Soviet Institution" presented to the Annual Convention of the American Historical Association

in San Francisco, Jan. 6–9, 1994. Mueller cites A. Kapustin's organization of the first "production review" by *Tverskaia pravda* that year as the origins of the mobilizing journalism of the 1930s.

5. In the spring of 1919, for example, *Pravda* and *Bednota* began running short notes on "Volunteer Saturdays" at railroad repair shops and other enterprises. On March 18, *Bednota* published a note about 130 engineers and mechanics who turned out to repair forty-nine railroad cars on a "Volunteer Saturday." The piece, headed "If Only Everyone Would Do This," ran next to an exhortation in boldface capital letters to volunteer for repair and maintenance work on the railroads "because the fate of the country depends on the condition of transport." On coverage of "Volunteer Saturdays," see Gershberg. For the example from *Bednota*, see *Bednota*, Mar. 18, 1919, 4.

6. See RGASPI, f. 17, op. 112, d. 261, ll. 22, 34; d. 275, ll. 12–13, 20–20ob, 25; d. 276, l. 12, on the Agitprop Department commission, which planned the state newspaper network and the Orgburo and Secretariat's approval of the project.

7. For the Eighth Party Congress resolution calling for a press that would expose "the crimes of various types of persons in high posts and institutions, showing the mistakes and shortcomings of Soviet and party organizations," see *O partiinoi i sovetskoi pechati: sbornik dokumentov* (Moscow: Izdatelstvo "Pravda," 1954), 212.

8. For reports to the CC Agitprop Department on work with correspondents from *Shveinik,Rabochaia gazeta,Gudok,Postroika* (organ of the construction workers' union), and *Na vakhte* (organ of the water transport workers' union), see RGASPI, f. 17, op. 60, d. 907, ll. 4–13; d. 935, ll. 1–2, 6–8ob, 9–12ob, 26–31. On *Rabochaia gazeta*'s organization of worker correspondents' conferences, see Julie Kay Mueller, "A New Kind of Newspaper: The Origins and Development of a Soviet Institution, 1921–1928" (Ph.D. diss., University of California–Berkeley, 1992), 270. See also RGASPI, f. 17, op. 60, d. 935, ll. 26–27.

9. TsKhDMO, f. 1, op. 23, d. 384, ll. 36–39.

10. TsKhDMO, f. 1, op. 3, d. 16, ll. 11–16.

11. Valentina Sergeevna Martynovskaia, "Iz vospominanii o brate," TMs, library of *Komsomolskaia pravda*, Moscow, 1977.

12. TsKhDMO, f. 1, op. 3, d. 19, ll. 73, 121–128.

13. My discussion of information flow and news production owes much to Mark Fishman's *Manufacturing the News* (Austin: University of Texas Press, 1980).

14. See the records of the Politburo's commission, headed by N. Baranskii, in GARF, f. 374 s. ch., op. 27 s., d. 23.

15. See Ingulov's opening speech to the Moscow Conference of Information Specialists *(Moskovskaia konferentsiia rabotnikov informatsii)* for his attack on the "Ukrainian comrades" supporting abolition of the reportorial profession (*Zhurnalist*, no. 3, 1926 [March]: 32). For a summary of Alekseev's article in *Proletarii*, see "Otkliki na diskussiiu," *Zhurnalist*, no. 4, 1926 (April): 69.

16. *Zhurnalist*, no. 3, 1925 (March): 21; no. 6–7, 1925 (June/July): 34–37, 87. For a characterization of the reporter as a "courier," see "O masterakh i podmasteriakh tsekha informatsii," *Zhurnalist*, no. 3, 1926 (March): 21. See also the summary of I. Alekseev's article run in *Zhurnalist*, no. 4, 1926 (April): 69.

17. *Krasnaia pechat*, no. 16, 1926 (August): 40, cited a case in which the People's

Commissariat of Agriculture Press Bureau prevented reporters from attending a conference of *vydvizhentsy* (blue collar workers promoted to white collar positions).

18. *Zhurnalist*, no. 2, 1926 (February): 56–57. In the case in question, a foreign correspondent was waiting in the foyer for an already scheduled interview with the "demi-Commissar," but had to go to the bathroom. While he was gone, the *Gudok* reporter got into the trust director's office by posing as him. The reporter's outrage was obviously increased by the ease with which the foreign newspaperman, who was from a minor power ("such as Greece") got access. Russian reporters frequently claimed that foreign correspondents had better access to Soviet institutions than they did.

19. *Zhurnalist*, no. 1, 1925 (January): 21–22.

20. *Zhurnalist*, no. 2, 1926 (February): 10.

21. Ibid.

22. Soviet enterprises were supposed to hold regular "production meetings" at which lower-level personnel could offer suggestions for improving work or criticize management procedures they were unhappy with. The production meeting was expected to be a forum for compromise between management and labor. Quote is from *Zhurnalist*, no. 2, 1926 (February): 55.

23. *Zhurnalist*, no. 3, 1923 (January); 33–34; September 1922: 28–29; no. 12, 1924 (June): 23–24; no. 14, 1924 (August/September): 53; no. 12, 1925 (December): 32–33; no. 2, 1927 (February): 42–43.

24. *Zhurnalist*, no. 2, 1927 (February): 42; no. 5, 1923 (March/April): 36; no. 3, 1923 (January): 34.

25. *Zhurnalist*, no. 3, 1926 (March): 33.

26. Louise McReynolds, *The News Under Russia's Old Regime* (Princeton: Princeton University Press, 1991), 162.

27. For this image of the bourgeois newspaperman, see *Zhurnalist*, no. 3, 1926 (March): 20. Evgenii Riabchikov, a reporter on aviation affairs for *Komsomolskaia pravda* and *Pravda*, reports that when he began his career in the central press in the early 1930s, "the word 'reporter' was taboo and detested, it was considered peculiar only to the bourgeois newspaper." (Evgenii Riabchikov, "Iz zapisok aviatsionnogo reportera," TMs, p. 3, library of *Komsomolskaia pravda*, Moscow, 1980).

28. *Zhurnalist*, no. 2, 1926 (February): 46.

29. *KP*, no. 16, 1926 (August): 35.

30. *Zhurnalist*, no. 3, 1926 (March): 36.

31. *Zhurnalist*, no. 2, 1926 (February): 47.

32. Ibid., 46.

33. *Zhurnalist*, no. 2, 1927 (February): 45.

34. "Moskovskaia konferentsiia rabotnikov informatsii," *Zhurnalist*, no. 3, 1926 (March): 33.

35. The term "agit-moral" is borrowed from a 1929 article by S. Rozval, a regular contributor to *Zhurnalist*. Rozval denounced the tendency to "look for nothing more than an 'agit-moral' in information and ignore the concrete facts." He provided one example of an "agit-moral": "Our country is rich in natural resources." See *Zhurnalist*, no. 21, 1929 (Nov. 1): 658.

36. *Zhurnalist*, no. 3, 1926 (March): 22.

37. *Zhurnalist*, no. 3, 1923 (January): 34–35.

38. GARF, f. 374s. ch., op. 27s., d. 1931, l. 72.

39. A. Kliachkin, "'Fitili' i 'gvozdi': iz zapisok reportera," in I. M. Afonichev, ed., *O vremeni i o sebe. Iz zhurnalistskikh bloknotov* (Leningrad: Lenizdat, 1984), 254.

40. "People of the past" is a direct translation of the Russian *byvshie liudi*, which referred to members of defunct social classes—the bourgeoisie, priests, nobles, and so on.

41. V. Verner, "Bezprizornye gazety: *Vecherniaia krasnaia gazeta,* " *Zhurnalist*, no. 4, 1926 (April): 55–56.

42. Ivan Gronskii, *Iz proshlogo . . . Vospominaniia* (Moscow: "Izvestiia," 1991), 108–110.

43. See Gronskii, 111–113, and the RKI's Dec. 10, 1925, report on *Izvestiia* in GARF, f. 374s. ch., op. 28s., d. 1450, ll. 9–10.

44. On November 27, 1926, for example, Skvortsov-Stepanov fired four of the Moscow Information Department reporters (GARF, f. 1244, op. 1, d. 12, l. 41). This move appears to have been in preparation for the department's merger with the All-Union News section, which occurred in December 1926 and January 1927. Beyond concerns strictly internal to the *Izvestiia* organization, this move may also have been prompted by a December 1926 Central Committee resolution calling for more coverage of Party Life in the newspapers. See Anatolii Mironovich Danilevich, "Gazeta *Izvestiia*. Stanovlenie. Tipologiia. (1917–1927g.g.)" (Ph.D. diss., Moscow State University, 1978), 116–121. On the appointment of new department editors at *Izvestiia* in August 1926, see Gronskii, 113, Danilevich, 116, and GARF, f. 1244, op. 1, d. 12, ll. 24–34.

45. GARF, f. 1244, op. 1, d. 12, l. 34.

46. *Zhurnalist*, no. 3, 1926 (March): 19. Lenin's "motto," *"travit negodnogo,"* refers to the use of denunciation and unmasking to expose incompetence and corruption within the state apparatus.

47. Graeme Gill, *The Origins of the Stalinist Political System* (Cambridge: Cambridge University Press, 1990), 129–130.

48. TsGAOD g. Moskvy, f. 190, op. 1, d. 1, l. 59ob.

49. Ibid.

50. Ibid.

51. Gershberg, 23.

52. GARF, f. 374sch., op. 27s., d. 1069, ll. 13–14.

53. "Khorosho provedennaia kampaniia," *Zhurnalist*, nos. 8–9, 1926 (August/September): 36.

54. *Torgovo-promyshlennaia gazeta* (*TPG*), Feb. 24, 1926, 1; Mar. 2, 1926, 1.

55. *TPG*, March 2, 1926, 1; *Zhurnalist*, no. 4, 1926 (April): 24–25.

56. See "O peregruzke spetsialistov," *TPG*, Feb. 23, 1926, 3; Feb. 20, 1926, 3.

57. "Proizvodstvo. O proizvoditel'nosti truda i izderzhkakh proizvodstva," *TPG*, Mar. 4, 1926, 3.

58. *Zhurnalist*, no. 5, 1926 (May): 49–51.

59. See GARF, f. 374sch., op. 27s., d. 1069, l. 4.

60. Gershberg, 23–24; "Novaia forma gazetnoi raboty," *Pravda*, Mar. 11, 1927, 3.

61. "Novaia forma gazetnoi raboty," *Pravda*, Mar. 11, 1927, 3.

62. Ibid.; Gershberg, 23–24.

63. Gershberg, 22.

64. RGASPI, f. 17, op. 60, d. 870, l. 28.

65. See Chapter 1 on the Orgburo directive prohibiting party newspapers from criticizing party committees higher in the hierarchy than themselves.

66. For an account of pre-1926 party policy toward the worker-peasant correspondents' movement, see Mueller, 326–344. For the views of Ingulov and Bukharin on the worker-peasant correspondents' movement see A. Zuev, "K pravilnomu rostu (posle 3-go vsesoiuznogo soveshchaniia rabselkorov)," *Zhurnalist*, nos. 6–7, 1926 (June/July): 3–4; S. Ingulov, "Neobkhodimo podlinnoe rukovodstvo," *Zhurnalist*, nos. 6–7, 1926 (June/July): 19–23.

67. *Zhurnalist*, nos. 8–9, 1926 (August/September): 63.

68. *Put rabselkora*, no. 1, 1926 (Mar. 15): 14.

69. Writers to *Put rabselkora* in 1926, including worker correspondents themselves, frequently described specific cases of party bureau appointments of wall newspaper editors and direct supervision of worker correspondents by party committees or cell representatives. See, for example, *Put rabselkora*, no. 1, 1926 (Mar. 15): 16–22. It was also claimed that most *village* wall newspapers were organs of local Komsomol cells (*Put rabselkora*, no. 1, 1926 (Mar. 15): 36.

70. According to a November 1925 investigation of wall newspaper editorial boards by the Press Subdepartment of the Sokolniki ward (*raion*) party committee, Moscow, there were 46 wall newspapers in the ward, 14 of them at factories, 13 at railroad depots and stations, 13 at Soviet institutions, and 6 in military detachments. A total of 271 persons were on the editorial boards, 225 of them (83 percent) male. Fifty percent of the board members belonged to the party or were candidate members, and 23 percent belonged to the Komsomol. Forty-four percent of board members were workers, 3 percent were peasants, and a whopping 53 percent were white-collar employees. In the vast majority of cases, editors were not elected by correspondents, but assigned to the position by local authorities. Cases were specifically noted where the wall newspaper came out only when the party cell secretary ordered the editors to put together an issue. See *Put rabselkora*, no. 1, 1926 (Mar. 15): 20–23.

71. In a file of letters sent to *Rabochaia gazeta* in the summer of 1924 on the reopening of factories closed by the revolution and the Civil War, much of the correspondence is *typed*, some of it on carbon paper, and signed by factory administrators or labor union committee members. Many of the "worker correspondents," in other words, were supervisory personnel who wrote in as representatives of their enterprise as a whole, not of the blue-collar workers. See RGASPI, f. 610, op. 1, d. 8, ll. 1–27, 64–109.

72. "Novaia forma gazetnoi raboty," *Pravda*, Mar. 11, 1927, 3.

73. For proof of Gusev's authorship of the *Pravda* piece, see his closing comments at the Fifth Plenum of the Press Workers' Subsection, GARF, f. 5566, op. 4, d. 3, l. 55.

74. See *Zhurnalist*, no. 12, 1927 (December): 57, and Gershberg, 24.

75. Gershberg, 26.

76. See Gershberg, 9, and RGASPI, f. 17, op. 113, d. 804, l. 12.

77. See Gershberg, 26–27. For evidence of Kapustin's attendance at a high-level session of the APPO (on Sept. 3, 1929), see GARF, f. 374sch., op. 27s., d. 1898, l. 63.

78. Gershberg, 38; *Bolshaia sovetskaia entsiklopedia* (Moscow: Gosizdat, 1975), s. v. "Pospelov."

79. Gersherg, 52, 187.

80. Ibid., 26, 144.

81. For Troitskii's appointment as head editor of *Komsomolskaia pravda*, see RGASPI, f. 17, op. 113, d. 831, l. 8. For biographical and personal details on Troitskii, see M. Dubrov, "Zametki nakanune iubileiia," TMs, library of *Komsomolskaia pravda*, Moscow, 1975.

82. See GARF, f. 374s.ch., op. 27s, d. 1567, ll. 8–8ob, 127.

83. Thus, a work agenda drawn up in the Leningrad Komsomol's Press Department in early 1927 included the following items: (1) working together with the city Komsomol paper *Smena* to prepare a report on the state of the local youth correspondents movement, (2) investigating the measures taken by enterprise wall newspapers to promote belt tightening, rationalization, and raising productivity, (3) working with *raion*-level Komsomol Committees to come up with new methods of mass work. See TsKhDMO, f. 1, op. 23, d. 737, ll. 10–13.

84. *Put rabselkora*, no. 17–18, 1926 (Nov. 30): 18.

85. On the earliest instances of *konkursy* and "shock brigades," see Rogachevskaia, 72–79.

86. See the Sekretariat's Nov. 5, 1927, resolution on a report by the Tambov Komsomol organ *Iunosheskaia pravda* (TsKhDMO, f. 1, op. 23, d. 737, ll. 157–159).

87. *Zhurnalist*, no. 13, 1929 (July 1): 386.

88. In late 1923 a Press Subdepartment report praised *Uralskii rabochii* (*UR*) as one of only five real provincial mass workers' newspapers in the USSR. Another subdepartment report produced about the same time commended Kiev's *Proletarskaia pravda* and *Uralskii rabochii* for effectively combining the functions of a leading and a mass workers' newspaper. The latter case is the first mention I have found of the notion of a combined mass/leading newspaper, a concept that would become the orthodox formula for Soviet newspapers in the early 1930s. See RGASPI, f. 17, op. 60, d. 870, ll. 5, 66.

89. *UR*, Mar. 5, 1926, 1.

90. See, for example, *UR*, Mar. 20, 1926, 2; Mar. 21, 1926, 2; Mar. 24, 1926, 3; or Mar. 26, 1926, 2.

91. *UR*, Apr. 23, 1926, 1.

92. Ibid.

93. *UR*, Mar. 16, 1926, 2, 7.

94. Ibid.

95. See, for example, *UR*, May 25, 1926, 3.

96. *UR*, July 20, 1927, 2; July 29, 1927, 4.

97. See, for example, *UR*, Aug. 17, 1927, 4; Aug. 25, 1927, 4.

98. RGASPI, f. 17, op. 113, d. 699, ll. 88–90; d. 786, l. 11.

99. Ibid., d. 637, ll. 124–26; RGASPI, f. 17, op. 114, d. 295, l. 116. See also F. A. Mikhailov's comments at the March 1926 Urals oblast Committee Plenum in *UR*, Mar. 16, 1926, 7.

100. See RGASPI, f. 17, op. 113, d. 826, l. 9 and d. 852, l. 7 for the appointments of Tumarkin and Filov. For evidence that Filov was head editor of *Uralskii rabochii* in 1927, see documentation on his dispute with the Sverdlovsk *oblast* Committee secretary Rumiantsev in May of that year, RGASPI, f. 17, op. 85, d. 72, ll. 3–25.

101. RGASPI, f. 17, op. 113, d. 795, ll. 146–147.

102. "I. Stanevskii: Kratkie svedeniia," TMs, library of *Komsomolskaia pravda*, Moscow, undated, ll. 1–2.

103. RGASPI, f. 17, op. 113, d. 831, l. 8.

104. RGASPI, f. 17, op. 114, d. 308, l. 243.

105. Boris Baianov, "Moia rabota v *Komsomolskoi pravde*, " and "Iarkii i samobytnyi (neskolko stranits o Vladimire Bubekine)," both TMs, library of *Komsomolskaia pravda*, Moscow, 1979. Also Aleksei Abramenkov, "Donbass, Kharkov, Moskva . . . ," TMs, library of *Komsomolskaia pravda*, Moscow, 1974, 1, 11.

106. Iurii Zhukov, *Liudi tridtsatykh godov* (Moscow: "Sovetskaia Rossiia," 1966), 41–43.

107. RGASPI, f. 17, op. 113, d. 800, ll. 3, 106.

108. Zhukov, 43; Gershberg, 189.

109. Abramenkov, 1–2, 6.

110. I have borrowed the use of the anthropological language of "sacred place" and "ritual" from Ken Jowitt, "'Moscow Centre,'" in *New World Disorder: The Leninist Extinction* (Berkeley: University of California Press, 1992), 164. However, I use the terms in a much looser way than Jowitt.

111. "Elite" should be understood here in a broad sense as *obshchestvennost*, translatable roughly as "official society," and meaning the collective body of activists and officials.

112. Results of the SRP survey are in GARF, f. 5566, op. 6, d. 27.

113. Ibid. l. 4, and capsule analysis of survey results in report to the Seventh Congress of the SRP (August 1930), GARF, f. 5566, op. 7, d. 1, l. 10.

114. GARF, f. 5566, op. 6, d. 27, l. 1–2.

115. Ibid., l. 11. Of 4,998 SRP members surveyed, 1,665 were members or candidate members of the party.

116. Interviews by author with subjects (Novoplianskii, Apr. 29, 1995; Kozhen, Aug. 10, 1995; Ortenberg, Apr. 19, 1995).

117. GARF, f. 5566, op. 6, d. 27, l. 11, T. H. Rigby, *Communist Party Membership in the USSR, 1917–1967* (Princeton: Princeton University Press), 116, and interviews by author with subjects (Novoplianskii, Apr. 29, 1995; Kozhen, Aug. 10, 1995; Ortenberg, Apr. 19, 1995). For biographical data on Karelshtein, see V. Shutkevich, ed., *Korrespondenty pobedy: Frontovaia 'Komsomolka' v dokumentakh i fotografiiakh* (Moscow: "Komsomol'skaia pravda," 1995), 34–35. For biographical citations on Tararukhin, see TsGAOD g. Moskvy, f. 374s. ch., op. 27s, d. 1921, ll. 22–30ob. For information on Sosnovskii, see *Deiateli SSSR i revoliutsionnogo dvizheniia Rossii. Entsiklopedicheskii slovar granat* (Moscow: Sovetskaia entsiklopediia, 1989), s.v. "Sosnovskii, Lev." Soviet definitions of "class background" and "social status" in the 1920s and early 1930s were malleable, manipulable, and negotiable (see Sheila Fitzpatrick, "Ascribing Class: The Construction of Social Identity in Soviet Russia," *Journal of Modern History* 65 [December 1993]: 745–770).

118. GARF, f. 5566, op. 7, d. 29, ll. 26–26ob.

119. For more on journalists' education levels in the 1920s, see Matthew Lenoe, "Stalinist Mass Journalism and the Transformation of Soviet Newspapers, 1926–1932." (Ph.D. diss.: University of Chicago, 1997), 616–619.

120. GARF, f. 5566, op. 6, d. 27, l. 11.

121. Ibid., ll. 4, 23, 26, 34.

122. Ibid.

123. For discussion of the failure of direct *vydvizhenie* at *Izvestiia* of blue-collar workers from inside the newspaper apparatus to white-collar positions, see records of the paper's party cell in TsGAOD g. Moskvy, f. 420, op. 1, d. 57, ll. 25–26, 84, 92–93, 99–102, 118–119, 133–134; d. 59, ll. 26, 52. For similar difficulties at *Rabochaia gazeta* in 1930, see TsGAOD g. Moskvy, f. 190, op. 1, d. 7, ll. 53–54, 82. For discussion of the same problem at the Seventh Plenary Session of the CC of the journalists' professional union, the SRP (Soiuz rabotnikov pechati), see GARF, f. 5566, op. 7, d. 1, l. 10; d. 4, ll. 40–41, 83.

124. David Novoplianskii, who eventually worked as a senior writer at *Komsomolskaia pravda* and *Pravda*, began writing for his factory newspaper as a young worker in Kharkov (David Novoplianskii, interview with the author, Apr. 29, 1995). David Ortenberg, editor of *Krasnaia zvezda* during World War II, began his career as a worker correspondent at the age of seventeen before becoming editor of a daily newspaper in the city of Nikolaevsk (David Ortenberg, interview with the author, Apr. 19, 1995). Semen Gershberg first wrote for a Ukrainian factory newspaper in Elizavetgrad (later Kirovgrad), and then for an *okrug* (province) newspaper (Gershberg, 4).

125. The above generalizations are based on my study of numerous biographies of individual journalists. Among these are Taras Kostrov, editor of *Komsomolskaia pravda* from 1925 to 1928 (see above); David Ortenberg, *Pravda* correspondent in the 1930s and editor of *Krasnaia zvezda* during World War II (author interview); David Novoplianskii, a reporter for *Komsomolskaia pravda* in the late 1930s (author interview); Valentin Kitain, a writer and editor at *Martenovka*, the workplace newspaper of the Hammer and Sickle factory in Moscow in the early 1930s (interview with the author, Moscow, May 16, 1995); Aleksei Kozhen, *Komsomolskaia pravda* correspondent from 1934 (with the author, Aug. 10, 1995); Semen Gershberg,

Pravda correspondent from the mid-1930s (Gershberg); Igor Maleev, editor and writer at *Komsomolskaia pravda* and *Rabochaia gazeta* from 1925 to 1928 (file "Igor Maleev," library of *Komsomolskaia pravda*, Moscow); A. Tararukhin, an editor at *Gudok* in 1929–1930 (see below); and others.

126. GARF, f. 374 s. ch., op. 27s., d. 1921, ll. 22–22ob.

127. Ibid., l. 22ob.

128. Ibid.

129. Ibid., ll. 22ob–23.

130. Ibid.

131. Ibid., ll. 23–24.

132. Ibid., l. 24.

133. Ibid., ll. 24–24ob.

134. Ibid., ll. 22, 27–30ob.

5. Mass Journalists, "Cultural Revolution," and the Retargeting of Soviet Newspapers

1. Sheila Fitzpatrick, ed., *Cultural Revolution in Russia, 1928–1931* (Bloomington: Indiana University Press, 1978). See especially Fitzpatrick, "Cultural Revolution as Class War" (8–40); Robert Sharlet, "Pashukanis and the Withering Away of the Law in the USSR" (169–188); and Susan Solomon, "Rural Scholars and the Cultural Revolution" (129–153).

2. See Michael David-Fox, *Revolution of the Mind: Higher Learning among the Bolsheviks, 1918–1929* (Ithaca: Cornell University Press, 1997), especially the conclusion, "The Great Break in Higher Learning," 254–272.

3. Michael David-Fox's claim that 1928–1931 saw an "intensification" of the party's "cultural project" reflects the campaign to Bolshevize nonparty institutions of higher education, most importantly the Academy of Sciences. This seems to me more like an effort to place dependable cadres in key positions than a drive to transform the psychology of the population as a whole. See David-Fox, *Revolution of the Mind*, 254–272.

4. For the Oct. 3, 1927, CC resolution, see *Zhurnalist*, no. 11, 1927 (November), 54–55. For a lead editorial in *Zhurnalist* condemning "bourgeois specialist" attitudes among newspapermen, see nos. 9–10, 1927 (September/October), 4–5.

5. RGASPI, f. 17, op. 113, d. 618, ll. 3, 128.

6. For the Oct. 3, 1927, CC resolution, see *Zhurnalist*, no. 11, 1927 (November): 54–55.

7. On the attacks on Bukharin and Ulianova at *Pravda*, see below.

8. See issues of *Zhurnalist* from January to July 1930, and in particular Ia. Tsirul, "Za zhurnalista—partiinogo rabotnika!," *Zhurnalist*, no. 5, 1930 (March), 135–136.

9. For an account of the conflict at *Cooperative Life*, see Matthew Lenoe,

"Stalinist Mass Journalism and the Transformation of Soviet Newspapers" (Ph.D. diss., University of Chicago, 1997), 487–495.

10. On events at *Evening Moscow*, see GARF, f. 374 s.ch., op. 27s., d. 1931, ll. 71–72; and RGASPI, f. 17, op. 113, d. 826, l. 5 (Volodin's appointment). See also "Dezinfektsionnaia kamera / 'Vecherniaia Moskva'," *Zhurnalist*, no. 13, 1930 (July), 24.

11. See RGASPI, f. 17, op. 113, d. 643, ll. 140–143; d. 644, l. 68. See also GARF, f. 374 s.ch., op. 27s., d. 1921, ll. 22–29. See also Tsirul, "Za zhurnalista—partiinogo rabotnika."

12. RGASPI, f. 17, op. 3, d. 670, l. 3.

13. RGASPI, f. 17, op. 3, d. 672, l. 7; E. H. Carr, *Foundations of a Planned Economy, 1926–1929*, vol. 2 (London: Macmillan, 1971), 63n.

14. RGASPI, f. 17, op. 3, d. 698, l. 7.

15. RGASPI, f. 89, op. 7, d. 6, ll. 3–4.

16. See the draft resolution of the *Pravda* editorial board on this dispute in RGASPI, f. 17, op. 85, d. 18, ll. 347–348.

17. See *Pravdist*, July 9, 1929, 1; and Carr, vol. 2, 62.

18. See "Nadezhda Sergeevna Alliluevoi lichno ot Stalina (perepiska 1928–1931 godov," *Rodina*, no. 10, 1992: 50–58.

19. See, for example, the Secretariat session of Dec. 21, 1928, documented in RGASPI, f. 17, op. 113, d. 687, l. 1.

20. On Kovalev's contact with Ingulov about staff appointments, see "O periakh iz khvosta. Mysli vslukh," *Pravdist*, Dec. 5, 1928, 3.

21. RGASPI, f. 17, op. 113, d. 685, ll. 27–30ob.

22. Ibid., ll. 1–3, 20–28.

23. Pravdist, June 22, 1929, 1.

24. See, for example, GARF, f. 374s.ch., op. 27s., d. 1898.

25. See Kapustin's call for *all* departments of *Pravda* to join the Party Life department in denouncing the Right Deviation, *Pravdist*, Mar. 13, 1929, 3.

26. *Pravdist*, Nov. 21, 1928, 3.

27. On the CC Secretariat's initiative to cut production costs at its newspapers, see RGASPI, f. 17, op. 113, d. 699, ll. 53–60ob.

28. RGASPI, f. 17, op. 113, d. 584, l. 3.

29. "Na novye puti," *Pravdist*, Dec. 19, 1928, 1.

30. *Zhurnalist*, no. 2, 1929 (Jan. 15): 56; no. 4, 1929 (Feb. 15): 109.

31. See, for example, *Pravda*, Jan. 1, 1929, 3, 5.

32. M. Bulyzhnik, "Propuskatelskii uklon," *Pravdist*, Dec. 29, 1928, 3.

33. *Pravdist*, Jan. 12, 1929, 3.

34. *Pravdist*, Jan. 5, 1929, 3.

35. Like many mass journalists, Naumov had been an organizer of worker correspondents. In 1927 he was a frequent contributor to the journal *Rabselkor* (see, for example, June 15, 1927, 35–37; and June 30, 1927, 32–33).

36. *Pravdist*, Jan. 12, 1929, 1, 3.

37. *Pravdist*, Nov. 10, 1928, 1; Feb. 9, 1929, 3.

38. *Pravdist*, Nov. 10, 1928, 1.

39. *Pravdist*, Dec. 1, 1928, 4; Jan. 9, 1929, 1; Feb. 20, 1929, 2–3; March 9, 1929, 3.

40. See, for example, *Pravdist*, Oct. 31, 1928, 3; Nov. 17, 1928, 2.

41. *Pravdist*, June 22, 1929, 1; June 29, 1929, 1; July 9, 1929, 2–3.

42. *Pravdist*, Nov. 14, 1928, 3; Dec. 5, 1928, 2; Dec. 12, 1928, 1; Dec. 22, 1928, 2.

43. On the close friendship between Ulianova, Rabinovich, and Ikhok, see Rabinovich's unpublished memoirs and Ulianova's correspondence in RGASPI, f. 14, op. 1, d. 322, especially ll. 1, 2, 7–13.

44. *Pravdist*, Oct. 31, 1928, 3; Nov. 10, 1928, 2; Nov. 14, 1928, 1; Nov. 28, 1928, 3; Dec. 12, 1928, 3.

45. *Pravdist*, Jan. 5, 1929, 1.

46. *Pravdist*, Feb. 2, 1929, 3.

47. *Pravdist*, Apr. 24, 1929, 2.

48. *Pravdist*, Aug. 1, 1929, 4.

49. *Pravdist*, June 22, 1929, 1; June 29, 1929, 1; July 9, 1929, 2–3.

50. RGASPI, f. 14, op. 1, d. 272, ll. 50–55.

51. Ivan Gronskii, *Iz proshlogo. Vospominaniia* (Moscow: "Izvestiia," 1991), 119.

52. Ibid., 133.

53. For example, at an April 1931 meeting of the *Izvestiia* editorial office party cell bureau, editor G. Ryklin referred to the newspaper's "specific peculiarities" in arguing against doing the same kind of mass work as *Rabochaia gazeta* and *Trud* did. Ryklin meant that *Izvestiia* targeted at educated white-collar city dwellers and purveyed a more neutral, less political brand of news than the latter two papers (see TsGAOD g. Moskvy, f. 420, op. 1, d. 58, ll. 57–58).

54. Danilevich, Anatolii Mironovich, "Gazeta '*Izvestiia*.' Stanovlenie. Tipologiia (1917–1927 g.g.)" (Ph.D. diss., Moscow State University, 1978), 115–116. On the appointment of A. Agranovskii as special correspondent for the Ukraine in the summer of 1926, see GARF, f. 1244, op. 1, d. 12, l. 24. By 1929 Agranovskii was a member of the editorial board (see GARF, f. 1244, op. 1, d. 31, l. 1).

55. On the purges at *Izvestiia* in 1926–1927, see Danilevich, 69–70, 116; Gronskii, 110; GARF, f. 1244, op. 1, d. 12, ll. 41, 56–57; d. 17, ll. 5–17; "Ratsionalizatsiiu po Izvestiinski," *Rulon*, Oct. 27, 1928, 2.

56. TsGAOD g. Moskvy, f. 420, op. 1, d. 56, ll. 8–9.

57. GARF, f. 1244, op. 1, d. 31, ll. 6–11 (emphasis added).

58. Ibid. ll. 13–14.

59. Ibid., l. 45.

60. TsGAOD g. Moskvy, f. 420, op. 1, d. 56, l. 2.

61. GARF, f. 1244, op. 1, d. 31, ll. 52–65ob.

62. Ibid., ll. 76–77; d. 33, l. 19.

63. In August 1929, for example, the head of *Izvestiia* 's Department of Culture and Society (the section that printed reviews, cultural criticism, popular science, and the like) reported to the editorial board that he frequently attended briefings at the Central Committee Agitprop Department on "culturo-political and art issues." See GARF, f. 1244, op. 1, d. 31, l. 19.

64. Ibid., l. 61.

65. *O partiinoi i sovetskoi pechati. Sbornik dokumentov* (Moscow: Izdatelstvo Pravda, 1954), 386–394.

66. On Gronskii's handling of demands for purges of non-Communists, see TsGAOD g. Moskvy, f. 420, op. 1, d. 56, ll. 1–1ob; and *Rulon*, the newspaper's employee *mnogotirazhka*, Jan. 4, 1930, 1. On the departure of journalists from *Izvestiia* in early 1930, see the closed meeting of the *Izvestiia* party collective on Mar. 3, 1930, TsGAOD g. Moskvy, f. 420, op. 1, d. 57, l. 1.

67. TsGAOD g. Moskvy, f. 420, op. 1, d. 57, ll. 10–12, 25, 28–29, 50–51.

68. Jeffrey Brooks, "Socialist Realism in *Pravda:* Read All About It!" *Slavic Review* 53, no. 4 (Winter 1994): 977.

69. For Krumin's first appearance at an *Izvestiia* editorial board meeting, see GARF, f. 1244, op. 1, d. 31, l. 97 (July 22, 1930).

70. See TsGAOD g. Moskvy, f. 420, op. 1, d. 57, l. 80 and GARF, f. 1244, op. 1, d. 31, ll. 98–99.

71. GARF, f. 1244, op. 1, d. 31, l. 97.

72. TsGAOD g. Moskvy, f. 420, op. 1, d. 57, ll. 16–22.

73. On conflict at the *Izvestiia* editorial offices between July 1930 and April 1931, see TsGAOD g. Moskvy, f. 420, op. 1, dd. 57–59, and Gronskii, *Iz proshlogo*, 134–135.

74. GARF, f. 1244, op. 1, d. 31, ll. 98–103.

75. Ibid., d. 39, ll. 1–47. Such direct intervention by the newspaper in economic planning and coordination had been pioneered by *Komsomolskaia pravda* at Leningrad's Krasnyi Putilovets Factory in early 1930. See M. Dubrov, "Zametki nakanune iubileiia," TMs, p. 12; *Komsomolskaia pravda* editorial office library, Moscow, 1975; and A. P. Rozhdestvenskii, "Stranitsy vospominaniia," TMs, pp. 4–6, *Komsomolskaia pravda* editorial office library, Moscow, 1976.

76. *O partiinoi i sovetskoi pechati*, 408–411.

77. TsGAOD g. Moskvy, f. 420, op. 1, d. 59, ll. 23–26, 36–39.

78. Ibid., ll. 45–49.

79. On GIZ's role in developing reader conferences and Iakov Shafir's criticism of same, see Shafir's report on reader studies to the CC Secretariat in RGASPI, f. 17, op. 85, d. 20, ll. 12–16. For an enthusiastic endorsement of newspaper reader conferences in the summer of 1928 by Sergei Ingulov, see RGASPI, f. 17, op. 113, d. 643, ll. 59–61.

80. See *Pravdist*, June 4, 1929, 1; *Zhurnalist*, no. 8 (Apr. 15), 1929: 239. See also V. Kuzmichev's *Organizatsiia obshchestvennogo mneniia* (Moscow: Rabotnik prosveshcheniia, 1929).

81. M. Bochacher, "O metodologii gazetovedeniia," *Zhurnalist*, no. 5, 1930 (Mar. 1): 156. For Bochacher's coverage of *Vyshka*, see *Zhurnalist*, no. 4, 1929 (Feb. 15): 118.

82. Ibid. For a summary account of Kuzmichev's and Rubakin's work, see Vadim Volkov, "The Politics of Reading in the Soviet Union, 1920s–1930s: Reflections on the Privatization of Life," TMs (photocopy), 8–10, paper presented to the Conference on Soviet Letters to Authority, Apr. 6–7, 1996, University of Chicago, Chicago, Illinois.

83. M. Gus, "Gazeta i chitatel,'" *Zhurnalist*, no. 5, 1930 (Mar. 1): 157–158.

84. *Zhurnalist*, no. 6, 1930 (Mar. 15): 192.

85. P. Cherepenin, "K informatsii," *Zhurnalist*, nos. 7–8, 1930 (April): 14–15.

86. B. Reznikov, "Polemicheskie zametki," *Zhurnalist*, no. 14, 1930 (July): 19–23.

87. On the 1930 debate about pedagogy at GIZh, see *Zhurnalist*, nos. 7–8, 1930 (April): 11–12; nos. 11–12, 1930 (June): 24–27; no. 13 (July), 1930: 30–35.

88. See *Komsomolskaia pravda*, June 7, 1930, 2; Aug. 23, 1930, 2; Oct. 24, 1930, 2. On the "Gus-Kurs Deviation" see A. Kotlyar, "Newspapers in the USSR: Reflections and Observations of a Soviet Journalist," Mimeographed Series no. 71, Research Program on the U.S.S.R. (New York: East European Fund, 1955), 55.

89. T. H. Rigby, *Communist Party Membership in the USSR, 1917–1967* (Princeton: Princeton University Press, 1968), 115.

90. For figures on the number of industrial workers in the Soviet Union, see Moshe Lewin, *The Making of the Soviet System* (New York: Pantheon Books, 1985), 225; and Hiroaki Kuromiya, *Stalin's Industrial Revolution* (Cambridge: Cambridge University Press, 1988), 88.

91. A. Zuev, "K pravilnomu rostu," *Zhurnalist*, nos. 6–7, 1926 (June/July): 3–4. The quote is from Zuev's account of Bukharin's speech, not from the speech itself.

92. See S. Ingulov, "Neobkhodimo podlinnoe rukovodstvo," *Zhurnalist*, nos. 6–7, 1926 (June/July): 19–23; *O partiinoi i sovetskoi pechati. Sbornik dokumentov* (Moscow: Izdatelstvo Pravda, 1954), 361.

93. GARF, f. 5566, op. 4, d. 4, l. 66.

94. *O partiinoi i sovetskoi pechati*, 374–375.

95. RGASPI, f. 17, op. 113, d. 643, ll. 81–84.

96. Ibid., d. 639, ll. 169–173; d. 694, ll. 166–167.

97. Ibid., d. 717, ll. 23–55; *O partiinoi i sovetskoi pechati*, 382–85. See ll. 3–31 of d. 717 for Ingulov's statement of the need to adjust *Bednota* to rural activists' reading level. The order to the newspaper to simplify its language was an unpublished supplementary point to the CC resolution.

98. See, for example, discussion of the need to defuse "peasant moods" among Moscow workers at a spring 1929 Moscow agitprop conference in TsGAOD g. Moskvy, f. 3, op. 10, d. 18, ll. 1–7, 10ob, 14–16ob, 37–38.

99. RGASPI, f. 17, op. 113, d. 643, ll. 55–68ob, esp. l. 58ob.

100. Ibid., ll. 55ob–56ob, 60–61.

101. For *Uchitelskaia gazeta*'s transformation into a mass organ, see RGASPI, f. 17, op. 113, d. 812, ll. 88–94 (January 1930).

102. Ibid., d. 796, l. 3.

103. Ibid., d. 815, ll. 4, 20–27.

104. Ibid., d. 840, ll. 74–78.

105. RGASPI, f. 17, op. 114, d. 273, ll. 4, 121–159.

106. RGASPI, f. 17, op. 114, d. 227, l. 137; d. 234, ll. 76–78, 82–83; d. 277, ll. 3, 104.

107. RGASPI, f. 17, op. 114, d. 234, ll. 76–83.

6. The Central Committee and Self-Criticism, 1928–1929

1. See Chapter 1.

2. On the reorganization of the Agitprop Department in early 1928, see Chapter 5.

3. See *Komsomolskaia pravda*, April 18, 1928, 2.

4. For Bukharin's speech, see *Komsomolskaia pravda*, April 19, 1928, 2; for Kosarev's speech, see *Komsomolskaia pravda*, April 22, 1928, 1; for Kostrov's speech, see *Komsomolskaia pravda*, April 24, 1928, 2.

5. Primary sources on this incident are RGASPI, f. 17, op. 113, d. 650, ll. 80–91; and GARF, f. 374 s. ch., op. 27 s., d. 1413, ll. 112–124.

6. TsGAOD g. Moskvy, f. 190, op. 1, d. 3., ll. 137–139.

7. Ibid., ll. 23–25.

8. Ibid., ll. 26–27.

9. TsGAOD g. Moskvy, f. 190, op. 1, d. 3, ll. 11–12. On Maleev biography, see Lev Igorevich Maleev (the journalist's son) to Sofiia Finger, Feb. 21, 1975, TMs, pp. 1–2, *Komsomolskaia pravda* editorial staff library, Moscow.

10. TsGAOD g. Moskvy, f. 190, op. 1, d. 4, ll. 16–17, 96–98, 105–106.

11. Ibid., d. 4, ll. 103–123; d. 7, ll. 2–8.

12. Ibid., d. 4, ll. 123; d. 7, ll. 6–7.

13. Ibid., d. 4, ll. 39–43.

14. Ibid., d. 4, ll. 140–41.

15. Ibid., l. 125.

16. Ibid.

17. Ibid., l. 156.

18. Ibid., ll. 157–158.

19. I. V. Stalin, *Sochineniia* (Moscow: Gosudarstvennoe izdatelstvo politicheskoi literatury, 1949), 11: 132.

20. Ibid., 11: 135–136.

21. TsKhDMO, f. 1, op. 3, d. 46, ll. 42–46.

22. TsKhDMO, f. 1, op. 3, d. 52, ll. 12, 159–160ob.

23. E. H. Carr, *Foundations of a Planned Economy, 1926–1929*, vol. 2 (London: Macmillan, 1971), 71–72.

24. For a summary account of Stalin and Kaganovich's attack on the VTsSPS leadership at the Eighth Congress of Labor Unions, see Carr, vol. 1, part 2, 558–563.

25. See for example *Komsomolskaia pravda*, Nov. 16, 1928, 1.

26. *Komsomolskaia pravda*, Nov. 14, 1928, 3.

27. Stalin, *Sochineniia*, 11: 137.

28. TsKhDMO, f. 1, op. 3, d. 52, ll. 12, 159–160ob.

29. Ibid., l. 158.

30. Ibid., ll. 183–184.

31. See *Komsomolskaia pravda*, Feb. 28, 1929, 3; Mar. 1, 1929, 2; May 9, 1929, 2.

32. See, for example, *Komsomolskaia pravda*, Apr. 11, 1928, 2; Jan. 1, 1929, 1.

33. *Komsomolskaia pravda*, June 7, 1929, 2; June 9, 1929, 4; June 12, 1929, 2; June 13, 1929, 1; June 14, 1929, 1; June 15, 1929, 4.

34. *Komsomolskaia pravda*, June 9, 1929, 4; June 16, 1929, 5.

35. *Komsomolskaia pravda*, June 13, 1929, 1.

36. *Komsomolskaia pravda*, June 16, 1929, 5.

37. *Komsomolskaia pravda*, Sept. 22, 1929, 2.

38. RGASPI, f. 17, op. 113, d. 643, l. 48.

39. Ibid., l. 53.

40. Ibid., ll. 58, 58ob, 64ob.

41. GARF, f. 374 s. ch., op. 27 s., d. 1621, ll. 1–21.

42. Ibid., ll. 259, 262, 264.

43. RGASPI, f. 17, op. 113, d. 678, ll. 20–26.

44. Ibid.

45. Ibid., ll. 18–19. See also *Pravda*, Dec. 5, 1928. Ingulov's article in this issue, titled "This is No Way to Tutor the Masses," praised the work of *Luganskaia pravda*, *Tverskaia pravda*, and other pioneers of mass journalism, but reprimanded the first paper along with *The Star* for their "mistakes."

46. See, for example, the resolution of the Sixteenth Party Conference (April 1929) headed "Ob itogakh i blizhaishchikh zadachakh borby s biurokratizmom," in *O partiinoi i sovetskoi pechati*, 391–392. See also the Central Committee Secretariat's June 1929 approval of a CCC resolution ordering *Pravda* to print a retraction of inaccurate charges of suppression of self-criticism and drunkenness against local party officials (RGASPI, f. 17, op. 113, d. 754, ll. 10, 33–34).

47. See, for example, *Pravda*, Aug. 30, 1929, 4.

48. *Pravda*, Sept. 1, 1929, 3.

49. *Pravda*, Sept. 3, 1929, 5; Sept. 5, 1929, 4.

50. *Komsomolskaia pravda*, Sept. 6, 1929, 1, 2; Sept. 8, 1929, 1.

51. *Komsomolskaia pravda*, Sept. 10, 1929, 1; Sept. 13, 1929, 1; *Pravda*, Sept. 11, 1929, 2; Sept. 14, 1929, 5; Sept. 18, 1929, 3. On the insurrections of mass journalists at *Pravda* and *Komsomolskaia pravda*, see Kultprop Department assistant

chief A. Gusev's January 1930 report on the self-criticism campaign to the Central Committee Orgburo in RGASPI, f. 17, op. 113, d. 815, ll. 104–104ob.

52. *Pravda*, Sept. 11, 1929, 2.

53. For Stalin's Sept. 9 letter to Molotov, see *Pisma I. V. Stalina V. M. Molotovu, 1925–1936 g.g.*, 161–162. In the Sept. 9 letter Stalin mentioned his suspicions that "Zinovev or one of Zinovev's pupils" was actually running *Pravda*. In a Dec. 25, 1929, letter he revealed that the "pupil" he was thinking of was Kovalev ("he has, they say, sympathies toward the Zinovevites"). For the Dec. 25 letter, see *Pisma I. V. Stalina V. M. Molotovu*, 172.

54. bid., 165.

55. "Nadezhda Sergeevne Alliluevoi lichno ot Stalina (perepiska 1928–1931 godov)," *Rodina*, no. 10, 1992: 50–58.

56. RGASPI, f. 85, op. 27, d. 108, ll. 8–11.

57. "Nadezhda Sergeevne Alliluevoi lichno ot Stalin."

58. TsGAOD g. Moskvy, f. 190, op. 1, d. 4, ll. 157–158.

59. Ibid.

60. "Nadezhda Sergeevna Allilueva lichno ot Stalina."

61. Ibid.

62. GARF, f. 374 s. ch., op. 27 s., d. 1898, l. 3. A. P. Mariinskii's account of the affair (a Sept. 16 letter to Ordzhonikidze at the CCC) was quite similar to Ingulov's. Mariinskii also claimed that Kovalev was behind the idea of exposing abuses in Leningrad, and had passed this on to Ingulov. However, as a CC Agitprop official, Mariinskii shared with Ingulov an interest in passing the buck to Kovalev. See RGASPI, f. 85, op. 27, d. 108, ll. 8–11.

63. Ibid., ll. 13–16ob.

64. Ibid., ll. 5–6.

65. Ibid., ll. 39–75ob.

66. RGASPI, f. 17, op. 113, d. 815, l. 104.

67. See Amy Knight, *Who Killed Kirov* (New York: Hill and Wang, 1999), 130–37.

68. *Pravda*, Oct. 8, 1929, 3.

69. *Zhurnalist*, no. 20, 1929 (Oct. 15): 615–616.

70. *Zhurnalist*, no. 21, 1929 (Nov. 1): 641.

71. TsGAOD g. Moskvy, f. 190, op. 1, d. 4, ll. 157–158.

72. Ibid., l. 158.

73. Ibid., ll. 158–160.

74. Ibid., l. 163.

75. *Pisma I. V. Stalina V. M. Molotovu*, ll. 171–174.

76. *Gazetnaia nedelia*, Oct. 5, 1929, 2.

77. On the CC Orgburo's confirmation of Troitskii's appointment to *Komsomolskaia pravda* in March 1930, see RGASPI, f. 17, op. 113, d. 831, l. 8.

78. On Kon's removal (at his own request), see RGASPI, f. 17, op. 113, d. 826, l. 9. For Agitprop Department chief Krinitskii's recommendation that Chagin be

fired from *Krasnaia gazeta* (probably in October 1929), see GARF, f. 374 s. ch., op. 27 s., d. 1898, l. 2. For Chagin's firing and expulsion from the party, see *Zhurnalist*, no. 22, 1929 (Nov. 15): 681.

79. See Institut mirovoi literatury imeni A. M. Gorkogo, *M. Gorkii i sovetskaia pechat*, vol. 2 (Moscow: Izdatelstvo "Nauka," 1965), 200.

80. On Naumov's appointment to *Sputnik agitatora*, see RGASPI, f. 17, op. 114, d. 205, l. 215.

81. On the reorganization of the Agitprop Department, see RGASPI, f. 17, op. 113, d. 809, ll. 1, 15–22, 25–91, 168–175ob. On Ingulov's "resignation" from the Agitprop Department on Sept. 21, 1929, see RGASPI, f. 17, op. 113, d. 781, ll. 193–195. On Stetskii's appointment to head the department, see RGASPI, f. 17, op. 113, d. 796, l. 9. On Gusev's appointment, see RGASPI, f. 17, op. 113, d. 786, l. 11.

82. RGASPI, f. 17, op. 113, d. 815, ll. 29–31.

83. Ibid., l. 58–60.

84. Ibid., ll. 61–67.

85. For a detailed examination of antiworker measures in practice and the "workerist" myths (i.e., stories of heroic "shock workers") promulgated by Left-leaning party leaders such as Trotskii and picked up later by Stalin, see Andrea Graziosi, "Stalin's Antiworker 'Workerism,' 1924–1931," *International Review of Social History* 40, part 2, 1995 (August): 223–258. Graziosi discusses "workerist" and "antiworkerist" strains that thread their way through Bolshevik rhetoric of the 1920s and 1930s.

7. Mass Journalism, "Soviet Sensations," and Socialist Realism

1. RGASPI, f. 17, op. 114, d. 232, ll. 224–230.

2. A word of explanation is due the reader about the distinction between the "proletarian literature" of the First Five-Year Plan years (1928–1931) and the "socialist realism" of 1932 and after. Although there are two names here, they both refer to the same phenomenon. Most of the tenets of socialist realism were formulated by RAPP critics and other writers and journalists between 1928 and 1931, as guidelines for the new "proletarian literature." In 1932 Maksim Gorkii, a number of Central Committee agitprop officials and newspaper editors, and Stalin himself were involved in the formulation of socialist realism as an official literary genre, but their instructions followed the earlier guidelines for proletarian literature closely. Also, proletarian literature was associated with RAPP, the Russian Association of Proletarian Writers, and socialist realism with its successor organization, the Soviet Writers' Union. However, the discontinuity between RAPP, which was harshly disciplined by Stalin in 1931–1932 for disruptive attacks on non-RAPP authors, and the Writers' Union has been much overdrawn in Western scholarship. In reality there was great continuity in leading personnel and literary doctrine between the two organizations.

3. Fedor Gladkov's *Cement*, first published in 1925, is considered the prototypical production novel (see Katerina Clark, *The Soviet Novel: History as Ritual* [Chicago: University of Chicago Press, 1981], 256–260). Because Gladkov's novel

predates the creation of mass journalistic genres, it would obviously be absurd to argue that mass journalism and factory-centered "media events" such as socialist competitions were *the* decisive influence on the development of the socialist realist production novel. However, I would contend that the example of factory-centered mass journalism prompted party Agitprop officials to demand a similar kind of factory-centered literature of fiction writers and to point to *Cement* as an example. Also, *Cement* does not contain mass journalistic elements present in later production novels, such as the role of socialist competitions and shock brigades in remaking worker consciousness and the obsession with rapid production tempos. Finally, it is also worth noting that *Cement* itself fit within an ongoing press campaign when it was written—the early NEP campaign to reopen factories closed down during the Civil War. In 1923 *Rabochaia gazeta* solicited and received hundreds of letters from worker correspondents on the theme of reopening factories (RGASPI, f. 610, op. 1, d. 8).

4. See Erica Wolf, "The Giant and the Builder: Fact and Fiction in the Story of a Worker at Magnitostroi," paper presented at Social Science Research Council symposium on "Self and Story in Russian History," La Jolla, Calif., Sept. 26–29, 1996.

5. See Boris Groys, *The Total Art of Stalinism. Avant-grade, Aesthetic, Dictatorship, and Beyond* (Princeton: Princeton University Press, 1992), especially pp. 3–34. See also Katerina Clark, *Petersburg, Crucible of Cultural Revolution* (Cambridge: Harvard University Press, 1995), Introduction and pp. 143–153, 305–307. Clark's indictment of the intelligentsia's disdain for commercial culture is broadly similar to Jeffrey Brooks's argument in *When Russia Learned to Read* (Princeton: Princeton University Press, 1985); and Louise McReynolds's discussion of intellectuals' attitude toward popular journalism in *The News Under Russia's Old Regime* (Princeton: Princeton University Press, 1991).

6. Clark, *The Soviet Novel*, 46–67, and Greg Carleton, "Genre in Socialist Realism," *Slavic Review* 53, no. 4 (Winter 1994): 992–1009.

7. Evgenii Dobrenko, "Iskusstvo prinadlezhat narodu. Formovka sovetskogo chitatelia," *Novyi Mir*, no. 12 (December), 1994: 193–213.

8. Andrei Sinyavsky, "On Socialist Realism," second part of *The Trial Begins and On Socialist Realism* (Berkeley: University of California Press, 1982), 147–219.

9. Sheila Fitzpatrick, "Becoming Cultured," in *The Cultural Front* (Ithaca: Cornell University, 1992), 216–237.

10. See, for example, A. Kemp-Welch, *Stalin and the Literary Intelligentsiia, 1928–1939* (New York: St. Martin's Press, 1991).

11. Clark, in *Petersburg*, makes a connection between 1920s movie star Douglas Fairbanks' roles as "the swashbuckler operating in exotic climes" and the "positive hero" of Gladkov's *Cement*, Gleb Chumalov.

12. For expressions of this concern, see *Zhurnalist*, no. 1, 1922 (Sept. 1): 5–9; no. 2, 1922 (Sept. 15): 38; no. 3, 1923 (January): 30–32. See also Julie Kay Mueller, "A New Kind of Newspaper" (Ph.D. diss., University of California–Berkeley, 1992), 76–77. Mueller points out that the Bolsheviks' anxiety about press content was associated with the legalization of advertising at the outset of the NEP and the fear that advertisers would exercise their "bourgeois" influence on editors.

13. Eric Naiman, *Sex in Public: The Incarnation of Early Soviet Ideology* (Princeton: Princeton University Press, 1997), 79–146.

14. For Komsomol CC officials' reprimands to the editors of the Leningrad Komsomol newspaper *Smena* for excessively sensationalistic coverage of the Chubarov Alley gang rape of 1926, see TsKhDMO, f. 1, op. 23, d. 589, ll. 76–82. For a more general criticism of the excessive sensationalism of the 1926 anti-hooliganism campaign in the press, see Sergei Ingulov, "Protiv khuliganstvo v pechati," *Zhurnalist*, no. 10, 1924 (October): 3–7. For the story of CCC chief Emelian Iaroslavskii's successful campaign to punish the Moscow Komsomol journal *Smena* (not to be confused with the Leningrad newspaper of the same name) for publishing "The Story of Irina" (1927), a boy-meets-girl tale that included some heavy sexual innuendo, see Matthew Lenoe, "Stalinist Mass Journalism and the Transformation of Soviet Newspapers, 1926–1932," (Ph.D. diss., University of Chicago, 1997) 848–852. This account is based on *Smena*, no. 15, 1927 (August): 13–14; and GARF, f. 374 s.ch., op. 27s., d. 328, ll.62–68.

15. In *Sex in Public* Naiman has shown that anxiety about NEP "pluralism" and the resurrection of individual desire as sex and commerce permeated official discourse in the 1920s. Naiman argues that party authorities sanctioned the spate of stories about sexual relations in 1926 to expose the "putrefaction" of NEP society. Although Naiman is undoubtedly right that there was a deliberate campaign to establish party control over private life, I would argue that the discussion and coverage of sex and rape spun far out of central control. Naiman views the disciplinary action taken against writers in the wake of the "excesses" as part of a deliberate program of "training"—training journalists and readers to submit previously personal matters to party monitoring. However, the furious reaction of Agitprop and CCC officials to the coverage of sex in Komsomol periodicals makes it doubtful that they were embarked on a conscious program of training. They were genuinely horrified by Komsomol journalists' open reporting and discussion of sex and violence.

16. Fedor Gladkov, *Cement* (New York: Frederick Ungar Publishing Co., 1974), 308.

17. Valentin Kataev, *Time, Forward!* (Evanston: Northwestern University Press, 1995), 193–199, 208–214, 322.

18. Gladkov, *Cement*, 57–74, 246–251.

19. See especially Kataev, *Time, Forward!*, 176–282, 215–219, 247–251.

20. For example, it is Badin's aggressiveness and coarseness that enables him to dominate the Cossack commander Borchi and force him to carry out a tough program of grain requisitions from the local peasantry (see Gladkov, *Cement*, 93–94).

21. Clark, *Petersburg*, 198.

22. Gladkov, *Cement*, 68.

23. See N. Frideva, "Chitatel Kievskikh politprosvetskikh bibliotek v 1926/27 g.," *Krasnyi bibliotekar*, no. 2, 1928 (February): 51–65; TsKhDMO, f. 1, op. 23, d. 861, ll. 38–39, 86–88; RGASPI, f. 17, op. 113, d. 637, ll. 31.

24. See Frideva, "Chitatel Kievskikh politprosvetskikh bibliotek"; "Chto chitaet rabochaia molodezh?" *Krasnyi bibliotekar*, no. 4, 1928 (April): 41–49; V. Budnev,

"Literatura dlia rabochei i krestianskoi molodezhi," *Knigonosha*, no. 8, 1925: 2–3; TsKhDMO, f. 1, op. 23, d. 588, ll. 38–40.

25. RGASPI, f. 17, op. 113, d. 637, l. 19.

26. Ibid., l. 21.

27. See the Orgburo's final resolution in ibid., ll. 8–13.

28. Ibid., ll. 8, 60.

29. Ibid., l. 61.

30. TsKhDMO, f. 1, op. 3, d. 4, ll. 49–52.

31. Ibid., l. 50.

32. TsKhDMO, f. 1, op. 3, d. 24, ll. 1, 8–12.

33. See Lev Lvovich Barkhash, "Desiat let v *Komsomolskoi pravde*, " TMs, 1977, library of *Komsomolskaia pravda* editorial offices, Moscow (including introductory notes by Sofiia Finger). On Komsomol TsK agitprop officials' determination to use youth interest in sports, technology, and exotic lands and peoples to attract and mobilize readers, see, for example, the Komsomol CC Agitprop Department's recommendations for improving the Siberian (Novosibirsk) Pioneer paper *Iunyi Leninets* ("Young Leninist") in TsKhDMO, f. 1, op. 23, d. 591, ll. 40–43 (dated late 1926 or early 1927). Here the Agitprop Department recommends the introduction of Aviation, Radio, and Chemistry departments, the enlargement of the Science and Technology department, and more coverage of the life of children of native tribes (*inorodtsy*). The report also notes the great popularity of the Physical Culture (sports) department. In October 1925, when the Komsomol Central Committee moved to make *Komsomolskaia pravda* more of a popular, mass newspaper and less of an official broadsheet, CC officials instructed the paper to strengthen and expand its department of Sport and Physical Culture, among other things (see TsKhDMO, f. 1, op. 3, d. 19, ll. 127–128). This was the point at which Taras Kostrov, Iakov Ilin, et al. were brought in to edit the paper, and it may be that Ilin's hiring of Barkhash from *Pravda* was directly connected with this instruction.

34. Evgenii Riabchikov, "Iz zapisok aviatsionnogo reportera," unpublished TMs, 1980, library of *Komsomolskaia pravda* editorial staff, Moscow. On aviation, modernization, and early Soviet culture, see Scott Palmer, "Modernizing Russia in the Aeronautical Age: Technology, Legitimacy, and the Structures of Airminded- ness, 1909–1939" (Ph.D. diss., University of Illinois–Urbana–Champaigne, 1997).

35. Ivan Gronskii, *Iz proshlogo. . . . Vospominaniia* (Moscow: "Izvestiia," 1991), 127–129.

36. Ibid.

37. See Chapter 5.

38. *Rulon*, Nov. 24, 1928, 3.

39. Ibid.

40. See Gronskii's account of the *Italia* rescue, cited above, and Iurii Zhukov, *Liudi tridtsatykh godov* (Moscow: Izdatelstvo "Sovetskaia Rossiia," 1966), 5–38.

41. See Gronskii, *Iz proshlogo*, 121–124; Mikhail Gus, *Bezumie svastiki* (Moscow: Sovetskii pisatel, 1971), 41–55; Anatolii Mironovich Danilevich, "Gazeta '*Izvestiia.*' Stanovlenie. Tipologiia. (1917–1927 g.g.)" (Ph.D. diss., Moscow State University, 1978), 134–136; *M. Gorkii i sovetskaia pechat*, vol. 1 (Moscow: Izdatelstvo

Nauka, 1964), 86–109 (correspondence between A. M. Gorkii and Artem Khalatov, October 1927 to March, 1927); *M. Gorkii i sovetskaia pechat*, vol. 2, 126–129 (correspondence between A. M. Gorkii and *The Worker Gazette* editor Konstantin Maltsev).

42. The editors of *M. Gorkii i sovetskaia pechat* claim that Gorkii's January 1928 letter to *Worker Gazette* editor Maltsev in December 1927 and January 1928 was "one of the earliest documents illuminating the first, preparatory period in the creation of the journal *Nashi dostizheniia*" (*M. Gorkii i sovetskaia pechat*, vol. 2, 126).

43. *M. Gorkii i sovetskaia pechat*, vol. 2, 128. On Gorky's exchange with the worker correspondents, see 126–127.

44. Ibid., 184–195.

45. Ibid., 194.

46. Ibid., 194–195.

47. According to a draft project for the journal prepared by Gorkii and Khalatov and dated July 5, 1928, the three primary departments of *Our Achievements* were to be Science, Technology and Production," and Culture and Daily Life. The Science department was to cover production-related breakthroughs rather than "theoretical and academic problems." The primary emphasis of the journal was thus to be on achievements in industrial production (see *M. Gorkii i sovetskaia pechat*, vol. 2, 196–197).

48. See Chapter 4.

49. *Komsomolskaia pravda*, Apr. 24, 1928, 2.

50. See the "Short List of Examplars" and Clark's list of the "canon" of socialist realism in Clark, *The Soviet Novel*, 4, 262; and TsKhDMO, f. 1, op. 3, d. 57, l. 29.

51. TsKhDMO, f. 1, op. 3, d. 57, l. 1.

52. Ibid., ll. 4–14.

53. Ibid., ll. 42–45.

54. TsKhDMO, f. 1, op. 23, d. 861, ll. 25–57.

55. Anne E. Gorsuch, "'A Woman Is Not a Man': The Culture of Gender and Generation in Soviet Russia, 1921–1928," *Slavic Review* 55, no. 3 (Fall 1996): 636–660.

56. Iu. Libedinskii, "Problema rabochei tematiki," *Na literaturnom postu* (*NLP*), no. 16, 1929: 14–15.

57. Vladimir Stavskii, "Kak zhe sobirat material?" *NLP*, no. 16, 1929: 16–17.

58. Ibid.

59. Mikhail Luzin, "Za perestroiku riadov, za novye metody raboty," *NLP*, no. 23, 1929: 7–16.

60. A. Isbakh, "O rabote v nizovykh kruzhkakh," *NLP*, nos. 15–16, 1930: 95–105.

61. "Za perestroiku RAPP. Za rabochee shefstvo nad pisatel skimi organizatsiiami," *NLP*, no. 17, 1930: 58–59.

62. Ibid.

63. Iu. Libedinskii, "Generalnaia zadacha proletarskoi literatury," *NLP,* no. 2, 1930: 5–14.

64. K. Driagin, "Ocherki kollektivizatsiia. Obzor ocherkov v broshiurakh i gazetakh," *NLP,* no. 9, 1930: 47–63.

65. See Libedinskii, "Generalnaia zadacha proletarskoi literatury." For biographical details on Stavskii and Chumandrin, see *Bolshaia sovetskaia entsiklopediia,* 1st edition (1929–1941), s. v. "Chumandrin, Mikhail Fedorovich," "Stavskii, Vladimir Petrovich." See also S. Dinamov, "Tvorchestvo Mikhaila Chumandrina," *NLP,* no. 12, 1930: 37–46.

66. L. Korelik, "Ocherk i feleton v gazete," *NLP,* no. 10, 1930: 56–59.

67. See Osip M. Brik, "Protiv romantiki," *Novyi lef,* no. 10, 1927: 1–2; S. Tretiakov, "S novym godom! S 'novym Lefom'!" *Novyi lef,* no. 1, 1928: 1–3; P. Neznamov, "Mimo gazety," *Novyi lef,* no. 5, 1928: 29–33; S. Tretiakov, "Chto proizoshlo v proletliterature," *Novyi lef,* no. 6, 1928: 1–3.

68. Boris Groys makes a similar point in *The Total Art of Stalinism,* 28–29.

69. Mikhail Rumer, "Otets rasskazyval . . . ," in *Bol i pamiat,* ed. V. S. Burkov and V. A. Miakushkov (Moscow: Izdatel stvo Respublika, 1993), 77–78.

70. M. Luzin, "Ob ocherke," *NLP,* no. 18, 1930: 92–111.

71. See, for example, Libedinskii, "Generalnaia zadacha proletarskoi literatury."

72. Luzin, "Ob ocherke."

73. See Luzin, "Ob ocherke," and Carleton, "Genre in Socialist Realism."

74. Carleton, "Genre in Socialist Realism," 1003.

75. Ibid., 1004–1006.

76. Boris Galin, *Stroitel novogo mira* (Moscow: Sovetskii pisatel, 1978), 429–495.

77. L. Kovalev, *Metro* (Moscow: Izdatel stvo Rabochaia Moskva, 1935).

78. "Novye zadachi 'Na literaturnom postu'," *NLP,* no. 1, 1931: 1.

79. "Proizvodstvennoe soveshchaniia ocherkistov," *NLP,* no. 4, 1931: 9–19.

80. V. Stavskii, "Novyi tip pisatel," *NLP,* no. 4, 1931: 13–17; B. Galin, "Za deistvennost ocherka," *NLP,* no. 4, 1931: 18–19.

81. "Za proletarskuiu literaturu," *NLP,* no. 13, 1931: 1–4.

82. "Strana dolzhna znat svoikh geroev," *Pravda,* May 18, 1931, 3.

83. See "Za pokaz geroev bolshevistskikh tempov," *NLP,* no. 17, 1931: 13–15; "Strana dolzhna znat svoikh geroev," *NLP,* no. 17, 1931: 21; "Za luchshii pokaz geroev piatiletki," *NLP,* no. 18, 1931: 45–46; Iu. Libedinskii, "O pokaze geroev i prizyve udarnikov," *NLP,* no. 28, 1931: 1–4.

84. "Za pokaz geroev bolshevistskikh tempov," *NLP,* no. 22, 1931: 31–32.

85. *NLP,* nos. 10–11, 1931.

86. See Sergei Vladimirovich Zhuravlev, "Istochniki po sozdaniiu 'Istorii fabrik i zavodov,' Moskvy v 1931–1938 gg.," (Ph.D. diss., Moscow State Historical-Archival Institute, 1989), 33–42.

87. For the resolution "On the Reconstruction of Literary and Artistic Organizations," see *O partiinoi i sovetskoi pechati*, 431.

88. On the Politburo commission that negotiated entry into the new writers' union with RAPP, see Gronskii, *Iz proshlogo*, 138–139, 334–338. For Gronskii's speech to the opening plenum of the Writers' Union Organizational Committee, see Gronskii, *Iz proshlogo*, 340–342; and *Sovetskaia literatura na novom etape. Stenogramma pervogo plenuma Orgkomiteta SSP* (Moscow 1933). For a summary of the statutes of the Soviet Writers' Union and of Zhdanov's speech to its First Congress, see Kemp-Welch, *Stalin and the Literary Intelligentsiia*, 169–170, 176–177.

Conclusion

1. I use the term here also to refer to *mnogotirazhki*, the workplace newspapers that were run off in low print runs on old platen presses, rather than just the hand-lettered broadsheets hung on the wall.

2. Roger Pethybridge in *The Social Prelude to Stalinism* discusses the connection between the Bolshevik social revolution and Stalinist culture, focusing on the low levels of literacy in the populace and the party. See Roger Pethybridge, *The Social Prelude to Stalinism* (New York: St. Martin's Press, 1974), 132–186 (Chapter 4). Moshe Lewin addresses the issue in terms of the regime's "contamination" by traditional Russian peasant values (Moshe Lewin, *The Making of the Soviet System* [New York: Pantheon, 1985], 57–87, 274–276. My argument is distinct in that I focus directly on the reading preferences of young Russian men, particularly young Communist activists, as revealed to higher-party officials by reader studies, intelligence reports, letters, etc.

3. See Nicholas Timasheff, *The Great Retreat* (New York: E. P. Dutton and Co., 1946) and Stephen Kotkin, *Magnetic Mountain: Stalinism as Civilization* (Berkeley: University of California Press, 1995), 4–7.

4. David Brandenberger has recently argued that the Stalinist leaders' reintroduction of Russian nationalist heroes and themes to mass culture in the mid-1930s was a pragmatic move and did not entail a personal commitment to Russian nationalism. See Brandenberger, "The 'Short Course' to Modernity: Stalinist History Textbooks, Mass Culture, and the Formation of Popular Russian National Identity, 1934–1956" (Ph.D. diss., Harvard University, 1999), 62–88, 117–144. See also David Brandenberger, *National Bolshevism: Stalinist Mass Culture and the Formation of Modern Russian National Identity, 1931–1956* (Cambridge: Harvard University Press, 2002).

5. Max Weber, *Economy and Society*, vol. 1 (Berkeley: University of California Press, 1978), 212–226.

6. Ibid., 241–245.

7. See Ken Jowitt, *New World Disorder: The Leninist Extinction* (Berkeley: University of California Press, 1992), 1–47.

8. Ibid., 121–158. Quote is from p. 139. For other explications of the neotra-

ditionalist image of Leninist societies, see Andrew Walder, *Communist Neotradition-alism: Work and Authority in Chinese Industry* (Berkeley: University of California Press, 1986); and Terry Martin, "Modernization or Neotraditionalism: Ascribed Nationality and Soviet Primordialism," in Sheila Fitzpatrick, ed., *Stalinism: New Directions* (New York: Routledge, 2000), 348–367. Much of my own thinking about neotraditionalism has been developed in discussions with Terry Martin, to whom I am greatly indebted.

9. Lewin, 12–18, 258–285.

10. See, for example, Jowitt, 13–25.

11. I borrow the phrase "neotraditional image" from Walder, *Communist Neo-Traditionalism*, xv, 2–8.

12. See Weber, *The Theory of Social and Economic Organization*, A. M. Henderson and Talcott Parsons, trans. (Glencoe: The Free Press, 1947), 124–127.

13. The sociologist Victor Zaslavsky, writing on the Brezhnev period, gives one of the most compelling descriptions of the Soviet status group hierarchy. See Victor Zaslavsky, *The Neo-Stalinist State: Ethnicity and Consensus in Soviet Society* (Armonk, N.Y.: M. E. Sharpe, Inc., 1994). On the ascription of status in the USSR, see also Sheila Fitzpatrick, "Ascribing Class: The Construction of Social Identity in Soviet Russia," *Journal of Modern History* 65 (December 1993): 745–770.

14. See, for example, Kotkin's reference to the "mechanisms by which the dreams of ordinary people and those of individuals directing the state found common ground in the Soviet version of the welfare state" (*Magnetic Mountain*, 23). See also his claim that in spite of the potentially divisive effects of the Stakhanovite movement and socialist competition, Bolshevik workplace practice and discourse about the ideal Soviet worker did shape a "new social identity grounded in . . . official language" even for the nonactivist workers (*Magnetic Mountain*, 201–225).

15. Jochen Hellbeck, "Speaking Out: Languages of Affirmation and Dissent in Stalinist Russia," *Kritika* 1, no. 1, 2000 (Winter 2000): 71–96.

16. See Sarah Davies, *Popular Opinion in Stalin's Russia* (Cambridge: Cambridge University Press, 1997); Sheila Fitzpatrick, *Stalin's Peasants* (New York: Oxford University Press, 1994); Matthew Payne, *Stalin's Railroad: Turksib and the Building of Socialism* (Pittsburgh: University of Pittsburgh Press, 2002); Karen Petrone, *"Life Has Become More Joyous, Comrades"* (Bloomington: Indiana University Press, 2000); and Jeffrey Rossman, "Worker Resistance under Stalin: Class and Gender in the Textile Mills of the Ivanovo Industrial Region, 1928–1932" (Ph.D. diss., University of California–Berkeley, 1997).

17. Anna Krylova, in a recent article in the journal *Kritika*, seems to suggest that to postulate opposition or even grumbling in the interwar USSR is to assume that Soviet subjects had "liberal personalities" or "liberal selves." She views the resisting "liberal self" as an ideological construct of liberal democratic regimes that scholars project inappropriately onto Soviet reality. Are we to assume, then, that "socialist selves" are incapable of resisting or grumbling? Or that "traditional peasant selves" are incapable of resisting or grumbling? See Anna Krylova, "The Tenacious Liberal Subject in Soviet Studies," *Kritika* 1, no. 1, 2000 (Winter 2000): 119–146.

18. See Alex Inkeles, *Public Opinion in Soviet Russia: A Study in Mass Persuasion*

(New York: Harvard University Press, 1958), 54–70. See also Vladimir Shlapen-tokh, *Soviet Public Opinion and Ideology. Mythology and Pragmatism in Interaction* (New York: Praeger, 1986), 69–70.

19. Karen Petrone's recent book reaches similar conclusions. See *Life Has Become More Joyous*, 120–125, 173–175.

20. Jowitt, 88–89, 221.

21. See Kotkin, 19–20.

22. Alexander Gerschenkron, *Economic Backwardness in Historical Perspective* (New York: Praeger, 1965). Gerschenkron's thinking is an important background to Jowitt's version of the neotraditionalist model. See Jowitt, 125.

23. I write "ideological" here deliberately because the commitment was quite often not practical. It was in words only.

Acknowledgments

I am very grateful to the many people who helped me with the research and writing of this book. I was extraordinarily fortunate to get into the University of Chicago's program in Russian history in 1992 and to have as my dissertation adviser Sheila Fitzpatrick. Professor Fitzpatrick was a dedicated, rigorous, and fair teacher who imposed no orthodoxies on her students. She was always ready to help us with careful reading of our work, professional advice, and strong support on the job market. Together with Richard Hellie and Ron Suny she ran a program where creative thinking, original research, and tough debate were valued above all. I would like to thank all three of these professors for their thorough reading of my dissertation manuscript (especially given that it was almost 1,000 pages long) and their support during and after graduate school. I would also like to thank Professor Wendy Griswold, now of Northwestern University, for her reading of the dissertation and her guidance on the "production of culture" approach to cultural studies.

My debt of gratitude to my fellow graduate students in the Chicago program is equally large. I doubt that I would have completed my Ph.D. had I not been in a community of such open, unpretentious, hardworking, and keen-witted colleagues. In classes, at the weekly Wilder House Russian History workshop, and at Jimmy's, they challenged me to hone my arguments, guided me to new sources, and taught me much about Soviet and world history. I'd like to thank all of my fellow students, including Alison Smith, Julie Gilmour, Chris Burton, Charles Hachten, Steven Harris, Stephen Bittner, John McCannnon, Nick Glossop, and Josh Sanborn. I'd also like to mention Jon Bone for guiding me to a number of sources, Julie Hessler for insightful critiques of sections of the book manuscript, and Julie Gilmour for making the contacts that enabled me to get access to the library of *Komsomolskaia pravda*. Finally, I will always remember and admire the quiet intelligence and sense of humor of Jennifer Stenfors, sadly now deceased.

I am especially grateful to Terry Martin, Matthew Payne, and Stewart Winger for companionship, no-holds-barred debate, professional advice, and intellectual stimulation. Terry and Matt have decisively influenced my own interpretations of Soviet history. Stewart has been a friend and intellectual companion since college. His enthusiasm for intellectual inquiry renewed my own at a critical juncture and motivated me to enter graduate school.

A number of scholars outside the University of Chicago have given me significant help with this book. Yuri Slezkine, James von Geldern, Owen Johnson, and Gregory Kasza all read and critiqued draft chapters. I thank Andrea Graziosi for his detailed and thoughtful comments on the entire book manuscript. Anonymous readers at Yale and Harvard University presses also provided very useful critiques of the work. Erica Wolf introduced me to her remarkable findings about the connections between Kataev's *Time, Forward!* and nonfiction journalism at Magnitogorsk. In 1999–2000 David Brandenberger, Eric Lohr, and other participants in the history workshops at Harvard's Davis Center for Russian and Eurasian Studies helped me refine my use of Ken Jowitt's and Janos Kornai's theories in my own work. Timothy Colton, director of the Davis Center, took seriously a manuscript that was not, on the face of it, very "sexy." My thanks also go to Peter Holquist and Jochen Hellbeck for propelling my own thinking forward with their fresh interpretations of Soviet history and to Dr. Hellbeck for taking the time to photocopy hundreds of pages of *Zhurnalist* for me in the winter of 1992–1993. I hope that Drs. Holquist and Hellbeck will take my challenges to their scholarly work in this book in the spirit of lively academic debate.

In Russia I had the help of dozens of archivists and researchers at the State Archive of the Russian Federation (GARF), the Russian State Archive of Social and Political History (RGASPI, formerly RTsKhIDNI), the archive of the Moscow party organization (TsGAOD g. Moskvy), the Lenin library, the Lenin library branch at Khimki, and the Komsomol Central Committee archive (TsKhDMO—now merged with RGASPI). Several Russian scholars were kind enough to share their archival expertise and interpretations of Soviet history with me. I'd like to thank Andrei Sokolov, Gennadii Bordiugov, and Oleg

Khlevniuk. Without the timely aid of V. A. Nevezhin I might never have found any of the veterans of 1920s and 1930s Soviet journalism I interviewed. My thanks also go to the journalists who agreed to speak with me—David Ortenberg, David Novoplianskii, Irina Rudenko, Kira Lavrova, Valentin Kitain, Aleksei Kozhen, Oleg Ignatev, and Iosif Lifshits. I am grateful to Anatolii Mironovich Danilevich at *Izvestiia* for access to that newspaper's library and his doctoral thesis. Finally, I owe thanks to a number of veteran journalists at *Komsomolskaia pravda* for arranging access to their library, a key source for my project. Kira Lavrova, Nikolai Dolgopolov, and especially Galina Ianchuk of the Reader Letters Department were tremendously helpful. Ms. Ianchuk provided essential assistance in arranging the publication of photographs from the *Komsomolskaia pravda* library in this book. I wish to thank *Komsomolskaia pravda* for permission to publish the photographs.

For friendship and hospitality in Moscow during my year of research (1994–1995) I owe thanks to Leonid Weintraub, Natasha Kriukova and her family, John, Wendy, and Kolya Kachur, Sergei Kriukov, Katherine Lahti, Francine Hirsch, Julie Gilmour, and Scott Palmer. Leonid Weintraub and John Kachur both helped me find sources, and Mr. Weintraub interviewed a number of people about their newspaper reading practices in the 1920s and 1930s.

I'd like to express my gratitude to several organizations that provided funds and logistical assistance for this project. First and foremost, the University of Chicago paid for my undergraduate and graduate education. Chicago was for me a kind of "Ivory Tower boot camp" where professors and students took rigorous argument, research, and intellectual effort with a seriousness now rare in American society. I owe the university an incalculable debt for a superb education. The Fulbright-Hays Doctoral Dissertation Research Abroad Program and the International Research and Exchanges Board funded my year of research in Moscow archives. I was enabled to do further research in Moscow in the summer of 1999 by a faculty research grant from the University of Arkansas—Little Rock.

My educational debts go back much further than college, and they are deeper obligations than grants and student loans. I'd like to extend my deepest thanks to five great teachers who shaped me as a scholar and as a human being. They are Robert Littlefield, my sixth-grade teacher at Doherty Elementary School in Andover, Massachusetts; Peter Anderson, my ninth-grade English teacher at Andover East Junior High; Lewis Bernieri, my tenth-grade English teacher and shot-put/discus coach at Phillips Academy—Andover; K. Kelly Wise, teacher of the

Novel and Drama seminar at Phillips Andover; and A. K. Ramanujan, now deceased, an inspired professor whose class in Reading and Writing Poetry I took at the University of Chicago.

I owe much to family and friends outside academia. My thanks to my mother, Susan Melder Lenoe, for passing on to me her love of literature and for watching our children, Simon and Eleanor Lenoe, so that I could write. My thanks also go to my aunt and uncle Priscilla and Calvin Rice, for their love and for handling my financial and legal affairs during my year of residence in Moscow. I lack the space to name the numerous friends who have helped me out along the way, and it seems invidious to single out only a few. Nonetheless I want to express thanks for companionship and kindness to Emi, Lorenzo, and Kenzo Esquivel and to Tom, Deena, Sean, and Paul Kinsky. I apologize to the many others I cannot name here.

This book has been a joint project with my wife, Mari Tsuchiya Lenoe, who worked to support us during graduate school, traveled with me to Moscow for a year, accepted the uncertainties of the academic job market, and tolerated moving almost every year between 1989 and 2003. Her wit, love of adventure, disdain for scholarly pretension, flexibility, and generosity are fantastic. My most heartfelt love and thanks go to her.

Portions of Chapters 1 and 4 appeared in my monograph "Agitation, Propaganda, and the 'Stalinization' of the Soviet Press, 1922–1930," Carl Beck Papers in Russian and East European Studies, no. 1305 (University of Pittsburgh Center for Russian and East European Studies, 1998). Chapter 2 was published in a slightly modified form in *Russian Review* 62, no. 4 (October 2003). I'd like to express my appreciation to The Carl Beck Papers and *Russian Review* for publishing these works.

Index